When should I travel to get the best airfare?
Where do I go for answers to my travel questions?
What's the best and easiest way to plan and book my trip?

frommers.travelocity.com

Frommer's, the travel guide leader, has teamed up with **Travelocity.com**, the leader in online travel, to bring you an in-depth, easy-to-use resource designed to help you plan and book your trip online.

At **frommers.travelocity.com**, you'll find free online updates about your destination from the experts at Frommer's plus the outstanding travel planning and purchasing features of Travelocity.com. Travelocity.com provides reservations capabilities for 95 percent of all airline seats sold, more than 47,000 hotels, and over 50 car rental companies. In addition, Travelocity.com offers more than 2,000 exciting vacation and cruise packages. Travelocity.com puts you in complete control of your travel planning with these and other great features:

> **Expert travel guidance from Frommer's** - over 150 writers reporting from around the world!
>
> **Best Fare Finder** - an interactive calendar tells you when to travel to get the best airfare
>
> **Fare Watcher** - we'll track airfare changes to your favorite destinations
>
> **Dream Maps** - a mapping feature that suggests travel opportunities based on your budget
>
> **Shop Safe Guarantee** - 24 hours a day / 7 days a week live customer service, and more!

Whether traveling on a tight budget, looking for a quick weekend getaway, or planning the trip of a lifetime, Frommer's guides and Travelocity.com will make your travel dreams a reality. You've bought the book, now book the trip!

Other Great Guides for Your Trip:

Here's what the critics say about Frommer's:

Montréal & Québec City

2001

by Herbert Bailey Livesey

IDG Books Worldwide, Inc.
An International Data Group Company
Foster City, CA • Chicago, IL • Indianapolis, IN • New York, NY

ABOUT THE AUTHOR

Herbert Bailey Livesey has written about travel and food for many publications, including *Travel & Leisure, Food & Wine,* and *Playboy.* He's the coauthor of several guidebooks, including *Frommer's Canada, Frommer's Europe from $70 a Day,* and *Frommer's New England.*

IDG BOOKS WORLDWIDE, INC.

An International Data Group Company
909 Third Avenue
New York, NY 10022

Find us online at **www.frommers.com**

ISBN 0-7645-6172-3
ISSN 1084-418X

Editor: Kate Shoup Welsh
Production Editor: Todd A. Siesky
Photo Editor: Richard Fox
Design by Michele Laseau
Cartographer: John Decamillis
Production by IDG Books Indianapolis Production Department

Front cover photo: Changing of the Guard at the Citadelle, with the Château Frontenac in the background (Québec City).

SPECIAL SALES

For general information on IDG Books Worldwide's books in the U.S., please call our Consumer Customer Service Department at 1-800-762-2974. For reseller information, including discounts, bulk sales, customized editions, and premium sales, please call our Reseller Consumer Service Department at 1-800-434-3422.

Manufactured in the United States of America

5 4 3 2 1

Contents

List of Maps

AN INVITATION TO THE READER

In researching this book, we discovered many wonderful places—hotels, restaurants, shops, and more. We're sure you'll find others. Please tell us about them, so we can share the information with your fellow travelers in upcoming editions. If you were disappointed with a recommendation, we'd love to know that too. Please write to:

Frommer's Montréal & Québec City 2001
IDG Books Worldwide, Inc.
909 Third Avenue
New York, NY 10022

AN ADDITIONAL NOTE

Please be advised that travel information is subject to change at any time—and this is especially true of prices. We therefore suggest that you write or call ahead for confirmation when making your travel plans. The authors, editors, and publisher cannot be held responsible for the experiences of readers while traveling. Your safety is important to us, however, so we encourage you to stay alert and be aware of your surroundings. Keep a close eye on cameras, purses, and wallets, all favorite targets of thieves and pickpockets.

WHAT THE SYMBOLS MEAN

✪ **Frommer's Favorites**
Our favorite places and experiences—outstanding for quality, value, or both.

The following abbreviations are used for credit cards:

AE	American Express	ER	enRoute
CB	Carte Blanche	JCB	Japan Credit Bank
DC	Diners Club	MC	MasterCard
DISC	Discover	V	Visa

FIND FROMMER'S ONLINE

www.frommers.com offers up-to-the-minute listings on almost 200 cities around the globe—including the latest bargains and candid, personal articles updated daily by Arthur Frommer himself. No other Web site offers such comprehensive and timely coverage of the world of travel.

The Best of Montréal & Québec City

The duality of Canadian life has been called the "Twin Solitudes." One Canada, English and Calvinist in origin, tends to be staid, smug, and work obsessed. The other, French and Catholic, is more creative, lighthearted, and inclined to see pleasure as the end purpose of labor. Or so go the stereotypes.

These two peoples live side by side throughout Québec and in the nine provinces of English Canada, but the blending occurs in particularly intense fashion in Québec province's largest city, Montréal. French speakers, known as Francophones, constitute 66% of the city's population, while most of the remaining population are speakers of English—Anglophones. (The growing number of residents who speak neither, or who have another primary tongue, are called *Allophones*.) Although both groups are decidedly North American, they are no more alike than Margaret Thatcher and Charles de Gaulle.

Montréal is a modern city in nearly every regard. Its downtown bristles with skyscrapers, but many of them are playful, almost perky, with unexpected shapes and shades of uncorporate colors. The city aboveground is mirrored by another below, where an entire winter can be avoided in coatless comfort. To the west and north of downtown are Anglo commercial and residential neighborhoods, centered around Westmount. To the east and north are Francophone *quartiers,* centered on Outremount and Plateau Mont-Royal. In between are the many dialects and skin tones of the immigrant rainbow, roiled by social conflicts and pressured to choose sides.

Over the past decade, there was an undeniable impression of decline in Montréal. A bleak mood prevailed, driven by lingering recession and uncertainty over the future. After all, it remains possible that Québec will yet choose to fling itself into an unknown independence from the rest of Canada. When yet another sovereignty referendum was held in 1995, the federalists won, but only by a razor-thin 1%. Secession would be a seismic event accompanied by even greater Anglo flight, loss of federal subsidies, economic uncertainty—even the highly remote but undiscountable possibility of civil war. Passions have cooled for the moment, though, especially after Québec's premier, Lucien Bouchard, although a devout separatist, declared that unemployment and the budget deficit demanded his attention.

Something worked. Ripples of optimism are spreading through the province and its largest city. Unemployment in Québec, long in double digits, shrank to under 7% in 2000, the lowest mark in more than 2 decades and below that of arch-rival Toronto. In a perhaps connected trend, crime in Montréal, already one of the safest cities in North America, hit a 20-year low. Favorable currency exchange and the presence of skilled workers have made the city a favored site for Hollywood film and TV production—recently attracting movies starring Bruce Willis, Robert DeNiro, John Travolta, and Eddie Murphy, among others—that brought in more than $700 million in revenue in a single year. That success inspired the construction of two major film studios, one now complete and another expected to be Canada's largest.

The rash of "For Rent" and "For Sale" signs that disfigured the city in the 1990s has evaporated, replaced by a welcome shortage of store and office space and a billion-dollar building boom that's filling up vacant plots all over downtown. The beloved old Forum hockey arena is undergoing expensive conversion to a dining and entertainment center, and an immense multimedia center for high-tech companies is rising near the St. Lawrence River. To be sure, not every project has enjoyed smooth sailing. A plan to build a downtown stadium for the Expos baseball team was on hold at last look, as was a new $900 million theme park called *Technodome* to be installed at the Port of Montréal.

Those stumbles won't matter to American visitors, for whom Montréal already might seem an urban near-paradise. The subway system, called the *Métro,* is modern and swift. Streets are clean and safe. Montréal's best restaurants are the equal of their south-of-the-border compatriots in almost every way, yet they are as much as 30% to 40% cheaper. And the government gives visitors back most of the taxes it collects from them.

Québec City is less sophisticated, more conservative, and more French. With its impressive location above the St. Lawrence River and its virtually unblemished Old Town of 18th- and 19th-century houses, it even looks French. Probably 95% of its residents speak the mother tongue, and far fewer are bilingual, as most Montréalers are. (In the province as a whole, about 81% of citizens are Francophone.) With that homogeneity and its status as the putative capital of a future independent nation, citizens seem to suffer less angst over what might happen down the road. They are also aware that a critical part of their economy is based on tourism, and they are far less likely to vent the open hostility toward visitors that Americans can experience in English Canada.

1 Frommer's Favorite Montréal & Québec City Experiences

MONTRÉAL

- **Exploring Vieux-Montréal.** The old city is redolent with old-world flavor. Wander Place Jacques-Cartier, the most engaging of the old city's squares; explore museums and the stunning architecture of its churches; and stroll along the revitalized waterfront.
- **Listening to Jazz.** Downtown, Old Town, all over, this is a favorite pastime of locals and visitors alike, especially in June during the renowned Montréal Jazz Festival.
- **Shopping.** Browse the shops of world-class domestic designers, from the up-and-coming to the well established; search for Inuit (Eskimo) sculptures of the highest

order, with prices to match; and take in the dozens of eclectic antique shops along rue Notre-Dame between rue Guy and rue des Seigneurs.

- **Savoring French and International Cuisine.** Dine in true French style, and in all its permutations—haute, bistro, original Québécois—as well as Cal-Asian hybrids and the offerings of the city's legion of ethnic restaurants representing dozens of foreign cuisines, notably Italian, Mexican, Thai, Chinese, Greek, Polish, and Indian.
- **Feasting on Table d'Hôte Specials.** Indulge in three or four courses for a fixed price that is only slightly more than the cost of an à la carte main course alone. Most full-service restaurants offer the table d'hôte, if only at midday.

QUÉBEC CITY

- **Strolling and Lounging on the Terrasse Dufferin.** Captivating Québec is at its best here, with the copper-spired Château Frontenac rearing up behind, the Lower Town below, and ferries, freighters, and pleasure craft moving on the broad, silvered river.
- **Lingering at an Outdoor Cafe.** Tables are set out at place d'Armes, in the Quartier du Petit-Champlain, and along the Grande-Allée—a quality-of-life invention the French and their Québécois brethren have perfected.
- **Relaxing in Battlefields Park.** The park is beautifully situated, overlooking the St. Lawrence River, and is particularly lively on weekends, when families and lovers come here to picnic and play.
- **Discovering the Blossoming Lower Town.** All but abandoned to shipping and grimy industry, the old riverside neighborhood is reborn, filling with antique shops, bistros, boutique hotels, and rehabilitated 18th- and 19th-century buildings.
- **Admiring the Skyline from the Lévis Ferry.** This provides quite a view for very little money, and passengers can stay on board and come right back without disembarking.

2 Best Hotel Bets

For full listings for these and many other hotels, see chapters 4 and 12.

MONTRÉAL

- **Best Historic Hotel:** No contest. **The Ritz-Carlton Montréal,** 1228 rue Sherbrooke Ouest (☎ **800/363-0366** or 514/842-4212), has been around since 1913, giving it a half-century lead on the nearest competition.
- **Best for Business Travelers:** A closer call, with several worthy candidates, but **La Reine Elizabeth/Queen Elizabeth,** 900 bd. René-Lévesque Ouest (☎ **800/ 441-1414** or 514/861-3511), gets the nod for its central location atop the railroad station, concierge floors, fully equipped health club, and excellent bus connections to the airports.
- **Best for a Romantic Getaway:** With ancient cut-stone walls, swags of velvet and brocade, and tilting floors that once were trod by Benjamin Franklin, as well as its baronial dining room and a breakfast nook under a peaked glass roof, the **Maison Pierre du Calvet,** 405 rue Bonsecours (☎ **514/282-1725**), provokes memories of lovers' hotels by the Seine.
- **Best Boutique Hotel:** As new as yesterday and as knowing as the Orient, **Le Germain,** 2050 rue Mansfield (☎ **514/849-2050**), brings a needed jolt of *shibui* panache to the too-often stodgy corps of downtown business hotels.

- **Best Lobby for Pretending That You're Rich:** A tie—the woody, hushed **Ritz-Carlton Montréal** (see "Best Historic Hotel" above) exudes old money, while the **Loews Vogue,** 1425 rue de la Montagne (☎ 800/465-6654 or 514/285-5555), caters to the cell-phone and Armani set.

- **Best for Families:** The **Delta Montréal,** 450 rue Sherbrooke Ouest (☎ 877/286-1986 or 514/286-1986), keeps the kids blissfully waterlogged with *two* pools—one inside, one outside. The young ones can also be placed under watchful eyes in the play center, giving their parents a break.

- **Best Moderately Priced Hotel:** True, there are no surprises here, but the management keeps tinkering with the formula and the cheapest rooms dip into the budget category (as low as US$80 for a double) at the **Holiday Inn Montréal Midtown,** 420 rue Sherbrooke Ouest (☎ 800/387-3042 or 514/812-6111 in Canada, 800/465-4329 in the U.S.).

- **Best Budget Hotel:** Rates at the **Lord Berri,** 1199 rue Berri (☎ 888/363-0363 or 514/845-9236), start low (a double goes for just US$55 in low season) and get lower the longer you stay. It's near St-Denis and just a 5-minute walk from Vieux-Montréal.

- **Best B&B:** Located in a 1723 house in Vieux-Montréal, **Auberge Les Passants du Sans Soucy,** 171 rue St-Paul Ouest (☎ 514/842-2634), is more upscale and stylish than most of its brethren, and near top restaurants and clubs in the old town.

- **Best Service:** It's tough to choose among the troops at the **Vogue** (see "Best Lobby for Pretending That You're Rich" above), the **Ritz-Carlton Montréal** (see "Best Historic Hotel" above), and the **Inter-Continental Montréal,** 360 rue St-Antoine Ouest (Bleury) (☎ 800/361-3600 or 514/987-9900). All three display an almost equal amount of grace and care when it comes to tending to their guests.

- **Best Location:** Airport buses leave regularly from the front door of **La Reine Elizabeth/Queen Elizabeth** (see "Best for Business Travelers" above), the main railroad station is just a couple of levels down in the hotel elevator, and most of the major corporate buildings are accessible through the corridors of the Underground City.

- **Best Health Club:** The **Omni Mont-Royal** (formerly the Four Seasons/Westin), 1050 rue Sherbrooke Ouest (☎ 800/228-3000 or 514/284-1110), lays on aerobics classes with instructors, free weights *and* weight machines, and Exercycles, as well as saunas, a steam room, whirlpools, and massages to recover from the workout.

- **Best Hotel Pool:** Most of the big downtown hotels have heated pools, but at the **Montréal Bonaventure Hilton,** 1 place Bonaventure (☎ 800/445-8667 or 514/878-2332), you can slip into the water indoors and stroke into the outdoors without leaving the water, even in January.

- **Best Views:** With 32 stories, the **Omni Mont-Royal** (see "Best Health Club" above) has some of the loftiest rooms, with the most panoramic views, in town.

QUÉBEC CITY

- **Best Historic Hotel:** The **Château Frontenac,** 1 rue des Carrières (☎ 800/828-7447 or 418/692-3861), is more than a century old. It was one of the first hotels built to serve railroad passengers and to encourage tourism at a time when most people stayed close to home, and it still rewards a visit.

- **Best for Business Travelers:** A tie. Both the **Hilton Québec,** 3 place Québec (☎ **800/445-8667** or 418/647-2411), and the **Radisson Gouverneurs,** 690 bd. René-Lévesque Est (☎ **800/463-2820** or 418/647-1717 from eastern Canada and Ontario, 800/333-3333 from elsewhere), are as central as can be found, with good fitness centers and executive floors with concierges and business services.
- **Best for a Romantic Getaway:** It's hard to beat curling up with a glass of wine beside the fire in the country-chic great room of the **Auberge Saint-Antoine,** 10 rue St-Antoine (☎ **800/692-2211** or 418/692-2211).
- **Best Boutique Hotel:** The sleek **Dominion 1912,** 126 rue Saint-Pierre (☎ **888/833-5253** or 418/692-2224), infusing a pre–World War I building with modernist design, continues a trend in designer hotels and inns in the Basse-Ville. It is especially fashionable among the younger business set.
- **Best Location:** Where else? For tourists, nothing can beat the **Château Frontenac** (see "Best Historic Hotel" above) for proximity to all the sights. In fact, the Château *is* one of the sights.
- **Best Health Club and Pool:** At the **Radisson Gouverneurs** (see "Best for Business Travelers" above), weights, Exercycles, and a workout room with instructors, as well as a whirlpool and sauna, will help you ease out the kinks. Slip into the heated pool inside and swim out to the open air.

3 Best Dining Bets

For full listings for these and many other recommended restaurants, see chapter 5 and chapter 13, and for a discussion of dining in Québec, see "Cuisine Haute, Cuisine Bas: Smoked Meat, Fiddleheads & Caribou" in the appendix.

MONTRÉAL

- **Best Spot for a Romantic Dinner:** Tucked into an 18th-century stone house in Vieux-Montréal is **La Marée,** 404 place Jacques-Cartier, near rue Notre-Dame (☎ **514/861-8126**), whose tables are bathed in candlelight and set with elegant crystal and silver. The food is excellent without being distracting, and the staff is professional and attentive but unobtrusive.
- **Best Spot for a Business Lunch:** The classic power place since 1958 has been **Le Beaver Club** in La Reine Elizabeth Hôtel, 900 bd. René-Lévesque Ouest (☎ **514/861-3511**), but because its men's-club air might be unpalatable to some women business travelers who have to entertain while on the road, the elegantly neutral **Café de Paris** at the Ritz-Carlton (see chapter 4), 1228 rue Sherbrooke Ouest, at rue Drummond (☎ **514/842-4212**), won't disappoint, at least in its deluxe setting and polished service.
- **Best Spot for a Celebration:** No need to rake in stacks of chips at the gambling tables in the casino to join the festive gatherings at **Nuances,** 1 av. du Casino (5th floor of the casino, ☎ **514/392-2708**), the gracious multistarred *temple d'cuisine* on the top floor. You'll get superb service, astonishing food, and spectacular views of the skyline to boot.
- **Best Wine List: Les Halles,** 1450 rue Crescent, between rue Ste-Catherine and boulevard de Maisonneuve (☎ **514/844-2328**), has a selection of more than 400 labels, carefully arranged not simply by such broad regional categories as Bourdeaux and Burgundy, but by appellation. Prices run well into three figures, but more moderately priced bottles are also available.

- **Best Decor:** With its exposed stone walls, wallpaper with delicate traceries, gilt and carved framed paintings of game, fireplaces ablaze much of the year, and velvet drapes at the windows, **La Marée,** 404 place Jacques-Cartier, near rue Notre-Dame (☎ 514/861-8126), pleases the eye at every turn.
- **Best View:** Assuming no one objects to rooms that move while its occupants are eating, the room with *the* vista is **Le Tour de Ville** in the Hôtel Delta Centre-Ville, 777 rue Université (☎ 514/879-1370). See chapter 9.
- **Best Value:** At lunch, the all-you-can-eat Indian buffet at **Le Taj,** 2077 rue Stanley, near rue Sherbrooke (☎ 514/845-9015), is a wonder. At dinner, even the *expensive* four-course table d'hôte at **Le Bourlingueur,** 363 St-François-Xavier, near rue St-Paul (☎ 514/845-3646), comes in under C$15.75 (US$10.85).
- **Best for Kids:** On the assumption that a kid who doesn't like pizza is as rare as fish feathers, get over to **Pizzédélic,** on The Main at 3509 bd. St-Laurent, near rue Sherbrooke (☎ 514/282-6784), among a growing number of branches. They have all manner of toppings, from the utterly conventional to just short of odd, and pastas, too—all to be eaten while looking out at the street or under umbrellas on the terrace in back.
- **Best French Cuisine: Les Halles** (see "Best Wine List" above) has clung to the crest of the haute pinnacle for more than a quarter century by judicious evolution in its cookery, not wrenching overhauls.
- **Best Italian Cuisine:** Superchic **Buona Notte,** 3518 bd. St-Laurent, near rue Sherbrooke (☎ 514/848-0644), may look as if it's more concerned with being a place to be seen than with what it sends out of the kitchen, but the pastas, focaccias, and risottos rival the occasional celebrity sightings.
- **Best Mexican Cuisine:** There's a party every night at **Casa de Matéo,** 440 rue St-François-Xavier, near rue St-Paul (☎ 514/844-4154), starting with the birdbath margaritas and dancing on through fried cactus, ceviche, and fish Veracruz. The infectious enthusiasm of the staff is often heightened by live mariachi music.
- **Best Thai Cuisine: Sawatdee,** 457 rue St-Pierre, near rue Notre-Dame (☎ 514/849-8854), purveys examples of a most complex Asian cooking style at good value in a setting of museum-quality Thai statuary and artworks.
- **Best Seafood:** Fish is the mainstay of Greek cooking, and is best when preparations are simplest. Grills are paramount at **Milos,** 5357 av. du Parc (☎ 514/272-3522), and the swimmers given that standard-setting treatment are as fresh as the dawn.
- **Best Pizza:** The name says it all: **Pizzédélic** (see "Best for Kids" above), where they do anything from same-old, same-old tomato and cheese to forward-edge designer concoctions with unlikely toppings, like snails.
- **Best Desserts:** With patisseries on every other corner, indulging in creamy, gooey, blissfully caloric sweets doesn't constitute a difficult search. But along boulevard St-Laurent, make the effort to seek out **Kilo,** 5206 bd. St-Laurent, between rue Maguire and rue Fairmount (☎ 514/277-5039).
- **Best Late-Night Dining:** Plateau Mont-Royal's most Parisian bistro, **L'Express,** 3927 rue St-Denis, near Rue Roy (☎ 514/845-5333), doesn't need a sign out front, since it stays full nightly until 3am (Sunday only until 1am). Simple but toothsome recipes with the freshest ingredients keep the night owls coming.
- **Best Outdoor Dining:** Serious food isn't primary at **Le Jardin Nelson,** 407 place Jacques-Cartier (☎ 514/861-5731), but you'll have music—classical or

jazz—as you partake of sweet or savory crepes or very good pizzas under the crabapple tree in the garden.

- **Best People Watching:** Any of a dozen cafes along St-Denis will fill this bill, especially on weekends, when the Plateau Mont-Royal boulevard comes alive. But **Le Café Cherrier,** 3635 rue St-Denis, at rue Cherrier (☎ 514/843-4308), might be the most fun, if you can find a seat on the wraparound terrace.

- **Best Afternoon Tea:** Gentility and correctness prevail at the **Café de Paris** in the Ritz-Carlton (see "Best Spot for a Business Lunch" above), where high tea is sublimely reassuring at any time of year, but best in spring and summer, when they move outdoors next to the duck pond.

- **Best Brunch:** Crepes with multitudes of fillings make for Frenchified brunches at **Le Jardin Nelson,** 407 place Jacques-Cartier, near rue de la Commune (☎ 514/861-5731), in the garden, inside, or on the terrace facing place Jacques-Cartier.

- **Best for Before-Theater Dinner:** The Polish cafe **Stash,** 200 rue St-Paul Ouest, near rue St-François-Xavier (☎ 514/845-6611), is only a block down the hill from the English-language Centaur Theatre, and it's open continuously from 11am to late evening.

- **Best Smoked Meat:** It'll only throw another log on a local controversy that's blazed for at least a century, but **Schwartz's** on The Main at 3895 bd. St-Laurent, north of rue Prince-Arthur (☎ 514/842-4813), serves up the definitive version of Montréal's untransplantable deli treat.

- **Best Fast Food:** Where else but **Chez Better,** 160 rue Notre-Dame, near place Jacques-Cartier (☎ 514/861-2617), where sausages and schnitzels dominate the card, washed down with any of dozens of foreign beers. Six branches and growing.

- **Best New Restaurant:** After making his bones in elite kitchens from France to Singapore, the chef and his young partner at **Jongleux Café,** 3434 av. St-Denis, near rue Sherbrooke (☎ 514/841-8080), are making waves with what he calls "updated bistro cooking." His creations soar well beyond that modest description, however.

- **Best Restaurant, Period:** Ever-questing Normand Laprise and partner Christine Lamarche keep **Toqué!,** 3842 rue St-Denis, near rue Roy (☎ 514/499-2084), in a league of its own. It's postmodern, it's postnouvelle, it's dazzling! Nipping at their heels, though, is **Nuances,** in the Casino de Montréal, Île Ste-Hélène (☎ 514/392-2708).

QUÉBEC CITY

- **Best Spot for a Romantic Dinner:** Stars above, tables illuminated by the flutter of candlelight and gas lamps, unobtrusive service, and even the name, **Le Saint-Amour,** 48 rue Ste-Ursule (☎ 418/694-0667), bespeak romance.

- **Best View:** Revolving rooftop restaurants rarely dish out food as elevated as their lofty venues, and **L'Astral** in the Loews Le Concorde hotel (see chapter 12), 1225 place Montcalm (☎ 418/647-2222), doesn't challenge that perception. Go for the views and a drink, and you shouldn't be disappointed.

- **Best Contemporary Cuisine: Laurie Raphaël,** 117 rue Dalhousie (☎ 418/692-4555), is named for the owners' children, a choice that isn't lost on those diners who devote great care to things they hold important—family, friends, and the tables around which they gather.

- **Best Seafood:** The owner of **Le Marie-Clarisse,** 12 rue du Petit-Champlain (☎ 418/692-0857), selects all the just-off-the-boat ingredients served at his comfortable bistro at the bottom of Breakneck Stairs. There's a fireplace inside and a terrace outside.

- **Best Pizza:** For conventional and unusual toppings on crispy-thin crusts that work better with a knife and fork than fingers, hit **Les Frères de la Côte,** 1190 rue St-Jean (☎ 418/692-5445).

- **Best People Watching:** **Le Marie-Clarisse's** few outdoor tables—perched above the main pedestrian intersection of le quartier Petit-Champlain—monopolize an unsurpassed observation point. See "Best Seafood" above.

- **Best Place to Take a Teenager:** Tasty pizzas and inventive pastas coupled with a thumping stereo and the noise level of a 20-lane bowling alley make **Les Frères de la Côte** (see "Best Pizza" above) a logical choice for parents with teens.

Planning Your Trip: The Basics

2

Montréal and Québec City have a stronger foreign flavor than other cities in Canada, and the first language of most residents is French. But once you decide to go, pulling together information on ways to get there, border formalities, exchanging money, climate, lodging possibilities, and related details is almost as easy as getting from Illinois to Florida. The information below and in the subsequent "Fast Facts" sections should help speed the process along.

1 Visitor Information & Entry Requirements

VISITOR INFORMATION

Québec tourism authorities produce volumes of detailed and highly useful publications, and they're easy to obtain by mail, by phone, or in person. To contact **Tourisme Québec,** write C.P. 979, Montréal, PQ H3C 2W3, or call ☎ **800/363-7777,** operator 806 (within the Montréal area, call ☎ **514/873-2015**). General information on travel in Canada can be obtained from the following offices:

Atlanta: Canadian Consulate General, Suite 400 South Tower, One CNN Center, Atlanta, GA 30303-2705 (☎ **404/577-6810** or 404/577-1512).

Boston: Canadian Consulate General, 3 Copley Place, Suite 400, Boston, MA 02116 (☎ **617/262-3760**).

Buffalo: Canadian Consulate General, 1 Marine Midland Center, Suite 3000, Buffalo, NY 14203-2884 (☎ **716/852-1247**).

Chicago: Consulate General, 2 Prudential Plaza, 180 N. Stetson Ave., Suite 2400, Chicago, IL 60601-6710 (☎ **312/616-1860**).

Dallas: Canadian Consulate General, 750 N. St. Paul, Suite 1700, Dallas, TX 75201 (☎ **214/922-9806**).

Detroit: Canadian Consulate General, 600 Renaissance Center, Suite 1100, Detroit, MI 48243-1704 (☎ **313/567-2085**).

Los Angeles: Canadian Consulate General, 300 S. Grand Ave., Suite 1000, Los Angeles, CA 90071 (☎ **213/687-7432**).

Minneapolis: Canadian Consulate General, 701 Fourth Ave. S., Suite 900, Minneapolis, MN 55415-1899 (☎ **612/333-4641**).

New York: Canadian Consulate General, 1251 Avenue of the Americas, 16th floor, New York, NY 10020-1175 (☎ **212/596-1600**).

Seattle: Canadian Consulate General, 412 Plaza 600, Sixth and Stewart sts., Seattle, WA 98101-1286 (☎ **206/443-1777**).

Washington, D.C.: Canadian Embassy, Tourism Section, 501 Pennsylvania Ave. NW, Washington, DC 20001 (☎ **202/682-1740**).

In addition, the Québec government maintains a number of offices in the United States and abroad, which can provide specific tourism information about the province:

New York: Délégation du Québec, 1 Rockefeller Plaza, 26th floor, New York, NY 10020-2201 (☎ **212/397-0200**).

Worldwide, there are offices ready to answer travelers' questions and provide literature:

London: Délégation du Québec, 59 Pall Mall, London SW1Y 5JH, England (☎ **071/930-8314**); High Commission of Canada, Canada House, Cockspur Street, Trafalgar Square, London SW1Y 5BJ, England (☎ **071/258-6600**).

Paris: Délégation du Québec, 4 av. Victor-Hugo, 75116 Paris, France (☎ **144/17-32-40**); Canadian Embassy, 35 av. Montaigne, 75008 Paris, France (☎ **14/143-2900**).

Besides these offices outside Québec, the province has a large office in Montréal, and there are convenient regional offices in Montréal and Québec City as well.

ENTRY REQUIREMENTS

DOCUMENTS　U.S. citizens or permanent residents of the United States require neither passports nor visas but will need some proof of citizenship, such as a birth certificate and a photo ID, both to enter Canada and to reenter the United States. A passport is the logical and preferred document, even though it isn't specifically required. Permanent U.S. residents who are not citizens must have their Alien Registration Cards (green cards) with them. If you plan to drive into Canada, be sure to have your car's registration handy.

An important point for teenage travelers: All persons under 19 require a letter from a parent or guardian granting them permission to travel to Canada. The letter must state the traveler's name and the duration of the trip. It is therefore essential that teenagers carry proof of identity. Otherwise, the letter from Mom and Dad is useless at the border.

Citizens of Australia, New Zealand, the United Kingdom, and Ireland need only carry a valid passport. Citizens of many other countries must have visas, applied for well in advance at their nearest Canadian embassy or consulate. Questions can be addressed to the **Canadian Immigration Division,** place du Portage, 140 Promenade du Portage, Phase 4, Hull, Québec K1A 1L1, or ☎ **819/994-2424.**

CUSTOMS　Regulations are flexible in most respects, but visitors can expect at least a probing question or two at the border or airport. Normal baggage

Siteseeing

Major Internet sites such as **Yahoo!** (**www.yahoo.com**), **Excite** (**www.excite.com**), **Lycos** (**www.lycos.com**), and **Infoseek** (**www.infoseek.com**) contain subcategories on travel, country/regional info, and culture. Search these for links to Web sites specializing in Montréal and Québec City. For further details on Web sites, see **"Planning Your Trip: An Online Directory"** following this chapter.

and personal possessions should be no problem, but tobacco and alcoholic beverages face limitations. Only 50 cigars, 200 cigarettes, and 400 grams of loose tobacco are allowed to individuals 16 years or over. In addition, an Imperial quart (just over a liter) of wine or liquor may be brought in, or a curiously generous case (24 cans) of beer, assuming the bearer is at or over the minimum drinking age in Québec, which is 18.

Pets with proper vaccination records may be admitted, but inquire in advance about necessary procedures at one of the Consulates General (see "Visitor Information" above, and "Pets" in "Fast Facts: Montréal" in chapter 3). Talk to U.S. Customs (see below) about bringing pets back home.

There are strict regulations regarding the import of plants, food products, and firearms. Hunters with valid licenses can bring in some gear, but handguns and fully automatic firearms are prohibited. Fishing tackle poses no problems, as long as the proper nonresident license is obtained.

For more detailed information concerning Customs regulations, write to **Canada Customs Office,** 400 place d'Youville, 2nd floor, Montréal, PQ H2Y 2C2 (☎ **514/283-2949** or 514/283-2959).

A car that is driven into Canada can stay for up to a year, but it must leave with the owner or a duty will be levied. The possession or use of a radar detector is prohibited, whether or not it is connected. Police officers can confiscate it and fine the owner C$500 to C$1,000 (US$333 to US$666).

For U.S. Citizens & Permanent Residents   Travelers who have been in Québec for fewer than 48 hours may bring back only US$200 worth of Canadian goods duty free. That limit may include only 50 cigarettes (2½ packs), 10 cigars, or 5 ounces of liquor.

Stays in Québec of more than 2 days have less strict limitations. Allowances expand to up to US$400 duty-free Canadian goods per person, including up to 100 cigars (but none from Cuba), a carton of cigarettes (200), and 1 liter (1.06 U.S. quarts) of liquor, assuming the carrier is 21 or older. Note that the liquor regulation is that of U.S. Customs; state laws may demand an additional tax or specify a different quantity limit, and the Customs officers enforce state laws as well as federal restrictions.

A flat duty of 10% is charged for the next $1,000 worth of purchases. Be sure to have receipts handy. But considering the substantial discounts available on domestic and foreign wine and liquor bottles at border duty-free stores, even paying the duty on a couple of extra bottles usually represents a savings. You cannot bring fresh foodstuffs into the United States; canned foods, however, are allowed. For more information, contact the **U.S. Customs Service,** 1301 Constitution Ave. (P.O. Box 7407), Washington, DC 20044 (☎ **202/927-6724**), and request the free pamphlet *Know Before You Go.* It's also available on the Web at **www.customs.ustreas.gov/travel/travel.htm**; click the Know Before You Go link.

Individual states may collect duty on each and every bottle travelers carry when crossing the border by car. When you're traveling by air, they won't, because Customs inspection by U.S.-government Customs agents takes place right there in Montréal's Dorval and Québec City airports before U.S. passengers board their planes, not when they arrive at their destinations. There are two U.S. Customs inspections in Dorval—one right after check-in and one past the duty-free shops on the way to the departure gate for carry-on luggage.

For U.K. Citizens   Citizens of the United Kingdom returning from Canada have customs allowances as follows: 200 cigarettes, 50 cigars, or 250g of smoking tobacco; 2 liters of still table wine; 1 liter of spirits or strong liqueur (over

22% volume); 2 liters of fortified wine, sparkling wine, or other liqueurs; 60cc (ml) perfume, 250cc (ml) of toilet water; and 145 pounds' worth of all other goods, including gifts and souvenirs. People under 17 cannot have the tobacco or alcohol allowance. For more information, contact **HM Customs & Excise,** Passenger Enquiry Point, 2nd Floor Wayfarer House, Great South West Road, Feltham, Middlesex, TW14 8NP (☎ **0181/910-3744;** from outside the U.K. 44/181-910-3744), or consult their Web site at **www.open.gov.uk**.

For Australian Citizens   The duty-free allowance in Australia is A$400 or, for those under 18, A$200. Personal property mailed back from Canada should be marked AUSTRALIAN GOODS RETURNED to avoid payment of duty. Upon returning to Australia, citizens can bring in 250 cigarettes or 250g of loose tobacco, and 1.125ml of alcohol. If you're returning with previously owned valuable goods, such as foreign-made cameras, file form B263. A helpful brochure, available from Australian consulates and Customs offices, is *Know Before You Go*. For more information, contact **Australian Customs Services,** GPO Box 8, Sydney, NSW 2001 (☎ **02/9213-2000**).

For New Zealand Citizens   The duty-free allowance for New Zealand is NZ$700. Citizens over 17 can bring in 200 cigarettes, or 50 cigars, or 250g of tobacco (or a mixture of all three if their combined weight doesn't exceed 250g), plus 4.5 liters of wine and beer, or 1.125 liters of liquor. New Zealand currency does not carry import or export restrictions. Fill out a certificate of export, listing the valuables you are taking out of the country; that way, you can bring them back without paying duty. Most questions are answered in a free pamphlet available at New Zealand consulates and Customs offices: *New Zealand Customs Guide for Travelers, Notice no. 4*. For more information, contact **New Zealand Customs,** 50 Anzac Ave., P.O. Box 29, Auckland (☎ **09/ 359-6655**).

2 Money

CURRENCY

Canadian money comes in graduated denominations of dollars and cents, but with a favorable balance for Americans, since the Canadian dollar is worth about 67¢ in U.S. currency, give or take a couple of points' daily variation. Put another way, one U.S. dollar buys about $1.50 in Canadian money, the exchange rate used to convert prices in this book. This means that U.S. dollars gain substantially more spending power the moment they are changed for local currency (a return, for example, of approximately C$525 Canadian for every US$350). And since prices are roughly on par with those in the States, the difference is real, not imaginary. Prices in this book, unless otherwise indicated, are given in both Canadian and U.S. dollars.

Visitors can bring in or take out any amount of money they wish, but if U.S. citizens import or export sums of US$5,000 or more, a report of the transaction must be filed with U.S. Customs.

Canadian coins are similar to their American counterparts: 1¢, 5¢, 10¢, 25¢. Bills—$1, $2, $5, $10, $20, $50, $100—are all the same size but have different colors, depending on the denomination. The gold-colored $1 coin (called a "loonie" by Canadians because of the depiction of a loon on one side) has all but replaced the $1 bill. A new $2 coin has appeared, with a bronze center surrounded by a nickel disk, meant to replace the old $2 bill, which is still in circulation. (It is sometimes called a "toonie," a reference to the next-smaller coin.) French speakers sometimes refer to a dollar as a "*piastre*."

Canadian & U.S. Dollar Equivalents

For U.S. Readers The rate of exchange used to calculate the dollar values given in this book was US$1 = approximately C$1.50 (or C$1 = US$0.667).

For British Readers The rate of exchange used to calculate the pound values in the accompanying table was £1 = approximately C$2.50 (or C$1 = 40p)

C$	U.S.$	U.K.£	C$	U.S.$	U.K.£
0.10	.07	.04	35.00	23.35	14.00
0.25	.17	.10	40.00	26.68	16.00
0.50	.33	.20	45.00	30.02	18.00
1.00	.67	.40	50.00	33.35	20.00
2.00	1.33	.80	55.00	36.69	22.00
3.00	2.00	1.20	60.00	40.20	24.00
4.00	2.67	1.60	65.00	43.36	26.00
5.00	3.34	2.00	70.00	46.69	28.00
6.00	4.00	2.40	75.00	50.02	30.00
7.00	4.67	2.80	80.00	53.36	32.00
8.00	5.34	3.20	85.00	56.70	34.00
9.00	6.00	3.60	90.00	60.03	36.00
10.00	6.67	4.00	95.00	63.37	38.00
15.00	10.00	6.00	100.00	66.70	40.00
20.00	13.34	8.00	150.00	100.05	60.00
25.00	16.68	10.00	200.00	133.40	80.00
30.00	20.00	12.00	250.00	167.50	100.00

Planning Basics

Many stores accept U.S. dollars, often posting a sign to that effect that gives the percentage rate they offer. Usually, that amount is less than what banks offer, but sometimes it is more favorable, because many establishments are eager to attract U.S. tourist dollars. As a rule, though, it's more advantageous to change money and traveler's checks at a bank, and better still to obtain cash at ATMs (see below).

ATMS

As ubiquitous in Québec as in the United States, ATMs are found in most of the same places, outside or inside bank branches, but also increasingly at other locations, including the province's new casinos. Look for signs reading GUICHET ATOMATIQUE or SERVICES AUTOMATISÉS.

The principal networks are **Cirrus** (☎ 800/424-7787; **www.mastercard. com/atm**) and **Plus** (☎ 800/843-7587; **www.visa.com/atms**) for withdrawing funds from home checking accounts. A four-digit PIN (personal identification number) is required, so people with fewer or more digits need to have another PIN assigned to their account(s) before leaving home. The exchange rate at ATMs is usually more favorable than that offered by banks. This advantage can be wiped out, however, if your home bank charges high transaction fees, so check with your bank before departing. When using ATMs to obtain cash advances on credit cards, remember that interest is charged from the day of withdrawal.

CREDIT CARDS

Credit cards are accepted as widely in Québec as in the States. Visa and MasterCard dominate the market, followed by the American Express card, Diners Club, and its Canadian cousin, enRoute. The Discover and Carte Blanche cards fall well behind the others in usage. Charge slips are written up in Canadian dollars, and card companies convert the amount to U.S. dollars when they credit the transaction to your account.

TRAVELER'S CHECKS

Reliable old traveler's checks are now something of an anachronism from the days before the ATM. The only sound alternative to traveling with large amounts of cash, traveler's checks were almost as reliable as currency, unlike personal checks, but could be replaced if lost or stolen, unlike cash. These days, traveler's checks are far less necessary because every city and large town in Québec has 24-hour ATMs that allow travelers to withdraw cash as needed.

If you still want the security of backup funds in the form of traveler's checks, they can be obtained at most banks. **American Express** offers denominations of $10, $20, $50, $100, $500, and $1,000. The service charge ranges from 1% to 4%. American Express traveler's checks are also available over the phone at ☎ **800/221-7282;** when using this number, Amex gold and platinum cardholders are exempt from the 1% fee. AAA members can obtain checks without a fee at most AAA offices.

Visa offers traveler's checks at Citibank locations nationwide, and at several other banks. The service charge ranges between 1.5% and 2%; checks come in denominations of $20, $50, $100, $500, and $1,000. **MasterCard** also offers traveler's checks. Call ☎ **800/223-9920** for a location near you.

THEFT

Almost every credit-card company has an emergency 800-number to call in the event your wallet or purse is stolen. They may be able to wire a cash advance immediately, and in many places, they can deliver an emergency credit card in a day or two. The issuing bank's 800-number is usually on the back of the credit card—though of course that doesn't help much if the card is stolen. Making photocopies of credit cards, key passport pages, and other important documents therefore makes sense. Visa cardholders should call ☎ **800/847-2911** in the U.S. and Canada. MasterCard holders should call ☎ **800/307-7309** in the U.S. and Canada. American Express cardholders should call ☎ **800/554-2639** in the U.S. or ☎ **301/214-8228** collect outside the U.S. for the Global Assist Hotline. Diners Club cardholders should call ☎ **303/799-1504** collect outside the U.S.; enRoute cardholders should call ☎ **800/363-3333** in Canada.

Odds are that if your wallet is gone, the police won't be able to recover it for you. However, after you realize that it's gone and you cancel your credit cards, it is still wise to inform them. Your credit-card company or insurer may require a police-report number.

3 When to Go

High season is late May through early September, when hotels are most likely to be full and charge their highest tariffs. Even then, though, weekends are cheaper and package plans reduce the bite, so advance planning has its rewards. The period from Christmas to New Year's is also busy (and more expensive), as are the days given to winter festivals in both Montréal and Québec City.

CLIMATE

Temperatures are usually a few degrees lower in Québec City than in Montréal. Spring, short but sweet, arrives around the middle of May. Summer (mid-June through mid-September) tends to be humid in Montréal, Québec City, and other communities along the St. Lawrence River, drier at the inland resorts of the Laurentians and Estrie. Intense but usually brief heat waves mark July and early August, but temperatures rarely remain oppressive in the evening. Autumn (September and October) is as short and changeable as spring, with warm days and cool or chilly nights. Canadian maples blaze with color for weeks. Winter brings dependable snows for skiing in the Laurentians, Estrie, and Charlevoix. After a sleigh ride or a ski run in Parc Mont-Royal, Montréal's Underground City is a climate-controlled blessing. Mid-February is the time for Québec City's robust Carnaval d'Hiver (Winter Carnival). Snow and slush are more-or-less constantly present from November to March.

Montréal's Average Monthly Temperatures (°F)

	Jan	Feb	Mar	Apr	May	June	July	Aug	Sept	Oct	Nov	Dec
High	21	25	34	52	65	74	78	77	70	56	43	26
Low	8	12	23	37	48	57	62	60	53	43	32	15

Québec City's Average Monthly Temperatures (°F)

	Jan	Feb	Mar	Apr	May	June	July	Aug	Sept	Oct	Nov	Dec
High	19	21	32	46	60	70	76	74	65	52	39	23
Low	5	8	19	32	43	53	57	56	48	37	28	12

Temperature Conversion

Celsius (°C):	-25	-20	-15	-10	-5	0	5	10	15	20	25	30	35
Fahrenheit (°F):	-13	-4	5	14	23	32	41	50	59	68	77	86	95

HOLIDAYS

In Québec province, the important public holidays are New Year's Day (Jan 1); Good Friday and Easter Monday (late March or April); Victoria Day (May 24 or nearest Monday); St-Jean-Baptiste Day, Québec's "national" day (June 24); Confederation, or Dominion, Day (July 1); Labour Day (first Monday in September); Canadian Thanksgiving Day (second Monday in October); Remembrance Day (November 11); and Christmas Day (December 25).

War & Remembrance

Canadian forces lost 60,000 dead in World War I, a tremendous loss for a country with a tenth the population of the United States, which lost 53,000 people in the same conflict. The Armistice that ended the war was signed on November 11, 1918, the 11th hour of the 11th day of the 11th month. It is commemorated as Remembrance Day, when Canadians wear red cloth poppies for days before and after. Again and again, lines are repeated from a poem written by John McCrae, a Canadian medical officer who himself died before war's end:

"In Flanders fields the poppies blow
Between the crosses, row on row."

Montréal & Québec City Calendar of Events

From June to September, only a serious misadventure in planning might allow visitors to miss a celebration of some sort in Montréal and Québec City. If something's not going on in one city, it's bound to be happening in the other, and it's easy to get from one to the other.

January

○ **La Fête des Neiges (Snow Festival), Montréal.** Montréal's answer to Québec City's Carnaval d'Hiver (Winter Carnival) features outdoor events such as harness racing, barrel jumping, racing beds on ice, canoe races, snowshoeing, skating, and cross-country skiing. The less athletically inclined can cheer from the sidelines and then inspect the snow and ice sculptures. The event, the first 2 weeks of February, takes places mostly on Île Notre-Dame, in the Port and Vieux-Montréal, and in Parc Maisonneuve. Call ☎ **514/872-4537** for details.

○ **Carnaval D'Hiver (de Québec), Québec City.** Usually Québec is courtly and dignified, but all that is cast aside when the symbolic snowman called Bonhomme ("Good Fellow") appears to preside over these 10 days of merriment in early February every year. During the event, more than a million revelers descend upon the city, eddying around the monumental ice palace and ice sculptures and attending a full schedule of concerts, dances, and parades. The mood is heightened by the availability of plastic trumpets and canes filled with a concoction called "Caribou," the principal ingredients of which are cheap whisky and sweet red wine. Perhaps its presence explains the eagerness with which certain Québecois participate in the canoe race across the treacherous ice floes of the St. Lawrence.

The Carnival is held in front of the Parliament Building, on grounds known during this time as Place du Palais—just outside the walls to the Old City—in early February. Hotel reservations must be made far in advance. Scheduled events are free. Call ☎ **418/626-3716** for details.

February/March

• **Festival Montréal en Lumière.** Filling a hole in the yearly schedule, the self-dubbed City of Festivals has created this "High Lights" celebration. It brings together a somewhat disparate collection of creative and performing events, from culinary competitions and special museum exhibitions to multimedia light shows and classical and pop concerts by international musical greats. Call ☎ **514/844-5400** for information. Mid-February to early March.

May/June

• **Festival de Théâtre des Amériques.** Two weeks of contemporary theater works from artists throughout the Americas, many on the cutting edge of creativity. Screenings are held at theaters throughout the city. Call ☎ **514/842-0704** for details. Late May to early June.

• **Montréal Bike Fest.** Early in June, more than 45,000 enthusiasts converge on Montréal to participate in a variety of cycling competitions, including a nocturnal bike ride, a 16-mile outing for up to 10,000 children, and the grueling Tour de l'Île, a day-long 70-kilometer race around the island before more than 120,000 spectators. The last event, which began in 1984, attracts almost as many women participants as men. Call ☎ **514/521-8356** for details. Usually the first Sunday in June.

- **Grand Prix Air Canada, Montréal.** International drivers lay rubber around the Gilles-Villeneuve race track on Île Notre-Dame in the only Formula I race in the country. Call ☎ 514/392-0000 for details. Second weekend in June.
- **St-Jean-Baptiste Day.** Honoring Saint John the Baptist, the patron saint of French Canadians, this *fête nationale* is marked by more festivities and far more enthusiasm throughout Québec province than national Dominion Day on July 1. It's their "national" holiday. In the past, its hallmark parade has been marred by considerable drunkenness and vandalism in both Montréal and Québec City. Last year, in a successful effort to control such problems, the parade was held along the streets of Vieux-Montréal the night before, June 23. Call ☎ 418/640-0799 for details. June 24.

July

✪ **Festival International de Jazz de Montréal.** Montréal has a long tradition in jazz, and this enormously successful festival has been celebrating America's one true art form since 1979. Miles Davis, Chet Baker, and Dizzie Gillespie have been among the many headliners in past years, but it costs money to hear stars of such magnitude. Fortunately, hundreds of other concerts are free, often given on the streets and plazas of the city. You can see events along rue Ste-Catherine and rue Jeanne-Mance. For information and tickets, call ☎ 514/871-1881. Late June to early July.

✪ **Festival d'Été International (International Summer Festival),** Québec City. The largest cultural event in the French-speaking world, this festival has attracted artists from Africa, Asia, Europe, and North America since it began in 1967. There are more than 250 events showcasing theater, music, and dance, with 600 performers from 20 countries. One million people come to watch and listen. Jazz and folk combos perform free in an open-air theater next to City Hall; visiting dance and folklore troupes put on shows; and concerts, theatrical productions, and related events fill the days and evenings. Call ☎ 418/532-4540 for details. Usually 10 days in mid-July.

- **Festival International Nuits d'Afrique, Montréal.** This World Beat musical event showcases nearly 300 musicians from the Caribbean, the Americas, and Africa. Performances take place in Club Soda, Club Balattou, and Place Berri. Call ☎ 514/499-9239 for details. Ten days in mid-July.

✪ **Festival Juste pour Rire (Just for Laughs Festival), Montréal.** This celebration strives to do for humor what the more famous jazz festival has done for that musical form. Comics perform in many venues, some free, some not. Both Francophone and Anglophone comics from many countries participate. It's held along rue St-Denis and elsewhere in the Latin Quarter. Call ☎ 514/845-3155 for details or check the Web site **www.hahaha.com**. Last 2 weeks of July.

- **Benson & Hedges International Competition d'Art Pyrotechnique (International Fireworks Competition), Montréal.** The open-air theater in La Ronde amusement park on Île Ste-Hélène is the best place to view the fireworks extravaganzas, although they can be enjoyed from almost any point overlooking the river. Tickets to the show also provide entrance to the amusement park. Kids, needless to say, love the whole explosive business. The 90-minute shows are staged by companies from several countries. Because parking is limited, it's best to use the Métro. Call ☎ 514/872-4537 for details. Saturdays in June, Sundays in July.

August

- **Grands Feux Loto-Québec, Québec City.** The capital has its own fireworks festival, overlapping the one in Montréal, and using the highly scenic Montmorency Falls as its setting. Five pyrotechnic teams are invited from as many different countries in this international competition. Their explosive displays are coordinated with appropriate music, as in Montréal. Call ☎ **418/692-3736.** Late July to mid-August.

- **Les Medievales de Québec (Québec Medieval Festival), Québec City.** Hundreds of actors, artists, entertainers, and other participants from Europe, Canada, and the United States converge on Québec City in period dress to re-create daily scenes from 5 centuries ago, playing knights, troubadours, and ladies-in-waiting during this event, a giant costume party. Parades, jousting tournaments, recitals of ancient music, and the Grand Cavalcade (La Grande Chevauchée), featuring hundreds of costumed equestrians, are just a few highlights. Fireworks are the one modern touch during this 5-day festival. Come in medieval attire, if you wish. Held in Québec City only in odd-numbered years. (In even-numbered years, its sister event, the Festival des Remparts, takes place in Dinan, France.) Held in the streets and public grounds of Old Québec. Call ☎ **418/692-1993** for details. Early to mid-August.

- **Festival des Films du Monde (World Film Festival), Montréal.** An international film event since 1976. Some 500 screenings take place over 12 days, including 200 feature films from more than 50 countries, drawing the usual throngs of directors, stars, and wannabes. It isn't as gaudy or as media-heavy as Cannes, but it's taken almost as seriously. Various movie theaters play host. Call ☎ **514/848-3883** for details. Late August to early September.

September

- **Fall Foliage.** The maple trees blaze in color, and a walk in the parks and squares of Montréal and Québec City is a refreshing tonic. It's a perfect time for a drive in the Laurentians or Estrie (near Montréal) and Île d'Orléans or up into Charlevoix from Québec City. Mid- to late September.

October

- **Festival International de la Nouvelle Danse, Montréal.** This 12-day showcase, held every 2 years (on odd years), invites troupes and choreographers from Canada, the United States, and Europe to various performance spaces. Call ☎ **514/287-1423** for details. Early October.

- **Festival du Nouveau Cinéma, Montréal.** Screenings of new and experimental films stimulate controversy and forums on the latest trends in film and video at halls and cinemas throughout the city. Call ☎ **514/843-4725** for details. Ten days in mid-October.

December/January

- **Christmas/New Year's.** Celebrating the holidays à la Française is a particular treat in Québec City, with its streets banked with snow and almost every ancient building sporting wreaths and decorated fir trees.

4 Tips for Travelers with Special Needs

FOR TRAVELERS WITH DISABILITIES

When calling to make an airline reservation or talking with a travel agent, inquire where a wheelchair will be stowed on the plane or train, or confirm that a Seeing Eye dog or hearing dog may accompany you. Remember that special meals can be preordered when making airline reservations. Québec regulations regarding accessibility for wheelchairs are similar to those in the United States, including curb cuts, entrance ramps, designated parking spaces, and specially equipped bathrooms. Access to the restaurants and inns housed in 18th- and 19th-century buildings, especially in Québec City, is often difficult or impossible, however.

A World of Options is a useful 658-page book of resources for travelers with disabilities; it covers everything from bicycle trips to scuba outfitters and costs $35 from **Mobility International USA,** P.O. Box 10767, Eugene, OR 97440 (☎ **541/343-1284,** voice and TDD; www.miusa.org).

FOR SENIORS

Senior discounts of 10% or 15% are offered by many airlines, but check to see if there are limited promotional fares that might constitute even greater savings. Amtrak offers seniors 62 and older a 15% discount on the U.S. segment of some of its fares between New York City and Montréal, a trip that takes 10 to 12 hours. Carry proof of age in order to obtain possible discounts at hotels, restaurants, and most museums and other attractions—driver's license, passport, Medicare card, and/or AARP membership card. While hotels, airlines, Amtrak, and car-rental agencies routinely give discounts to AARP members, you must ask. For membership, write to the **American Association of Retired Persons (AARP),** 601 E St. NW, Washington, DC 20049 (☎ **800/ 424-3410** or 202/434-2277).

To meet other people and combine travel with learning, look into **Elderhostel** educational programs, which many seniors find worthwhile. Those qualified to participate must be 60 years of age or older, while their accompanying spouses, "significant others," relatives, or friends need only be of adult age, as a rule. For more information, contact Elderhostel, 75 Federal St., Boston, MA 02110 (☎ **617/426-7788;** www.elderhostel.org).

FOR SINGLES

Two problems crop up most often for solo travelers: added costs and feelings of isolation, especially on Friday and Saturday nights, when everyone else seems to be out and about in numbers divisible by two. Check the sections in this book on popular local bars (see chapters 9 and 17), possibilities for meeting locals and engaging in some lively conversation. Jazz and folk-music spots, especially those that charge no cover—and most in Montréal and Québec City do not—are also fertile grounds for meeting and chatting with Québecois.

Bed-and-breakfast inns are often a good choice for meeting people, and both Montréal and Québec City have them. Guests come together over breakfast and might end up going out to explore or dine together. Prices are often (but not always) lower than those at hotels, many of which charge the same rate for a room whether it's occupied by one or two people. Other budget alternatives are the YMCA or YWCA in Montréal, more desirable than many of their number in other cities and affording a relaxed way to encounter other travelers. Guided walking tours are another excellent way to explore the city and enjoy a couple of hours of social interaction at the same time.

FOR GAYS & LESBIANS

In Montréal, gay and lesbian travelers may enjoy the Gay Village, primarily along rue Ste-Catherine Est between rue St-Hubert and rue Papineau, where there are numerous meeting spots, shops, cafes, bars, and clubs. Useful telephone services are the **Gay Line** (☎ **514/866-5090** or 888/505-1010 outside the 514 area code), which describes current events and activities in English daily from 7 to 10pm, and the **Gay and Lesbian Association of UQAM** (Québec University) at ☎ **514/987-3039.** To increase the chances of meeting people, try to visit the city during the annual **Gay & Lesbian Pride Festival;** it takes place at the end of July, with a parade, concerts, parties, and art shows (☎ **514/285-4011**). During the second week of October in Montréal, the **Black & Blue Festival** is 7 days of gay benefit parties at various locations throughout the city (☎ **514/875-7026**).

The gay community in Québec City is relatively small, centered in the Upper Town just outside the city walls, near Porte (Gate) Saint-Jean.

FOR FAMILIES

Montréal and Québec City offer an abundance of family oriented activities, many of them outdoors, even in winter. Dogsledding, water sports, river cruises, and frequent festivals and fireworks displays are among the possibilities. The walls and fortifications of Québec City are fodder for imagining the days of knights and princesses, and both cities have horse-drawn sightseeing carriages, a surefire hit with most youngsters. Many museums make special efforts to address children's interests and enthusiasms.

FOR STUDENTS

Many of the tips that apply to single travelers apply to students (who may or may not be traveling solo). Always carry a university or similar ID card to obtain the many available discounts, especially at museums and other attractions. Both Montréal and Québec City have their designated Latin Quarters, centrally located university areas filled with students.

To save money on lodging, consider the YMCA or the YWCA in Montréal and the youth hostels in Québec City. For information about the 16 youth hostels in Québec province, contact **Regroupment Tourisme Jeunesse,** 4545 av. Pierre-de-Coubertin C.P. 1000, Succursale, Montréal, Canada H1V 3R2.

5 Getting There

Served by highways, transcontinental trains and buses, and three international airports, Montréal and Québec City are easily accessible from any part of the United States and Europe.

BY PLANE

TO MONTRÉAL   Dorval International Airport is served by most of the world's major airlines, more than 50 in all. (Mirabel Airport, farther from the city, now accepts only air freight and some charter flights.) Most visitors fly into Dorval from other parts of North America on **Air Canada** (☎ **514/ 393-3333** or 800/776-3000 outside Canada), **American** (☎ **800/ 433-7300**), **Canadian** (☎ **800/665-1177** or 514/847-2211), **Continental** (☎ **800/231-0856**), **Delta** (☎ **800/221-1212** or 514/337-5520), **Northwest** (☎ **800/441-1818**), or **US Airways** (☎ **800/428-4322**). In the United States, Air Canada flies out of New York (Newark and LaGuardia), Miami, Tampa, Chicago, Los Angeles, and San Francisco.

Other carriers that serve Montréal via Dorval include **Air France** (☎ **800/ 847-1106**), **British Airways** (☎ **800/247-9297**), and **Swissair** (☎ **800/ 879-9154**). Regional airlines, such as Air Atlantic, American Eagle, and Inter-Canadian, also serve the city.

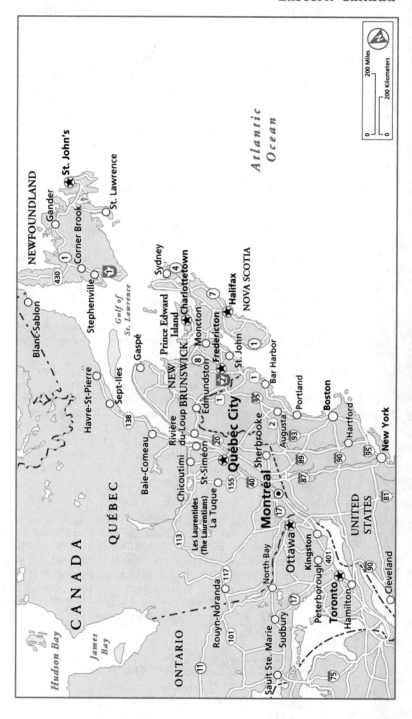

Flying for Less: Tips for Getting the Best Airfare

Passengers within the same airplane cabin rarely pay the same fare for their seats. Business travelers who need to purchase tickets at the last minute, change their itinerary at a moment's notice, or get home before the weekend pay the premium rate, known as the *full fare.* Passengers who can book their tickets long in advance, who don't mind staying over Saturday night, or who are willing to travel on a Tuesday, Wednesday, or Thursday after 7pm will pay a fraction of the full fare. On most flights, even the shortest hops, the full fare is close to $1,000 or more, but a 7-day or 14-day advance purchase ticket is closer to $200 to $300. Here are a few other easy ways to save:

1. Periodically airlines lower prices on their most popular routes. Check your newspaper for advertised discounts, or call the airlines directly and ask if any **promotional rates** or special fares are available. You'll almost never see a sale during the peak summer vacation months of July and August, or during the Thanksgiving or Christmas seasons; but in periods of low-volume travel, you should pay no more than $400 for a cross-country flight. If your schedule is flexible, ask if you can secure a cheaper fare by staying an extra day or by flying midweek. (Many airlines won't volunteer this information.) If you already hold a ticket when a sale breaks, it may even pay to exchange your ticket, which usually incurs a $50 to $75 charge.

   Note, however, that the lowest-priced fares are often nonrefundable, require advance purchase of 1 to 3 weeks and a certain length of stay, and carry penalties for changing dates of travel.

2. **Consolidators,** also known as *bucket shops,* are a good place to find low fares. Consolidators buy seats in bulk from the airlines and then sell them back to the public at prices below even the airlines' discounted rates. Their small ads usually run in the Sunday travel sections of most major newspapers. Before you pay, however, ask for a confirmation number from the consolidator, and then call the airline itself to confirm your seat. Be prepared to book your ticket with a different consolidator—there are many to choose from—if the airline can't

TO QUÉBEC CITY Québec City is served from the United States by a number of major airlines, notably Air Canada, but most air traffic comes by way of Montréal or Toronto (see above). Direct flights are available from New York (Newark) on **Air Alliance,** a connector airline for Air Canada (☎ **800/361-8620** in Canada, or 800/776-3000 outside Canada), and from Boston on **Northwest Airlink/Precision** (☎ **800/225-2525**). **Canadian Airlines** flies into Québec City from international destinations outside the U.S. (☎ **800/363-7530** in Canada, or 800/426-7000 outside Canada).

BY TRAIN

For **VIA Rail** information from the United States, call ☎ **800/561-3949** or log on to **www.viarail.ca.** In Canada, call ☎ **514/989-2626.**

TO MONTRÉAL Montréal is a major terminus on Canada's **VIA Rail** network, with its station, **Gare Centrale,** at 935 rue de la Gauchetière Ouest (☎ **514/871-1331**). The city is served by comfortable VIA Rail trains—some equipped with dining cars, sleeping cars, and cellular telephones—from other confirm your reservation. Also be aware that bucket-shop tickets are usually nonrefundable or rigged with stiff cancellation penalties, often as high as 50% to 75% of the ticket price.

Council Travel (☎ 800/226-8624; www.counciltravel.com) and STA Travel (☎ 800/781-4040; www.statravel.com) cater especially to young travelers, but their bargain-basement prices are available to people of all ages. Travel Bargains (☎ 800/AIR-FARE; www.1800airfare.com) was formerly owned by TWA but now offers the deepest discounts on many other airlines, with a 4-day advance purchase. Other reliable consolidators include 1-800-FLY-CHEAP (www.1800flycheap.com); TFI Tours International (☎ 800/745-8000 or 212/736-1140), which serves as a clearinghouse for unused seats; and "rebators" such as Travel Avenue (☎ 800/333-3335 or 312/876-1116) and the Smart Traveller (☎ 800/448-3338 in the U.S., or 305/448-3338), which rebate part of their commissions to you.ctoid.

3. Search the Internet for cheap fares—but know that it's still best to compare your findings with the research of an experienced travel agent, if you're lucky enough to have one, especially when you're booking more than just a flight. For full details on surfing the Web, see "Planning Your Trip: An Online Directory" following this chapter.

4. Great last-minute deals are also available through free e-mail services provided directly by the airlines. Each week, the airline sends you a list of discounted flights, usually leaving the upcoming Friday or Saturday, and returning the following Monday or Tuesday. You can sign up for all the major airlines at once by logging on to Smarter Living (www.smarterliving.com), or go to each individual airline's Web site.

The way to get the cheapest flight of all may be to book an escorted tour or a package that includes airfare and accommodations. See "Packages & Escorted Tours" below for details.

cities in Canada. There is scheduled service to Québec City via Trois-Rivières, and to and from Ottawa, Toronto, Winnipeg, and points west. Amtrak (☎ 800/872-7245; www.amtrak.com) has one train a day to Montréal from Washington and New York that makes intermediate stops. While it is a no-frills, coach-only affair, its scenic route passes along the eastern shore of the Hudson River and west of Lake Champlain. The *Adirondack* takes about 10½ hours from New York, if all goes well, but delays aren't unusual.

Passengers from Chicago can get to Montréal most directly by taking Amtrak to Toronto, then switching to VIA Rail.

The Queen Elizabeth/Le Reine Elisabeth hotel is located directly above the train station in Montréal, and less expensive lodging is only a short cab or Métro ride away. Seniors 62 and older are eligible for a 15% discount on some Amtrak trains, on the U.S. segment of the trip. VIA Rail also has a senior discount. Don't forget to bring along proof of citizenship (a passport or birth certificate) to use when crossing the border.

TO QUÉBEC CITY Québec City's train station, the **Gare du Palais,** is in the Lower Town at 450 rue de la Gare-du-Palais ([tel] **418/692-3940**). Four commuter trains run between Montréal and Québec City daily between 7am and 6pm, and they have snack and beverage services. Travel time between the two cities is about 3 hours. One-way fares vary substantially, with many kinds of discounts for seniors, students, and days of departure, but generally run from about C$30 (US$20) for supersaver economy class to around C$80 (US$53) for first-class, which provides meal service and more leg room.

BY BUS

TO MONTRÉAL Montréal's main bus terminal is the **Terminus Voyageur,** 505 bd. de Maisonneuve Est (☎ **514/842-2281**). The Voyageur company operates buses between here and all parts of Québec, with frequent runs through the Eastern Townships to Sherbrooke, to the various villages in the Laurentians, and to Québec City. Morning, noon, early afternoon, and midnight buses cover the distance between Toronto and Montréal in less than 7 hours. From Boston or New York, there is daily bus service to Montréal on **Greyhound** (☎ **800/231-2222** or 514/843-8495; **www.greyhound.com**). The trip from Boston takes about 8 hours; from New York City, with five departures daily, it takes 9 hours.

TO QUÉBEC CITY From New York or Boston, take **Greyhound** (☎ **800/231-2222**) to Montréal and change for the bus to Québec City, a 3-hour ride away. The bus traffic between Québec City and Montréal is heavy, with the express buses of **Orléans Express** (☎ **514/842-2281** in Montréal, or 418/524-4692 in Québec City), running almost every hour on the hour from 7am to 1am. The bus line also links Québec City to the rest of Québec province, with connections to the rest of Canada. Ask about excursion tickets and discounts for seniors and children.

BY CAR

Highway distances and speed limits are given in kilometers (km) in Canada. The speed limit on the autoroutes (limited-access highways) is 100 kilometers per hour (62 mph), although enforcement is lax. In the event you are stopped, there is a stiff penalty for not wearing seatbelts. And if you possess a radar detector, it can be confiscated. Passengers must buckle up in the backseat as well as in the driver's and passenger's seats up front.

Members of the **American Automobile Association (AAA)** should bring along their membership cards. The 24-hour hot line for emergency service provided by the **Canadian Automobile Association (CAA),** which is affiliated with AAA, is ☎ **514/861-7575** in Montréal and ☎ **418/624-0708** in Québec City. Headquarters for CAA-Québec is 444 rue Bouvier, Québec City, PQ G2J 1E3.

For information on road conditions in and around Québec City from November through mid-April, there is a 24-hour hot line (☎ **418/643-6830**). For the same information in Montréal, call ☎ **514/636-3026;** outside Montréal, call ☎ **514/636-3248.**

TO MONTRÉAL Interstate 87 runs due north from New York City to link up with Canada's Autoroute 15 at the border, and the entire 400-mile journey is on expressways. Likewise, from Boston, I-93 north joins I-89 just south of Concord, New Hampshire. At White River Junction there is a choice between continuing on I-89 to Lake Champlain, crossing the lake by roads and bridges to join I-87 and Canada Autoroute 15 north, or picking up I-91 at White

River Junction to go due north toward Sherbrooke, Québec. At the border, I-91 becomes Canada Route 55 and joins Canada Route 10 west through Estrie to Montréal. The Trans-Canada Highway, which connects both ends of the country, runs right through the city. From Boston to Montréal is about 320 miles; from Toronto, 540 kilometers (350 miles); from Ottawa, 190 kilometers (120 miles). Once you're in Montréal, Québec City is an easy 3-hour drive.

TO QUÉBEC CITY   Québec City is slightly more than 500 miles from New York, and less than 400 miles from Boston. Coming from New York and points farther south, pick up Interstate 91 at New Haven, and follow it right up to the Canadian border. From Boston, take I-93 out of the city and link up with I-91 at St. Johnsbury, Vermont. After crossing the border, I-91 becomes Québec Autoroute 55, to Sherbrooke and Drummondville. From Sherbrooke, there is a choice. To make the trip quickly, take Autoroute 55 to Autoroute 20. But Route 116, which heads northeast from Richmond, midway between Sherbrooke and Drummondville, is more scenic, if a bit slower.

On the approach to the city, follow signs for Pont (Bridge) Pierre-Laporte. After crossing the bridge, turn right onto boulevard Wilfrid-Laurier (Route 175), which later changes names and becomes the Grande-Allée. Past the Old City walls it becomes rue St-Louis, which leads straight to the Château Frontenac. For the most scenic entrance into the city, take an immediate exit onto boulevard Champlain after crossing the bridge, and turn left at the entrance to Parc des Champs-de-Bataille (Battlefields Park), up a steep hill to follow Chemin Grande-Allée to the Musée du Québec. Drive halfway around the circle in front of the museum, and then take avenue Montcalm-Wolfe to the Grande-Allée and turn right.

When you're driving to Québec City from Montréal (a car can be rented in the train station), Autoroute 40, which runs along the north shore of the St. Lawrence, is faster than Autoroute 20, on the south shore. The trip takes less than 3 hours without stops.

6 Packages & Escorted Tours

Before you start your search for the lowest airfare, you may want to consider booking your flight as part of a travel package such as an escorted tour or a package tour. What you lose in adventure, you'll gain in time and money saved when you book accommodations, and maybe even food and entertainment, along with your flight.

ESCORTED TOURS & CRUISES

There are ample reasons for taking an escorted tour: to save money, to have someone else make the arrangements and deal with glitches in a foreign language, and to travel with built-in companions. There are disadvantages, too, however: arising, eating, and sleeping on someone else's schedule; abiding by the decisions of the group and the tour guide; and traveling in a unilingual bubble that works against interplay with members of the native population. In Québec, the pros aren't as strong as they might be in, say, India or Egypt. While French is the dominant language, there's almost always someone nearby who speaks English. The money is easy to comprehend, since it uses essentially the same denominations as in the United States, and prices are lower than at home. And the Québec tourism authorities are as helpful and forthcoming as can be found anywhere in the world.

Some people love escorted tours, however. They let you relax and take in the sights while a bus driver fights traffic for you; they spell out your costs up front; and they take you to the maximum number of sights in the minimum amount of time with the least amount of hassle.

The following are some reputable escorted-tour operators. Make sure to ask as many questions as necessary; be sure especially to find out exactly what is included in the price and what the cancellation policy is.

Air Canada (☎ **800/925-4016,** ext. 8097) assembles custom packages that include round-trip air, lodging, sightseeing, and some meals in Québec City, Montréal, and Laurentian resorts.

Tauck Tours (☎ **800/468-2825** or 203/226-6911) has a 7-day, 6-night tour that includes Vermont, New Hampshire, Montréal, and Québec City. It's offered spring through mid-October, and it is to be recommended for the opportunity to view the fall foliage in both countries.

Yankee Holidays (☎ **800/468-2825** or 203/226-6911) has 10-day package tours taking in Montréal, Québec City, Ottawa, and Toronto, as well as an 8-day rail excursion that starts in Montréal and continues along the St. Lawrence to Gaspé. An 8-day cruise sails from Rochester, New York, through the St. Lawrence Seaway to Montréal and on to Québec City. Among the participating hotels are the Queen Elizabeth and Bonaventure Hilton in Montréal and the Château Frontenac in Québec City.

Cruises from New York and New England through the Maritime Provinces and down the St. Lawrence to Québec City and Montréal are increasingly popular, especially from June through the foliage season. Among the lines offering these cruises, usually from 6 to 10 days long, are **Clipper** (☎ **888-278-4732**), **Holland America** (☎ **800/426-0327**), **Norwegian** (☎ **800/327-7030**), **Princess** (☎ **800/774-6237**), **Seabourn** (☎ **800/528-6273**), and **Silversea** (☎ **888/313-8883**).

PACKAGE TOURS

Package tours are not the same thing as escorted tours. They are simply a way to buy airfare and accommodations at the same time. For popular destinations like Montréal and Québec City, they are a smart way to go, because they can save you a lot of money. In many cases, a package that includes airfare, hotel, and transportation to and from the airport will cost you less than just the hotel alone would have, had you booked it yourself. That's because packages are sold in bulk to tour operators—who resell them to the public at a cost that drastically undercuts standard rates.

Packages, however, vary widely. Some offer a better class of hotels than others. Some offer the same hotels for lower prices. Some offer flights on scheduled airlines, while others book charters. In some packages, your choice of accommodations and travel days may be limited. Some packages let you choose between escorted vacations and independent vacations; others will allow you to add on just a few excursions or escorted day trips (also at lower prices than you could locate on your own) without booking an entirely escorted tour. Each destination usually has one or two packagers that are cheaper than the rest because they buy in even greater bulk. If you spend the time to shop around, you will save in the long run.

FINDING A PACKAGE DEAL The best place to start your search is the travel section of your local Sunday newspaper. Also check the ads in the back of national travel magazines like *Travel & Leisure, National Geographic Traveler,* and *Condé Nast Traveller.* **Liberty Travel** (☎ **888/271-1584** to be connected with the agent closest to you; **www.libertytravel.com**), one of the biggest packagers in the Northeast, often runs a full-page ad in the Sunday papers. You won't get much in the way of service, but you will get a good deal. **American Express Vacations** (☎ 800/241-1700; http://travel.americanexpress.com) is another option. Check out its **Last Minute Travel Bargains** site, with deeply discounted vacations packages and reduced airline fares.

Another good resource is the airlines themselves, which often package their flights together with accommodations. Fly-by-night packagers are uncommon, but they do exist; when you buy your package through the airline, however, you can be pretty sure that the company will still be in business when your departure date arrives. Among the airline packagers, your options include **American Airlines FlyAway Vacations** (☎ 800/321-2121), **Delta Dream Vacations** (☎ 800/872-7786), and **US Airways Vacations** (☎ 800/455-0123). Pick the airline that services your hometown most often.

Planning Your Trip:
An Online Directory

by Lynne Bairstow

Lynne Bairstow is the coauthor of *Frommer's Mexico* and the editorial director of *e-com* magazine.

Day by day, the Internet becomes more integrated into our lives—including the way we plan and book our travel. By early 2000, one in every 10 trips was being booked online, a trend that's sure to accelerate.

The Internet not only provides a wealth of destination information but also gives you the chance to compare experiences with fellow travelers, ask experts for pretrip advice, seek out discounted fares once accessible only to travel-industry insiders, and stay in touch via e-mail while you're away. The instant communication and storehouse of information have revolutionized the way travel is researched, reserved, and realized.

This Online Directory will help you take better advantage of the travel planning information available online, and it's best used in conjunction with this book. Part 1 lists general Internet resources that can make any trip easier, such as sites for obtaining the best possible prices on airline tickets. In part 2 you'll find some top online guides for Montréal and Québec City, organized first by city and then by category.

Keep in mind this isn't a comprehensive list but a discriminating selection to get you started. Recognition is given to sites based on their content value and ease of use and aren't paid for—unlike some Website rankings, which are based on payment. Finally, remember this is a press-time snapshot of leading Web sites—some undoubtedly will have evolved, changed, or moved by the time you read this.

1 Top Travel-Planning Web Sites

Although the Internet was once a conglomerate of sites for researching places to visit, several key companies have emerged that offer comprehensive travel planning and booking. In addition to the Frommer's Online (see box, above), we list the other top online travel agencies below, along with some more specialized services.

WHY BOOK ONLINE?

Online agencies have come a long way over the past few years, now providing tips for finding the best fare and giving suggested dates or times to travel that yield the lowest price if your plans are flexible. Other sites even allow you to establish the price you're willing to pay, and they check the airlines' willingness to accept it. However, in some cases, these sites may not always yield the best price. Unlike a travel agent, for example, they may not have access to charter flights offered by wholesalers.

What You'll Find at the Frommer's Site

We highly recommend **Arthur Frommer's Budget Travel Online (www. frommers.com)** as an excellent travel planning resource. Of course, we're a little biased, but you'll find indispensable travel tips, reviews, monthly vacation giveaways, and online booking. Among the site's most popular features is the regular "Ask the Expert" bulletin boards, which feature one of the Frommer's authors answering your questions via online postings.

Subscribe to Arthur Frommer's Daily Newsletter (**www.frommers. com/newsletters**) to receive the latest travel bargains and inside travel secrets in your e-mailbox every day. You'll read daily headlines and articles from the dean of travel himself, highlighting last-minute deals on airfares, accommodations, cruises, and package vacations. You'll also find great travel advice by checking our Tip of the Day or Hot Spot of the Month.

Search our Destinations archive (**www.frommers.com/destinations**) of more than 200 domestic and international destinations for great places to stay, tips for traveling there, and what to do while you're there. Once you've researched your trip, the online reservation system (**www.frommers.com/ booktravelnow**) takes you to Frommer's favorite sites for booking your vacation at affordable prices.

Online booking sites aren't the only places to reserve airline tickets—all major airlines have their own Web sites and often offer incentives—bonus frequent-flyer miles or Net-only discounts, for example—when you buy online or buy an e-ticket.

The new trend is toward conglomerated booking sites. A consortium of U.S. and European airlines is planning to launch an as-yet-unnamed Web site that will offer fares lower than those available through travel agents. United, Delta, Northwest, and Continental have initiated this effort, based on their success at selling airline seats at their own online sites.

The best of the travel-planning sites are now highly personalized; they store your seating preferences, meal preferences, tentative itineraries, and credit-card information, allowing you to plan trips or check agendas quickly.

In many cases, booking your trip online can be better than working with a travel agent. It gives you the widest variety of choices, control, and the 24-hour convenience of planning your trip when you choose. All you need is some time—and often a little patience—and you're likely to find the fun of online travel research will greatly enhance your trip.

WHO SHOULD BOOK ONLINE?

Online booking is best for travelers who want to know as much as possible about their options, those who have flexibility in their travel dates and are looking for the best price, and bargain hunters driven by a good value who are open-minded about where they travel.

One of the biggest successes in online travel for both passengers and airlines is the offer of last-minute specials, such as American Airlines' weekend deals or other Internet-only fares you must purchase online. Another advantage is that you can cash in on incentives for booking online, such as rebates or bonus frequent-flyer miles.

More people still would rather look online than book online, partly due to fear of putting their credit-card numbers out on the Net. Secure encryption and increasing experience buying online have removed this fear for most travelers. In some cases, however, it's simply easier to buy from a local travel agent who can deliver your tickets to your door (especially if your travel is last minute or you have special requests). You can find a flight online and then book it by calling a toll-free number or contacting your travel agent, though this is somewhat less efficient. To be sure you're in secure mode when you book online, look for a little icon of a key (in Netscape) or a padlock (in Internet Explorer) at the bottom of your Web browser.

Business and other frequent travelers also have found numerous benefits in online booking, as the advances in mobile technology provide them with the ability to check flight status, change plans, or get specific directions from hand-held computing devices, mobile phones, and pagers. Some sites will even e-mail or page passengers if their flights are delayed.

Online booking is increasingly able to accommodate complex itineraries, even for international travel. The pace of evolution on the Net is rapid, so you'll probably find additional features and advancements by the time you visit these sites. What the future holds for online travelers is ever-increasing personalization, customization, and reaching out to you.

TRAVEL PLANNING & BOOKING SITES

Below are listings for sites for planning and booking travel. The sites offer domestic and international flight, hotel, and rental-car bookings, plus news, destination information, and deals on cruises and vacation packages. Free (one-time) registration is required for booking.

✪ Travelocity (incorporates Preview Travel). **www.travelocity.com; www.previewtravel.com; www.frommers.travelocity.com**

Travelocity is Frommer's online travel planning/booking partner. Travelocity uses the SABRE system to offer reservations and tickets for more than 400 airlines, plus reservations and purchase capabilities for more than 45,000 hotels and 50 car-rental companies. An exclusive feature of the SABRE system is its **Low Fare Search Engine,** which automatically searches for the three lowest-priced itineraries based on a traveler's criteria. Last-minute deals and consolidator fares are included in the search. If you book with Travelocity, you can select specific seats for your flights with online seat maps and also view diagrams of the most popular commercial aircraft. Its hotel finder provides street-level location maps and photos of selected hotels. With the **Fare Watcher** e-mail feature, you can select up to five routes and receive e-mail notices when the fare changes by $25 or more.

Travelocity's **Destination Guide** includes updated information on some 260 destinations worldwide—supplied by Frommer's.

Note to AOL Users: You can book flights, hotels, rental cars, and cruises on AOL at keyword: Travel. The booking software is provided by Travelocity/ Preview Travel and is similar to the Internet site. Use the AOL "Travelers Advantage" program to earn a 5% rebate on flights, hotel rooms, and car rentals.

Expedia. www.expedia.com
Expedia is Travelocity's major competitor. It offers several ways of obtaining the best possible fares: **Flight Price Matcher** allows your preferred airline to match an available fare with a competitor; a comprehensive **Fare Compare** area shows the differences in fare categories and airlines; and **Fare Calendar** helps you plan your trip around the best possible fares. Its main limitation is that like many online databases, Expedia focuses on the major airlines and hotel chains, so don't expect to find too many budget airlines or one-of-a-kind B&Bs here.

TRIP.com. www.trip.com
TRIP.com began as a site geared toward business travelers, but its innovative features and highly personalized approach have broadened its appeal to leisure travelers as well. It is the leading travel site for those using mobile devices to access Internet travel information.

TRIP.com includes a trip-planning function that provides the average and lowest fare for the route requested, in addition to the current available fare. An on-site "newsstand" features breaking news on airfare sales and other travel specials. Among its most popular features are Flight TRACKER and intelliTRIP. **Flight TRACKER** allows users to track any commercial flight en route to its destination anywhere in the United States, while accessing real-time FAA-based flight monitoring data. **intelliTRIP** is a travel search tool that allows users to identify the best airline, hotel, and rental-car rates in less than 90 seconds.

In addition, the site offers e-mail notification of flight delays, plus city resource guides, currency converters, and a weekly e-mail newsletter of fare updates, travel tips, and traveler forums.

Yahoo! Travel. travel.yahoo.com
Yahoo! is currently the most popular of the Internet information portals, and its travel site is a comprehensive mix of online booking, daily travel news, and destination information. The **Best Fares** area offers what it promises, plus provides feedback on refining your search if you have flexibility in travel dates or times. There is also an active section of message boards for discussions on travel in general and specific destinations.

Online Directory

Airline Web Sites

Below are the Web sites for the major airlines serving Montréal and Québec City. These sites offer schedules and flight booking, and most have pages where you can sign up for e-mail alerts for weekend deals and other late-breaking bargains.

Air Canada. **www.aircanada.ca**
American. **www.americanair.com**
British Airways. **www.british-airways.com**
Canadian Airlines. **www.cdnair.ca**
Continental. **www.continental.com**
Delta. **www.delta.com**
Northwest. **www.nwa.com**
US Airways. **www.usairways.com**

SPECIALTY TRAVEL SITES

Although the sites listed above provide the most comprehensive services, some travelers have specialized needs that are best met by a site catering specifically to them.

For adventure travelers, **iExplore** (www.iexplore.com) is a great source for information and booking adventure and experiential travel, as well as related services and products. The site combines the secure Internet booking functions with hands-on expertise and 24-hour live customer support by seasoned adventure travelers, for those interested in trips off the beaten path. The company is a supporting member of the Ecotourism Society and is committed to environmentally responsible travel worldwide.

Another excellent site for adventure travelers is **Away.com** (www.away.com), which features unique vacations for challenging the body, mind, and spirit. Trips may include cycling in the Loire Valley, taking an African safari, or assisting in the excavation of a Mayan ruin. For those without the time for such an extended exotic trip, offbeat weekend getaways are also available. Services include a customer-service center staffed with experts to answer calls and e-mails, plus a network of over 1,000 prescreened tour operators. Trips are categorized by cultural, adventure, and green travel. Away.com also offers a Daily Escape e-mail newsletter.

GORP (Great Outdoor Recreation Pages; www.gorp.com) has been a standard for adventure travelers since its founding in 1995 by outdoor enthusiasts Diane and Bill Greer. Tapping their own experiences, they created this Web site that offers unique travel destinations and encourages active participation by fellow GORP visitors through the sophisticated menu of online forums, contests, and discussions.

For travelers who prefer unique accommodations, **InnSite** (www.innsite.com) offers listings for inns and B&Bs in all U.S. states and dozens of countries around the globe. Find an inn at your destination, have a look at images of the rooms, check prices and availability, and then send e-mail to the innkeeper if you have further questions. This is an extensive directory of bed-and-breakfast inns but includes listings only if the proprietors submitted one (*Note:* It's free to get an inn listed). The descriptions are written by the innkeepers, and many listings link to the inn's own Web site, where you can find more information and images.

Another good resource for mostly one-of-a-kind places in the United States and abroad is **Places to Stay** (www.placestostay.com), which focuses on resort accommodations.

"Have Kids, Still Travel!" is the motto of the **Family Travel Forum** (FTF; www.familytravelforum.com), a site dedicated to the ideals, promotion, and support of travel with children. FTF is supported by memberships, which are available in flexible prices from a $2.95 monthly fee to a heftier annual fee for more comprehensive services. Since no advertising is accepted, FTF provides its members with honest, unbiased information, informed advice, and practical tips designed to make traveling with children a healthy, safe, hassle-free experience, not to mention a better value.

TOP VACATION PACKAGE SITES

Both **Expedia** and **Travelocity** (see above) offer excellent selections and searches for complete vacation packages. Travelers can search by destination and desired dates coupled with how much they're willing to spend. Travelocity has a valuable "Cruise Critic" function, to help would-be cruisers obtain first-hand accounts of the quality and details of a cruise from recent passengers.

Travel wholesalers, such as **Apple Vacations** (**www.applevacations.com**) and **Funjet** (**www.funjet.com**), are also good starting points, but they still require that the final booking be handled through a travel agent.

As travel agents tend to be more expert at sorting through the values in vacation packages, you might find **Vacation.com** (**www.vacation.com**) helpful in previewing packages and finding an appropriate agent to help you book the deal. This site represents a nationwide network of 9,800 local travel agencies that specialize in finding the best values in cruises, vacation packages, tours, and other leisure travel services. To find a Vacation.com member agency, enter your ZIP code, and the Vacation.com Agency Finder will locate a nearby office.

LAST-MINUTE DEALS & OTHER ONLINE BARGAINS

There's nothing airlines hate more than flying with lots of empty seats. The Net has enabled airlines to offer last-minute bargains to entice travelers to fill those seats. Most of these are announced on Tuesday or Wednesday and are valid for travel the following weekend, but some can be booked weeks or months in advance. You can sign up for weekly e-mail alerts at airlines' sites (for their Web sites, see "Airline Web Sites," above) or check sites that compile lists of these bargains, such as **Smarter Living** or **WebFlyer** (see below). To make it easier, visit a site that'll round up all the deals and send them in one convenient weekly e-mail. But last-minute deals aren't the only online bargains; other sites can help you find value even if you haven't waited until the eleventh hour. Increasingly popular are services that let you name the price you're willing to pay for an air seat or vacation package, and travel auction sites.

Cheap Tickets. www.cheaptickets.com
Cheap Tickets has exclusive deals that aren't available through more mainstream channels. One caveat about the Cheap Tickets site is that it'll offer fare quotes for a route and later show that the fare isn't valid for your dates of travel—most other Web sites, such as Expedia, consider your dates of travel before showing what fares are available. Despite its problems, Cheap Tickets can be worth the effort because its fares can be lower than those offered by its competitors.

Bid for Travel. www.bidfortravel.com
Bid for Travel is another of the travel auction sites, similar to Priceline (see below), which are growing in popularity. In addition to airfares, Internet users can place a bid for vacation packages and hotels.

Go4less.com. www.go4less.com
Specializing in last-minute cruise and package deals, Go4less has some excellent offers. The **Hot Deals** section gives an alphabetical listing by destination of superdiscounted packages.

LastMinuteTravel.com. www.lastminutetravel.com
Suppliers with excess inventory come to this online agency to distribute unsold airline seats, hotel rooms, cruises, and vacation packages. It's got great deals, but you have to put up with excessive advertisements and slow-loading graphics.

Moment's Notice. www.moments-notice.com
As the name suggests, Moment's Notice specializes in last-minute vacation and cruise deals. You can browse for free, but if you want to purchase a trip you have to join Moment's Notice, which costs $25. Go to **World Wide Hot Deals** for a complete list of special deals in international destinations.

✪ **onetravel.com.** **www.onetravel.com**

Here you'll find deals on domestic and international flights, cruises, hotels, and all-inclusive resorts like Club Med. 1travel.com's **Saving Alert** compiles last-minute air deals so you don't have to scroll through multiple e-mail alerts. A feature called "Drive a little using low-fare airlines" helps map out strategies for using alternate airports to find lower fares. And **Farebeater** searches a database that includes published fares, consolidator bargains, and special deals exclusive to 1travel.com. *Note:* The travel agencies listed by 1travel.com have paid for placement.

✪ **Priceline.com.** **www.priceline.com**

Even people who aren't familiar with many Web sites have heard about Priceline.com. Launched in 1998 with a $10-million ad campaign featuring William Shatner, Priceline lets you "name your price" for domestic and international airline tickets and hotel rooms. In other words, you select a route and dates, guarantee with a credit card, and make a bid for what you're willing to pay. If one of the airlines in Priceline's database has a fare lower than your bid, your credit card will automatically be charged for a ticket.

The downside? You can't say when you want to fly—you have to accept any flight leaving between 6am and 10pm on the dates you selected, and you may have to make a stopover. No frequent-flyer miles are awarded, and tickets are nonrefundable and can't be exchanged for another flight. So if your plans change, you're out of luck. Priceline can be good for travelers who have to take off on short notice (and thus are unable to qualify for advance-purchase discounts). But be sure to shop around first, because if you overbid, you'll be required to purchase the ticket—and Priceline will pocket the difference between what it paid for the ticket and what you bid.

Priceline says that more than 35% of all reasonable offers for domestic flights are being filled on the first try, with much higher fill rates on popular routes (New York to San Francisco, for example). They define "reasonable" as not more than 30% below the lowest generally available advance-purchase fare for the same route.

SkyAuction.com. **www.skyauction.com**

This auction site has categories for airfare, travel deals, hotels, and much more.

Smarter Living. **www.smarterliving.com**

Best known for its e-mail dispatch of weekend deals on 20 airlines, Smarter Living also keeps you posted on last-minute bargains on everything from Windjammer Cruises to flights to Iceland.

Travelzoo.com. **www.travelzoo.com**

At this Internet portal, more than 150 travel companies post special deals. It features a Top 20 list of the best deals on the site, selected by its editorial staff

---

Know When the Sales Start

Although most people learn about last-minute weekend deals from e-mail dispatches, it can be best to find out precisely when these deals become available. Because the deals are limited, they can vanish within hours—sometimes even minutes—so it pays to log on as soon as they're obtainable. Check the pages devoted to these deals on airlines' Web pages to get the info. An example: Southwest's specials are posted at 12:01am Tuesdays (central time). So if you're looking for a cheap flight, stay up late and check Southwest's site to grab the best new deals.

One of the best sources of travel information is word-of-mouth from someone who has just been there. Internet discussion groups are offering an unprecedented way for travelers around the globe to connect and share experiences. The **Frommer's Online** site (**www.frommers.com**) offers these message boards, as well as areas where you can pose questions to the guidebook writers themselves in the section "Ask the Expert." **Yahoo! Travel, Expedia,** and **Travelocity** are other good sources of online travel discussion groups.

The granddaddy of specialized discussions on particular topics, is **Usenet,** a collection of more than 50,000 newsgroups. You'll find a comprehensive listing at **Deja News** (**www.dejanews.com/usenet/**) or at **www.liszt.com**.

---

each Wednesday night. This list is also available via an e-mailing list, free to those who sign up.

WebFlyer. www.webflyer.com

WebFlyer is a comprehensive online resource for frequent flyers and also has an excellent listing of last-minute air deals. Click on **Deal Watch** for a roundup of weekend deals on flights, hotels, and rental cars from domestic and international suppliers.

ONLINE TRAVELER'S TOOLBOX

Veteran travelers usually carry some essential items to make their trips easier. The following is a selection of online tools to smooth your journey.

CDC Travel Information. www.cdc.gov/travel/index.htm

This site features health advisories and recommendations for inoculations from the U.S. Centers for Disease Control and Prevention. The CDC site is good for an overview, but it's best to consult your personal physician to get the latest information on required vaccinations or other health precautions.

✪ Foreign Languages for Travelers. www.travlang.com

Here you can learn basic terms in more than 70 languages and click on any underlined phrase to hear what it sounds like. (*Note:* Free audio software and speakers are required.) It also offers hotel and airline finders with excellent prices and a simple system to get the listings you're looking for.

Intellicast. www.intellicast.com

Here you'll find weather forecasts for all 50 states, as well as cities around the world. Note that temperatures are in Celsius for many international destinations, so don't think you'll need that winter coat for your next trip to Athens.

✪ Mapquest. www.mapquest.com

The best of the mapping sites lets you choose a specific address or destination, and in seconds it'll return a map and detailed directions. It really is easier than calling, asking, and writing down directions. The site also links to special travel deals and helpful sites.

Net Café Guide. www.netcafeguide.com/mapindex.htm

Stop here to locate Internet cafes at hundreds of locations around the globe. Catch up on your e-mail, log on to the Web, and stay in touch with the home front, usually for just a few dollars per hour.

Tourism Offices Worldwide Directory. www.towd.com

This is an extensive listing of tourism offices, some with links to these offices' Web sites.

Online Directory

Checking E-mail at Internet Cafes

Until a few years ago, most travelers who checked their e-mail while traveling carried a laptop—an expensive and often technologically problematic option. Thankfully, Web-based free e-mail programs have made it much easier to check your mail.

Just open an account at any one of the numerous "free-mail" providers—the original leaders continue to be **Hotmail** (hotmail.com), **Excite** (www.excite.com), and **Yahoo! Mail** (mail.yahoo.com), though many are available. AOL users should check out **AOL Netmail,** and USA.NET (**www.usa.net**) comes highly recommended for functionality and security. You can find hints, tips, and a mile-long list of free-mail providers at **www.emailaddresses.com**. Then all you'll need to check your mail is a Web connection, easily available at Net cafes and copy shops around the world. After logging on, just point the browser to your free-mail's Internet address, enter your user name and password, and you'll have access to your mail. From these sites, you can download all your e-mail—even from office accounts—or your local or national Internet service provider address. There'll be a section generally called "check other mail" that allows you to add the names of other e-mail servers.

The downside is that most Web-based e-mail sites allow a maximum of only 3MB capacity per mail account, which can fill up quickly. Also, message sending and receiving isn't immediate; some messages may be delayed by several hours or even days.

Internet cafes have become ubiquitous, so for a few dollars an hour you'll be able to check your mail and send messages from virtually anywhere in the world. Interestingly, these cafes tend to be more common in very remote areas, where they may offer the best form of access for an entire community, especially if phone lines are difficult to obtain.

Travelers' Tales. www.travelerstales.com
Considered the best in compilations of travel literature, *Travelers' Tales* is an award-winning series of books grouped by destination (Mexico, Italy, France, China.) or by theme (Love & Romance, The Ultimate Journey, Women in the Wild, The Adventure of Food). It's a new kind of travel book that offers a description of a place or type of journey through the experiences of many travelers. It makes for a perfect traveling companion.

The Travelite FAQ. www.travelite.org
Here you'll find tips on packing light, choosing luggage, and selecting appropriate travel wear—helpful if you always tend to pack too much or are a compulsive list maker.

Universal Currency Converter. www.xe.net/ucc
Come here to see what your dollar or pound is worth in more than 100 other countries.

U.S. Customs Service Traveler Information.
   www.customs.gov/travel/travel.htm
Wondering what you're allowed to bring in to the United States? Check at this thorough site, which includes maximum allowance and duty fees.

U.S. State Department Travel Warnings.
  travel.state.gov/travel_warnings.html
You'll find reports on places where health concerns or unrest might threaten U.S. travelers. Keep in mind that these warnings can be somewhat dated and conservative. You can also sign up to receive State Department briefings via e-mail.

Web Travel Secrets. www.web-travel-secrets.com
If this list leaves you yearning for more travel-oriented sites, Web Travel Secrets offers one of the best compilations around. One section offers advice and tips on how to find the lowest prices for airlines, hotels, and cruises. The other section provides a comprehensive listing of Web travel links for airfare deals, airlines, booking engines, cars, cruise lines, discount travel and best deals, general travel resources, hotels and hotel discounters, search engines, and travel magazines and newsletters.

Visa. www.visa.com/pd/atm/

MasterCard. www.mastercard.com/atm
Use these sites to find ATMs in hundreds of cities in the United States and around the world. Both include maps for some locations and both list airport ATM locations, some with maps. *Tip:* You'll usually get a better exchange rate using ATMs than exchanging traveler's checks at banks, but check in advance to see what kind of fees your bank will assess for using an overseas ATM.

2 Top Web Sites for Montréal

Information updated by Herbert Bailey Livesey

Herbert Bailey Livesey is coauthor of *Frommer's Canada, Frommer's Europe from $70 a Day,* and *Frommer's New England.*

On sites specific to Canada, note that the suffix **.ca** often replaces the familiar .com and .org, so if you have difficulty logging on to a specific site, using .ca may open it. There is, for example, a Yahoo.ca address for the popular search engine.

PROVINCIAL GUIDES

✪ Bonjour Québec. www.tourisme.gouv.qc.ca
The official site of the government of the Province of Québec, this endeavors to be a comprehensive information bank about all things Québec, and nearly succeeds. On the board are upcoming events, ongoing attractions, and planned activities. Hotel searches are made by as many qualifiers as you want to try—region, price range, size, B&B or hotel, among them—and you can reserve online.

Destination Québec. www.destinationquebec.com
Listed here are more than 3,000 restaurants and 2,500 lodgings throughout the province, as well as vacation packages, golf courses, cultural events, transportation, and diverse outdoor activities. The site is full of suggestions and detailed information.

Yellow Pages. www.yellowpages.ca
Key in the business or person you want to find, the city, and the province, and the number and address pop up, along with a neighborhood map and a list of nearby shops and restaurants.

CITY GUIDES

✪ **Bonjour à la Montréal. www.tourism-montreal.org**
Another official tourism site, this constitutes a first source that hits the highlights but skims, rather than delves at depth. Click the "traveler" box to get a directory to attractions, guided tours, entertainment, accommodations, and restaurants.

Gay Canada: Montréal. www.cglbrd.com/cities/qc/montreal
No need to pore over the back pages of alternative newsweeklies to find the local gay/lesbian scene. This useful Web guide points you right to Montréal's gay-friendly community groups, hotels, bars, clubs, coffee shops, restaurants, and more. It outlines, for example, almost 30 hotels and B&Bs in and near Montréal's Gay Village.

Montréal E-Guide. www.pagemontreal.qc.ca/meg
Take a district-by-district tour of Montréal online, visiting the historic Old Montréal spots and the Latin Quarter's cafes and such attractions as Olympic Park and the Biodôme. Each section of the guide includes a helpful map, a snippet of history, hotel and restaurant listings, and sightseeing suggestions. A decent first source, but more details would be useful.

Montréal Live. www.montreal-live.com
Though serving mostly as an advertising venue for dining, lodging, recreation, and tourism businesses, this site does offer perks such as weather forecasts, online reservations at more than 50 accommodations, and direct links to companies' sites. Needs updating.

✪ **Montréal Online. www.montrealonline.com**
Seeking fun in the city? Look no further. This abundant site, a service of *The Gazette,* offers festival schedules, a slew of theater and dance reviews, a searchable and review-speckled restaurant directory, interactive music listings, a bar guide, and movie listings. Can't decide? Let the site's condensed "Very Best of Montréal" section guide you.

The Montréal Page. www.pagemontreal.qc.ca
This directory links to 6,676 Web sites ("and counting," it claims) representing local arts and entertainment, bars and restaurants, businesses, community groups, schools, media, events, and tourist attractions. If don't have time to sort through them all, check out the guide's list of must-see sites.

Montréal.com: Your City on the Web. www.montreal.com
Although the hotel and restaurant pages are merely rosters of establishments, with no reviews or descriptions, the up-to-date listings of events are especially useful. Check, too, the visitors' guide to Internet cafes and things for kids.

The Student's Guide to Montréal. www.studentsguide.com/montreal
Whether you're stopping in Montréal for a short vacation or a long education, this guide can be of moderate use. Essentially a directory of links, here you'll find everything from schools and libraries to sushi bars and cinemas. The entertainment section lists things you can do for less than $5.

The Ultimate Montréal Travel Page. users.nac.net/jmessina
A frequent traveler to the bustling Canadian city shares personal observations and spotty reviews of bars and restaurants, a currency converter, Montréal Web cameras, maps, weather reports, and a guide to tourist attractions. With the intro page, you hear "Canadian Sunset."

NEWSPAPERS & MAGAZINES

Hour. www.hour.qc.ca
This Montréal culture magazine highlights local happenings in the worlds of film, music, comedy, dance, visual arts, and gay culture. Read entertainingly grumpy and often profane takes on current events from several columnists, as well as updated restaurant and film reviews.

The Montréal Gazette. www.montrealgazette.com
The city's English-language daily posts each day's news and views so visitors can know what's on Montréalers' minds. The paper also produces the highly useful Web site, Montréal Online, described above.

Montréal Mirror. www.montrealmirror.com
Designed in kitschy fashion with vivid colors and doll icons, this culture magazine's fun site covers general entertainment as well as local happenings. "Got an opinion?" it asks. Then answers, "Shove it down our editors' throat." Determinedly iconoclastic columnists comment on current events.

DINING GUIDES

Canada's Restaurant Guide. www.restaurant.ca
Eleven Canadian cities are covered in this informative site, including Montréal and Québec City. Very few worthwhile restaurants are excluded, and you can search by several criteria, including neighborhood, type of cuisine, price range, and ambience; they even offer ratings.

Dining in Montréal. www.homepagers.com/montreal/dine.html
The site isn't much to look at, but it does provide bare facts about restaurants listed by food category.

Montréal Bar and Restaurant Page. www.bar-resto.com
Sort through descriptions about 70 selected bars and restaurants of wildly varied quality, many of the pubby variety and few that might be described as serious establishments. Hyperlinks often reveal helpful material, such as maps, menus, photos, and coupons.

TOP ATTRACTIONS

Canadian Centre for Architecture. www.cca.qc.ca
All architecture all the time. The center hosts exhibitions, publications, public programs, a library, and more. If you'd like to take a tour, first check out this site to find out what's on display—permanently or short-term.

Montréal China Town Internet. www.trendmaker.com/mcti.htm
Get a taste of China in the midst of Montréal. With considerable overstatement, this site promises to tell you all you want to know about Chinatown, but does lead visitors to some of the neighborhood's restaurants, bookstores, magazines and newspapers, radio stations, and businesses.

Montréal Museum of Fine Art (Musée des Beaux-Arts). www.mmfa.qc.ca
Pay a virtual visit to the museum via QuickTime VR, or check out the simpler yet detailed text-and-photo guide to collections (including Canadian and Amerindian art) and special exhibitions. This site also covers the museum's history, hours and fees, tours, and special programs.

Montréal Planetarium (Planétarium de Montréal). www.planetarium. montreal.qc.ca
See the stars and learn what and where they are in the night sky. The planetarium puts on three or four new shows a year and hosts workshops and school

programs. Learn about all of them, as well as admission rates, hours, and show schedules.

Musée David M. Stewart au Fort de l'Île Sainte Hélène. www.Mlink. NET/~stewart

The European settlement and development of Canada is shown through this collection of military and naval weaponry and artifacts, uniforms, and housewares, displayed in a fort built after the War of 1812. Exhibitions, special programs, events, services, and tours are described.

Musée McCord d'Histoire Canadienne. www.musee-mccord.qc.ca

Collector and Montréal native David Ross McCord started this museum with the intent of reflecting the history and varied cultures of Canada. The site provides tastes of the extensive collections, which include more than 29,000 articles of clothing and other artifacts and 750,000 photographs. Also find out about special exhibitions, tours, hours, admission, events, and publications.

Olympic Park. www.rio.gouv.qc.ca

Find out what's up at the Montréal venue erected for the 1976 Olympic games. (For one thing, its survival, for it is rumored to be a candidate for the wrecker's ball.) Along with an events calendar, this site provides a history of the park and stadium, tour-package information, a map, and a guide to the Sports Centre's programs.

Pointe-à-Callière. www.musee-pointe-a-calliere.qc.ca

The site digs beyond the exhibits of this archaeology and history museum, one of Montréal's most engaging, to take a look at research programs, architectural components, and special events. Get a preview of the permanent collections and multimedia show online.

Vieux-Montréal. www.vieux.montreal.qc.ca

If you're planning to stop by the historic city center of old Montréal, be sure to visit this entertaining site first to find out about attractions, events, and lodging or to read about the district's history. An animated tour with sound zips around the *quartier* and there's a live cam shot of Place Jacques-Cartier.

GETTING AROUND

Montréal Airports. www.admtl.com/index-e.html

Get help finding your way through Montréal's Mirabel and Dorval airports. Call up current arrivals and departures, as well as contact information for the airlines whose planes land there. Check the **Smart-Trip Planner** page to find online ticket agents. From parking lots to shuttle bus schedules, little relevant info is left out.

STCUM. www.stcum.qc.ca

Here's your Montréal guide to local transport: buses, the Métro, transportation for riders with disabilities, commuter trains, and schedules. An online navigation tool called **Tous Azimuts** recommends public-transportation itineraries based on arrival/destination points and the time of day.

3 Top Web Sites for Québec City

CITY GUIDES

Québec: Une Histoire d'Amour. www.quebecregion.com

The Greater Québec Area Tourism and Convention Bureau promises Québec City visitors an unforgettable experience. To help facilitate it, they provide a Web site full of information about accommodations, attractions, sports, shopping, dining, history, and culture, all frequently updated. Each section features a directory searchable by region or other preferences; vacation packages are described.

Télégraphe de Québec. www.telegraphe.com
Find out what's on in the capital region on this useful (if slow-loading) site: festivals, art exhibits, concerts, sports events, and other Québec City happenings. In addition to descriptions of major events, check out this ad-spotted site's guides to outdoor activities, lodging, dining, shopping, parks and gardens, plays, music, and art. Also get Web cam views, weather reports, and connections to today's front pages of national newspapers.

DINING GUIDE

TorDine: Old Québec City. www.tordine.com/ontheroad/quebec/ oldquebec
Each entry in this restaurant directory features photos of the establishment and facts on its type of food, average price, degree of formality, hours, parking availability, and credit-card policy. While the listings aren't comprehensive, they cover most of the better-known places. Links are included where available. See also Canada's Restaurant Guide at **www.restaurant.ca**.

TOP ATTRACTIONS

Fortifications of Québec. parcscanada.risq.qc.ca/fortifications_e
Québec City is surrounded by walls and ramparts, the only walled city north of Mexico. Check out these sturdy remnants from the days of early French and English military defense during your travels. Get a sneak preview online. Also find historical information and tour schedules.

Grands Feux Loto-Québec. www.lesgrandsfeux.com
If you like your fireworks with appropriately stirring music, this event is for you. This huge musical pyrotechnical competition, which goes on for a couple of weeks every summer, takes place above the Montmorency Falls north of Québec City. Check the site for a detailed program of this year's performances, ticket information, directions, and, of course, photos. You can reserve tickets online.

La Citadelle (Québec Citadel). www.qbc.clic.net/~citadel/english.html
At the Citadel, you can take a 1-hour guided tour that includes a visit to the Royal 22e Regiment Museum within an 1841 British military prison. Get schedules and fees at their site.

Musée du Québec. www.mdq.org
Pay a virtual visit to one of Québec's two most important museums to see examples of its 20,000 pieces of early, modern, and contemporary art, a collection ranging from Ozias Leduc to Michel Goulet. If you want to visit the MDQ in person, find out about its location, hours, admission costs, and current exhibitions.

Musée de la Civilisation (Museum of Civilization). www.mcq.org
This superb museum's site highlights its permanent exhibits (like the cool kids' exhibition called "Growing Up"), as well as its more loftier attractions, which examine societal matters such as human rights, politics, employment, and art trends. The history of Canada is examined in enchanting detail from the first European arrivals through the 19th century.

3

Getting to Know Montréal

For a city of more than a million inhabitants, getting to know and getting around Montréal is remarkably easy. Dorval Airport is only 14 miles away, and once you're in town, the Métro (subway) system is fast and efficient. Walking, of course, is the best way to enjoy and appreciate this vigorous, multidimensional city, neighborhood by neighborhood.

1 Orientation

ARRIVING

BY PLANE   The **Aéroport de Dorval** (☎ 514/633-3105, or 800/465-1213 from Québec and eastern Ontario) is 14 miles (22km) southwest of downtown, and it now accepts nearly all commercial flights. A new $145 million annex is planned for international flights, with completion expected by 2003. The ride into town takes less than 30 minutes if traffic isn't tangled and costs about C$28 (US$19.30) plus tip by taxi. Montréal's **Aéroport Mirabel** (☎ 514/476-3010, or 800/465-1213 from Québec and eastern Ontario), 34 miles (55km) northwest of the city, which used to accept most international carriers from outside North America, now receives only freight and charter flights. The ride into the city from there takes about 45 minutes in normal traffic and costs about C$55 (US$38) by taxi.

Both airports are served by **L'Aérobus** (☎ 513/931-9002) shuttles between the airports and the downtown terminal at 777 rue de la Gauchetiére Ouest, near La Reine Elizabeth Hotel. Free minibuses take passengers from there to many major hotels. Buses from Dorval cost C$11 (US$7.60) one way, C$19.75 (US$13.60) round-trip. The fare between Mirabel and Dorval is C$15 (US$10.35) one way, C$19.75 (US$13.60) round-trip. Schedules are changed frequently, but buses usually operate every 20 to 30 minutes from Dorval between 5:10am and 11:10pm.

BY TRAIN   Montréal has one intercity rail terminus, **Gare Centrale** (Central Station), situated directly beneath La Reine Elizabeth Hotel at the corner of boulevard René-Lévesque and rue Mansfield (☎ 514/871-1331). Central Station is part of the underground city and is thus connected to the Métro (Bonaventure Station).

BY BUS   The **Terminus Voyageur** (☎ 514/842-2281) has a bar, a cafeteria, and a travel agency. There are also a rental-car desk and a tourism-information booth. Beneath the terminal is the Berri-UQAM Métro station, the junction of several important Métro lines and a good starting point for trips to most quarters of the city. (UQAM—pronounced "*oo*-kahm"—stands for Université de Québec à Montréal.) Alternatively, taxis usually line up outside the terminal building.

BY CAR   For driving directions to Montréal, see "Getting There" in chapter 2.

VISITOR INFORMATION

The main information center for visitors in Montréal is the large and efficiently organized **Infotouriste,** at 1001 rue du Square-Dorchester (☎ **800/363-7777** from anywhere in Canada and the U.S., or 514/873-2015), between Peel and Metcalfe streets in the downtown hotel and business district. To get there, take the Métro to the Peel stop. The office is open daily June to early September 8:30am to 7:30pm, and early September to May 9am to 6pm. Employed by the Québec Ministry of Tourism, the bilingual staff workers are quite knowledgeable, and the center is a useful information resource regarding dining, accommodations, and attractions throughout the province and in Montréal itself. In addition to the large number of brochures and publications on hand, there are counters for tour companies, hotel reservations, currency exchange, and car rental.

The city has its own convenient **information bureau** in Old Montréal at 174 rue Notre-Dame (corner of place Jacques-Cartier), near the monument to Lord Nelson (☎ **514/871-1595**). It's open daily Easter to mid-October, 9am to 7pm; mid-October to Easter, Thursday to Sunday 9am to 5pm.

CITY LAYOUT

For the duration of your visit, it makes sense to accept local directional conventions. The city borders the **St. Lawrence River.** As far as its citizens are concerned, that's south, looking toward the United States, although the river in fact runs more nearly north and south at that point, not east and west. For that reason, it has been observed that Montréal is the only city in the world where the sun rises in the south. Don't fight it: Face the river. That's south. Turn around. That's north. When examining a map of the city, note that such prominent thoroughfares as rue Ste-Catherine and boulevard René-Lévesque are said to run "east" and "west," the dividing line being boulevard St-Laurent, which runs "north" and "south." To ease the confusion, the directions given below conform to local tradition, since they are the ones that will be given by natives.

MAIN ARTERIES & STREETS   In **downtown Montréal,** the principal streets running east-west include boulevard René-Lévesque, rue Ste-Catherine (*rue* is the French word for "street"), boulevard de Maisonneuve, and rue Sherbrooke; the north-south arteries include rue Crescent, rue McGill, rue St-Denis, and boulevard St-Laurent, the line of demarcation between east and west Montréal (most of the downtown area of interest to tourists and businesspeople lies to the west). In **Plateau Mont-Royal,** northeast of the downtown area, major streets are avenue du

Greater Montréal

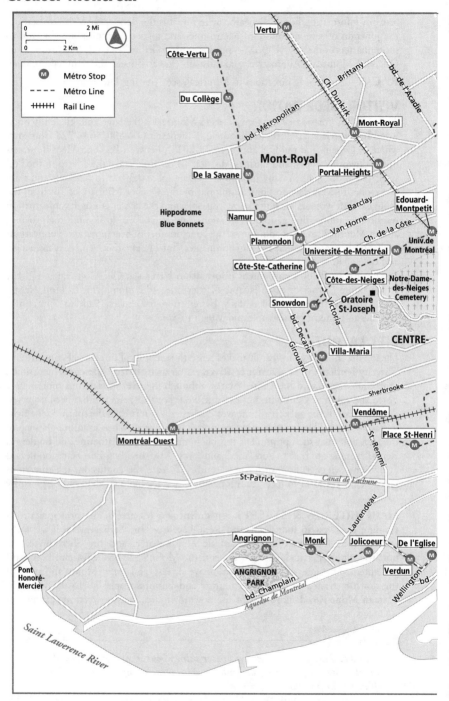

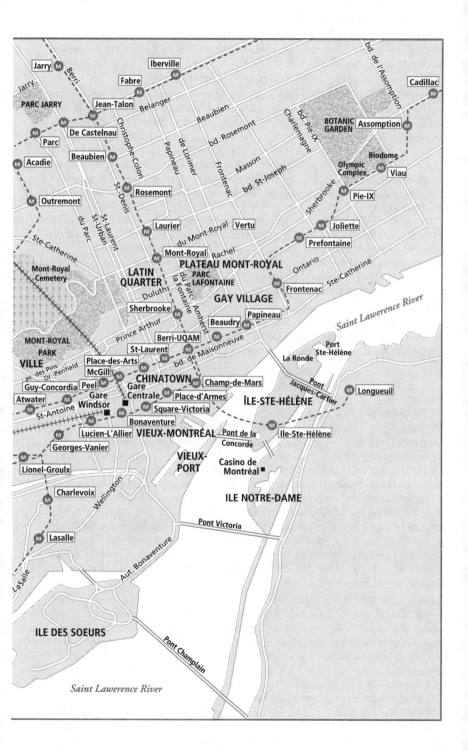

Mont-Royal and avenue Laurier. In **Vieux-Montréal** (Old Montréal), rue St-Jacques, rue Notre-Dame, and rue St-Paul are the major streets, along with rue de la Commune, which hugs the park that borders the St. Lawrence River.

FINDING AN ADDRESS   Boulevard St-Laurent is the dividing point between east and west (*est* and *ouest*) in Montréal. There's no equivalent division for north and south (*nord* and *sud*)—the numbers start at the river and climb from there, just as the topography does. For instance, when you're driving along boulevard St-Laurent and passing number 500, that's Vieux-Montréal, near rue Notre-Dame; number 1100 is near boulevard René-Lévesque; number 1500 is near boulevard de Maisonneuve; and number 3400 is near rue Sherbrooke. Even numbers are on the west side of north-south streets and the south side of east-west streets; odd numbers are on the east and north sides, respectively.

In earlier days, Montréal was split geographically along ethnic lines: Those who spoke English lived predominantly in the city's western regions, and French speakers were concentrated to the east. Things still do sound more French as you walk east: Street names and Métro station names change from Peel and Atwater to St-Laurent and Beaudry. While boulevard St-Laurent is the east-west dividing line for the city's street-numbering system, the "spiritual split" comes farther west, roughly at avenue de Bleury/avenue de Parc.

STREET MAPS   Good street plans are found inside the free tourist guide supplied by the **Greater Montréal Convention & Tourism Bureau** and distributed widely throughout the city. The bureau also provides a large foldout city map free.

Neighborhoods in Brief

DOWNTOWN   This area contributes the most striking elements of the dramatic Montréal skyline and contains the main railroad station, as well as most of the city's luxury and first-class hotels, principal museums, corporate headquarters, and largest department stores. Loosely bounded by rue Sherbrooke to the north, boulevard René-Lévesque to the south, boulevard St-Laurent to the east, and rue Drummond to the west, downtown Montréal incorporates the neighborhood formerly known as "The Golden Square Mile," an Anglophone district once characterized by dozens of mansions erected by the wealthy Scottish and English merchants and industrialists who dominated the city's politics and social life well into this century. Many of those stately homes were torn down when skyscrapers began to rise here after World War II, but some remain, often converted to institutional use. At the northern edge of the downtown area is the urban campus of prestigious McGill University, which retains its Anglophone identity.

THE UNDERGROUND CITY   During Montréal's long winters, life slows on the streets of downtown. The people escape down escalators and stairways into *la ville souterraine,* what amounts to a parallel subterranean universe. Down there, in a controlled climate that's eternally spring, it's possible to arrive at the railroad station, check into a hotel, go out for lunch at any of hundreds of fast-food counters and full-service restaurants, see a movie, attend a concert, conduct business, go shopping, and even take a swim—all without unfurling an umbrella or donning an overcoat.

This underground "city" evolved when major building developments in the downtown area such as Place Ville-Marie, Place Bonaventure, Complexe Desjardins, Palais des Congrès, and Place des Arts put their below-street-level areas to profitable use, leasing space for shops and other purposes. Over time, in fits and starts and with no master plan in place, these spaces became connected with Métro stations and with each other. It became possible to ride long distances and walk the shorter ones, through mazes of corridors, tunnels, and plazas. There are now more than 1,600 shops, 40 banks, 200 restaurants, 10 Métro stations, and about 30 cinemas down there.

Admittedly, the term *underground city* is not entirely accurate, since some parts—such as Place Bonaventure and Complexe Desjardins—define their own spaces, which may have nothing to do with "ground level." In Place Bonaventure, passengers may leave the Métro and then wander around on the same level only to find themselves, at one point, peering out a window several floors above the street.

The city beneath the city has obvious advantages, including the elimination of traffic accidents and avoidance of the need to deal with winter slush or summer rain. But it covers a vast area, without the convenience of a logical street grid, and can be confusing at times. There are plenty of signs, but it's wise to make careful note of landmarks at key corners along your route in order to get back to your starting point. Expect to get lost anyway—but, being that you're in an underground maze, that's part of the fun.

RUE CRESCENT   One of Montréal's major dining and nightlife districts lies in the western shadow of the massed phalanxes of downtown skyscrapers. It holds hundreds of restaurants, bars, and clubs of all styles between Sherbrooke and René-Lévesque, centering on rue Crescent and spilling over onto neighboring streets. From east to west, the Anglophone origins of the quarter are evident in the surviving street names: Stanley, Drummond, de la Montagne (changed from "Mountain"), Crescent, Bishop, and MacKay. The party atmosphere that pervades after dark here never quite fades, and it builds to crescendos as weekends approach, especially in warm weather, when its largely 20- and 30-something denizens spill out into sidewalk cafes and onto balconies in even greater numbers than during the winter months.

VIEUX-MONTRÉAL   The city was born here in 1642, down by the river at Pointe-à-Callière, and today, especially in summer, activity centers around place Jacques-Cartier, where cafe tables line narrow terraces and where sun worshipers, flower sellers, itinerant artists, street performers, and strolling locals and tourists congregate. The area is larger than it might seem at first, bounded as it is on the north by rue St-Antoine, once the "Wall Street" of Montréal and still home to some banks, and on the south by the recently developed Vieux-Port (Old Port), a linear park bordering rue de la Commune that gives access to the river and provides welcome breathing room for cyclists, in-line skaters, and picnickers. To the east, Vieux-Montréal is bordered by rue Berri, and to the west by rue McGill. Several small but intriguing museums are housed in historic buildings, and the architectural heritage of the district has been substantially preserved. Its restored 18th- and 19th-century structures have been adapted for use as shops, studios, cafes, bars, offices, and apartments.

ST-DENIS   Rue St-Denis, from rue Ste-Catherine Est to avenue du Mont-Royal, running from downtown to the Plateau Mont-Royal section, is the thumping central artery of Montréal's Latin Quarter, thick with cafes, bistros, offbeat shops, and lively night spots. It is to Montréal what boulevard St-Germain is to Paris, and indeed, once you're here, it isn't difficult to imagine yourself transported to the Left Bank. At the southern end of St-Denis, near the concrete campus of the Université du Québec à Montréal (UQAM), the avenue is decidedly student-oriented, with alternative rock cranked up in the inexpensive bars and clubs, and kids in jeans and leather swapping philosophical insights and telephone numbers. Farther north, above Sherbrooke, a raffish quality persists along the facing rows of three- and four-story row houses, but the average age of residents and visitors nudges past 30. Prices are higher, too, and some of the city's better restaurants are located here. This is a district for taking the pulse of Francophone life, not for absorbing art and culture of the refined sort, for there are no museums or important galleries on St-Denis, nor is most of the architecture notable. But, then, that relieves visitors of the chore of obligatory sightseeing and allows them to take in the passing scene—just as the locals do—over bowls of café au lait at any of the numerous terraces that line the avenue.

PLATEAU MONT-ROYAL Northeast of the downtown area, this may be the part of the city where Montréalers feel most at home—away from the chattering pace of downtown and the crowds of heavily touristed Vieux-Montréal. Bounded roughly by boulevard St-Joseph to the north, rue Sherbrooke to the south, avenue Papineau to the east, and rue St-Dominique to the west, it has a vibrant ethnicity that fluctuates in tone and direction with each new surge in immigration. rue St-Denis (see above) runs the length of the district, but boulevard St-Laurent, running parallel to rue St-Denis, has the more polyglot flavor. Known to all as "The Main," it was once the boulevard first encountered by foreigners tumbling off ships at the waterfront. They simply shouldered their belongings and walked north on St-Laurent, peeling off into adjoining streets when they heard familiar tongues, saw people who looked like them, or smelled the drifting aromas of food they once cooked in the old country. New arrivals still come here to start their lives again, and in the usual pattern, most work hard, save their money, and move to the suburbs. But some stay on. Without its people and their diverse interests, St-Laurent would be just another paper-strewn urban eyesore. But these ground-floor windows are filled with glistening golden chickens, collages of shoes and pastries and aluminum cookware, curtains of sausages, and even the daringly farfetched garments of those designers on the edge of Montréal's active fashion industry. Many warehouses and former tenements have been converted to house this panoply of shops, bars, and low-cost eateries, and their often-garish signs draw eyes from the still-dilapidated upper stories above. (See chapter 7 for a detailed walking tour of this fascinating neighborhood.)

PRINCE-ARTHUR & DULUTH These two essentially pedestrian streets connect boulevard St-Laurent with St-Denis, 8 blocks to the east. The livelier rue Prince-Arthur is lined with ethnic restaurants, primarily Greek and Portuguese, but with Asian establishments looking to take their place. Many allow customers to bring their own wine, readily available from nearby convenience stores. Mimes, jugglers, and street musicians try to wrest what spare change passersby can be persuaded to divest. Four blocks north of rue Prince-Arthur, rue Duluth is fairly quiet in the blocks near St-Laurent, but more engaging near St-Denis. The mix of cuisines is much like that on Prince-Arthur. Tourists are evident in greater numbers on Prince-Arthur, many of them attracted by menus promising bargain lobster dinners for less than C$12 (US$8.30) during some times of the year.

PARC DU MONT-ROYAL Not many cities have a mountain at their core. Okay, reality insists that it's just a tall hill, not a true mountain. Still, Montréal is named for it—the "Royal Mountain"—and it's a soothing urban pleasure to drive, walk, or take a horse-drawn calèche to the top for a view of the city, the island, and the St. Lawrence River, especially at dusk. The famous American landscape architect Frederick Law Olmsted, who created New York City's Central Park and Brooklyn's Prospect Park, among others, designed Parc du Mont-Royal. On its far slope are two cemeteries— one Anglophone, one Francophone—silent reminders of the linguistic and cultural division that persists in the city. With its skating ponds, hiking and running trails, and even a short ski run, the park is well used by Montréalers, who refer to it simply and affectionately as "the mountain."

You can't throw a stone in Montréal without hitting stained glass.

—Attributed to Mark Twain

CHINATOWN   Just north of Vieux-Montréal, south of boulevard René-Lévesque, and centered on the intersection of rue Clark and rue de la Gauchetière (pedestrianized at this point), Montréal's pocket Chinatown is mostly restaurants and a tiny park, with the occasional grocery, laundry, church, and small business. Knots of old men stand on street corners discussing the day's events. For the benefit of outsiders, most signs are in French or English as well as Chinese. Community spirit is strong—it has had to be to resist the bulldozers of commercial proponents of redevelopment—and Chinatown's inhabitants remain faithful to their traditions despite the encroaching modernism all around them. Concerned investors from Hong Kong, wary of their uncertain future as part of mainland China, have poured money into the neighborhood, producing signs that its shrinkage has been halted, even reversed. Signaling that optimism, there are new gates to the area on boulevard St-Laurent, guarded by white stone lions.

THE GAY VILLAGE   The city's gay and lesbian enclave runs east along rue Ste-Catherine from rue St-Hubert to rue Papineau. A small but vibrant district, it's filled with clothing stores, small eateries, a bar/club complex in a former post-office building, and the Gay and Lesbian Community Centre, at 1301 rue Ste-Catherine Est.

ÎLE STE-HÉLÈNE   St. Helen's Island in the St. Lawrence River was altered extensively to become the site of Expo '67, Montréal's very successful world's fair. In the 4 years before Expo opened, construction crews reshaped the island and doubled its surface area with landfill, then went on to create beside it an island that hadn't existed before, Île Notre-Dame. Much of the earth needed to do this was dredged up from the bottom of the St. Lawrence River, and 15 million tons of rock from the excavations for the Métro and the Décarie Expressway were carried in by truck. The city built bridges and 83 pavilions. When Expo closed, the city government preserved the site and a few of the exhibition buildings. Parts were used for Olympic Games events in 1976, and today the island is home to Montréal's popular new casino and an amusement park, La Ronde.

2 Getting Around

BY METRO

For speed and economy, nothing beats Montréal's Métro system for getting around. Clean, relatively quiet trains whisk passengers through an expanding network of underground tunnels, with 65 stations at present and more scheduled to open. **Single rides** cost C$2 (US$1.40), while a strip of six tickets costs C$8.25 (US$5.70). Depending on how you plan to use the system, you can save money with a *carte touristique* (tourist card) for unlimited rides during the specified period, either the **1-day pass** for C$7 (US$4.85) or the **3-day pass** for C$14 (US$9.65). Buy tickets at the booth in any station, and then slip one into the slot in the turnstile to enter the system. Take a transfer (*correspondence*) from the machine just inside the turnstiles of every station, which allows transfers from a train to a bus at any other Métro station for no additional fare. Remember to take the transfer ticket at the station where you first enter the system. (When starting a trip by bus and intending to continue on the

Métro, ask the bus driver for a transfer.) Connections from one Métro line to another can be made at the Berri-de Montigny, Jean-Talon, Lionel-Groulx, and Snowdon stations. The Métro runs from about 5:30am to 12:30am Sunday through Thursday, and until 1am on Friday and Saturday.

BY BUS

Buses cost the same as Métro trains, and Métro tickets are good on buses, too. Exact change is required to pay bus fares in cash. Although they run throughout the city (and give riders the decided advantage of traveling above ground), buses don't run as frequently or as swiftly as the Métro.

BY TAXI

There are plenty of taxis run by several different companies. Cabs come in a variety of colors and styles, so their principal distinguishing feature is the plastic sign on the roof. At night, the sign is illuminated when the cab is available. Fares aren't too expensive, with an initial charge of C$2.50 (US$1.70) at the flag drop, C$1.20 (US85¢) per kilometer, and C40¢ (US30¢) per minute of waiting. A short ride from one point to another downtown usually costs about C$5 (US$3.45). Tip about 10% to 15%. Members of hotel and restaurant staffs can call cabs, many of which are dispatched by radio. They line up outside most large hotels or can be hailed on the street.

BY CAR

Montréal is an easy city to navigate by car. Visitors arriving by plane or train, however, will probably want to rely on public transportation and cabs rather than rent a car. A rental car can come in handy, though, for trips outside of town or if you plan to drive to Québec City.

RENTALS   Terms, cars, and prices for rentals are similar to those in the United States. All the larger U.S. companies operate in Canada or have affiliates (National is represented by Tilden, for instance). Basic rates are about the same from company to company. A charge is usually levied when you return a car in a city other than the one in which it was rented. All of the companies listed below have counters at Dorval Airport.

  Major car-rental companies include **Avis,** 1225 rue Metcalfe (☎ **800/879-2847** or 514/866-7906); **Budget,** Gare Centrale (☎ **800/268-8900** or 514/866-7675); **Hertz,** 1073 rue Drummond (☎ **800/263-0600** or 514/938-1717); **Thrifty,** 1076 rue de la Montagne (☎ **800/367-2277** or 514/989-7100); **National/Tilden,** 1200 rue Stanley (☎ **800/227-7368** or 514/878-2771); and **Enterprise,** 4028 Ste-Catherine Ouest (☎ **800/736-8222** or 514/931-3722).

GASOLINE   Gasoline and diesel fuel are sold by the Imperial gallon or, more often, the liter, at prices somewhat higher than those in the United States. One Imperial gallon equals 1.2 U.S. gallons, or 4.546 liters. Gas in Québec costs about C$25 (US$17.25) to fill the tank of a small car with the lowest grade of unleaded gasoline. To convert the approximate cost of Canadian gas to familiar U.S. standards, multiply the cost per liter in Canadian dollars by four. Then convert the price to U.S. dollars.

PARKING   It can be difficult to park on the heavily trafficked streets of downtown Montréal, but there are plenty of metered spaces, with varying hourly rates. (Look around before walking off without paying. Meters are set well back from the curb so they won't be buried by plowed snow in winter.) Check for signs noting restrictions, usually showing a red circle with a diagonal slash. The words *"livraison seulement,"* for example, mean "delivery only." Most downtown shopping complexes have underground parking lots, as do the big downtown hotels. Some of the hotels don't charge

extra to take cars in and out of their garages during the day, which can save money for those who plan to do a lot of sightseeing by car.

DRIVING RULES The limited-access expressways in Québec are called *autoroutes,* and distances and speed limits are given in kilometers (km) and kilometers per hour (kmph). Some highway signs are in French only, although Montréal's autoroutes and bridges often bear dual-language signs. Seat-belt use is required by law while driving or riding in a car in Québec. Turning right on a red light has been prohibited in Montréal and the province of Québec, except where specifically allowed by an additional green arrow, but there is discussion about changing the law. Ask upon arrival.

Fast Facts: Montréal

American Express Offices of the American Express Travel Service are located at 1141 bd. de Maisonneuve Ouest near rue Stanley (☎ **514/284-3300**), and in La Baie (The Bay) department store, 585 rue Ste-Catherine Ouest (☎ **514/ 281-4777**). For lost or stolen cards, call ☎ **800/268-9824.**

Area Code Montréal's telephone area code is 514. It isn't necessary to dial a country code when calling from the United States.

Baby-sitters Nearly all large hotels offer baby-sitting services (*garderie des enfants*). In the smaller hotels and guest houses, managers often know of sitters they believe to be reliable. Give as much notice as possible, and make certain about rates and extra charges, such as car fare, before making a commitment.

Bookstores   Montréal has many bilingual bookstores. **Chapters** (☎ 514/ 849-8825) is a large chain that resulted from a merger between Smithbooks and Coles booksellers. The flagship unit is at 1171 rue Ste-Catherine Ouest, and branches are scattered throughout the city. **Indigo,** in place Montréal Trust at 1500 av. McGill College (☎ **514/281-5549**), carries both books and CDs and has a second-floor cafe. For travel-related books, guidebooks, maps, and travel accessories, try **Ulysse,** in the Latin Quarter at 4176 rue St-Denis, near rue Duluth (☎ **514/843-9447**), and near the Delta Montréal Hotel at 560 av. du Président-Kennedy (☎ **514/843-7222**).

Business Hours   Most **stores** are open from 9 or 10am to 6pm Monday through Wednesday, 9am to 9pm on Thursday and Friday, and 9am to 5pm on Saturday. Many stores are now also open on Sunday from noon to 5pm. **Banks** are usually open Monday through Friday from 8 or 9am to 4pm.

Currency Exchange   There are currency-exchange offices near most locations where they're likely to be needed: at the airports, in the train station, in and near Infotouriste at Dorchester Square, and near Notre-Dame Basilica at 86 rue Notre-Dame. The **Bank of America Canada,** 1230 rue Peel, also offers foreign-exchange services Monday through Friday 8:30am to 5:30pm and on Saturday 9am to 5pm.

Doctors & Dentists   The front desks at hotels can contact a doctor quickly. If it's not an emergency, call your country's consulate and ask for a recommendation (see "Embassies & Consulates" below). Consulates don't guarantee or certify local doctors, but they maintain lists of physicians with good reputations. Even if the consulate is closed, a duty officer should be available to help. For dental information, call the hot line at ☎ **514/288-8888** or the 24-hour dental clinic at ☎ **514/342-4444**. In an emergency, dial ☎ **911**.

Drugstores   Open 24 hours a day, 365 days a year, the branch of **Pharmaprix** at 5122 Côte-des-Neiges, at Chemin Queen Mary (☎ **514/738-8464**), has a fairly convenient location.

Electricity   Canada uses the same electricity (110–120 volts, 60 cycles) as the United States and Mexico, with the same flat-prong plugs and sockets.

Embassies & Consulates   All embassies are in Ottawa, the national capital. In Montréal, the American consulate general is at 1155 rue St-Alexandre (☎ **514/ 398-9695**). The United Kingdom has a consulate general at 1000 rue de la Gauchetière Ouest, Suite 4200 (☎ **514/866-5863**). Other English-speaking countries (Australia and New Zealand) have their embassies or consulates in Ottawa.

Emergencies   Dial ☎ **911** for the police, firefighters, or an ambulance.

Hospitals   Hotel staffs and consulates can offer advice and information. Hospitals with emergency rooms are **Hôpital Général de Montréal,** 1650 rue Cedar (☎ **514/937-6011**) and **Hôpital Royal Victoria,** 687 av. des Pins Ouest (☎ **514/842-1231**). **Hôpital de Montréal pour Enfants** (☎ **514/934-4400**) is a children's hospital with a poison center. Other prominent hospitals are **Hôtel-Dieu,** 209 av. des Pins Ouest (☎ **514/843-2611**), and **Hôpital Notre-Dame,** 1560 rue Sherbrooke Est (☎ **514/281-6000**).

Hotlines   For the **Sexual Assault Center** 24-hour crisis line, call ☎ **514/934-4604;** for the **Suicide Action** line, call ☎ **514/723-4000;** and for the **Poison Centre,** dial ☎ **800/463-5060.**

Internet Access   The **CyberGround NetCafé,** 3672 bd. St-Laurent (☎ **514/842-1726**), has 16 computers with easy Internet access for C$8 (US$5.50) an hour. Hours are Monday through Friday 10am to 11pm, Saturday and Sunday 11am to 11pm. Another possibility is **Cybermac Café Internet,** 1425 rue Mackay (☎ **514/287-9100**).

Liquor Laws   All hard liquor and spirits in Québec are sold through official government stores operated by the Québec Société des Alcools (look for maroon signs with the acronym "SAQ"). Wine and beer can be bought in grocery stores and convenience stores, called *dépanneurs*. The legal drinking age in the province is 18.

Luggage Storage & Lockers   Luggage can be checked at Gare Centrale, the main railroad station. Most hotels and guest houses will store their clients' luggage for a day or two.

Mail   All mail posted in Canada must bear Canadian stamps. That might seem painfully obvious, but apparently large numbers of visitors use stamps from their home countries, especially the United States. To receive mail in Montréal, have it addressed to you, c/o Poste Restante, Station "A," 1025 rue St-Jacques Ouest, Montréal, PQ H3C 1G0, Canada. It can be claimed at the main post office (see below). Take along valid identification, preferably with a photo.

Newspapers & Magazines   Montréal's primary English-language newspaper is the *Montréal Gazette.* (To familiarize yourself with events in the city and province before your arrival, log on to the paper's Web site, **www.montrealgazette.com.**) Most large newsstands and those in the larger hotels also carry *The Wall Street Journal, The New York Times, USA Today,* and the *International Herald Tribune.* So do the several branches of the **Maison de la Presse Internationale,** two of which are at 550 and 728 rue Ste-Catherine Ouest. In Plateau Mont-Royal, a similar operation called **Multimags,** at 3550 av. St-Laurent, sells hundreds of foreign newspapers and magazines. For information about current happenings in Montréal, pick up the Friday or Saturday edition of the *Gazette,* or the free bimonthly booklet called *Montréal Scope,* available in some shops and many hotel lobbies.

Pets   Dogs and cats can be taken into Québec, but the Canadian Customs authorities at the frontier will want to see a rabies vaccination certificate less than 3 years old signed by a licensed veterinarian. If a pet is less than 3 months old and obviously healthy, the certificate isn't likely to be required. Check with U.S. Customs about bringing your pet back into the States. Most hotels in Montréal do not accept pets, so inquire about their policy before booking a room.

Police   Dial ☎ **911** for the police. There are three types of officers in Québec: municipal police in Montréal, Québec City, and other towns; Sûreté de Québec officers, comparable to state police or highway patrol in the United States; and RCMP (Royal Canadian Mounted Police), who are similar to the FBI and handle cases involving infraction of federal laws. RCMP officers speak English and French. Other officers are not required to know English, though many do.

Post Office   The main post office is at 1250 rue University, near Ste-Catherine (☎ **514/395-4909**), open Monday through Friday 8am to 6pm. A convenient post office in Old Montréal is at 155 rue St-Jacques (at rue St-François-Xavier). At this writing, it costs C46¢ (US32¢) to send a first-class letter or postcard within Canada, and C55¢ (US38¢) to send a first-class letter or postcard from Canada to the United States. First-class airmail service to other countries costs C95¢ (US66¢) for the first 20 grams (about ⅔ ounce). These prices are increased by the astonishing imposition of a *sales tax,* another C8¢ (US6¢) for a first-class stamp!

Radio   For English-language radio programming, tune to 600 AM (talk and pop), 800 AM (talk), 990 AM (oldies), 92.5 FM (pop-rock), 93.5 FM (classical music), and 98.1 FM or 88.5 FM (CBC public radio). A French station playing classical music is 100.7 FM. Some American AM and FM stations can be tuned in as well.

Rest Rooms   With so many shopping complexes throughout the city, convenient rest rooms are usually available (the up-front Québecois just call them toilets). But when in dire need, duck into the nearest hotel or buy a cup of coffee in a handy cafe and use their facilities.

Safety   Montréal is a far safer city than its U.S. counterparts of similar size, but common sense insists that visitors stay alert to their surroundings and observe the usual urban precautions. There are reports of escalating road-rage incidents, so expressions of impatience and anger with the actions of other drivers can be unwise.

Smoking   It is statistically true that French-speaking Québecers smoke more than other Canadians, despite heavy taxes on tobacco, and the province has not yet clamped down on smoking in public places with the determination of municipal governments in English Canada and the United States. Still, a growing number of restaurants have set aside nonsmoking sections, and cigar lounges are a fading fad.

Taxes   Most goods and services in Canada are taxed 7% by the federal government. On top of that, the province of Québec has an additional 7.5% tax on goods and services, including those provided by hotels. In Québec, the federal tax appears on the bill as the TPS (elsewhere in Canada, it's called the GST), and the provincial tax is known as the TVQ. Tourists may receive a rebate on both the federal and provincial tax on items they have purchased but not used in Québec, as well as on lodging. To take advantage of this refund, request the necessary forms at duty-free shops and hotels, and submit them, with the original receipts, within a year of the purchase. Contact the Canadian consulate or Québec tourism office for up-to-the-minute information about taxes and rebates.

Telephones   The telephone system, operated by Bell Canada, closely resembles the American model. All operators (dial ☎ **0—0** to get one) speak French and English, and respond in the appropriate language as soon as callers speak to them. Pay phones in Québec require C25¢ (US17¢) for a 3-minute local call. Directory information calls (dial ☎ **411**) are free of charge. Both local and long-distance calls usually cost more from hotels—sometimes a lot more, so check. Directories (*annuaires des téléphones*) come in white pages (residential) and yellow pages (commercial).

Television   Though most channels broadcast in French, Montréal has two English-language channels—6 and 12—and cable-equipped TVs also receive some American stations with network affiliations, including CBS from Burlington,

Vermont (Channel 3); NBC from Plattsburgh, New York (Channel 5); and ABC from Burlington, Vermont (Channel 22).

Time   Montréal, Québec City, and the Laurentians are all in the eastern time zone. Daylight saving time is observed as in the States, moving clocks ahead an hour in the spring and back an hour in the fall.

Tipping   Practices are similar to those in the United States: 15% to 20% of restaurant bills, 10% to 15% for taxi drivers, C$1 per bag for porters, C$1 per night for the hotel room attendant. Hairdressers and barbers expect 10% to 15%. Hotel doormen should be tipped for calling a taxi or other services.

Transit Information   Dial "AUTOBUS" (☎ 514/288-6287) for information about the Métro and city buses. For airport transportation, call L'Aérobus (☎ 514/931-9002).

Useful Telephone Numbers   For Alcoholics Anonymous, call ☎ 514/376-9230; for the Institute for the Blind, call ☎ 514/529-2040; for transport for disabled persons, call ☎ 514/280-5341; for the Poison Centre, call ☎ 800/463-5060; for the 24-hour pharmacy, call ☎ 514/738-8464; for the Sexual Assault Center, call ☎ 514/934-4504; for Canadian Customs, call ☎ 514/283-9000; for U.S. Customs, call ☎ 514/636-3875.

Water   Unless specifically labeled *nonpotable,* the drinking water is as safe as in the States.

4 Where to Stay in Montréal

Montréal hoteliers make everyone welcome, at least in part because there are more hotel rooms proportionally here than in other North American cities of similar size, and still more are opened every year. Those rooms, more than 23,000, have to be filled throughout the year, and with that competition and the continued robust value of the U.S. dollar in relation to its Canadian counterpart, this is the place to splurge, or at least step up in class.

Accommodation options range from soaring glass skyscrapers to grand boulevard hotels to converted row houses in Vieux-Montréal. Except in bed-and-breakfasts, visitors can almost always count on discounts and package deals, especially on weekends, when the hotels' business clients have packed their bags and gone home. B&Bs offer cozier settings at somewhat lower prices and give visitors the opportunity to get to know a Montréaler or two. By the nature of the trade, bed-and-breakfast owners are among the most outgoing and knowledgeable guides one might want.

Stylish inns and boutique hotels are appearing in increasing numbers, several of them recommended below, but for information about more conventional downtown bed-and-breakfasts, contact **Bed & Breakfast Downtown Network,** 3458 av. Laval (at rue Sherbrooke), Montréal, PQ H2X 3C8 (☎ **800/267-5180** or 514/289-9749; **www. bbmontreal.qc.ca**). This is a referral agency for homeowners who have one or more rooms available for guests. It represents about 30 properties with 50 guest rooms; doubles are C$65 to C$75 (US$45 to US$52) for rooms that share bathrooms, C$100 to C$135 (US$69 to US$93) for rooms with private bathrooms. Accommodations and the rules of individual homeowners vary significantly, so it's wise to ask all pertinent questions up front, such as if children are welcome, if smoking is permitted, or if all guests share bathrooms. Deposits are usually required, with the balance payable upon arrival. American Express, Visa, and MasterCard are accepted.

Nearly all hotel staff members, from front-desk personnel to porters, are reassuringly bilingual. Rare exceptions are the recent immigrants in menial positions who speak little French *or* English.

The highest room rates are applied from May through October, with the busiest times in July and August, especially during the frequent summer festivals, during annual holiday periods (Canadian or American), and when Montréal and Québec City hold their winter carnivals. At those times, reserve well in advance, especially if special

Best Hotel Bets

For a roundup of my favorite Montréal hotels, in categories ranging from the "Best Historic Hotel" to the "Best Hotel Pool," see chapter 1.

rates or packages are desired. Most other times, expect to find plenty of available rooms.

Three useful Web sites for both exploring lodging possibilities and making reservations online are **www.tourism-montreal.org**, **http://celestia.all-hotels.com**, and **www.destinationquebec.com**.

CATEGORIES   For convenience, the recommendations below have been categorized first by neighborhood, then by price. At most hotels and inns, the price differential from low to high season is rarely more than 15% or 20%, so in the listings below, the lowest price is for a January stay, the highest for a room in summer. A star beside an entry signifies an establishment that is one of my particular favorites and generally represents good value in its respective category. All rooms have private bathrooms unless otherwise noted. In the very expensive and expensive hotels, cable color TV and in-room movies are to be expected, as are restaurants, bars, meeting rooms, and parking garages. Business centers, health clubs, pools, and concierges are common but less certain, so inquiries should be made if any of these services or facilities are required.

TAXES   The provincial government imposes a 7.5% tax on accommodations (TVQ) in addition to the 7% federal goods and services tax (TPS). Foreign visitors can get most of the hotel tax back, assuming they save their receipts and file the necessary refund form. Unless specifically noted, prices given here do *not* include taxes—federal or provincial.

1 Downtown

VERY EXPENSIVE

✪ **Loews Vogue.** 1425 rue de la Montagne (between bd. de Maisonneuve and rue Ste-Catherine), Montréal, PQ H3G 1Z3. ☎ **800/465-6654** or 514/285-5555. Fax 514/ 849-8903. www.loewshotels.com/vogue.html. E-mail: loewsvogue@loewshotels.com. 142 units. A/C MINI-BAR TV TEL. C$195–C$430 (US$134–US$297) double; from C$425 (US$293) suite. Children under 16 stay free in parents' room. Lower weekend rates. AE, DC, ER, MC, V. Valet parking C$15 (US$10.35). Métro: Peel.

The Vogue created quite a stir when it opened in late 1990 after completion of a stunning conversion of an undistinguished office building. Not a few observers felt it instantly displaced the Ritz-Carlton at the apex of the local luxury-hotel pantheon. Confidence resonates from every member of its staff, and luxury breathes from its lobby to its well-appointed guest rooms. Although some guests find it chilly in look and tone, that's difficult to reconcile with the feather pillows and duvets that dress the oversized beds, the fresh flowers and cherry wood furniture, and the marble bathrooms with Jacuzzis with every unit—double-sized in suites. Other room amenities include fax machines, modem access, safes, hair dryers, in-room movies, bathroom TVs, and plush robes. All of this suits most of the international clientele to a tee.

Dining/Diversions: Société Café serves three meals a day, with outside tables in summer. The lobby bar, L'Opéra, has piano music Thursday through Saturday and an outdoor terrace in summer.

Amenities: Concierge, 24-hour room service, dry-cleaning and laundry, baby-sitting, secretarial services, express checkout, small exercise room, and coin-operated laundry.

Montréal Bonaventure Hilton. 1 place Bonaventure (corner of Gauchetière and Mansfield), Montréal, PQ H5A 1E4. ☎ **800/445-8667** or 514/878-2332. Fax 514/878-1442. www.hiltonmontreal.com. E-mail: info@hiltonmontreal.com. 395 units. A/C MINIBAR TV TEL. C$145–C$350 (US$100–US$241) double. Children 18 and under stay free in parents' room. Weekend packages available. AE, CB, DC, ER, MC, V. Self-parking C$14 (US$9.65); valet C$22 (US$15.15). Métro: Bonaventure.

The Hilton's main entrance is at de la Gauchetière and Mansfield, but the lobby is on the 17th floor, for the three stories of the hotel constitute what amounts to a penthouse above the Place Bonaventure Exhibition Hall. It has elevator access to Central Station and the Underground City. From aloft, the hotel looks as if it has a square hole in its top. That's the 3-acre rooftop garden, with strolling pheasants, paddling ducks, and a heated pool. All guest rooms have color TVs in the bedrooms and many have black-and-white sets in the compact bathrooms; views are of the city or the garden. Hair dryers, ironing boards, and data ports are standard. There are no-smoking rooms and an executive floor. All rooms, public and private, have recently undergone renovation.

Dining: Le Castillon is the hotel's French restaurant. Another, La Bourgade, is less expensive. Both have summer dining terraces.

Amenities: Concierge, 24-hour room service, baby-sitting, year-round heated outdoor pool, fitness center with sauna, and business center.

✪ **Omni Mont-Royal.** 1050 Sherbrooke Ouest (at rue Peel), Montréal, PQ H3A 2R6. ☎ **800/228-3000** or 514/284-1110. Fax 514/845-3025. www.omnihotels.com. E-mail: dumaberg@microtec.net. 329 units. A/C MINIBAR TV TEL. C$149–C$259 (US$99.35–US$172.65) double; from C$370 (US$246.65) suite. Rates include breakfast. Children under 18 stay free in parents' room. Weekend rates and special packages available. AE, CB, DC, ER, MC, V. Self-parking C$11 (US$7.85); valet C$19 (US$13.55). Métro: Peel.

This used to be the Le Quatre Saisons hotel, and, briefly, the Westin Mont-Royal, but in whatever corporate guise, it's a worthy competitor to the nearby Ritz-Carlton, especially after an ongoing all-floors $5.5-million renovation by the new owners. The coolly austere lobby, lined with marble, is softened by statuary and banks of plants and flowers. Rooms are large, with fresh furnishings, but make sure that you are assigned one of the refurbished units. They are offered in escalating categories of relative luxury, from standard to premium. Robes are ready for guests' use and there are in-room safes. On-demand movies can be chosen from a library of more than 60 titles. There are 12 no-smoking floors.

Dining/Diversions: Zen, an upscale Chinese restaurant, offers lunch and dinner daily, as does the light-filled Opus II, which has featured a form of world cuisine through frequent chef changes. Buffet breakfasts and lunches are served in the lobby bar, L'Apèro, which features piano music in the evenings.

Amenities: Concierge, 24-hour room service, in-room massage, twice-daily maid service, car and limo rentals, secretarial services, and boutiques. The impressive health club features a heated outdoor pool, open all year, with morning coffee and juice, aerobics classes, weight machines, whirlpool, sauna, and workout gear or swimsuits on request.

✪ **Ritz-Carlton Montréal.** 1228 Sherbrooke Ouest (at rue Drummond), Montréal, PQ H3G 1H6. ☎ **800/363-0366** in Canada and the U.S., or 514/842-4212. Fax 514/842-2268. www.ritzcarlton.com. E-mail: ritz@citenet.net. 229 units. A/C MINIBAR TV TEL. C$215–C$425

(US$148–US$293) double; C$395–C$675 (US$272–US$466) suite. Children under 14 stay free in parents' room. Packages available. AE, CB, DC, ER, MC, V. Self-parking or valet C$17.25 (US$12), with in/out privileges. Pets accepted (deposit required). Métro: Peel.

In 1912, the Ritz-Carlton opened its doors to the carriage trade, and that clientele has remained faithful. Over the years, however, their Pierce-Arrows gave way to Rolls-Royces and Lamborghinis. A few of these (or at least a Cadillac limo or a couple of Mercedes) are always parked in readiness near the front door. A needed $10-million renovation completed in 1999 has restored the gloss the hotel long held, and a perceived skid in service standards has been arrested. Male patrons used to be required to wear jackets in public rooms after 5pm, but management has eased up on that requirement. Bathrooms are equipped with robes, makeup mirrors, hair dryers, and speakers carrying TV sound. Fax machines are available on request, phones have data ports, and rooms have safes and irons with boards, and even umbrellas.

Dining/Diversions: The Café de Paris is favored for its high tea, weekend brunches, and weekday power breakfasts. Meals are served on the terrace in summer, next to the famous duck pond. An adjacent room spreads a luncheon buffet. There's piano music in the Ritz Bar and Le Grand Prix, with dancing nightly in the latter.

Amenities: Concierge, 24-hour room service, same-day dry cleaning and laundry, twice-daily maid service, baby-sitting, express checkout, secretarial services, modest fitness room, barber shop, newsstand, and gift shop.

EXPENSIVE

Delta Centre-Ville. 777 rue University (at rue St-Antoine), Montréal, PQ H3C 3Z7. ☎ **800/ 361-8155** or 514/879-1370. Fax 514/879-1761. www.deltahotels.com. E-mail: Mbouchard@ deltahotels.com. 550 units. A/C TV TEL. C$195–C$225 (US$135–US$155) double. AE, DC, DISC, ER, MC, V. Parking nearby. Métro: Square Victoria.

Within walking distance of Gare Centrale, downtown offices, and Vieux-Montréal, this new Delta, formerly a Radisson, serves both businesspeople and families well. There are both an indoor pool and in-room movies for the kids, a fitness center with Nautilus machines and a sauna for their parents, and a special floor for execs with minibars in the rooms. All rooms have hair dryers, modem ports, voice mail, and irons and ironing boards. Twenty-eight floors up is the city's only revolving restaurant, **Tour de Ville,** fun for a drink at sunset even if you eat elsewhere. One floor down, the once-public bar has become a private lounge to complement the executive Signature Club. There is a direct connection with the Underground City and the Métro.

✪ **Delta Montréal.** 450 Sherbrooke Ouest (at rue City Councillors), Montréal, PQ H3A 2T4. ☎ **800/268-1133** or 514/286-1986. Fax 514/284-4342. www.deltamontreal.com. E-mail: reservat@istar.ca. 453 units. A/C MINIBAR TV TEL. C$149–C$290 (US$103–US$200) double; from C$350 (US$241) suite. Children under 18 stay free in parents' room. Weekend packages available. AE, DC, DISC, ER, MC, V. Parking C$13 (US$8.95). Métro: Place des Arts or McGill.

This carefully maintained unit of the Canadian chain, with its expansively equipped business center, is targeted to the business traveler. However, its supervised children's crafts and games center and outdoor pool (open July and August) make it clear that families are welcome, too. Rooms have angular dimensions, escaping the boxiness of many contemporary hotels. Most have small balconies; all have coffeemakers and voice mail. The better-than-average health club has an aerobics instructor, an indoor lap pool, and two squash courts. For an extra C$30 (US$21), upgrade to the Signature executive floor. Enter the 23-story tower from Avenue du President-Kennedy.

Dining: Le Bouquet Bistro is open most of the day, with a popular luncheon buffet, while the adjacent dining room is more formal, with an international menu. Drinks, light meals, and a weekday lunch buffet are offered in the casual Le Cordial.

Downtown Montréal Accommodations

PARC DU MONT-ROYAL

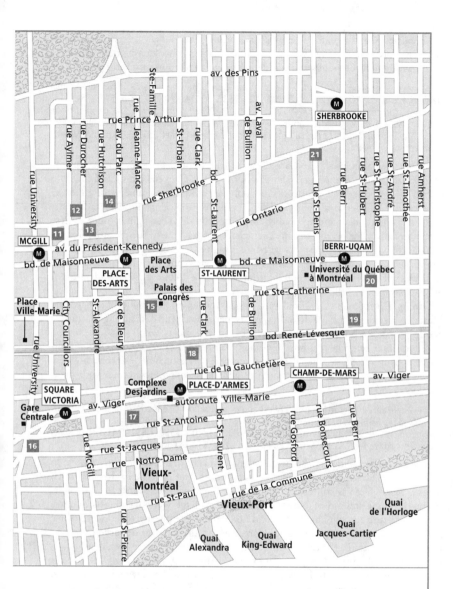

Le Centre Sheraton **8**
Le Germain **5**
Loews Vogue **7**
Lord Berri **19**
Montagne **6**
Montréal Bonaventure Hilton **10**

Omni Mont-Royale **4**
Ritz-Carlton Montréal **2**
Travelodge Montréal
  Centre **18**
Wyndham Montréal **15**
YMCA **20**

Amenities: Concierge, room service, dry-cleaning and laundry service, indoor and outdoor pools, fitness center, whirlpool, sauna, massage, two squash courts, business center with rental computers and translation service, and courtesy airport transport.

Le Centre Sheraton. 1201 bd. René-Lévesque Ouest (between rue Drummond and rue Stanley), Montréal, PQ H3B 2L7. ☎ **800/325-3535** or 514/878-2000. Fax 514/878-3958. www.sheraton.com. 864 units. A/C TV TEL. C$119–C$320 (US$82–US$221) double; from C$290 (US$200) suite. Children under 17 stay free. Weekend rates available. AE, DC, DISC, ER, MC, V. Self-parking C$12 (US$8.25) with in/out privileges; valet C$15 (US$10.35). Métro: Bonaventure or Peel.

Le Centre Sheraton rises near Gare Centrale (the Central Station), a few steps off Dorchester Square, and within a short walk of the rue Crescent dining and nightlife district. A high glass wall transforms the lobby atrium into an immense greenhouse, big enough to shelter royal palms and a luxuriance of tropical plants. The staff is efficient, and the rooms are comfortably corporate in style. That figures, since earnest people in suits make up most of the clientele. They gravitate to the executive Towers section, which bestows upon its guests complimentary breakfast, newspapers of choice, and an expansive private lounge with great views and free evening hors d'oeuvres. Half of the rooms have minibars; all have robes, coffeemakers, and in-room movies. Seventeen of the 35 floors are reserved for nonsmokers.

Dining/Diversions: The Boulevard restaurant serves three meals a day; the Musette, breakfast and lunch only. Jazz is performed Tuesday through Saturday evenings in the Impromptu Bar, and there's a separate sports bar.

Amenities: Concierge in Towers, 24-hour room service, same-day dry-cleaning and laundry, baby-sitting, secretarial services, express checkout, valet parking, business center, and airport transport. Indoor pool and sixth-floor fitness center with pool, whirlpool, and sauna.

✪ **Le Germain.** 2050 rue Mansfield (west end of av. President Kennedy), Montréal, PQ H3A 1Y9. ☎ **514/849-2050.** Fax 514/849-1437. www.hotelgermain.com. E-mail: reservations@ hotelgermain.com. 101 units. A/C MINIBAR TV TEL. C$210–C$550 (US$145–US$379). Rates include breakfast. AE, DC, ER, MC, V. Parking C$15 (US$10.35). Métro: Peel.

This latest undertaking by the owner of two equally desirable boutique hotels in Québec City and suburban Ste-Foy brings a fresh shot of panache to the downtown lodging scene. She has converted a small office tower with her sturdy sense of style; the result is a magical mix of Asian minimalism with all the Western comforts an international executive might anticipate…and not. Among the unexpected, discover three polished apples sitting in designated depressions on their shelves opposite the elevators. Help yourself. In the capacious rooms, find a vase with a fresh orchid, as well as hair dryers, desktop modem ports, irons and boards, CD players, big wicker chairs with fat cushions, and beds that will cure insomnia, piled with pillows and comforters. Self-serve breakfasts are set out on the mezzanine, with perfect croissants, a machine that makes excellent café au lait, and choices of newspapers in French and English. The location is near every downtown sightseeing and shopping destination.

Dining: The bar serves a limited menu from 4:30 to 10pm, featuring Asian soups, salads, sandwiches, and a couple of light main courses.

Amenities: Room service, dry-cleaning and laundry, and express checkout.

✪ **Le Reine Elizabeth/Queen Elizabeth.** 900 bd. René-Lévesque Ouest (at rue Mansfield), Montréal, PQ H3B 4A5. ☎ **800/441-1414** or 514/861-3511. Fax 514/954-2258. www. cphotels.ca. E-mail: gehres@geh.cphotels.ca. 1,080 units. A/C MINIBAR TV TEL. C$139–C$229 (US$96–US$158) double; concierge-level rates about C$80 (US$55) higher; from C$325 (US$224) suite. Children 18 and under stay free in parents' room. Various discounts, weekend, and excursion packages available. AE, CB, DC, DISC, ER, MC, V. Parking C$15 (US$10.35). Métro: Bonaventure.

Montréal's largest hotel has lent its august presence to the city since 1958. Its 21 floors sit atop VIA Rail's Gare Centrale, with place Ville-Marie, place Bonaventure, and the Métro all accessible by underground arcades. That desirable location makes it a frequent choice for heads of state and touring celebrities, even though other hotels in town offer higher standards of personalized pampering. Those who can afford it close the gap by staying on the Entree Gold 19th floor, which has a private concierge and check-in and a lounge serving complimentary breakfasts and cocktail-hour canapés to go with the honor bar. Less exalted rooms on floors 4 through 17 are entirely satisfactory, with most of the expected comforts and gadgets (including in-room movies, hair dryers, coffeemakers, and voice mail), in price ranges to satisfy most budgets. No-smoking floors are available.

Dining/Diversions: Le Beaver Club (see chapter 5) features a combo for dancing on Saturday nights. Several other more casual bistro/bars serve meals in a variety of settings.

Amenities: Concierge, 24-hour room service, dry-cleaning and laundry service, baby-sitting, business center, beauty salon, and shopping arcade. Large well-equipped health club with indoor pool and Jacuzzi, steam room, and instructors.

Wyndham Montréal. 1255 rue Jeanne-Mance, Montréal, PQ H5B 1E5. ☎ **800/361-8234** or 514/285-1450. Fax 514/285-1243. www.wyndham.com. E-mail: info@wyndham-mtl.com. 600 units. A/C MINIBAR TV TEL. C$126–C$189 (US$87–US$130) double; from C$350 (US$241) suite. Children under 18 stay free in parents' room. Packages available. AE, DC, ER, MC, V. Self-parking C$10 (US$6.90); valet C$15 (US$10.35). Métro: Place des Arts.

This used to be Le Meridien and then, briefly, the Complexe Desjardins, but nothing much besides the name has changed. It is still an integral part of the striking Complexe Desjardins, across the street from the Place des Arts and the Montréal Museum of Contemporary Art. Four hundred of the 600 rooms and suites have just enjoyed $15 million in renovations, so ask for one of them. They have hair dryers, voice mail, and modem access. Glass-enclosed elevators glide up to bedrooms and down to the lower levels of the complex, which contains a shopping plaza and an indoor pool cantilevered over garden terraces. Chinatown is a block away, and Vieux-Montréal, the downtown district, and the ethnic neighborhoods along The Main are within easy walking distance. The hotel is often the official headquarters of Montréal's annual jazz festival. No-smoking floors are available.

Dining/Entertainment: Café Fleuri provides all meals, while Le Club, with a French menu, serves only lunch and dinner. Le Bar overlooks Complexe Desjardins and has piano music nightly.

Amenities: Concierge, baby-sitting, 24-hour room service, dry-cleaning and laundry service, express checkout, indoor pool (about to be enlarged), fitness center with whirlpool and sauna, and business center.

MODERATE

Château & Hôtel Versailles. 1659 (north side) and 1808 (south side) rue Sherbrooke Ouest (at St-Mathieu), Montréal, PQ H3H 1E5. ☎ **888/933-8111** or 514/933-8111. Fax 514/ 933-6967. www.versailleshotels.com. E-mail: hotelinfo@versailleshotels.com. 65 units in the town houses, 107 units in the hotel. A/C MINIBAR TV TEL. C$144–C$214 (US$99–US$148) double. Children under 17 stay free in parents' room. Special packages Nov–May. AE, CB, DC, ER, MC, V. Valet parking C$14.50 (US$10). Métro: Guy.

This has long been a local favorite, despite a long, genteel decline. None too soon, it was decided that changes were needed, and the facility has been completely overhauled, leaving little resemblance to what it was. The Château portion of the property

---

⊕ Family-Friendly Hotels

Courtyard Marriott Montréal (*see p. 64*) Parents will appreciate the self-service laundry and their children the indoor pool; all of them like the choices of the buffet breakfast.

Delta Montréal (*see p. 59*) The Activity Centre for supervised play and crafts making is a big draw for small kids, along with the swimming pool and (for bigger kids) an electronic-games room.

Holiday Inn Montréal Midtown (*see p. 65*) Two kids under 19 stay free with parents, kids under 12 eat free, and everyone gets to enjoy free in-room movies and the big swimming pool; special packages for families.

Wyndham Montréal (*see p. 63*) The glass-enclosed elevators scooting up and down the heart of the complex are fun for kids, as are the indoor pool and the subterranean levels of the Underground City. Children stay free with their parents.

YMCA (*see p. 66*) It has three family rooms, a cafeteria that serves three meals a day, and a big indoor pool that guests may use.

---

began as a European-style pension in 1958, subsequently expanding into adjacent pre–World War I town houses. Those have been given the full decorator treatment, with voluptuous colors, fine modern furnishings with faint Deco tinges and some Second Empire touches. Only one deficiency remains—the lack of an elevator to deal with the three floors. Some years ago, a modern tower was acquired across the street and made into a motel-ish hotel. Guest rooms in both sections are of good size, equipped with hair dryers, safes, and coffeemakers. A few antiques are spotted around the public rooms. Breakfast and afternoon tea are served in a small dining room with a fireplace. There are two no-smoking floors and a French restaurant in the tower. Price and location (near Sherbrooke shopping and the Museum of Fine Arts) keep both popular, so reserve well in advance.

Courtyard Marriott Montréal. 410 rue Sherbrooke Ouest (at av. du Parc), Montréal, PQ H3A 1B3. ☎ **800/449-6654** or 514/844-8855. Fax 514/844-0912. E-mail: info@ courtyardmontreal.com. 181 units. A/C TV TEL. C$109–C$299 (US$75–US$206). AE, CB, DC, ER, MC, V. Valet parking C$12.75 (US$8.80). Métro: Place des Arts.

Formerly La Citadelle, this fulfills the Marriott chain's promise of providing service to business travelers at moderate cost. While the mid-rise slab can hardly be described as grand, needed renovations have perked it up. Rooms now provide hair dryers, coffeemakers, and telephones with voice mail. Junior suites provide space for longer stays; some of them have extra fax and modem lines. The compact fitness center has Nautilus machines, a sauna, and a steam room. The restaurant sets out a buffet breakfast (not included in room rate) each morning. With a self-service Laundromat and an indoor pool, the Courtyard also appeals to families on tight budgets.

Four Points. 475 Sherbrooke Ouest (at rue Aylmer), Montréal, PQ H3A 2L9. ☎ **800/ 325-3535** or 514/842-3961. Fax 514/842-0945. 195 units. A/C TV TEL. C$115–C$149 (US$79–US$103) double; C$155–C$195 (US$107–US$135) suite. Children under 17 stay free in parents' room. Packages available. AE, CD, DC, ER, MC, V. Parking C$12 (US$8.25). Métro: Place des Arts.

A new brand-name division of the Starwood hotel colossus (which also owns the Westin and Sheraton chains), this midpriced business hotel is a refurbished Howard

Johnson. Such is the ever-in-flux nature of the lodging trade in Montréal. In any event, it accomplishes its mission without breathing hard. That is, it provides a modest exercise room with aerobic devices, and roomy suites for businesspeople (and families) on longer stays, with fax machines, copiers, and computer on call—all at reasonable prices. Rooms have hair dryers, Nintendo PlayStations, unstocked fridges, coffeemakers, and irons and ironing boards, and the newspaper of your choice is made available. Towels are unaccountably skimpy, though, and bathroom lighting is often dim. The ground-floor Bistro le Monde sets out an appetizing buffet breakfast and has economical lunch and dinner table d'hôtes (fixed-price meals) of C$9.95 (US$6.85) and C$18.95 (US$13.05).

✪ **Holiday Inn Montréal Midtown.** 420 Sherbrooke Ouest (at av. du Parc), Montréal, PQ H3A 1B4. ☎ **800/387-3042** in Canada, 800/465-4329 in the U.S., or 514/842-6111. Fax 514/842-9381. www.rosdevhotels.com. E-mail: himidtown@hospitalitequebec.com. 486 units. A/C TV TEL. C$109–C$194 (US$75–US$134) double. Children 19 and under stay free in parents' room. Summer and family packages available. AE, DC, DISC, ER, MC, V. Parking C$13.50 (US$8.70). Métro: Place des Arts.

Not to be confused with the Holiday Inn in the Quartier Chinois (Chinatown), this midlevel entry stands among the clutch of similar hotels that cluster around the intersection of Sherbrooke and rue Durocher (which include the two described immediately above). Like them, it's among the city's best values in its class, especially for families. Self-operated washers and dryers, for example, are provided for guests' use, rare in the city. Bathrooms are compact. No-smoking and executive floors are available. A large heated indoor pool is attended by a lifeguard. The adjoining fitness center has weights, exercise bikes, whirlpool, and sauna.

Le Cantlie Suites. 1110 rue Sherbrooke Ouest (at rue Peel), Montréal, PQ H3A 1G9. ☎ **800/567-1110,** 888/CANTLIE, or 514/842-2000. Fax 514/844-7808. www.hotelcantlie. com. 229 units. A/C TV TEL. C$109–C$190 (US$75–US$131) double; from C$153 (US$106) suite. Extra person C$25 (US $17.25). Children 14 and under stay free in parents' room. Weekly and monthly rates available. AE, MC, V. Valet parking C$13.50 (US$9.30). Métro: Peel.

A neighbor to the Ritz-Carlton, this converted apartment house offers elbow room and a prime location at reasonable prices. Despite the name, accommodations range from standard doubles they call "studios" to one- and two-bedroom suites, which have either a full-size kitchen or a kitchenette. Most units have in-room fax, data port, work area, hair dryer, and iron and board. The rooftop pool (open in summer only) offers a fine view of the city, and guests have access to a nearby health club. There's a terrace cafe in warm months and a complete business center. Even casual requests at the front desk are likely to result in discounted room rates.

✪ **Montagne.** 1430 rue de la Montagne (north of Ste-Catherine), Montréal, PQ H3G 1Z5. ☎ **800/361-6262** or 514/288-5656. Fax 514/288-9658. www.intermatch.qc.ca/ hoteldelamontagne. 138 units. A/C TV TEL. C$145–C$155 (US$96.65–US$103.35) double. AE, CB, DC, DISC, ER, MC, V. Parking C$12 (US$8). Métro: Peel.

Two white lions stand sentinel at the front door, with a doorman in a pith helmet. The fauna fixation continues in a crowded lobby that incorporates a pair of 6-foot carved elephants, two gold-colored crocodiles, and a nude female figure with stained-glass butterfly wings sitting atop a splashing fountain. Clearly we are not in Kansas. Up on the mezzanine is the main dining room, Le Lutétia. Light meals are available beside the pool on the roof, 20 stories up, and there's dancing under the stars. Off the lobby, a cabaret lounge featuring a piano player and jazz duos (Monday to Saturday) leads into Thursday's, a bar/restaurant with a spangly disco and a terrace on rue Crescent. After all that, the relatively serene bedrooms seem downright bland. Given all these inducements, a stay here is a genuine bargain, especially in contrast to the expensive Hotel Vogue across the street.

Travelodge Montréal Centre. 50 bd. René-Lévesque Ouest (at rue Clark), Montréal, PQ H2Z 1A2. ☎ **800/363-6535** or 514/874-9090. Fax 514/874-0907. www.travelodge.com. E-mail: travelodge@mtl. 242 units. A/C TV TEL. C$69–$160 (US$48–US$110) double. Children under 18 stay free in parents' room. AE, CB, DC, DISC, ER, MC, V. Parking C$10 (US$6.90). Métro: Place des Arts or Place d'Armes.

An anonymous mid-rise bulk midway between east and west Montréal, near China-town and Old Montréal, the former Hotel Arcade's low rates and convenient location are its primary virtues. The guest rooms are small but bright, with double or twin beds (some rooms have up to four beds), cable TV with remote, and coffeemakers. All have showers, none have tubs. There's a lobby bar, and the dining room one flight up serves breakfast and dinner daily, but not lunch. There are two no-smoking floors.

INEXPENSIVE

Castel St-Denis. 2099 rue St-Denis, Montréal, PQ H2X 3K8. ☎ **514/842-9719.** Fax 514/843-8492. www.castelsaintdenis.qc.ca. E-mail: anne-marie@castelsaintdenis.qc.ca. 18 units. A/C TV. C$55 (US$38) double. Extra person C$10 (US$6.90). MC, V. No parking available. Métro: Berri-UQAM or Sherbrooke.

Among the budget choices in the Latin Quarter, the Castel St-Denis is one of the more desirable. It's a little south of Sherbrooke, among the cafes of the lower reaches of the street, and 2 long blocks from the Terminus Voyageur. Most of the rooms are fairly quiet, and all are tidy and simply decorated, if hardly chic—flowered coverlets and wood dadoes. The bilingual owner is a good source for guidance about nearby restaurants and attractions.

✪ **Lord Berri.** 1199 rue Berri (between bd. René-Lévesque and rue Ste-Catherine), Montréal, PQ H2L 4C6. ☎ **888/363-0363** or 514/845-9236. Fax 514/849-9855. www.lordberri. com. E-mail: info@lordberri.com. 154 units. A/C TV TEL. C$75–C$82 (US$52–US$57) double. Extra person C$10 (US$6.90). AE, DC, ER, MC, V. Outdoor parking C$10 (US$6.90). Métro: Berri-UQAM.

After a stint as a Days Inn, this economy hotel has returned to its old name, along with some needed upgrading of the furnishings and wallpaper. The resulting decor is still as interesting as a bus schedule, but you can't argue with the low rates, which is why this place has a star for value. If you don't plan to spend much time in your room, then this is one of your best budget options in the city. Its Latin Quarter location and 5-minute walk from Vieux-Montréal help make up for its limitations. Rooms have full bathrooms and offer in-room movies. Hair dryers and coffeemakers are provided. Several floors are set aside for nonsmokers.

YMCA. 1450 rue Stanley (between bd. de Maisonneuve and rue Ste-Catherine), Montréal, PQ H3A 2W6. ☎ **514/849-8393.** Fax 514/849-7821. www.ymcamontreal.qc.ca. 331 units. C$46–C$50 (US$32–US$35) double. AE, MC, V. Parking nearby. Métro: Peel.

This cavernous "Y" has more than 420 beds in 331 austere rooms in an assortment of configurations, most with telephone and color TV (the higher rate above is for rooms with TV) and without. There are no private bathrooms. Common bathrooms are located on each floor. Men, women, and families can be accommodated. An inexpensive cafeteria is available for all meals. Guests may use the training room, indoor pool, saunas, squash courts, and jogging track free. Self-service laundry machines are available. Reserve at least a week ahead. There's no curfew. The restaurants and nighttime distractions of the rue Crescent district are right around the corner.

2 Vieux-Montréal (Old Montréal)

VERY EXPENSIVE

✪ **Inter-Continental Montréal.** 360 rue St-Antoine Ouest (at rue de Bleury), Montréal, PQ H2Y 3X4. ☎ **800/361-3600** or 514/987-9900. Fax 514/847-8550. www.montreal.interconti. com. E-mail: montreal@interconti.com. 357 units. A/C MINIBAR TV TEL. C$180–C$345 (US$124–US$238) double; from C$350 (US$241) suite. Packages available. AE, CB, DC, DISC, ER, MC, V. Valet parking C$19 ($13.10). Small pets accepted. Métro: Square Victoria.

Only a few minutes' walk from Notre-Dame Basilica and the restaurants and nightspots of Vieux-Montréal, this striking luxury hotel opened in 1991 and became an instant candidate for inclusion among the top properties in town. Its tower houses the sleek reception area and guest rooms, while the restored annex, the 1888 Nordheimer building, contains a bar-bistro and some of the hotel's function rooms. (Take a look at the early 19th-century vaults down below.) Guest rooms are quiet and well lit, with photographs and lithographs by local artists on the walls and with in-room movies. The turret suites are fun, with their round bedrooms and wraparound windows. All rooms have coffeemakers and two or three telephones. Robes and hair dryers are supplied. Four floors are reserved for nonsmokers, and there are executive floors with a lounge.

Dining/Diversions: Les Continents serves all three meals and Sunday brunch. Le Cristallin, the lobby-level piano bar, offers a light menu and has music nightly. In the Nordheimer building is congenial Chez Plume, popular for lunch and after work weekdays.

Amenities: Concierge, 24-hour room service, same-day laundry/valet Monday through Friday, complimentary newspaper, nightly turndown, express checkout, business center, and health club with small enclosed rooftop lap pool, sauna and steam rooms, massage, and weight room.

EXPENSIVE

✪ **Auberge du Vieux-Port.** 97 rue de la Commune Est (near rue St-Gabriel), Montréal, PQ H2Y 1J1. ☎ **888/660-7678** or 514/876-0081. Fax 514/876-8923. www.aubergeduvieuxport. com. E-mail: info@aubergeduvieuxport.com. 27 units. A/C MINIBAR TV TEL. C$135–C$260 (US$93–US$179) double. Extra person C$15 (US$10.35). Rates include full breakfast. AE, DC, DISC, ER, MC, V. Valet parking C$13.50 (US$9.30). Métro: Place d'Armes.

Expanding on their own fine example, the owners of Sans Soucy (below) helped produce this larger, more luxurious inn in an 1882 building, adding a romantic cellar restaurant. Although it's gone through four managers in a short period, that doesn't seem to have affected performance. Polished hardwood floors, exposed brick walls, massive beams, and the original windows shape the hideaway bedrooms. Fifteen rooms face the waterfront and 22 have whirlpool baths. All rooms are no-smoking; they have hair dryers and the phones have data ports. Room service is available from 7:30am to 10pm. Drinks and sandwiches are served on the rooftop terrace, which has unobstructed views of the Old Port, a particular treat when fireworks are scheduled at La Ronde amusement park. Rates are lowest November to mid-April, except for the Christmas period.

Dining: The restaurant, **Les Ramparts** (☎ **514/392-1649**), sticks to traditional French fare in fixed-price meals carefully prepared and adroitly served. At one end of the room is an excavated fragment of the colonial fortification.

✪ **La Maison Pierre du Calvet.** 405 rue Bonsecours (at rue St-Paul), Montréal, PQ H27 1Z5. ☎ **514/282-1725.** Fax 514/282-0456. www.pierreducalvet.ca. E-mail: calvet@ pierreducalvet.ca. 9 units. A/C TEL. C$165–C$225 (US$114–US$155); C$450 (US$310) suite.

Vieux-Montréal Accommodations

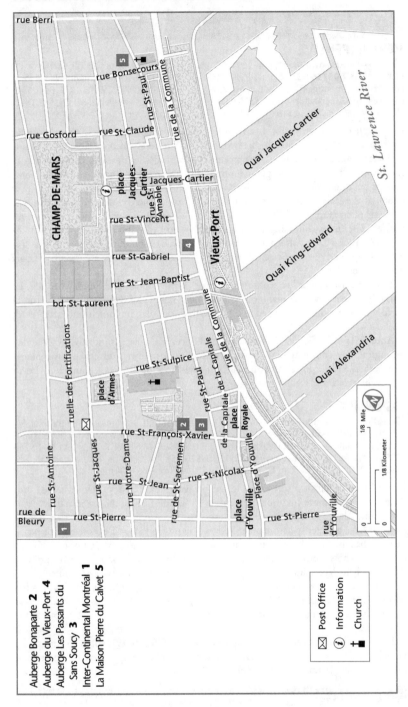

Auberge Bonaparte **2**
Auberge du Vieux-Port **4**
Auberge Les Passants du
Sans Soucy **3**
Inter-Continental Montréal **1**
La Maison Pierre du Calvet **5**

☒ Post Office
ⓘ Information
✝■ Church

Extra person C$35 (US$24). Rates include full breakfast. AE, MC, V. Parking C$10 (US$6.90). Métro: Place d'Armes.

When Ben Franklin was here in 1775 during his attempt to enlist Canada in the revolt against the British, the house was already 50 years old. After a stint as the theme restaurant Les Filles du Roi, the same owners made it into an inn that bids to transport guests to an elegant *manoir* beside the Loire. The beamed public rooms are furnished with copious antiques, not reproductions, including carpets on the ancient stone floors, leather sofas, gilt-framed portraits, a marquetry-topped reception desk, ship models, and a gloriously romantic dining room that refers to no specific era but suggests a 19th-century ducal hunting lodge. Bedrooms are no less opulent, some with fireplaces and heavily carved four-poster canopied beds. TV sets would only spoil the ambience. Food and service don't always live up to the setting, but Vieux-Montréal has plenty of places to eat. A 50% deposit is required.

MODERATE

Auberge Bonaparte. 447 rue St-François-Xavier (north of St-Paul), Montréal, PQ H2Y 2T1. ☎ **514/844-1448.** Fax 514/844-0272. E-mail: bonaparte@securenet.net. 31 units. A/C TV TEL. C$145–C$195 (US$100–US$135) double; C$325 (US$224) suite. Extra person C$15 (US$10). Rates include full breakfast. AE, MC, V. Métro: Place d'Armes or Square Victoria.

The restaurant of the same name on the ground floor has long been one of Old Montréal's favorites. Romantic and faded in a Left Bank way, it has now undergone massive renovation. While they were at it, the owners undertook to transform the overhead floors into this modish urban inn, opened in 1999. Even the smallest rooms are surprisingly spacious, and they have a variety of combinations of furniture—queen, king, and double beds—that are useful for families. Of the eight units on each floor, four have whirlpool baths with separate showers. Hair dryers are available. Spring for the handsome suite on the top floor and get superb views of Notre-Dame, cloistered gardens, and cobblestone streets. Room service is available around the clock, including the possibility of a full dinner at 3am.

✪ **Auberge Les Passants du Sans Soucy.** 171 rue St-Paul Ouest, Montréal, PQ H2Y 1Z5. ☎ **514/842-2634.** Fax 514/842-2912. www.relativedata.com/getaways/sanssoucy. 9 units. A/C TV TEL. C$110–C$145 (US$76–US$100) double; C$180 (US$124) suite. Extra person C$10 (US$6.90). Rates include full breakfast. AE, DC, ER, MC, V. Parking C$11.50 (US$7.95). Métro: Place d'Armes.

This delightful bed-and-breakfast in Vieux-Montréal is a 1723 house on even older foundations craftily converted by the bilingual owners. (Its seemingly misspelled name is a play on the name of one of them, Daniel Soucy.) Exposed brick, beams, and a marble floor form the entry area, which serves as an art gallery and reception area and leads to a breakfast nook with a skylight. Nine guest rooms are upstairs, and each has mortared stone walls, a buffed wood floor, a clock radio, a hair dryer, fresh flowers, lace curtains, and a wrought-iron or brass bed. Four rooms have Jacuzzis, and gas fireplaces have been added to three others. The inn is 8 blocks from Place Jacques-Cartier. The substantial breakfasts include chocolate croissants and café au lait.

3 Plateau Mont-Royal

Auberge de La Fontaine. 1301 rue Rachel Est (at rue Chambord), Montréal, PQ H2J 2K1. ☎ **800/597-0597** or 514/597-0166. Fax 514/597-0496. www.aubergedelafontaine.com. E-mail: info@aubergedelafontaine.com. 21 units. A/C TV TEL. C$135–C$184 (US$93–US$127) double; C$170–C$234 (US$117–US$161) suite. Extra person C$15 (US$10.35).

Children under 12 stay free in parents' room. Rates include buffet breakfast. AE, CB, DC, ER, MC, V. Limited free parking behind the inn or on the street. Métro: Mont-Royal or Sherbrooke.

For those who prefer to stay away from frenetic downtown districts, this urban inn may be just the ticket. Situated at the northern edge of Lafontaine Park, it's a bit far from the action (except in summer, when there are free concerts in the park and the tennis courts and jogging and cycling paths are well used). The inn has clean, sprightly rooms in bright colors; bathrooms are equipped with hair dryers. The small suites have whirlpool baths, while many of the other rooms have terraces or balconies. Those in the new section are roomier; units in back are quieter. Guests may use the terrace on the third floor, and they have access to a small kitchen that's kept stocked with complimentary cookies, tea, and juice. The lobby gets quite crowded for breakfast. There's a long staircase to negotiate and no elevator.

Where to Dine in Montréal 5

With well over 4,000 eating places, Montréal is filled to the brim with dining choices. Until only a few years ago, they were overwhelmingly French, in the several variations and subcategories that culinary tent covers. A few *temples d'cuisine* delivered haute standards of gastronomy, numerous accomplished bistros served up humbler ingredients in less grand settings, and folksy places featured the hearty fare of the colonial era, which employed the ingredients available in New France—game, maple syrup, and root vegetables. Everything else was ethnic. Yes, some places offered Asian and Mediterranean cooking, but they didn't enjoy the same favor they did in other cities of North America. Québec was French, and that was that.

While recurring waves of food crazes washed over Los Angeles, Chicago, Toronto, and New York in the 1980s, introducing their citizens to Cajun, Tex-Mex, Southwestern, and the fusion cuisines variously known as Franco-Asian, Pacific Rim, and Cal-Ital, the diners of Montréal were resolute. They stuck to their Francophilic traditions. Now that's changed, dramatically. The recession of the early 1990s put many restaurateurs out of business and forced others to reexamine and streamline their operations. Immigration continued to grow, and along with it, the introduction of still more foreign cooking styles. Montréalers began sampling the exotic edibles emerging in new storefront eateries all around them—Thai, Moroccan, Vietnamese, Portuguese, Turkish, Mexican, Indian, Creole, Szechuan, Japanese.

Innovation and intermingling of styles, ingredients, and techniques were inevitable. The city, long among the world's elite gastronomic centers, is now as cosmopolitan in its tastes and offerings as any on the continent. True, some of the silliness that has attended culinary innovation elsewhere has afflicted chefs here, too. Plates arrive in towering overwrought presentations that might well incorporate spiky fans of snow peas amid ponds of raspberry-beet coulis beneath timbales of wild rice and minced portobello mushrooms from which grow minigroves of rosemary and thyme. But what still is paramount to most chefs is the freshness and appropriateness of ingredients, and novelty is secondary.

Deciding where to dine among the many tempting choices can be bewildering. The establishments recommended in this chapter should help you get started, because they include some of the most popular and honored restaurants in town. Getting to any of them involves

Best Dining Bets

See chapter 1 for a list of my favorite Montréal restaurants, whether you're looking for a room with a view, the best French cuisine, or the best spot to rekindle a romance.

passing many other worthy possibilities, for numbers of good restaurants often cluster in concentrated neighborhoods or along particular streets, such as rue Crescent, St-Denis, or St-Laurent. Nearly all of them have menus posted outside, prompting the local tradition of stopping every few yards for a little mouthwatering reading and comparison shopping before deciding on a place for dinner.

It's a good idea, and an expected courtesy, to make a reservation to dine at one of the city's top restaurants. Unlike larger American and European cities, however, a few hours or a day in advance is usually sufficient. A hotel concierge can make the reservation, even though nearly all restaurant reservationists will switch immediately into English when they sense that a caller doesn't speak French. Dress codes are all but nonexistent, except in a handful of luxury restaurants, but adults who show up in the equivalent of T-shirts and jeans should feel uncomfortably out of place at the better establishments. Montréalers are a fashionable lot, and manage to look smart even in casual clothes.

Few people want to dine in five-fork restaurants all the time. This city's moderately priced bistros, cafes, and ethnic joints offer often outstanding food, congenial surroundings, and amiable service at reasonable prices. And, speaking of value, the city's table d'hôte (fixed-price) meals are eye-openers. Entire two- to four-course meals, often with a beverage, can be had for little more than the price of an à la carte main course alone. Even the best restaurants offer them, so tables d'hôte represent a considerable savings and the chance to sample some excellent restaurants without breaking the bank. Having your main meal at lunch instead of dinner keeps costs down too, and is the most economical way to sample the top establishments. The delectable bottom line of dining in Montréal is that a meal here can be the equal in every dimension to the best offered in Los Angeles, Chicago, or New York—for about one-third less.

Alcohol-based beverages are heavily taxed, imported varieties even more so than domestic versions. To save a little, buy Canadian. That's no deprivation when it comes to beer, for there are many breweries, micro to national, that produce highly palatable products. Wine is another matter, largely due to a climate inhospitable to the essential grapes. Given the price differential with California and European pressings, though, you might want to try bottles from Estrie (east of Montréal), from British Columbia, and from the Niagara Frontier. The vineyards near the famous Falls actually take advantage of the frigid winters, allowing grapes to freeze in order to make the sweet dessert "ice wines." If you drink more than one glass of wine with dinner, the half- or quarter-liter of house wine offered at many restaurants is a better deal than ordering by the glass.

Québec cheeses richly deserve your attention, and many can only be sampled there, for they are often unpasteurized, in the French manner, and cannot be imported into the United States. Of the many available, often as a separate course in better restaurants, you might try Mimolette Jeune (firm, fragrant, orange in color), Oka (semisoft, pleasantly smelly, made of cow's milk in a monastery), Le Migneron (semisoft, from goat's milk), and Le Chèvre Noire (a sharp goat variety covered in black wax).

When "cuisine" is the last thing on your mind and what you want is a quick meal that will do minimal damage to your credit-card balance, Montréal doesn't disappoint, either. Numerous places serve sandwiches and snacks for only a few dollars. Many of them go by the generic name *casse-croûte*—which means, literally, "break crust." They couldn't be simpler: often just a few stools at a counter, with a limited number of menu items that might be just soup and *chien chaud* (hot dog) augmented by such homey Québecois favorites as *tourtière* and *poutine*. In addition, a number of mostly ethnic eateries serve two-course lunch specials for under C$8 (US$5.50). Look, in particular, to Thai, Chinese, and Indian restaurants for all-you-can-eat lunch buffets at that price.

For a more extended discussion of Québec dining, see "Cuisine Haute, Cuisine Bas: Smoked Meat, Fiddleheads & Caribou" in the appendix following chapter 18.

PRICES   The restaurants recommended below have been categorized by neighborhood and then by the cost of an average dinner for one person. Prices listed for main courses in these entries are for dinner unless otherwise indicated (luncheon prices are usually lower). Prices *do not* include wine, tip, nor the 7% federal tax and 7.5% provincial tax that are added to the restaurant bill. Food purchased in a market or grocery store is not taxed, by the way.

PARKING   Because parking space is at a premium in most restaurant districts in Montréal, take the Métro or a taxi to the restaurant (most are within 1 or 2 blocks of a Métro station). Alternatively, when making a reservation, ask if valet parking is available.

SMOKING   The Québecois are the heaviest smokers in Canada, despite the high cost of the demon weed. But even in addicted Montréal, no-smoking areas in restaurants are increasingly available, if far from common. The government decree that restaurants must provide smoke-free sections won't take full effect for several more years. In the meantime, larger restaurants are the most likely to have set aside blocks of tables away from the nicotine haze.

1 Restaurants by Cuisine

BELGIAN
L'Actuel (p. 75)
Witloof (p. 88)

BREAKFAST/BRUNCH
Le Café Cherrier (p. 93)
Eggspectation (p. 92)

CHINESE
La Maison Kam Fung (p. 79)

DELI
Bens (p. 92)
Chez Schwartz Charcuterie
    Hébraïque de Montréal (p. 88)

FRENCH
Le Beaver Club (p. 74)
Les Halles (p. 75)

FRENCH BISTRO
Boris Bistro (p. 81)
Chez Lévêsque (p. 91)
La Chronique (p. 91)
La Gargote (p. 81)
Le Bourlingueur (p. 84)
Le Paris (p. 78)
L'Express (p. 87)

FRENCH CONTEMPORARY
Jongleux Café (p. 86)
La Marée (p. 80)
Nuances (p. 90)
Toqué! (p. 85)

GERMAN
Chez Better (p. 84)

GREEK
Milos (p. 85)

INTERNATIONAL
Baba-Reeba (p. 87)
Mövenpick (p. 80)

ITALIAN
La Sila (p. 78)

ITALIAN CONTEMPORARY
Buona Notte (p. 87)
Pavarotti (p. 83)

JAPANESE
Katsura (p. 75)
Na Go Ya (p. 83)

KOREAN
Na Go Ya (p. 83)

LIGHT FARE
La Brioche Lyonnaise (p. 92)
Le Café Cherrier (p. 93)
Eggspectation (p. 92)
Le Jardin Nelson (p. 84)
Kilo (p. 92)
Santropol (p. 93)
St-Viateur Bagel & Café (p. 93)
Wilensky Light Lunch (p. 90)

MEXICAN
Casa de Matéo (p. 81)

NORTH AFRICAN
Au Coin Berbère (p. 86)

NORTHERN INDIAN
Le Taj (p. 78)

PIZZA
Pizzédélic (p. 89)

POLISH
Stash (p. 85)
Mazurka (p. 89)

SEAFOOD
Chez Delmo (p. 80)
Gibbys (p. 80)
Maestro S.V.P. (p. 88)
Magnan (p. 91)

STEAK
Gibbys (p. 80)
Magnan (p. 91)

SZECHUAN/CANTONESE
La Maison Kam Fung (p. 79)

THAI
Sawatdee (p. 83)

VEGETARIAN
Le Commensal (p. 79)

---

2 Downtown

VERY EXPENSIVE

✪ **Le Beaver Club.** In Le Reine Elisabeth Hotel, 900 René-Lévesque Ouest. ☎ **514/ 954-2214.** Reservations recommended. Men are expected to wear jackets. Main courses C$28–C$35 (US$19.30–US$24.15); table d'hôte lunch (Mon–Fri) C$17.50–C$22.75 (US$12.05–US$15.70), dinner (Fri–Sat only) C$39–C$46 (US$26.90–US$31.70). AE, CB, DISC, MC, V. Mon noon–3pm; Tues–Fri noon–3pm and 6–11pm; Sat 6–11pm (late June through Aug, Tues–Sat 6–11pm only). Métro: Bonaventure. FRENCH.

The restaurant takes its name from an organization of socially prominent explorers and trappers established in 1785, which is why you dine under the stuffed heads of bison and moose. Their wilderness adventures are depicted in a stained-glass mural and carved wood panels that reveal the L-shaped room's 1950s origins. They are scheduled for updating, but still undergird the clubby ambience of the room. With widely spaced tables allowing a measure of privacy, it has long been a magnet for the city's power brokers (although, with 225 seats to fill, it's hardly exclusive). Lunch is the time for the gentlest prices. The menu changes twice a year, always including the trademark roast beef, but expanding from the former meat-and-potatoes regimen to lighter, more fetchingly presented fish and fowl. The lobster carpaccio and chilled carrot soup with mint are typical of this contemporary approach. On Saturday evenings, a trio plays for dancing.

✪ **Les Halles.** 1450 rue Crescent (between rue Ste-Catherine and bd. de Maisonneuve). ☎ **514/844-2328.** Reservations recommended. Main courses lunch C$14.50–C$26 (US$10–US$17.95), dinner C$25–C$35 (US$17.25–US$24); table d'hôte lunch C$25 (US$17.25), dinner C$35 (US$24) or C$47 (US$32). AE, CB, DC, DISC, ER, MC, V. Tues–Fri 11:45am–2:30pm; Mon–Sat 6–11pm. Closed Dec 23–Jan 19. Métro: Guy-Concordia or Peel. FRENCH.

Les Halles continues to thrive as one of the most accomplished French restaurants in town, despite its unlikely location, squeezed into the most frenetic block of Crescent Street, right up against the Hard Rock Cafe, of all places. It's unquestionably pricey, however, so consider having lunch here instead of dinner. Despite the prices, this isn't an "event" establishment, draped with brocade and glinting with Baccarat. Tables are close, service is correct but chummy, and animated conversations often start up between strangers—all of which promote the idea (if not the reality) of a mainstream, not fancy, establishment. Alberta beef, Québec lamb, and such game dishes as red deer and guinea hen are stars on the menu, but seafood, including snowy halibut and wall-eye, simply prepared, is also good. Ingredients are rarely exotic, yet the kitchen dresses them in unexpected ways. Main courses and desserts come in such hefty portions you don't really need appetizers, but the table d'hôte lunch is a good deal. The wine cellar has more than 10,000 bottles of 400 wines.

EXPENSIVE

Katsura. 2170 rue de la Montagne (between bd. de Maisonneuve and rue Sherbrooke). ☎ **514/849-1172.** Reservations recommended. Main courses C$11–C$27 (US$7.60–US$18.60); table d'hôte lunch C$8.75–C$15 (US$6.05–US$10.35), dinner C$27–C$31 (US$18.60–US$21.40). AE, DC, ER, MC, V. Mon–Fri 11:30am–2:30pm and 5:30–10pm (Fri until 11pm); Sat 5:30–11pm; Sun 5:30–9:30pm. Métro: Peel or Guy-Concordia. JAPANESE.

A tuxedoed maître d' greets patrons at the door and leads them to one of the large convivial tables in the front room, to the smaller areas in back, or to the three-sided marble sushi bar in the middle (which serves as a refuge for those who arrive without a reservation). Whatever you choose, waitresses in kimonos move quickly and quietly to serve and, if asked, to explain the extensive menu. Katsura has been around long enough to claim credit for introducing sushi to Montréal. Although no longer a novelty, sushi and sashimi are still prepared with close attention to craft by the three able chefs working behind the bar; part of the pleasure of dining here is watching those practi-tioners at work. It's a common gesture, by the way, to give them a small gratuity separate from that added to the bill. Depending upon choices, a meal here can be relatively economical. Sample a lot of their creations, though, and the bill shoots into a much costlier category.

MODERATE

L'Actuel. 1194 rue Peel (on Square Dorchester). ☎ **514/866-1537.** Main courses C$12.50–C$33 (US$8.60–US$22.75); table d'hôte lunch and dinner C$13.50–$17 (US$9.30–US$11.70). AE, MC, V. Mon–Tue noon–10pm; Wed noon–10:30pm; Thurs–Fri noon 11pm; Sat 5–11pm. BELGIAN.

Dine one flight up, where the most desirable of a sea of tables overlook the square. Fit-tingly for a Belgian restaurant, mussels are the expected house specialty, in more than a dozen variations, Provençal to curried, for C$16 to C$23 (US$11.05 to US$15.85), and in uniformly big portions. They are brought to the table in the cast-iron pot in which they were cooked. Double-fried potatoes are the delectable accompaniment,

Downtown Montréal Dining

PARC DU MONT-ROYAL

McGill University

ATWATER

GUY-CONCORDIA

PEEL

LUCIEN-L'ALLIER

BONAVENTURE

Place Bonaventure

GEORGES-VANIER

Gare Windsor

Métro Ⓜ

Baba-Reeba **10**

Boris Bistro **25**

Bens **6**

Buona Notte **14**

Chez Schwartz **11**

Eggspectation **4**

Jongleux Café **18**

Katsura **3**

L'Actuel **8**

L'Express **17**

La Brioche Lyonnaise **22**

La Maison Kam Fung **23**

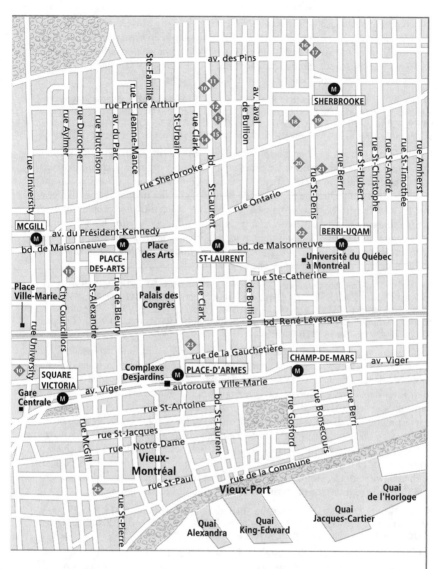

and complimentary second helpings are customary. A sturdy Muscadet goes well with mussels, and there are two good ones on the list. If mollusks aren't to your liking, other options include club steaks and tournedos in 18 different sauces and preparations; there's also a spicy steak tartare. Although the establishment is very popular, there's almost always an available table, even on a Saturday night.

La Sila. 2040 rue St-Denis (north of Rue Ontario). ☎ **514/844-5083.** Reservations recommended on weekends. Main courses C$8–C$15 (US$5.50–US$10.35); table d'hôte lunch C$9.95–C$18.95 (US$6.85–US$13.05), dinner C$12.95–C$49.95 (US$8.95–US$34.45). AE, DC, ER, MC, V. Mon–Fri 11:30am–2:30pm; Mon–Sun 5:30–11pm. Métro: Sherbrooke. ITALIAN.

If you've spent much time on Earth, you've been in at least 30 places just like this. Apart from dilution of the heavier cream sauces it once served, this restaurant remains a stout traditionalist on Montréal's dining scene, right down to Ol' Blue Eyes on the stereo. Reasons to go are the pastas, made in-house, and the trademark milk-fed veal that practically parts with a loving look. Service is by careerists, not people stopping in for a few paychecks, a difference gratifying to behold. Redecoration has brightened the interior and added a bar, and the terrace still invites diners in the warm months. Little on the menu is likely to disappoint. There's limited free parking in the back, useful along this gaudy strip below Sherbrooke.

Le Paris. 1812 rue Ste-Catherine Ouest (near rue St-Marc). ☎ **514/937-4898.** Main courses C$14–C$24 (US$9.65–US$16.55); table d'hôte lunch C$10–C$22 (US$6.90–US$15.15), dinner C$14–C$25 (US$9.65–US$17.25). AE, DC, ER, MC, V. Mon–Thurs noon–3pm and 5:30–10:30pm; Fri–Sat noon–3pm and 5:30–11pm; Sun 5:30–10:30pm. Métro Guy-Concordia. FRENCH BISTRO.

If you spent your salad days at the Sorbonne 40 years ago and found yourself with a few extra francs to upgrade from your usual meal of soup and half a baguette, you could nip around the corner to a place much like this. It's been open that long, and they haven't redecorated since—just some random old photos and posters and a few slaps of paint when required. The welcome is friendly and casual, as if you were here just last night, and there's accordion music on the stereo. On the menu are such bistro staples as *foie de veau* (calf's liver), *boudin noir* (blood sausage), and *brandade de morue* (salt cod mousse), but if they seem a little *too* French, wait for grain-fed roast chicken on Saturdays and steak *au poivre* all the time. Dishes are simple and unadorned, washed down with glasses from a selection of nine wines that go for as little as C$4.75 (US$3.30). Save room for the board of Québecois and French cheeses.

✪ Le Taj. 2077 rue Stanley (near rue Sherbrooke). ☎ **514/845-9015.** Main courses C$9–C$17 (US$6.20–US$11.70); luncheon buffet C$9 (US$6.20). AE, DC, ER, MC, V. Sun–Fri 11:30am–2:30pm; daily 5–10:30pm. Métro: Peel. NORTHERN INDIAN.

A large relief temple sculpture occupies pride of place in this dramatic setting of cream and apricot. In the glassed cubicle in the corner, a chef works diligently over a pair of tandoor ovens. His specialty is the mughlai repertoire of the northern Indian subcontinent. Seasonings of the dishes he sends forth tend more toward the tangy than the incendiary, but say you want your food spicy and you'll get it. (And watch out for the innocent-looking green coriander sauce.) Whatever the level of heat, dishes are perfumed with selections of turmeric, saffron, ginger, sumin, mango powder, and garam masala. For a rare treat, order the marinated lamb chops roasted in the tandoor; they arrive at the table sizzling and nested on braised vegetables. Vegetarians have a choice of eight dishes, the chickpea-based *channa masala* among the most complex. Main courses are huge, arriving in a boggling array of bowls, saucers, cups, and dishes, all with nan, the pillowy flat bread, and basmati rice. Evenings are quiet, and lunchtimes are busy but not hectic.

ⓘ Family-Friendly Restaurants

Pizzédélic *(see p. 89)*   Pizza never fails to please the younger set, and this place caters to any taste, with toppings that stretch the imagination.

Magnan *(see p. 91)*   Known especially for its supercheap all-you-can-eat lobster and beef extravaganzas, the menu also has lots of sandwiches and other simple foods kids like. Parents don't have to worry about the inevitable messes, especially since they'll be making big ones themselves.

McDonald's—For something familiar, but with a twist, this McDonald's, only a block from Notre-Dame Basilica at the corner of rue Notre-Dame and boulevard St-Laurent, deserves a mention. Located in a house that was once the home of Antoine Lamet de la Mothe Cadillac, the founder of Detroit and a governor of Louisiana, it offers the usual menu, along with pizzas and the Québec favorite, *poutine* (french fries doused with gravy and cheese nuggets).

Mövenpick *(see p. 80)*   This something-for-everyone emporium has a dozen stations selling omelettes, pizzas, burgers, and just about anything a youngster might crave, in a Disneyland setting with a romper room, games, and no fear about making too much of a mess.

INEXPENSIVE

La Maison Kam Fung. 1008 rue Clark (near Gauchetièrie Est). ☎ **514/878-2888.** Main courses C$7.25–C$14 (US$5–US$9.65). AE, DC, ER, MC, V. Daily 7am–3pm and 5–10:30pm. Métro: Place d'Armes. SZECHUAN/CANTONESE.

Weekends are the event days, when Chinese families that dispersed throughout the suburbs return for a wallow in their comfort food. Although regular meals are served in the evening, the morning to midafternoon hours are reserved for dim sum. That's the time to go. Here's the drill: Go to the second floor, obtain a ticket from the young woman at the podium, and wait. Once summoned to a table, be alert to the carts being trundled out of the kitchen. They are stacked with covered baskets and pots, most of which contain dumplings of one kind or another, such as balls of curried shrimp or glistening envelopes of pork nubbins or scallops, supplemented by such items as fish puree slathered on wedges of sweet pepper and, for the adventuresome, steamed chicken feet and squid. Order until sated. Resist the desire to gather up the first five items that appear. Much more is on the way.

Le Commensal. 1204 av. McGill College (at rue Ste-Catherine). ☎ **514/871-1480.** Reservations not accepted. Dishes priced by weight: C$1.95 (US$1.35) per 100g (about 3.5 oz.). AE, MC, V. Daily 11am–11pm. Métro: McGill. VEGETARIAN.

Le Commensal serves vegetarian fare buffet-style. Most of the dishes are so artfully conceived, with close attention to aroma, color, and texture, that even avowed meat eaters don't feel deprived. The only likely complaint is that those dishes that are supposed to be hot are too often lukewarm. Patrons circle the table helping themselves, then pay the cashier by weight. The second-floor location affords a view, which compensates for the utilitarian decor. There is no tipping.

Le Commensal has been expanding, with nine branches scattered around the greater Montréal area and in Toronto. One of the most convenient in-town locations is at 1720 St-Denis and Sherbrooke (☎ **514/845-2627**).

Mövenpick. Rue University at rue Cathcart. ☎ **514/861-8181.** Most items under C$15 (US$10.35). MC, V. Daily 7:30am–2am. Métro: McGill or Bonaventure. INTERNATIONAL.

The central gimmick of this outpost of the Swiss chain, long a successful presence in Toronto, is its theme-park simulation of a European market. Placed at intervals around the 30,000-square-foot space are more than a dozen food stations where diners line up for pizzas, crepes, sushi, coffee, pastas, omelettes, waffles, salads, rôtisserie birds, grilled meats, baked goods, and seafood, including freshly opened oysters. Faux grapevines, fake flowers, and an ersatz tree are meant to evoke a Mediterranean setting. Never mind that. In essence, this is a playland cafeteria, and the food, much of it prepared to order, ranges from satisfactory to pretty good. Upon entrance, you are handed a "passport," which the servers stamp with the prices of the items ordered. Pay up when you leave. Eat a course at a time or load a tray with a complete meal and take it to the nearby tables. Children are welcome in the designated romper room, and chess and scrabble sets are available to lingerers. The bistro has table service, and two bars serve wine, beer, and spirits. Almost everything is available for takeout.

3 Vieux-Montréal (Old Montréal)

VERY EXPENSIVE

Gibbys. 298 place d'Youville (at rue St-Pierre). ☎ **514/282-1837.** Reservations required. Main courses C$25.95–C$44.75 (US$17.90–US$30.85). AE, DC, DISC, ER, MC, V. Sun–Thurs 4:30–11pm; Fri–Sat 4:30–11:30pm. Free Valet Parking. Métro: Square Victoria. STEAK/SEAFOOD.

Given its popularity and situation in this touristy quarter, Gibby's is routinely dismissed as an overpriced snare for out-of-towners. That's closer to the truth of late, now that they've eliminated lunch and jacked up their prices (that C$44.75 is for filet mignon and scampi, a jazzed-up surf-and-turf). Still, it's a handsome place, a 2-century-old stone-and-beam setting that's much larger than it looks from the outside. And if your taste buds cry out for a break from the novelties of fusion cookery, then this is your place. Everything comes in strapping portions, cuts of beef and lamb rearing 2 inches off the plate and slabs of fish as wide as a catcher's mitt. Grilling is usually precise and to order, often the best choice for the several daily choices of fresh fish as well as the meats.

☼ La Marée. 404 place Jacques-Cartier (near rue Notre-Dame). ☎ **514/861-8126.** Reservations required. Main courses C$26–C$35 (US$17.95–US$24.15); table d'hôte lunch C$14–C$19 (US$9.65–US$13.10). AE, CB, DC, DISC, ER, MC, V. Mon–Fri noon–3pm; daily 5:30–11:30pm. Métro: Champ-de-Mars. FRENCH CONTEMPORARY.

Despite the T-shirted masses who fill the May-to-October terrace of this historic 1807 house on the west side of Old Montréal's busiest plaza, dining of a high order takes place behind these stone walls. It begins with the setting: fireplaces, paintings of fish and game, delicately figured wallpaper, and furnishings recall the eras of Louis XIII and the Sun King. Candlelight enhances the mood for romantic couples in the evening, while power lunches prevail at midday. Known especially for its refined and precise treatment of seafood, the kitchen is lauded—correctly—for such fabrications as grilled halibut on caramelized onions, and stir-fried chopped lobster in its shell. Natural flavors are allowed to prevail, and presentations are not so flashy that they bring conversation to a screeching halt. In cooler weather, chateaubriand (C$68/US$47) and roasted pheasant for two with goose liver and truffles (C$58/US$40) top the list. Service is disciplined and professional. There's no dress code, but you'll want to look at least casually stylish.

EXPENSIVE

Chez Delmo. 211 rue Notre-Dame (near rue St-François-Xavier). ☎ **514/849-4061.** Reservations recommended. Main courses C$15.75–C$29.95 (US$10.85–US$20.65). AE, MC, V.

Mon 11:30am–2:30pm; Tues–Fri 11:30am–2:30pm and 5:30–10pm; Sat 5:30–10:30pm. Métro: Square Victoria. SEAFOOD.

This venerable fish house has resisted change for decades. But that's a good thing: It's an atmospheric retreat that evokes a time nearly lost, when the freshest available fruits of the sea were quickly broiled, poached, baked, grilled or sautéed and presented with wisps of saucing and not a fennel brush or oven-dried tomato in sight. Enter a dim room with twin facing bars and their lines of stools, just the place for single diners in search of a light lunch of opened-to-order oysters (still only in months with an "R," even though they are now available year-round). Other diners are funneled into the larger, relatively characterless back room where full meals are served. Salmon from the Maritime Provinces, halibut, Arctic char, and real Dover sole are often featured, substantial in portion and lacking in flash, the better to lubricate the insider talk of deal makers from nearby law offices and brokerage houses.

MODERATE

Boris Bistro. 465 av. McGill (near rue des Récollets). ☎ **514/848-9575.** Reservations suggested weekend nights. Main courses at lunch and dinner C$12–C$14 (US$8.30–US$9.65). AE, MC, V. Daily 11:30am–11pm (may close Sun and Mon nights in winter). Metro: Square Victoria. FRENCH BISTRO.

"Boris" is the owner's dog, depicted in the restaurant logo as a canine sophisticate in a turtleneck. Putting aside questions of Gallic relationships with their pets, this very new and immediately popular eatery is taking full advantage of the excitement evident in the resurgent far western end of Vieux-Montréal (a new multimedia center has already prompted the building of two new hotels). Not much work has gone into the interior, a brutalist environment with bare concrete floor and beams and exposed vents. Despite the surroundings, the staff and patrons transform it into a lighthearted space, aided in great part by very reasonable prices and such bistro classics as *blanquette de veau, bouillabaise,* beef tartar, and mussels *du jour.* Don't pass up the super *frites* with mayo. If it's good weather, head straight for the courtyard and tables that seat 160 under big square patio umbrellas.

✪ Casa de Matéo. 440 rue St-François-Xavier (near rue St-Paul). ☎ **514/844-4154.** Reservations suggested weekend nights. Main courses C$14.95–C$21.50 (US$10.30–US$14.85); daily lunch specials C$11 (US$7.60). AE, CB, DC, ER, MC, V. Mon–Fri 11:30am–10pm; Sat–Sun 11am–11pm. Métro: Place d'Armes. MEXICAN.

Stepping into Casa de Matéo feels like wandering into a party in progress, especially on Friday and Saturday evenings, when mariachis come to kick the fiesta up a notch. Get in the mood with a birdbath-sized frozen margarita, which arrives with chips and salsa at the center horseshoe bar that's encased with rough terra-cotta tiles. The cheerful staff from Mexico, Guatemala, and other Latin American countries lends authenticity, and most are delighted to be addressed in even a few words of Spanish. With these generous servings, appetizers can be skipped—but that would mean missing the *plato Mexicano,* a sampler of all the starters. Because the plato Mexicano is a meal in itself, some diners may want to stop there—but *that* would mean missing the *pescado Veracruzano:* whole red snapper quickly marinated and fried and served with a nest of crisp vegetables. The usual burritos and enchiladas are easy to forget.

La Gargote. 351 place d'Youville (at rue St-Pierre). ☎ **514/844-1428.** Main courses and luncheon table d'hôte C$11.95–C$14.95 (US$7.95–US$9.96). MC, V. Mon–Fri noon–2pm and 5:30–10pm; Sat–Sun 5:30–10pm. Métro: Square-Victoria. FRENCH BISTRO.

Even though it's right across the street from the Montréal history museum, tourists haven't yet discovered this spirited little bistro. That's just as well, since it's already packed with locals and businesspeople, especially at lunch, when the staff is pressed

Vieux-Montréal Dining

Casa de Matéo **6**
Chez Better **10**
Chez Delmo **1**
Gibby's **5**
La Gargote **4**
La Marée **11**
Le Bourlingueur **9**
Le Jardin Nelson **12**
Na Go Ya **2**
Pavarotti **7**
Sawatdee **3**
Stash **8**

Post Office
Information
Church

hard to deal with the crush. When said patrons pay attention to their plates and not their companions, they are sure to be satisfied by such classics as duck sausage l'orange and lamb and merguez couscous, along with less familiar possibilities such as *paupiettes* of pheasant with mushrooms and currants. A featured bottle of a decent burgundy goes for C$32 (US$22). The surroundings are the Vieux-Montréal norm, relying on stone and brick walls and rough-cut rafters overhead, warmed by a fireplace in winter. Meals are also put together for takeout—meant for offices, but useful for a picnic in the nearby waterfront park. Better still is lunch at the tables set out in the plaza from late May to mid-September.

Na Go Ya. 140 rue Notre-Dame Ouest (at rue St-François-Xavier). ☎ **514/845-5864.** Main courses C$3.95–C$10.95 (US$2.70–US$7.55); table d'hôte lunche C$9.95–C$12.95 (US$6.85–US$8.95). Daily 11am–3pm and 5–9pm (until 10pm Fri–Sun). Metro: Square Victoria. JAPANESE/KOREAN.

Here's a worthy alternative for those who crave sushi but want to avoid the higher prices and hauteur of fancier purveyors in town. A stool at the short bar in front entitles you to one of the economical lunch packages. One is comprised of five pieces of sushi, five maki, and a handroll of rice around spicy tuna for only C$9.95 (US$6.85); the other, three sashimi and four pieces of sushi for C$12.95 (US$8.95). (Hint: Eat the ones wrapped in seaweed first, while they're still warm—they get chewy if you save them for later.) They are put together by chatty chefs who are in sharp contrast to the truculent fellows at the posher places. For about the same prices, you can opt for a "lunch box" of grilled beef, chicken, or salmon, each of which comes with miso soup, rice, salad, and fruits. In the three dining areas that trail out toward the back, complete meals for two are available for C$24.95 to C$53.95 (US$17.20 to US$37). That food is Korean, the ethnic background of the chef and the owners, and if you haven't experienced that cuisine, you're in for a pleasant surprise.

Pavarotti. 408 rue St-François-Xavier (north of rue St-Paul). ☎ **514/844-9656.** Reservations recommended on weekends. Main courses C$11.50–C$16.25 (US$7.95–US$11.20). AE, DC, ER, MC, V. Mon 11am–3pm; Tues–Thurs 11am–9pm; Fri 11am–10pm; Sat 5–10pm. Métro: Square Victoria. CONTEMPORARY ITALIAN.

Dean Martin sings about a moon hitting your eye like a big pizza pie and basso profundos commit arias. The interior of this 125-year-old stone house has a thrown-together quality, with brick walls, old photos of the port, ship models, hanging bundles of herbs, and a candle chandelier that would do justice to the lair of the Phantom of the Opera—all of which is so dimly lit that the menu is hard to make out. That's okay. Take a blind poke; you probably won't be disappointed. There isn't anything too odd, and servings are ample. The bruschetta is typical, not one or two pieces of toast, but a ring of six, with a do-it-yourself heap of chopped tomato, onion, garlic, and olives in the middle. After that, plates of feathery pasta, made right there, become evening specials, like the one that came with a tumble of clams, mussels, and shrimp. The soupy house risotto supports your choice of seafood or vegetables. By midevening, the place is a friendly babble, orchestrated by the always-present owner.

✪ Sawatdee. 457 rue St-Pierre (near rue Notre-Dame). ☎ **514/849-8854.** Main courses C$8.95–C$12.95 (US$6.15–US$8.95); table d'hôte dinner for 2 C$29.90 and C$39.90 (US$21 and US$28). AE, MC, V. Mon–Wed 11:30am–2:30pm and 5–10:30pm; Thurs 11:30am–3pm and 5–10:30pm; Fri 11:30am–3pm and 5–11pm; Sat 5–11pm; Sun 5–10:30pm. Métro: Square Victoria or Place d'Armes. THAI.

Before it moved here from its first location near Atwater Market, this was proclaimed one of the 100 best restaurants in Canada. It wasn't then, and isn't now, but Sawatdee is still a welcome addition. The owners brought along the impressive collection of museum-quality statuary and embroidered tapestries, which deserves closer examination. At C$8.95 (US$6.15), the lunch buffet is cheap and filling, but hardly amazing. Dinner is the more memorable meal, especially if you make it clear that you want authentic Thai seasonings, not the wan "Canadian" versions usually served to non-Asians. Several dishes involve whole fish.

INEXPENSIVE

✪ Chez Better. 160 rue Notre-Dame (near place Jacques-Cartier). ☎ **514/861-2617.** Main courses C$7.50–C$11.50 (US$5.15–US$7.95); table d'hôte C$13.75–C$15.75 (US$9.50–US$10.85). AE, DC, ER, MC, V. Daily 11am–10pm. Métro: Champ-de-Mars. GERMAN.

They aren't making a half-hearted boast with the name of this place. This and the other five outposts of this local chain are named for the founder, a Canadian born in Germany. Presumably he grew homesick for tastes of his native land and opened his first restaurant in this 1811 building near the top of Place Jacques Cartier to assuage that hunger. Think multiple variations of knackwurst, chipolata, kasseler, sauerkraut, and 100 brands of beer—that gives the general outline of the menu. Forget grease and oozing globules of fat, though, for these are lighthearted sausages, brightly seasoned with herbs, curry, hot pepper, and even truffle shavings. A special lunchtime sampler of bratwurst, cevapcici, and diable comes with fries and kraut and costs just C$7.50 (US$5.15)—a terrific deal. Three jars of mustard sit on each table. While sausage plates are the stars, there are also mixed grills, chicken schnitzels, grilled smoked pork chops, salads, and mussels nine ways. Service can be disjointed, but rarely to the point of irritation. Two other branches tourists are likely to encounter are at 4382 bd. St-Laurent (☎ **514/845-4554**) and 1430 rue Stanley (☎ **514/848-9859**).

✪ Le Bourlingueur. 363 St-François-Xavier (at rue St-Paul). ☎ **514/845-3646.** Reservations recommended on weekends. Table d'hôte lunch or dinner C$10.25–C$14.50 (US$7.05–US$10). MC, V. Mon–Fri 11:30am–9pm; Sat–Sun 5–9pm. Métro: Place d'Armes. FRENCH BISTRO.

Although it doesn't look especially promising upon first approach, this place is a real find in Vieux-Montréal. I give it a star for the almost unbelievably low prices they charge for several four-course meals daily. The blackboard menu changes depending on what's available at the market that day, making it possible to dine here twice a day for a week without repeating anything except the indifferent salad. Roast beef and *choucroute garnie* are likely to show up, but the specialty of the house is seafood— watch for the cold lobster with herb mayonnaise. Well short of chic, it doesn't make the most of its stone walls and old beams, but at least they've banished the old white chairs and maroon tablecloths. That hardly matters though, not at these prices and relative quality. The crowd is diverse—you'll be dining with the widest possible range of ages, genders, and occupations here. They have a no-smoking section.

✪ Le Jardin Nelson. 407 place Jacques-Cartier (at rue de la Commune). ☎ **514/861-5731.** Reservations accepted only by phone, not by walkup. Main courses C$10.25–C$14.95 (US$7.05–US$10.30). MC, V. May–Labour Day daily 11:30am–3am; Labour Day–Early Nov daily 11:30am–midnight (later on weekends); Mid-Nov–Apr weekends 11:30am–5pm. Métro: Place d'Armes. LIGHT FARE.

Near the foot of the hill, a passage leads into the garden court in back of a stone building dating from 1812. More a place to spend a pleasant hour or two than for serious dining, there's jazz most nights and weekend afternoons and classical chamber groups Monday to Friday during lunch hours in the good months. A crabapple tree shades the garden, a horticultural counterpoint to the music. Food takes second place, but the kitchen does right by its individual pizzas and crepes with both sweet and savory fillings (including lobster), as well as soups, omelettes, pastas, salads, and sandwiches. There's a covered people-watching porch in front and dining rooms and a bar inside.

✪ Stash. 200 rue St-Paul Ouest (at rue St-François-Xavier). ☎ **514/845-6611.** Reservations recommended on weekends. Main courses C$8.25–C$14.75 (US$5.70–US$10.15); table d'hôte lunch and dinner C$18.75–C$24.50 (US$12.50–US$16.90). AE, CB, DC, ER, MC, V. Daily 11:45am–11pm (until 10pm in winter). Métro: Place d'Armes. POLISH.

Even after moving from its former spot beside Notre-Dame Basilica, this *restauracja polska* continues to draw enthusiastic diners for its munificent portions and low prices. The current setting has brick-and-stone walls, colorful hanging lamps, new carpeting, wooden refractory tables and upholstered pews rescued from a convent, and shelves of secondhand books and newspapers to peruse. Roast wild boar is featured in addition to an ample card of pierogies (a kind of Polish ravioli stuffed with meat or cheese), potato pancakes, borscht with sour cream, roast duck, and beef Stroganoff. A jolly tenor pertains, enforced by such menu admonitions as "anything tastes better with wodka, even wodka. Read, eat, and enjoy."

4 Plateau Mont-Royal
VERY EXPENSIVE
✪ Milos. 5357 av. du Parc (between rue St-Viateur and av. Fairmont). ☎ **514/272-3522.** Reservations recommended. Main courses C$22.50–C$28.95 (US$15.50–US$19.95); table d'hôte C$29.95 (US$21). AE, MC, V. Mon–Fri noon–3pm and 5–11pm; Sat 5–11pm; Sun 5–10pm. Métro: Outremont, then a 12-block walk. GREEK/SEAFOOD.

Avenue du Parc used to be a virtual Little Mykonos, lined with Hellenic fish houses. That culinary population has thinned out, but the top dog remains and still holds to a standard higher than its rivals are ever likely to achieve. Inside, it is what a taverna at a picturesque Aegean fishing port would look like if it had the necessary drachmas. White plaster walls, bleached wooden floors, Greek vases, blue tiles, stations for salad prep and cooking, a holding room downstairs for busy nights, and refrigerated cases for the finny main events. The freshest available fish, flown in from wherever they are at peak, are the reason Milos prevails. Show the slightest interest and you'll be taken on a tour of the iced and clear-eyed denizens offered for your pleasure—Icelandic char, sushi-quality yellowfin tuna, Nova Scotia lobsters, Florida pompano, Mediterranean *loup-de-mer,* and cephalopods. Food is priced by the pound; you can pick your very own meal or leave it to the chefs. They'll even cook a veal chop if you absolutely insist. With drinks comes grilled bread, the waiter pouring a dish of fragrant olive oil and snipping fresh oregano into it. Order the excellent Greek salad as a first course. The main course will be along soon, brushed with olive oil and charcoal-grilled—validation once again that the most memorable meals are often the simplest. The waiters can be brusque at first, but they warm up as the meal proceeds. Expect to part with about C$150 (US$103) for two with tax, wine, and tip—it's worth it.

✪ Toqué! 3842 rue St-Denis (at rue Roy). ☎ **514/499-2084.** Reservations essential. Menu dégustation C$70 or C$80 (US$48 or US$55), C$97 or C$107 (US$67 or US$74) with wine. Main courses C$28–C$32 (US$19.30–US$22). AE, DC, ER, MC, V. Daily 5:30–11pm. Closed Dec 24–Jan 6. Métro: Sherbrooke. FRENCH CONTEMPORARY.

Toqué! is the sort of adornment that can single-handedly raise the gastronomic expectations of an entire city. A meal here is virtually obligatory for anyone who admires superb food dazzlingly presented. Normand Laprise teamed with Christine Lamarche to create a place as modernist in its cuisine as in its decor, which combines bright colors and minimalist fixtures, with a wall down the middle to separate smokers from nonsmokers. "Postnouvelle" might be an apt description of their creations, for while presentations are eye-openers, the portions are quite sufficient and the singular combinations of ingredients are intensely flavorful. Asian and related fusion influences are more evident these days, but experimentation is kept on a tether, and they are still working within the dictates of the contemporary French kitchen. That professionalism is applied exclusively to top-of-the-bin ingredients, some of them rarely seen on a plate—foie gras with milkweed buds, for only one example. The menu is never set in stone. If fiddleheads are good at morning market, they might well replace the listed asparagus that night. Consider just one recent dish: roasted *bas-du-fleuve* saddle of lamb joined by a lentil compote moistened with juices of the meat and combining butternut squash, cipollini onion, carrots, Jerusalem artichoke, and wilted bok choy. Duck, veal, quail, and venison are memorable in whatever fabrications the kitchen has conjured, while salmon and Arctic char are often the most desirable fish. Unless you are highly knowledgeable about wines, my recommendation is to choose one of tasting menus, where each of the four or five courses are accompanied by different wines carefully selected to complement those specific preparations. The restaurant fills up later than most, with prosperous-looking suits and women who sparkle at throat and wrist, so while there is no stated dress code, you'll want to look your best. Service is efficient, helpful, and not a whit self-important. Allow 2 hours for dinner and call at least a day ahead for reservations.

EXPENSIVE

✪ **Jongleux Café.** 3434 av. St-Denis (north of rue Sherbrooke). ☎ **514/841-8080.** Main courses C$19–C$25 (US$13.10–US$17.25); table d'hôte C$18–C$29 (US$12.40–US$20). AE, CB, DC, ER, MC, V. Mon–Fri noon–2pm and 6–10pm; Sat 6–11pm. Métro: Sherbrooke. FRENCH CONTEMPORARY.

One of the city's best new restaurants doesn't look like it from the sidewalk of this raffish district. Things perk up inside the door, though, its two levels calm beneath Milanese-style wire lighting. The young co-owner and her cheerful wait staff greet patrons warmly, a welcome not always followed up with efficiency in bringing drinks and menus. Those lapses aside, her previously peripatetic partner was trained in prestigious kitchens in France, Singapore, and Montréal, and it shows on every plate. His claim merely to be updating traditional bistro cooking is belied by his remarkable paella of snails and crisp-fried sweetbreads and by the salmon tournedos in a tapenade crust accompanied by saffron-touched chickpea raviolis. It may require a small leap of faith to order the braised pig cheeks, but that rich silken flesh is a revelation, draped with delicate pasta envelopes flavored with Camembert. Unsalted butter, unusual in Québec, comes with the excellent chewy bread; wines by the glass cost C$6 to C$8 (US$4.15 to US$5.50). Most patrons tend to be on the silvery side of 40, looking for a jolt to sophisticated taste buds, but food this good deserves a wider audience.

MODERATE

Au Coin Berbère. 73 rue Duluth (east of bd. St-Laurent). ☎ **514/844-7405.** Main courses C$9.25–C$16.75 (US$6.40–US$11.55). MC, V. Tues–Wed 5–11pm; Thurs–Sun 5pm–midnight. Métro: Mont-Royal or Sherbrooke. NORTH AFRICAN.

This earnest little retreat may be all but empty, but don't let that deter you. Couscous is the specialty, the name of both the North African dish and of the grain pasta that's its one essential ingredient. Here, it is both tasty and a bargain, and it may be particularly appealing to vegetarians eager for something other than salads. The staff pushes the most expensive versions as shamelessly as in a Moroccan medina, but accepts your decision to take the cheaper one with falling-off-the-bone duck, scented with cilantro and mint and zinged with optional harisa sauce. Dates stuffed with almond paste are dessert, and mint tea a perfect topper. It's fully licensed.

Baba-Reeba. 3614 bd. St-Laurent (near rue Prince Arthur). ☎ **514/281-6913.** Main courses C$7.25–C$18.95 (US$5–US$13.05). AE, MC, V. Tues–Wed 11:30am–11pm; Thurs–Sat 11:30am–1am (or 2am). Metro: St-Laurent. FUSION.

Hybrid establishments, places that defy ready classification, abound along The Main. This cheerful multipurpose joint combines the functions of kicked-back cafe, contemporary bistro, and festive *boîte de nuit.* It takes partial inspiration from Barcelona tapas bars (there's an unaffiliated Baba-Reeba in that Catalan city), but only as a launching pad. Very few items on the long menu would be identifiable to a Spaniard, but assuming you aren't a stickler for authenticity, the appetizer-sized tapas prove to be uniformly tasty, from the grilled chicken nubbins with a honey-based Asian dipping sauce to *patatas bravas* that are actually potato skins layered with cheese. While sipping and nibbling, take in a virtual history of lighting fixtures, including wall sconces, fringed lamps, wrought-iron chandeliers, pinlights, even a lava lamp. Bar action picks up around 9pm, when friends and strangers make contact and later drift upstairs to the Gypsy Club, a disco playing music from the seventies to now and occasionally staging a flamenco show to sustain the Spanish connection.

✪ **Buona Notte.** 3518 bd. St-Laurent (near rue Sherbrooke). ☎ **514/848-0644.** Reservations recommended. Main courses C$10.25–C$24 (US$7.05–US$16.55); table d'hôte C$19–C$29 (US$13.10–US$20). AE, DC, MC, V. Mon–Wed 11:30am–midnight; Thurs–Sat 11:30am–1am; Sun 5pm–midnight. Métro: St-Laurent. ITALIAN CONTEMPORARY.

With its high ceiling masked by electric fans and heating ducts, Buona Notte could easily be in New York's SoHo district. A principal component of the remaining decor is a collection of plates painted by celebrity diners, among them Ben Kingsley, Danny DeVito, Winona Ryder, and Nicolas Cage. They are boxed (the plates, that is) and arrayed along the walls. Funk and hip-hop thump over the stereo, and the dishy waitresses look ready to depart on the next fashion shoot. They are in black (with splashes of carefree gray), as are most of their customers, cell phones at the ready. The front opens up in warm weather. Although the food inevitably takes second place to preening, it's surprisingly worthwhile. Pastas prevail, tumbled with crunchy vegetables or silky walnut sauce or any of 10 or more other combinations. The kitchen exhibits less reliance on meat than the norm and makes an imaginative risotto with two cheeses and two sauces. Service is stretched thin at dinner, especially on the weekends, and the noise level cranks up after 7pm. The active bar in back features single-malt scotches; it stays open until 2am Sunday to Wednesday, until 3am Thursday to Saturday.

If the velvet rope is up at Buona Notte, there are several other similar spots on the half block from there to Sherbrooke, including **Mediterraneo** (3500 bd. St-Laurent, ☎ **514/844-0027**), **Primadonna** (3479 bd. St-Laurent, ☎ **514/282-6644**), and **Globe** (3455 bd. St-Laurent, ☎ **514/284-3823**).

✪ **L'Express.** 3927 rue St-Denis (at rue Roy). ☎ **514/845-5333.** Reservations recommended. Main courses C$10.85–C$17.35 (US$7.50–US$11.95). AE, CB, DC, ER, MC, V. Mon–Fri 8am–3am; Sat 10am–3am; Sun 10am–2am. Métro: Sherbrooke. FRENCH BISTRO.

No obvious sign announces the presence of this restaurant, only its name discreetly spelled out in white tiles embedded in the sidewalk. There's no need to call attention to itself, since *tout* Montréal knows exactly where it is. While there are no table d'hôte menus, the food is fairly priced for such an eternally busy place and costs the same at midnight as at noon. Substantial starters that include bone marrow with coarse salt and a potted chicken pâté may suggest one of the lighter main courses, such as the ravioli *maison,* round pasta pockets flavored, more than stuffed, with a mixture of beef, pork, and veal. Larger appetites might step up to full-flavored duck breast with chewy chanterelles in a sauce with the scent of deep woods. Or simply stop by for a *croque monsieur* or a bagel with smoked salmon and cream cheese. Although reservations are usually necessary for tables, single diners can often find a seat at the zinc-topped bar, where meals are also served. Breakfast is served from 8 to 11:30am.

Maestro S.V.P. 3615 St-Laurent (near rue Sherbrooke). ☎ **514/842-6447.** Reservations recommended. Main courses C$13–C$39 (US$8.95–US$27). AE, DC, MC, V. Mon–Wed 11am–11pm; Thurs–Fri 11am–midnight; Sat 4pm–midnight; Sun 4–11pm. Métro: Sherbrooke. SEAFOOD.

You could eat well for a week on the 2 blocks of The Main north of Sherbrooke. Make this store-front bistro one of those stops. The name of the place and the musical instruments mounted on the walls have no particular relevance to the menu or the owner, unless you count the jazz trio she brings in Sunday evenings at 6:30. Those are only a few of the attractions likely to get your attention; others include the dozen oysters proffered during the generously defined happy hour—11am to 7pm—for only C$7 (US$4.80). Or on Mondays only, drop in for all-you-can-eat mussels for C$9.99 (US$6.90). They come in several preparations, from Thai to Provençal. Two black-boards list the recommended wines of the day, in glasses costing C$6.25 to C$11.50 (US$4.30 to US$7.95). Service is casual, but alert, and there is valet parking Thursday through Saturday.

Witloof. 3619 rue St-Denis (at rue Sherbrooke). ☎ **514/281-0100.** Reservations recom-mended. Main courses C$13.95–C$17.95 (US$9.60–US$12.35); table d'hôte C$29.95–C$35.95 (US$21–US$25). AE, DC, MC, V. Mon–Fri 11:30am–3pm and 5–10pm; Sat–Sun 5–10pm. Métro: Sherbrooke. BELGIAN & FRENCH.

The name is Flemish for endive, and Witloof has long specialized in Belgian dishes. Now, with a new associate chef from the south of France, it has solidified its standing as one of the most gratifying restaurants in town. It remains at the border between casual and elegant, as exemplified by snowy linen tablecloths covered with butcher paper. Steaming casseroles of mussels in six versions, with tents of *frites* on the side, are deservedly the most popular items on the menu, but the classic Belgian fish stew, *waterzooi*, is a close second. Because it is always busy, the kitchen can fall behind on orders, but the convivial atmosphere dissuades grousing. Several Belgian beers are available, including the Blanche de Bruges, and go well with most of this food. Desserts range from crème caramel to praline crepes. Many diners take advantage of the early bird table d'hôtes to soak up the late-afternoon sun on the terrace.

INEXPENSIVE

⭕ **Chez Schwartz Charcuterie Hébraïque de Montréal.** 3895 bd. St-Laurent (north of rue Prince-Arthur). ☎ **514/842-4813.** Most items C$5–C$12 (US$3.45–US$8.30). No credit cards. Mon–Thurs 9am–12:30am; Fri 9am–1:30am; Sat 9am–2:30am; Sun 9am–12:30am. Métro: St-Laurent. DELI.

The imposition of French-first laws turned this old-line delicatessen into this linguistic mouthful, but it's still known simply as Schwartz's to its many ardent fans. They are convinced it is the only place on the continent to indulge in the guilty treat of smoked meat. Housed in a long, narrow space, it has a lunch counter and a collection of simple tables and chairs crammed almost impossibly close to each other. Any empty seat is up for grabs. Few mind the inconvenience or proximity to strangers, for they are soon delivered plates described either as small (meaning large) or large (meaning humon-gous) heaped with slices of the trademark delicacy, along with piles of rye bread. Most people also order sides of french fries and one or two mammoth garlicky pickles. There is a handful of alternative edibles, but tofu and leafy green vegetables aren't among

March of the Tongue Troopers

When the separatist Parti Québecois took power in the province in 1976, they wasted no time in undertaking to make Québec unilingual. They promptly passed Bill 101, which made French the sole official language of government and sharply restricted the use of other languages in education and commerce. Since about 20% of the population had English as a primary language, one out of five Québecers felt themselves declared instant second-class citizens. Francophones responded that it was about time *les Anglais,* aka *les autres* (the others), knew what that felt like and set about enforcing the new law.

The vehicle was *L'Office de la Langue Française.* Its agents fanned out across the province, scouring the landscape for linguistic insults to the state and her people. No offense was too slight for their stern attention. MERRY CHRISTMAS signs were removed from storefronts, and department stores were forced to come up with a new name for Harris Tweed. Any merchant who put up a GOING OUT OF BUSINESS poster faced the possibility of a fine to accompany his already-dour situation. By fiat and threat of punishment, hamburgers became *hambourgeois,* a hot dog was rechristened *le chien chaud,* a funeral parlor was transformed into a *salon funéraire,* and Schwartz's Montréal Hebrew Delicatessen became *Chez Schwartz Charcuterie Hebraïque de Montréal.* Particular scrutiny was accorded the Eastern Townships, on the south side of the St. Lawrence River. They had been settled by United Empire Loyalists, Americans faithful to the British Crown who fled to Canada at the time of the Revolution. The region, known henceforth as either Estrie or Les Cantons de l'Est, had a Tea Table Island and a Molasses Lake, which became *Île Table à Thé* and *Lac à Mélasse.*

Eventually, it might be assumed, there would be no more Anglophone words to conquer. But bureaucrats will be bureaucrats. Required definitions describe every object in the known world. One is a *petit gâteau de forme rectangulaire, aromatisé au chocolat, dont la texture se situe entre le biscuit sec et le gâteau spongieux.*

Or, in a word, a brownie.

---

them. Most days, and especially weekends, expect a wait. Schwartz's has no liquor license, but it does have a no-smoking section.

Mazurka. 64 rue Prince Arthur Est (near bd. St-Laurent). ☎ **514/844-3539.** Reservations for 4 or more only. Main courses C$5.15–C$12.50 (US$3.55–US$8.60); Mon–Thurs table d'hôte lunch C$5.75 and C$8.25 (US$3.95 and US$5.70). AE, MC, V. Daily 11:30am–midnight. Métro: Sherbrooke. POLISH.

Even among the low-priced eateries that line both sides of pedestrianized Prince Arthur, this old-timer (opened 1952) is an eye-widening bargain. Do the Mazurka double-take, for example, with the mixed plate of pierogies, sausage, bigos, a potato pancake, and stuffed cabbage, all for only C$10.25 (US$7.05). Usually costly veal shank goes for the same price, and they've been known to offer two lobsters for the same price that their competitors charge for one. Service is glum and rushed, as might be expected, but that doesn't deter the throngs of students, artists, frugal execs, and night people who fill the place 12 hours a day.

✪ **Pizzédélic.** 3509 bd. St-Laurent (near rue Sherbrooke). ☎ **514/282-6784.** Pizzas and pastas C$6.95–C$12.95 (US$4.80–US$8.95); table d'hôte lunch C$8.95–14.95

(US$6.15–US$10.30). MC, V. Sun and Wed–Thurs 11:30am–1am; Tues 11:30am–2am; Fri–Sat 11:30am–3am. Métro: St-Laurent. PIZZA.

Pizza here runs the gamut from traditional to as imaginative as anyone might conceive, with toppings from feta cheese to escargots to artichokes to pesto. All arrive on thin, not-quite-crispy crusts. The difference over ordinary pizzerias is the use of fresh, not canned, ingredients, as in the antipasto plate of grilled vegetables and calamari strips. Pastas and meat dishes are also available. The front opens in warm weather, and there's a terrace in back. It's a growing chain, with units all over town, but two other conveniently located Pizzédélics are at 1329 Ste-Catherine (☎ **514/526-6011**) and 370 av. Laurier Ouest (☎ **514/948-6290**).

Wilensky Light Lunch. 34 rue Fairmount Ouest (at rue Clark). ☎ **514/271-0247.** Most items C$2–C$3.25 (US$1.40–US$2.30). No credit cards. Mon–Fri 9am–4pm. Closed 2 weeks in July, 2 weeks in Feb. Métro: Laurier; then walk about 12 blocks. Bus: 55 to St-Laurent and Fairmount; then walk a block. LIGHT FARE.

Wilensky's has been a Montréal tradition since 1932, known for its grilled-meat sandwiches, low prices, curt service, and utter lack of decor. Expect to find nine stools at a counter. Scenes from the film *The Apprenticeship of Duddy Kravitz* were shot here, for this is Mordecai Richler territory, and the ambience is Early Immigrant. The food selections are limited to a few sandwiches—not much more than bologna, salami, and mustard thrown on a bun and squashed on a grill—and hot-dog sandwiches, also squashed. They're washed down with root beer or a drink jerked from the rank of syrups, like the old-time soda fountain it is. Cherry-pineapple is a possibility. I'm talking tradition, not cuisine. Pay when served.

5 Outer Districts

VERY EXPENSIVE

✪ **Nuances.** 1 av. du Casino (in the Casino de Montréal, Île Ste-Hélène). ☎ **514/392-2708.** Reservations strongly recommended. Main courses C$29–C$41 (US$20–US$28); table d'hôte C$49 (US$34) or C$62 (US$43). AE, DC, ER, MC, V. Daily 5:30–11pm. Métro: Île Ste-Hélène. CREATIVE FRENCH.

Unlikely as it may seem, here is haute cuisine in a gambling casino, ensconced atop four floors of bleeping buzzers, blinking lights, and the crash of cascading jackpots. This elegant entry in Montréal's gastronomic sweepstakes quickly shouldered its way to the top of the pyramid. The designers didn't stint on what they deemed the appropriate trappings, not with this mahogany paneling, soaring ceiling, Villery & Boch china, and lavish deployment of leather and linen and gleaming brass. A maître d' seats you, a captain explains the evening's possibilities, and a waitress takes your order and serves. All of them are qualified to advise on appropriate wines from the extensive list to accompany each course. After the ever-changing *amuse-bouche,* you might want to start with the wrapped round stockade of thin asparagus spears topped with greens and surmounted by the meat of a small lobster claw. Among the rhapsody of main course choices are the perfect rosy slices of loin of lamb baked in clay and the sushi-quality tuna barely touched to flame and resting on a platform of pureed fennel. The five-course menu dégustation (C$62/US$43) allows the kitchen to show off to your benefit. While you're blowing the budget, accept the accompanying selected wines, a different one with each course for another C$41 (US$28). The *plateau de fromage* has several admirable Québec-produced cheeses. Make it all the way to dessert after all that, and the waitress might suggest a dish of praline mousse and chocolate sherbet. A stiffened dress code keeps out guys attired in baggy shorts and tank tops.

MODERATE

Chez Lévêsque. 1030 rue Laurier Ouest (near Durocher, in Outremont). ☎ **514/279-7355.** Reservations recommended. Main courses C$14.95–C$26.95 (US$10.30–US$18.60); table d'hôte lunch C$9.95–C$25 (US$6.85–US$17.25), dinner C$14.95–C$27.95 (US$10.30–US$19.25). AE, CB, DC, ER, MC, V. Mon–Fri 8am–midnight; Sat–Sun 10:30am–midnight. Métro: Laurier. FRENCH BISTRO.

In the brasserie tradition, this place opens for breakfast and doesn't shut down until late. Drop by and stay a while. Have a coffee, write a poem, peruse *Le Monde,* dig through a full four courses. It's a place to hang out. That isn't to say it hasn't kept up with the times. There's bouillabaisse, salmon tartar, and lamb Provençal on the card, but someone in charge thinks fusion ideas and healthy living are important, too. The local fad for *Le Plat Montignac* is featured here—that is, the trimming of fat and related nasties by the flesh-on-greens device. It shows up as Chilean sea bass laid over a comforter of mixed vegetables and the brace of quail infused with a peppery honey-soy marinade and set upon a nest of greens. Nonsmokers even have their allotted space, past the chummy bar, and a fireplace blazes much of the year in the upstairs room. In warm weather, the front is opened up. Sunday brunch is a five-course winner at only C$24.50 (US$16.90).

La Chronique. 99 rue Laurier Ouest, near Durocher, in Outremont. ☎ **514/271-3095.** Main courses C$19–C$27 (US$13.10–US$18.60); table d'hôte C$14–C$28 (US$9.65–US$19.30). DC, MC, V. Tues–Fri 11:30am–2:30pm and 6–10pm; Sat 6–10pm. Metro: Laurier. FRENCH BISTRO.

Two of Montréal's top chefs recommend this modest-looking storefront bistro. I hope that revealing their enthusiastic approbation won't spoil the place for the prosperous Francophones who are its steady custom, but this is too good to skip. For one thing, in a city of heavy smokers, that habit is entirely excluded. For another, the chef allows you to discover how remarkable traditional bistro dishes can be when in the hands of a master. Diners who are leery of organ meats, for only one example, will find the veal sweetbreads a revelation, their silkiness paired with slices of spicy chorizo. The menu isn't hidebound, by any means, with ceviche, gazpacho, and Southwestern flavors appearing. Lobster lovers will be wowed by the *Douceurs de la Mer* menu, which employs the flesh of that crustacean in three different courses. With dessert, expensive ingredients like foie gras, and wines chosen to complement each offering, the price per person is C$92 (US$64). A small but judicious selection of cheeses may precede or replace the tantalizing desserts, which look as if they might take flight. Menus are only in French, but the cordial waiters speak English.

Magnan. 2602 rue St-Patrick, Pointe St-Charles. ☎ **514/935-9647.** Main courses C$4.95–C$18.50 (US$3.40–US$12.80). DC, ER, MC, V. Tavern: Mon–Sat 8am–midnight; Sun and holidays 9am–11pm. Restaurant: Mon–Fri 11am–10pm; Sat–Sun 4–10pm. By car or taxi, drive west on rue St-Jacques, turn left on rue Atwater, following it around to the right of Atwater Marché (Market) and under the Lachine Canal; take the first exit at the sign for rue St-Patrick, turn right on St-Patrick, and go 3 blocks to the restaurant, on the right. STEAK/SEAFOOD.

This rough-hewn roadhouse on the south side of the Lachine Canal has resin tables under umbrellas next to the parking lot, a ground-floor *taverne* with neon beer signs and several TV sets, and a slightly more formal dining room in the basement. So forget elegance and skip the forgettable appetizers and go straight for the twin lobsters. They come cold and split, with potatoes or rice and mayo or garlic butter. Monsters of the deep, they aren't, but when was the last time you had 2 pounds of lobster for under US$10? On about 20 days in May and June, they up the stakes with all-you-can-eat lobster and roast-beef nights, with all the trimmings for C$48.50 (US$33) per person, *including taxes and service.* (Better call now to reserve a table.) Kids are welcome in the dining room, where there are plenty of sandwiches and the simple foods they like, and parents don't need to worry about the inevitable mess, especially since they'll be making big ones themselves.

6 Early-Morning & Late-Night Bites

When the yen for coffee and a pastry or a sandwich strikes, you are never far from an outpost of one of the three major cafe chains: **A.L. Van Houtte, Presse Café,** or **Second Cup** (which is usually open 24 hours). All have reasonable prices for decent food, and many have tables indoors and out for resting tired feet or plotting next sightseeing moves.

Bens. 990 bd. de Maisonneuve (at rue Metcalfe). ☎ **514/844-1000.** Most items under C$12 (US$8.30). MC, V. Sun–Wed 7:30am–2am; Thurs 7:30am–3am; Fri–Sat 7:30am–4am Métro: Peel. DELI.

This deli-restaurant was founded by Ben and Fanny Kravitz in 1908 and is still in the family. That progress through the decades is attested by autographed photos of celebrities from the period of its greatest notoriety, including Burl Ives, the Ink Spots, and Ed Sullivan. Current owners persist in the claim that this is where Montréal's famous smoked meat originated. Besides the inevitable variations on that much-loved ingredient, the menu meanders through cheese blintzes, potato latkes, corned beef and cabbage, bagels and lox, and much more. They are fully licensed.

Eggspectation. 1313 av. de Maisonneuve Ouest (at rue de la Montagne). ☎ **514/842-3447.** Most items under C$12 (US$8.30). MC, V. Daily 6am–5pm (until 6pm Sat–Sun). Métro: Laurier. BREAKFAST/BRUNCH/LIGHT FARE.

Let the dopey name deter you and you'll miss a meal that may constitute one of your best food memories of Montréal, at least if you're of the breakfast-is-best school of gastronomy. Prices are low and portions are huge, ensuring crowds from early morning to late afternoon. One reader lauds the thick, creamy slices of French toast spiked with Grand Marnier and joined with mounds of fresh fruits. Eggs any way are special, too, even if they are tagged with names like *eggscaliber* and *eggsileration*. Sandwiches and pastas are also on the card. The spiffy decor aids in establishing a sense of well-being. In summer, it stays open into the evening. The ever-expanding chain has additional branches at 198 rue Laurier Ouest, near rue St-Denis, and at 213 rue St-Jacques in Vieux-Montréal.

✪ Kilo. 5206 bd. St-Laurent (between rue Maguire and rue Fairmount). ☎ **514/277-5039.** Most items under C$10 (US$6.90). MC, V. Mon 5pm–midnight; Tues–Thurs 10:30am–midnight; Fri–Sun 1pm–2am. Métro: Laurier. DESSERTS/LIGHT FARE.

When dining in this neighborhood, skip the last course and make a beeline to Kilo. The mousses, cakes, and pies sold here are arrayed as enticingly as jewels in a display case. Light lunches are served, but it's the desserts, sweet and creamy or tartly piquant, that draw the crowds and constitute a direct challenge to the most determined dieters among them. Strong coffee laced with cognac, amaretto, or Grand Marnier is often chosen to complement. They have a branch at 1495 rue Ste-Catherine Est (☎ 514/596-3933).

La Brioche Lyonnaise. 1593 rue St-Denis (near bd. de Maisonneuve). ☎ **514/842-7017.** Most items under C$12 (US$8.30). AE, MC, V. Daily 8:30am–midnight. Métro: Berri-UQAM. LIGHT FARE/PASTRIES.

There are many delightful patisseries—pastry shops—in this French city, and this, deep in the Quartier Latin, is one of the most popular. Most of them serve light items—quiches, salads, and sandwiches—but patrons often settle for just a sweet cake or a croissant and coffee, perhaps a bowl of café au lait. They stop in after dinner, UQAM classes, or a show at the theater across the street, or simply for a break in sightseeing. Check out what's available in the display case—from Marie Claires to megameringues—and then find a table in one of the several seating areas. As in most patisseries, there's no pressure to move on.

✪ Le Café Cherrier. 3635 rue St-Denis (at rue Cherrier). ☎ **514/843-4308.** Main courses C$6–C$12.50 (US$4.15–US$8.60); table d'hôte C$12.50–C$16.50 (US$8.60–C$11.40). AE, MC, V. Mon–Fri 8am–11pm; Sat–Sun 9am–11pm (to 3am in summer); brunch Sat–Sun 8:30am–3pm. Métro: Sherbrooke. BREAKFAST/BRUNCH/LIGHT FARE.

The tables on the terrace wrapped around this corner building are filled whenever there's even a slim possibility that a heavy sweater and a bowl of café au lait will fend off frostbite. In summer, the loyalists get to stay out until way past midnight, and in winter, all the same people squeeze inside. Brunch is popular, even if the food is unexceptional, but consider this place any time a snack or a light meal is in order. Portions are ample and inexpensive. An easygoing atmosphere prevails, and it's said to be popular with musicians, actors, artists, and journalists; contrive to look mysterious or celebrated.

St-Viateur Bagel & Café. 1127 Mont-Royal Est (near rue de la Roche). ☎ **514/528-6361.** Most items under C$10 (US$6.90). No credit cards. Daily 6am–midnight. Métro: Mont-Royal. BAGELS/LIGHT FARE.

The bagel wars flare as hotly as Montréal's eternal smoked-meat controversy, but this, an offshoot of a beloved old bakery, is easily among the top contenders. Bagels in these parts are thinner, smaller, and crustier than the bloated, cottony monsters nowadays posing as the real thing in most parts of the republic south of the border. These are hand-rolled, twist-flipped into circles, dusted with sesame seeds or whatever, and baked in big wood-fired ovens right on premises. Try them, in or out. Sandwiches on-site come with soup or salad. Expect a short wait on weekends and not infrequently during the week.

Santropol. 3990 rue St-Urbain (at Rue Duluth). ☎ **514/842-3110.** Most items under C$10 (US$6.90). No credit cards; debit cards accepted. Mon–Thurs 11:30am–midnight; Fri 11:30am–1am; Sat noon–1am; Sun noon–midnight. Métro: Mont-Royal; then walk through Jeanne Mance Park. LIGHT FARE.

Mostly vegetarian sandwiches, salads, and pot pies come in hefty proportions at this flavorsome favorite. The composition of the clientele is hinted in the sign that reads, HEY STUDENTS—BRING OUR CUTLERY BACK, but families and oldsters drop by in substantial numbers, too. They dawdle at tables with chairs that don't even bear a family resemblance amid lots of stamped tin on walls and ceilings and offhanded sculptures beholden to no school. Herbal teas, coffees, and 18 different kinds of milk shakes (almond, mint, maple, and peach-apricot are among the choices) constitute the available nonalcoholic beverages. Occupying a timeworn redbrick house, the restaurant has several dining nooks, along with a recently expanded tree- and fern-filled courtyard in summer. One percent of the bill is sent to organizations that ease hunger in Québec and developing nations. Takeout is available.

7 Picnic Fare: Where to Get It, Where to Eat It

When planning a picnic or a meal to eat back in your hotel room, consider a stop at **La Vieille Europe,** 3855 bd. St-Laurent near St-Cuthbert (☎ **514/842-5773**), a compact storehouse of culinary sights and smells. Choose from wheels of pungent cheeses, garlands of sausages, pâtés, cashews, honey, fresh peanut butter, or dried fruits.

Coffee beans are roasted in the back, adding to the admixture of maddening aromas. A stroll to the north along St-Laurent reveals other possibilities for mobile edibles.

In the rue Crescent area, the **Faubourg Ste-Catherine,** on rue Ste-Catherine Ouest between Guy and St-Mathieu, is a market and fast-food complex that sells a substantial variety of prepared takeout foods such as sushi and sandwiches, as well as breads, fresh fruits, pastries, and ice cream. You'll find similar bounty underground at **Les Halles de la Gare,** an accumulation of food stalls, delis, and cafes beneath the Queen Elizabeth hotel and adjacent to the main concourse of the railroad station. Among them is an SAQ wine store. Downtown, the new **Marché Mövenpick,** at the corners of Cathcart and University and Mansfield and René Lévésque, sells just about everything from its various food stalls for takeout, including sushi, panini, fruits, baked goods, cheeses, pizzas, and grills.

Better still, make the short excursion by Métro (the Lionel-Grouix stop) to **Marché Atwater,** the public market at 3025 St-Ambroise, open 7 days a week. The long shed is bordered by stalls of gleaming produce and flowers, the two-story center section given to wine purveyors, food counters, bakeries, and cheese stores. The best representatives of the last two are **La Fromagerie** (☎ 514/932-4653), whose highly knowledgeable attendants know every detail of production of the 450 to 550 different North American and European cheeses on offer, and the **Boulangerie Première Moison** (☎ 514/932-0328), which fills its space with the tantalizing aromas of baskets of breads and cases of pastries. (There is another branch of the bakery in the Gare Centrale.) From either location, it isn't far by taxi to Parc du Mont-Royal, a wonderful place to enjoy a picnic.

In Vieux-Montréal, pick up supplies at the new food market in the historic **Marché Bonsecours** (☎ 514/872-4560) on rue de la Commune and take them to the linear park of the Vieux-Port, only steps away. That park can also be the picnic destination from **Olive & Gourmando** (☎ 514/350-1083) at 351 rue St-Paul Ouest, open Tuesday through Saturday from 8am to 6pm. Primarily a bakery, it placed third in a *Gazette* reader's poll only months after it opened. That was for its baguettes, but many breads, croissants, and pastries are available. Put your sandwiches together from the cheeses and sausages in the cold case, or choose from their interesting compositions, including a grilled portobello mushroom with a puree of olives and goat cheese. A lot of the bread is out the door by midmorning. If you want wine or beer with your lunch, there's a new *dépanneur* (convenience store), **Le Quartier** (☎ 514/392-1299), at 321 rue Notre-Dame Est (near rue Bonsecours). There's much greater choice at the **SAQ Selection,** 440 bd. de Maisonneuve (Métro: McGill).

Exploring Montréal 6

Montréal is a feast of choices, able to satisfy the desires of both physically active and culturally curious visitors. Depending upon what interests you and how much time you have, you can hike up imposing Mont-Royal in the middle of the city, cycle beside the Lachine Canal, take in the artworks and ephemera of some 20 museums and as many historic buildings, attend a Canadiens hockey match or an Expos baseball game, party toward dawn on rue Crescent and The Main, or soak up the concrete and spiritual results of some 400 years of conquest and immigration. And with riverboat rides, the fascinating Biodôme, a sprawling amusement park, puppet and magic shows, and the unique Cirque du Soleil, few cities assure kids of as good a time as this one.

Once you've decided what you want to do, getting from hotel to museum to attraction is pretty easy: The superb Métro system, a fairly logical street grid, wide boulevards, and the vehicle-free Underground City all aid in the swift, largely uncomplicated movement of people from place to place.

Montréal's 350th birthday was celebrated in 1992 by the opening or expansion of many of the attractions described in this chapter. Efforts to enhance cultural opportunities have continued since then, as with the Biosphère, which opened in 1995 on Île Ste-Hélène. To help boost public awareness of Montréal's museum collections, a Montréal Museums Day has been inaugurated. On this day, usually the last Sunday in May, most museums are open to all free, and free shuttle buses carry visitors to most of them. Of greater utility is the **Montréal Museums Pass,** which allows entry to 20 of the city's museums and is available year-round. Good for 2 out of 3 consecutive days, the pass costs C$20 (US$13.80). It is sold at all participating museums, the Infotouriste Centre on Square Dorchester, and at many Montréal hotels. For further information, call ☎ **800/363-7777** from outside Montréal or 514/845-6873 within the metropolitan area.

When planning visits, you might want to note in the listings below which museums have restaurants, a few of which are pretty good. Most museums are closed Mondays.

Suggested Itineraries

If You Have 1 Day

Explore the oldest part of town, called **Vieux-Montréal.** It borders the recently resuscitated port, with many restored buildings dating from the 18th and 19th centuries. Don't miss the unusual interior of the stunning **Notre-Dame Basilica.** The **Pointe-à-Callière,** Montréal's Museum of Archaeology and History, opened in 1992 and provides a clever and engaging orientation to the city in its early years, enthralling kids and adults alike.

Then, for contrast, stroll through the downtown sections of the modern city, including its vibrant vest-pocket **Chinatown,** and visit the **Musée des Beaux Arts** (Museum of Fine Arts), which has a modern pavilion and a big bookstore and gift shop. Enjoy a table d'hôte lunch or dinner in one of the city's fine downtown restaurants.

If You Have 2 Days

On the second day, take the Métro to the **Olympic Complex,** which has an inclined tower and observation deck. Across the street is the **Botanical Garden,** its carefully cultivated acres providing hours of peaceful meditation. While there, see the Chinese Garden and take the informative open-air train tour. While in the neighborhood, don't miss the fascinating **Biodôme,** which replicates four distinct ecosystems, complete with live flora and fauna. In summer, make an island day of it on **Île Ste-Hélène** by visiting the old fort, with its museum and changing-of-the-guard ceremony, and perhaps the new **Biosphère.** Afterward, go to **La Ronde Amusement Park,** where fireworks displays are mounted many evenings. Or head that night to Vieux-Montréal and take in a performance at the English-language **Centaur Theatre,** listen to jazz or folk in one of the clubs along Rue St-Paul, or, if it's in town, thrill to the magic of the acclaimed **Cirque du Soleil.**

If You Have 3 Days

On the morning of Day 3, take an exhilarating jet-boat ride through the **Lachine Rapids,** or a calmer harbor cruise aboard *Le Bateau-Mouche.* Get to know the Montréal of natives by wandering along **boulevard St-Laurent,** the axis of the city's ethnic neighborhoods, to rue Prince-Arthur and rue Duluth, then through Carré St-Louis (St. Louis Square) to the **Latin Quarter,** the center of activity for the Francophone population. In the evening, dine in one of the fine restaurants in adjacent **Plateau Mont-Royal** and cap the night with a club crawl.

If You Have 4 Days or More

On the fourth day, fit and athletic visitors might choose to climb **Mont-Royal** from rue Peel and admire the view of the city and river from the lookout, then stroll or take a picnic in the surrounding park. (If the prospect of that hike is daunting, take the Métro to the Guy station, then bus no. 165.) In the afternoon, take in a specialized museum, perhaps the **McCord Museum of Canadian History** or the **Canadian Centre for Architecture.**

On day five, visit the **Oratoire St-Joseph,** the city's most prominent shrine, which gives a glimpse of the spiritual life of devout Montréalers. If the weather's good, rent a bike and follow the **Lachine Canal** for 7 miles (11km) to Lake St-Louis. If the weather turns dicey, descend to the climate-controlled world of Montréal's **Underground City,** a labyrinth of passages, subway tunnels, shops, and cinemas, all of which can be enjoyed without once stepping outdoors.

1 The Top Attractions

DOWNTOWN

✪ **Musée des Beaux-Arts.** 1379–1380 rue Sherbrooke Ouest (at rue Crescent). ☎ **514/285-2000.** www.mmfa.qc.ca. Permanent collection free; temporary exhibitions C$15 (US$10.35) adults, C$7.50 (US$5.20) seniors and students, C$3 (US$2.05) children 12 and under. AE, MC, V. Half-price Wed 5:30–9pm. Tues and Thurs–Sun 11am–6pm; Wed 11am–9pm. Métro: Peel or Guy-Corcordia.

The Museum of Fine Arts, Montréal's most prominent museum, was opened in 1912 in Canada's first building designed specifically for the visual arts. The original neoclassical pavilion is on the north side of Sherbrooke. Years ago, museum administrators recognized that the collection, now totaling more than 30,000 works, had outgrown the building, and curators were forced to make painful decisions about which items could be placed on view at any one time. Resulting exhibits often seemed sketchy and incomplete. That problem was solved in late 1991 with the completion of the stunning new annex, the Jean-Noël Desmarais Pavilion, directly across the street. Designed by Montréal architect Moshe Safdie, who first gained international notice with his Habitat housing complex at the 1967 Expo, the new pavilion tripled exhibition space, adding two sub–street-level floors and underground galleries that connect the new building with the old.

For the best look at the results, enter the new annex, take the elevator to the top, and work your way down. The permanent collection is largely devoted to international contemporary art and Canadian art created after 1960, and to European paintings, sculpture, and decorative arts from the Middle Ages to the 19th century. On the upper floors are many of the gems of the collection. On the fourth floor alone are paintings by Hogarth, Reynolds, Brueghel, El Greco, and Ribera. (For a bonus, be sure to walk to the sculpture court for a splendid panoramic view of the city.) On subsequent levels, view examples—representative if not world-class—of more recent artists, including Renoir, Monet, Picasso, Roualt, Cézanne, and Rodin. On the subterranean floors are works by 20th-century modernists, primarily those who rose to prominence after World War II, including the abstract expressionists and those who followed.

From the lowest level of the new pavilion, follow the under-street corridor past primitive artworks from Oceana and Africa, and then up the elevator into the old building, with its displays of pre-Columbian ceramics, Inuit carvings, and Amerindian crafts. The rest of that building is used primarily for traveling exhibitions assembled by some of the world's great museums. Throughout, works are nearly always dramatically mounted, carefully lit, and diligently explained in both French and English. Across the street are a street-level store—with an impressive selection of quality books, games, and folk art—and a cafe.

Musée McCord d'Histoire Canadienne. 690 rue Sherbrooke Ouest (at rue Victoria). ☎ **514/398-7100.** www.musee-mccord.qc.ca. Admission C$7 (US$4.85) adults, C$5 (US$2.75) students, C$1.50 (US$1.05) ages 7–11, free for children under 7, C$14 (US$9.65) families. Free admission Sat 10am–noon. Tues–Fri 10am–6pm; Sat–Sun 10am–5pm (summer daily from 9am). Métro: McGill. Bus: 24.

Associated with McGill University, the McCord Museum of Canadian History showcases the eclectic—and not infrequently eccentric—collections of scores of 19th- and 20th-century benefactors. Objects from its holdings of 29,000 costumes, artifacts, and 750,000 historical photographs are rotated in and out of storage, so it isn't possible to be specific about what will be on view at any given time. In general, expect to view furniture, clothing, china, silver, paintings, photographs, and folk art that

Downtown Montréal Attractions

Basilique Notre-Dame **12**
Cathédrale-Basilique
  Marie-Reine-du-Monde **6**
Cathédral Christ Church **9**
Centre Canadien d'Architecture **1**
Centre d'Histoire de Montréal **13**
Chapelle Notre-Dame-de-Bonsecours **21**
Hôtel de Ville **18**

Interactive Science Center **15**
Marché Bonsecours **17**
Musée d'Art
  Contemporain de Montréal **10**
Musée des Hospitalières **8**
Musée de la Banque
  de Montréal **11**
Musée des Beaux-Arts **2**

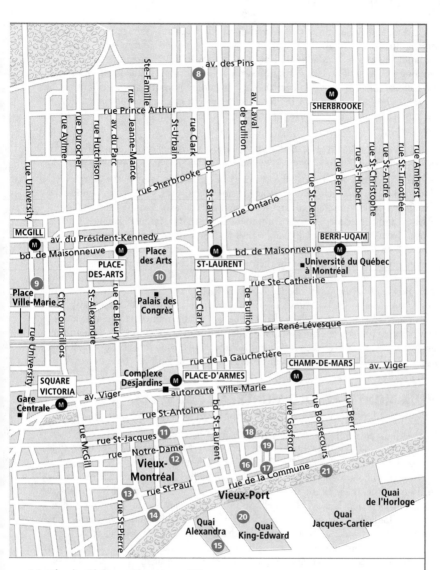

- Musée du Château Ramezay **19**
- Musée McCord d'Histoire Canadienne **5**
- Musée Redpath **4**
- Parc du Mont-Royal **3**
- Place Jacques-Cartier **16**
- Planétarium de Montréal **7**
- Pointe-à-Callière **15**
- Vieux-Port **20**

reveal rural and urban life as it was lived by English-speaking immigrants of the past three centuries. The original 1905 building was disemboweled and rebuilt, to its benefit, and a new wing was added during renovations in 1992, providing galleries for temporary exhibits. The First Nations room displays portions of the museum's extensive collection of ethnology and archaeology, including jewelry and meticulous beadwork. Exhibits are intelligently mounted, with texts in English and French, although the upstairs rooms are of narrower interest. There's a popular cafe near the front entrance.

Parc du Mont-Royal. ☎ **514/844-4928** (general information) or 514/872-6559 (special events). Daily 6am–midnight. Métro: Mont-Royal. Bus: No. 11; hop off at Lac des Castors.

Montréal is named for the 761-foot (232m) hill that rises at its heart—the "Royal Mountain." Joggers, cyclists, dog walkers, skaters, and others use it throughout the year. On Sundays, hundreds congregate around the statue of George-Étienne Cartier to listen and sometimes dance to improvised music. In summer, Lac des Castors (Beaver Lake) is surrounded by sunbathers and picnickers (no swimming allowed, however). In wintertime, cross-country skiers follow the miles of paths, snowshoers tramp along other trails laid out for their use, and there's a tow for the short downhill skiing run above the lake. In the cold months, the lake fills with whirling ice skaters of various levels of aptitude. The large, refurbished Chalet Lookout near the crest of the hill provides both a sweeping view of the city from its terrace and an opportunity for a snack. Up the hill behind the chalet is the spot where, tradition has it, de Maisonneuve erected his wooden cross in 1642. Today the cross is a 100-foot-high steel structure visible from all over the city, illuminated at night. Park security is provided by mounted police. There are three cemeteries on the northern slope of the mountain—Catholic, Protestant, and Jewish.

VIEUX-MONTRÉAL (OLD MONTRÉAL)

For further information about this quarter, log on to **www.vieux.montreal.qc.ca**.

✪ **Basilique Notre-Dame.** 110 rue Notre-Dame Ouest (on place d'Armes). ☎ **514/842-2925.** Basilica C$2 (US$1.40) adults, free for praying. MC, V. June 24 to Labour Day daily 7am–8pm; rest of the year daily 7am–6pm; tours all year. Métro: Place d'Armes.

Big enough to hold 4,000 worshipers, and breathtaking in the richness of its interior furnishings, this magnificent structure was designed in 1824 by an Irish American Protestant architect, James O'Donnell. So profoundly was he moved by the experience, O'Donnell converted to Catholicism after the basilica was completed. The impact is understandable. None of the hundreds of churches on the island of Montréal approaches this interior in its wealth of exquisite detail, most of it carved from rare woods delicately gilded and painted. O'Donnell, one of the proponents of the Gothic Revival style in the early decades of the 19th century, is the only person honored by burial in the crypt.

The main altar was carved from linden wood, the work of Victor Bourgeau. Behind it is the Chapelle Sacré-Coeur (Sacred Heart Chapel), much of it destroyed by a deranged arsonist in 1978 but rebuilt and rededicated in 1982. It is such a popular place for weddings that couples have to book it 18 months in advance. The altar was cast in bronze by Charles Daudelin of Montréal, with 32 panels representing birth, life, and death. A 10-bell carillon resides in the east tower, while the west tower contains a single massive bell. Nicknamed "Le Gros Bourdon," it weighs more than 12 tons and has a low, resonant rumble that vibrates right up through the feet. It is tolled only on special occasions.

Although you can go through on your own, there are guided tours in English starting at 8am and leaving at various times through the day, but usually on the hour and half hour during tourist season. At this writing, the church's small museum is temporarily closed for renovations.

Interactive Science Centre (iSci). King Edward Pier, Vieux-Port. ☎ **514/496-4724.** www.isci.ca. C$9.95–C$21.95 (US$6.85–US$15.15) adults, C$8.95–C$18.95 (US$6.15–US$13.05) ages 13–17 and 60 and over, C$7.95–C$16.95 (US$5.50–US$11.70) ages 4–12. Summer daily 10am–9pm; rest of year Sun–Thurs 10am–6pm, Fri–Sat 10am–9pm (hours subject to change). Metro: Square Victoria, Place d'Armes, or Champ-de-Mars.

Occupying a newly completed steel-and-glass building running the length of King Edward Pier, this ambitious $49-million complex was inaugurated in May 2000. Focusing on science and technology, it employs a variety of interactive displays and a cinema as well as a preexisting IMAX theater to enlighten visitors about the life sciences, energy conservation, and 21st-century communications. Assessment of its success in fulfilling its mission needs to await the seasoning of another year or so. For the moment, its most popular component by far is the IMAX. Admission fees vary according to a variety of combinations of exhibits and attractions.

Vieux-Port. 333 rue de la Commune Ouest (at rue McGill). ☎ **514/496-7678.** www. oldportofmontreal.com. Port and interpretation center, free. Interpretation Center mid-May to early Sept daily 10am–9pm; hours for specific attractions vary. Métro: Champ-de-Mars, Place d'Armes, or Square-Victoria.

Montréal's Old Port, a once-dreary commercial wharf area, was transformed in 1992 into an appealing 1.2-mile-long, 133-acre promenade and park with public spaces, bicycle paths, tram rides, exhibition halls, and a variety of family activities. Cyclists, in-line skaters, joggers, strollers, lovers, and sunbathers all make use of the park in good weather. There's a large-scale, wraparound IMAX theater incorporated into the new Interactive Science Centre. A variety of harbor cruises leave from here. To get an idea of all there is to see and do, hop aboard the small Balade tram that travels throughout the port. At the far eastern end of the port is a 1922 clock tower, La Tour de l'Horloge, with 192 steps leading past the exposed clockworks to observation decks at three different levels (admission is free). Most cruises, entertainment, and special events take place from mid-May to October. Information booths with bilingual attendants assist visitors during that period. The Old Port stretches along the waterfront from rue McGill to rue Berri. Quadricycles, bicycles, and in-line skates are available for rent.

Place Jacques-Cartier. Between rue Notre-Dame and rue de la Commune. Métro: Place d'Armes.

Across the street from the Hôtel de Ville (City Hall) is the focus of summer activity in Vieux-Montréal. The most active of the old city's plazas has two recently repaved streets bracketing a center promenade that slopes down to the port past venerable stone buildings surviving from the 1700s. Its outdoor cafes, street performers, flower sellers, and the horse-drawn carriages that gather at its base recall the Montréal of a century ago. Montréalers insist they would never go to a place so thronged by tourists—which begs the question of why so many of them in fact congregate here. They take the sun and sip sangría on the bordering terraces on warm days, enjoying the unfolding pageant just as much as visitors do.

✪ **Pointe-à-Callière (Montréal Museum of Archaeology and History).** 350 place Royale (at rue de la Commune). ☎ **514/872-9150.** www.musee-pointe-a-calliere.qc.ca. Admission C$8.50 (US$5.85) adults, C$6 (US$4.15) seniors, C$5.50 (US$3.85) students, C$3 (US$2.05) children 6–12, free for children under 6, C$17 (US$11.70) families. AE, MC, V.

June 24–Sept 6, Tues–Fri 10am–6pm, Sat–Sun 11am–6pm; rest of year Tues–Fri 10am–5pm, Sat–Sun 11am–5pm. Métro: Place d'Armes.

A first visit to Montréal might best begin here. Built on the very site where the original colony was established in 1642 (Pointe-à-Callière), the modern Museum of Archaeology and History engages visitors in rare, beguiling ways. The striking new building echoes the triangular Royal Insurance building (1861) that stood here for many years. Go first to the 16-minute multimedia show in an auditorium that actually stands above exposed ruins of the earlier city. Images pop up, drop down, and slide out on rolling screens accompanied by music and a playful bilingual narration that keeps the history slick and utterly painless, with enough quick cuts and changes to keep even the youngest viewers from fidgeting.

Pointe-à-Callière was the point where the St-Pierre River merged with the St. Lawrence. Evidences of the many layers of occupation at this spot—from Amerindians to French trappers to Scottish merchants—were unearthed during archaeological digs that persisted here for more than a decade. They are on view in display cases set among ancient building foundations and burial grounds below street level. The bottom shelves of the cabinets are for items dating from before 1600, and there are other shelves for consecutive centuries. Wind your way on the self-guided tour through the subterranean complex until you find yourself in the former Custom House, where there are more exhibits and a well-stocked gift shop. Allow at least an hour for a visit.

New expansion has incorporated the Youville Pumping Station, across from the main building. Dating from 1915, it has been restored to serve as an interpretation center. The main building contains L'Arrivage cafe and affords a fine view of Old Montréal and the Old Port.

ELSEWHERE IN THE CITY

✪ **Biodôme de Montréal.** 4777 av. Pierre-de-Coubertin (next to Olympic Stadium). ☎ **514/868-3000.** www.ville.montreal.qc.ca/biodome. Admission C$9.50 (US$6.55) adults, C$7 (US$4.80) seniors and students over 17, C$4.75 (US$3.25) children 6–17, free for children under 6. AE, MC, V. Daily 9am–5pm (until 7pm in summer). Métro: Viau.

Near Montréal's Botanical Garden and next to the Olympic Stadium is the engrossing Biodôme, possibly the only museum of its kind. Originally built as the velodrome for the 1976 Olympics, it has been refitted to house replications of four distinct ecosystems—a Laurentian forest, the St. Lawrence marine system, a tropical rain forest, and a polar environment—complete with appropriate temperatures, flora, fauna, and changing seasons. All four re-creations are allowed a measure of freedom to grow and shift, so the exhibits are never static. With more than 6,000 creatures of 210 species and 4,000 trees and plants, the Biodôme incorporates exhibits gathered from the old aquarium and the modest zoos at the Angrignon and LaFontaine parks. Among these are specimens of certain threatened and endangered species, including macaws, marmosets, and tamarins, while the Polar World has puffins and four kinds of penguins. Biodôme also has a game room for kids called Naturalia, a shop, a restaurant, and a cafeteria.

✪ **Jardin Botanique.** 4101 rue Sherbrooke Est (opposite Olympic Stadium). ☎ **514/872-1400.** www.ville.montreal.qc.ca/jardin. For the outside gardens, greenhouses, and insectarium, May–Oct C$9.50 (US$6.55) adults, C$7 (US$4.85) seniors and students, C$4.75 (US$3.30) children 6–17; Nov–Apr C$6.75 (US$4.65) adults, C$5.25 (US$3.60) seniors and students, C$3.50 (US$2.40) children. A ticket for the Botanical Garden, Insectarium, and Biodôme, good for 30 days, C$15.25 (US$10.50) adults, C$11.25 (US$7.75) seniors, C$7.75 (US$5.35) children. MC, V. Daily 9am–5pm (until 7pm in summer). Métro: Pie-IX; then walk up the hill to the gardens, or from mid-May to mid-Sept take the shuttle bus from Olympic Park (Métro: Viau).

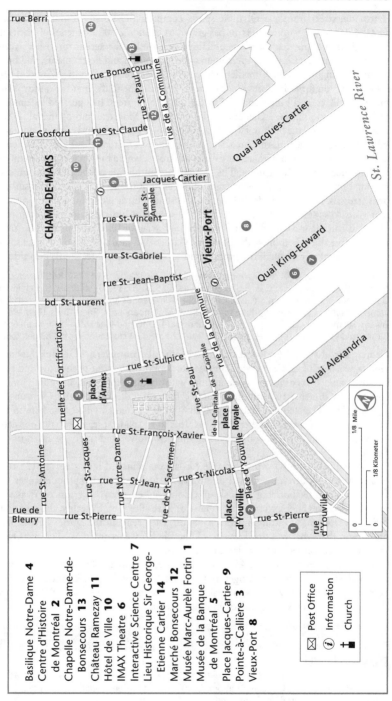

CHAMP-DE-MARS

rue Berri

rue Bonsecours

rue Gosford

rue St-Claude

Jacques-Cartier

rue St-Vincent

rue St-Gabriel

rue St- Jean-Baptist

bd. St-Laurent

rue St-Sulpice

rue St-François-Xavier

St-Jean

rue St-Nicolas

rue St-Antoine

rue St-Jacques

rue Notre-Dame

rue de St-Sacremen

rue de Bleury

rue St-Pierre

place d'Armes

place Royale

place d'Youville

Vieux-Port

rue de la Commune

rue St-Paul

Quai Jacques-Cartier

Quai King-Edward

Quai Alexandria

St. Lawrence River

Place d'Youville

rue d'Youville

rue St-Pierre

rue St-Amable

de la Capitale, de la Capitale

Basilique Notre-Dame **4**

Centre d'Histoire
de Montréal **2**

Chapelle Notre-Dame-de-
Bonsecours **13**

Château Ramezay **11**

Hôtel de Ville **10**

IMAX Theatre **6**

Interactive Science Centre **7**

Lieu Historique Sir George-
Etienne Cartier **14**

Marché Bonsecours **12**

Musée Marc-Aurèle Fortin **1**

Musée de la Banque
de Montréal **5**

Place Jacques-Cartier **9**

Pointe-à-Callière **3**

Vieux-Port **8**

⊠ Post Office

ⓘ Information

✝■ Church

1/8 Mile

1/8 Kilometer

Across the street from the Olympic sports complex, the Botanical Garden spreads across 180 acres. Begun in 1931, it has grown to include 21,000 varieties of plants in 31 specialized segments, ensuring something beautiful and fragrant for visitors year-round. Ten large conservatory greenhouses shelter tropical and desert plants, and bonsai and penjings, from the Canadian winter. One greenhouse, called the Wizard of Oz, is especially fun for kids. Roses bloom here from mid-June to the first frost, May is the month for lilacs, and June is for the flowering hawthorn trees. Inaugurated in summer 1991, the 6-acre Chinese Garden, a joint project of Montréal and Shanghai, is the largest of its kind ever built outside Asia, with pavilions, inner courtyards, ponds, and myriad plants indigenous to China. The serene Japanese Garden fills 15 acres and contains a cultural pavilion with an art gallery, a tearoom where the ancient tea ceremony is performed, and a Zen garden. The grounds are also home to the Insectarium, displaying some of the world's most beautiful insects, not to mention some of its sinister ones (see "Especially for Kids" below). Birders should bring along binoculars on summer visits to spot some of the more than 130 species of birds that spend at least part of the year in the garden. In summer, an outdoor aviary is filled with butterflies. Year-round, a free shuttle bus links the Botanical Garden and nearby Olympic Park; a small train runs regularly through the gardens and is worth the small fee charged to ride it.

Stade Olympique. 4141 av. Pierre-de-Coubertin (bd. Pie IX). ☎ **514/252-8687.** www.rio. gouv.qc.ca. Funicular ride, C$9 (US$6.20) adults, C$5.50 (US$3.80) students and children. Guided tours of the stadium are available. Public swim periods are scheduled daily, with low admission rates. Cable car mid-June to early Sept, Mon noon–6pm, Tues–Thurs 10am–9pm, Fri–Sat 10am–11pm; early Sept to mid-Jan and mid-Feb to mid-June, Mon–Sun noon–6pm. Closed mid-Jan to mid-Feb. Métro: Pie-IX or Viau (choose the Viau station for the guided tour).

Centerpiece of the 1976 Olympic Games, Montréal's controversial Olympic Stadium and its associated facilities provide considerable opportunities for both active and passive diversion. It incorporates a natatorium with six different pools, including one of competition dimensions with an adjustable bottom and a 50-foot-deep version for scuba diving. The stadium seats 60,000 to 80,000 spectators, who come here to see the Expos, rock concerts, and trade shows. It is to be made at least partially obsolete, however, by a proposed new baseball stadium downtown, and might be razed in the future.

The stadium has a 65-ton retractable Kevlar roof winched into place by 125 tons of steel cables, which are attached to a 626-foot inclined tower that looms over the arena like an egret bobbing for fish in a bowl. When everything functions as was intended, it takes about 45 minutes to raise or lower the roof. In reality, the roof malfunctions frequently, and high winds have torn large rents in the fabric. That is only one reason that what was first known as "The Big O" was scorned as "The Big Owe" after cost overruns led to heavy increases in taxes.

The tower, which leans at a 45° angle, also does duty as an observation deck, with a funicular that whisks 90 passengers to the top in 95 seconds. On a clear day, the deck bestows a 35-mile view over Montréal and into the neighboring Laurentides. A free shuttle bus links the Olympic Park and the Botanical Garden.

2 More Attractions

DOWNTOWN

Christ Church Cathedral. 635 rue Ste-Catherine (at rue University). ☎ **514/843-6577** (office) or 514/288-6421 (recorded information). Free admission; donations accepted. Daily 8am–6pm; services Sun 8am, 10am, and 4pm. Métro: McGill.

This Anglican cathedral, reflected in the postmodernist Maison des Coopérants office tower, stands in glorious Gothic contrast to the city's glassy downtown skyscrapers. Sometimes called the "floating cathedral" because of the many tiers of malls and corridors of the Underground City beneath it, the building was completed in 1859. The original steeple, too heavy for the structure, was replaced by a lighter aluminum version in 1940. Christ Church Cathedral hosts concerts throughout the year, notably from mid-January through August on Wednesdays at 12:30pm.

Cathédrale-Basilique Marie-Reine-du-Monde. Bd. René-Lévesque (at rue Mansfield). ☎ **514/866-1661.** Free admission; donations accepted. Mon–Fri 7am–7:30pm; Sat 7:30am–8:30pm; Sun 8:30am–7:30pm. Métro: Bonaventure.

No one who has seen both will confuse Montréal's Mary Queen of the World Cathedral with St. Peter's Basilica in Rome, but a scaled-down homage was the intention of its guiding force. Bishop Ignace Bourget was moved to act in the middle of the last century, after the first Catholic cathedral burned to the ground in 1852. Construction lasted from 1875 to 1894, delayed by his desire to place it not in Francophone east Montréal but in the heart of the Protestant Anglophone west. The resulting structure covers less than a quarter of the area of its Roman inspiration, and there are no curving arcades to embrace a sweeping plaza in front—the stairs to the entrance are only a few yards away from the boulevard. Most impressive is the 252-foot-high dome, about half the size of the original. A local touch is provided by the statues standing on the roofline, representing patron saints of the region. The interior is less rewarding visually than the outside. A planned restoration is expected to cost at least $7.5 million.

Musée d'Art Contemporain de Montréal. 185 rue Ste-Catherine Ouest. ☎ **514/847-6226.** www.macm.org. Admission C$6 (US$4.15) adults, C$4 (US$2.75) seniors, C$3 (US$2.05) students, free for children under 12, C$12 (US$8.30) families; free to all Wed 6–9pm. Tues–Sun 11am–6pm (until 9pm Wed). Métro: Place des Arts.

The Museum of Contemporary Art of Montréal, the only such repository in Canada devoted exclusively to contemporary art, moved into this new facility at the Place des Arts in 1992 after years in an isolated riverfront building. "Contemporary" is defined here as art produced since 1939. About 60% of the permanent collection of some 6,000 works is composed of the work of Québecois artists, but it also includes examples of such international artists as Jean Dubuffet, Max Ernst, Jean Arp, Larry Poons, and Antoni Tàpies, as well as photographers Robert Mapplethorpe, Ansel Adams, and Montréaler Michel Campeau. A few larger pieces are seen on the ground floor, but most are one flight up, with space for temporary exhibitions to the left and selections from the permanent collection on the right. No single style prevails, so expect to see installations both small and room-filling; video displays; evocations of Pop, Op, and abstract expressionism; and accumulations of objects simply piled on the floor. That the works often arouse strong opinions signifies a museum that is doing something right.

The museum's restaurant La Rotonde features a menu of Provençal food and has a summer dining terrace.

VIEUX-MONTRÉAL (OLD MONTRÉAL)

Hôtel de Ville. 275 rue Notre-Dame (at the corner of rue Gosford). ☎ **514/872-3355.** Free admission. Daily 8:30am–4:30pm. Métro: Champ-de-Mars.

City Hall, finished in 1878, is relatively young by Vieux-Montréal standards. The French Second Empire design makes it look as though it was imported stone by stone from the mother country. Balconies, turrets, and mansard roofs detail the exterior, seen to particular advantage when illuminated at night. It was from the balcony above the awning that an ill-mannered Charles de Gaulle proclaimed, "Vive le Québec Libre!" in 1967, thereby pleasing his immediate audience but straining relations with the Canadian government for years. Fifteen-minute guided tours are given throughout the day on weekdays May through October. The Hall of Honour is made of green marble from Campagna, Italy, and houses art deco lamps from Paris and a bronze-and-glass chandelier, also from France, that weighs a metric ton. In the display cabinet to the left by the elevator are gifts from mayors of other cities from around the world. Council Chamber meetings, on the first floor, are open to the public. The chamber has a hand-carved ceiling and five stained-glass windows representing religion, the port, industry and commerce, finance, and transportation. The mayor's office is on the fourth floor. There are infrequently scheduled guided tours.

Chapelle Notre-Dame-de-Bon-Secours/Musée Marguerite-Bourgeoys. 400 rue St-Paul Est (at the foot of rue Bonsecours). ☎ **514/282-8670.** Chapel free; museum C$5 (US$3.45) adults, C$3 (US$2.05) seniors and students, C$2 (US$1.40) ages 6–12, free for children under 6. May–Oct Tues–Sun 10am–5pm; Nov–Jan 15 and Mar 15–Apr 30 Tues–Sun 11am–3:30pm. Closed Jan 15–Mar 15. Métro: Champ-de-Mars.

Just to the east of Marché Bonsecours, Notre Dame de Bonsecours Chapel is called the Sailors' Church because of the special attachment to it felt by fishermen and other mariners. That devotion is manifest in the many ship models hanging inside. A revered 16th-century 6-inch-high carving of the Madonna is once again on display. The first church building, the project of an energetic teacher named Marguerite Bourgeoys, was built in 1678. She arrived with de Maisonneuve to undertake the education of the children of Montréal in the latter half of the 17th century. Later on, she and several sister teachers founded a nuns' order called the Congregation of Notre-Dame, Canada's first. The pioneering Bourgeoys was recognized as a saint in 1982. There's an excellent view of the harbor and the old quarter from the church's tower.

The present church, which dates from 1773, incorporates a museum and a restored 18th-century crypt, an archaeological site that has unearthed ruins and materials from the earliest days of the colony. Admission to both the museum and the archaeological site is C$8 (US$5.50). Mandatory guided tours are limited to seven people; tours in English are Thursday through Sunday at 2pm.

Marché Bonsecours. 350 rue St-Paul Est (at the foot of rue St-Claude). ☎ **514/872-7730.** www.marchebonsecours.qc.ca. Free admission. Sat–Thurs 10am–6pm, Thurs–Fri 10am–9pm. Métro: Champ-de-Mars.

Bonsecours Market, an imposing neoclassical building with a long facade, a colonnaded portico, and a silvery dome, was built in the mid-1800s and first used as Montréal's City Hall, then for many years after 1878 as the central market. It has never been decided with finality what it will be since then. Essentially abandoned for much of the 20th century, it was restored in 1964 to house city government offices, and in 1992 became the information and exhibition center for the celebration of the city's 350th birthday. It continues to be used as an exhibition space, and room was made for shopping stalls and a sidewalk cafe. Currently, it has a fairly large food market, too, to serve the growing resident population of Vieux-Montréal. The architecture alone makes a brief visit worthwhile.

Musée du Château Ramezay. 280 rue Notre-Dame (east of Place Jacques-Cartier). ☎ **514/861-3708.** www.chateauramezay.qc.ca. Admission C$6 (US$4.15) adults, C$5 (US$3.45) seniors, C$4 (US$2.75) students, free for children under 6, C$12 (US$8.30) families. MC, V. June–Sept daily 10am–6pm; Oct–May Tues–Sun 10am–4:30pm. Métro: Champ-de-Mars.

Claude de Ramezay, the 11th governor of the colony, built his residence at this site in 1705. The château was the home of the city's royal French governors for almost 4 decades, but in 1745, his heirs sold it to a trading company. They apparently rebuilt it, using portions of the original structure. Fifteen years later, it was taken over by the British conquerors. In 1775 an army of American revolutionaries invaded and held Montréal, using the château as their headquarters. Benjamin Franklin, sent to persuade Québecois to rise with the American colonists against British rule, stayed in the château for a time, but failed to persuade the city's people to join his cause. After the American interlude, the house was used as a courthouse, a government office building, a teachers' college, and headquarters for Laval University before being converted into a museum in 1895. Old coins and prints, portraits, furnishings, tools, a loom, Amerindian artifacts, and other memorabilia related to the economic and social activities of the 18th century and first half of the 19th century fill the main floor. In the cellar are the vaults of the original house. Descriptive placards are in both French and English. Across rue Notre-Dame is the City Hall.

PLATEAU MONT-ROYAL

For further information about this region, log on to **www.tpmr.qc.ca**.

Musée des Hospitalières de l'Hôtel-Dieu de Montréal. 201 av. des Pins Ouest. ☎ **514/849-2919.** Admission C$5 (US$3.45) adults, C$3 (US$2.05) seniors and students 12 and over, free for children 11 and under. Mid-June–mid-Oct Tues–Fri 10am–5pm, Sat–Sun 1–5pm; mid-Oct–mid-June Wed–Sun 1–5pm. Métro: Sherbrooke. Bus: 144.

Opened in 1992 to coincide with the city's 350th birthday, this unusual museum, in the former chaplain's residence of Hôtel-Dieu Hospital, traces the history of Montréal from 1659 to the present and focuses on the evolution of health care spanning 3 centuries in the history of the hospital, including an exhibit of medical instruments. It bows to the missionary nurse Jeanne Mance, who arrived in 1642 and founded of the first hospital in Montréal, the only woman among the first settlers who left France with Sieur de Maisonneuve. The museum's three floors are filled with memorabilia, including paintings, books, reliquaries, furnishings, and a reconstruction of a nun's cell. Its architectural high point is a marvelous "floating" oak staircase brought to the New World in 1634 from the Maison-Dieu hospital in La Flèche, France. The original Hôtel-Dieu was built in 1645 near the site of the present Notre-Dame Basilica, in Vieux-Montréal. This building was erected in 1861. Guided tours are Sundays at 2pm.

Parc Lafontaine. Rue Sherbrooke and av. Parc Lafontaine. ☎ **514/872-2644.** Free admission; small fee for use of tennis courts. Always open. Tennis courts summer daily 9am–10pm. Métro: Sherbrooke.

The European-style park near downtown is one of the city's oldest. Illustrating the dual identities of the city's populace, half the park is landscaped in the formal French manner, the other in the more casual English style. Among its several bodies of water is a lake used for paddleboating in summer and ice skating in winter. Snowshoeing and cross-country trails curl through the trees. An open amphitheater, the **Théâtre de Verdure,** is the setting for free outdoor theater and movies in summer. Joggers, bikers, picnickers, and tennis buffs (there are 14 outdoor courts) share the space.

Oratoire St-Joseph. 3800 Chemin Queen Mary (on the north slope of Mont-Royal). ☎ **514/733-8211.** www.saint-joseph.org. Free admission, but donations are requested. Daily 6am–9:30pm; museum daily 10am–5pm. The 56-bell carillon plays Wed–Fri noon–3pm; Sat–Sun noon–2:30pm. Métro: Côtes-des-Neiges.

This huge basilica with a giant copper dome was built by Québec's Catholics to honor St. Joseph, patron saint of Canada. Dominating the north slope of Mont-Royal, its imposing dimensions are seen by some as inspiring, by others as forbidding. It came into being through the efforts of Brother André, a lay brother in the Holy Cross order who enjoyed a reputation as a healer. By the time he had built a small wooden chapel in 1904 near the site of the basilica, he was said to have affected hundreds of cures. Those celebrated powers attracted supplicants from great distances, and Brother André performed his work until his death in 1937. His dream of building this shrine to his patron saint became a reality only years after his death, in 1967. He is buried in the basilica and was beatified by the Pope in 1982, a status one step below sainthood. The basilica is largely Italian Renaissance in style, its dome recalling the shape of the Duomo in Florence, but of much greater size and less grace. Inside is a museum where a central exhibit is the heart of Brother André. Outside, a Way of the Cross lined with sculptures was the setting of scenes for the Canadian film *Jesus of Montréal*. Brother André's wooden chapel, with his tiny bedroom, is on the grounds and open to the public. Pilgrims, some ill, come to seek intercession from St. Joseph and Brother André and often climb the middle set of 100 steps on their knees. At 862 feet (263m), the shrine is the highest point in Montréal. A cafeteria and snack bar are on the premises. Ninety-minute guided tours are offered in several languages at 10am and 2pm daily in summer and on weekends in September and October (donation only).

ÎLE STE-HÉLÈNE

La Biosphère. 160 Chemin Tour-de-l'Isle (Île Ste-Hélène). ☎ **514/283-5000.** Admission C$6.50 adults (US$4.50), C$5 (US$3.45) seniors and students, C$4 (US$2.75) children 7–17, free for children under 7, C$16 (US$11.05) families. June 24–Labour Day daily 10am–6pm; Sept–May Tues–Sun 10am–5pm. Métro: Île Ste-Hélène, then a short walk or the shuttle bus.

Not to be confused with the Biodôme at Olympic Park, this facility is located in the geodesic dome designed by Buckminster Fuller to serve as the American Pavilion for Expo '67. A fire destroyed the acrylic skin of the sphere in 1976, and it served no purpose other than as a harbor landmark until 1995. The motivation behind the Biosphère is unabashedly environmental, with four exhibition areas, a water theater, and an amphitheater, all devoted to promoting awareness of the St. Lawrence–Great Lakes ecosystem. Multimedia shows and hands-on displays invite the active participation of visitors, and there is an exhibition related to the activities of the ocean explorer Jacques-Yves Cousteau. In the highest point of the so-called Visions Hall is an observation level with an unobstructed view of the river. Connections Hall offers a "Call to Action" presentation employing six giant screens and three stages. There is a preaching-to-the-choir quality to all this that slips over the edge into zealous philosophizing. But the various displays and exhibits are put together thoughtfully and will divert and enlighten most visitors, at least for a while. Just don't make a special trip.

Musée David M. Stewart. Vieux Fort, Île Ste-Hélène. ☎ **514/861-6701.** www.stewart-museum.org. Admission May–Oct C$10 (US$6.90) adults, C$7 (US$4.85) seniors and students, C$20 (US$13.80) families, free for children under 7; Nov–Apr C$6 (US$4.15) adults, C$4 (US$2.75) seniors and students, C$12 (US$8.30) families. May–mid-Oct daily 10am–6pm; late Oct–mid-May Wed–Mon 10am–5pm. Métro: Île Ste-Hélène, then a 15-minute walk. By car: Take the Jacques-Cartier Bridge to the Parc des Îles exit, then follow signs to Vieux Fort.

After the War of 1812, the British prepared for a possible future American invasion by building this moated fortress, which now houses the David M. Stewart Museum. The duke of Wellington ordered its construction as another link in the chain of defenses along the St. Lawrence. Completed in 1824, it was never involved in armed conflict. The British garrison left in 1870, after confederation of the former Canadian colonies. Today the low stone barracks and blockhouses contain the museum, which displays maps and scientific instruments that helped Europeans explore the New World, as well as military and naval artifacts, weaponry, uniforms, housewares, and related paraphernalia from the time of Jacques Cartier (1535) through the end of the colonial period. Useful labels are in both French and English.

From late June through late August, the fort comes to life with reenactments of military parades and retreats by La Compagnie Franche de la Marine and the 78th Fraser Highlanders, at 11am, 3pm, and 4:30pm. The presence of the French unit is an unhistorical sop to Francophone sensibilities, since New France had become English Canada almost 65 years before the fort was erected. If you absolutely must be photographed in stocks, they are provided on the parade grounds.

3 Especially for Kids

IMAX Theatre. Vieux-Port, Quai King Edward (end of bd. St-Laurent). ☎ **800/349-4629** or 514/496-4629 (information and tickets). www.isci.ca/en/imax/mixte.htm. Admission C$9.95 (US$6.85) adults, C$8.95 (US$6.15) seniors and students 13–17, C$7.95 (US$5.50) children 4–11. MC, V. Daily. Call for current schedule of shows in English. Métro: Place d'Armes.

The images and special effects are larger than life, sometimes in 3-D and always visually dazzling, thrown on a new seven-story screen in the renovated theater. Recent films made the most of charging elephants, underwater scenes around the Galapagos, cameras swooping low over Alaska wildlife and glaciers, and, lately, the acrobats and performers of the Cirque du Soleil. Running time is usually under an hour. Arrive for shows at least 10 minutes before starting time, earlier on weekends and evenings. Tickets can be ordered online.

Insectarium. Botanical Garden, 4101 rue Sherbrooke (bd. Pie IX). ☎ **514/872-1400.** www.ville.montreal.qc.ca/insectarium. May–Oct C$9.50 (US$6.55) adults, C$7 (US$4.85) seniors, C$4.75 (US$3.30) children 6–17; Nov–Apr C$6.75 (US$4.65) adults, C$5.25 (US$3.65) seniors, C$3.50 (US$2.40) children. MC, V. Summer daily 9am–7pm; rest of year daily 9am–5pm. Métro: Pie-IX; walk up the hill to the gardens, or in summer take the shuttle bus from Olympic Park. Métro: Viau.

A relatively recent addition to the Botanical Garden, this two-level structure near the Sherbrooke gate exhibits the collections of two avid entomologists: Georges Brossard (whose brainchild this place is) and Father Firmia Liberté. More than 3,000 mounted butterflies, scarabs, maggots, locusts, beetles, tarantulas, and giraffe weevils are displayed, and live exhibits feature scorpions, tarantulas, crickets, cockroaches, and praying mantises. Needless to say, kids are delighted by the creepy critters. Their guardians are apt to be less enthusiastic, except in summer in the Butterfly House, when beautiful live specimens flutter among the nectar-bearing plants.

La Ronde Amusement Park. Parc des Îles, Île Ste-Hélène. ☎ **800/797-4537** or 514/ 872-4537. Unlimited all-day pass C$24.35 (US$16.25) for those 12 and over, C$12.60 (US$8.40) under 12, C$12.40 (US$8.25) grounds admission only. Reserved seating for fireworks, from C$26.10 (US$17.40) including all rides. Last week in May, Sat–Sun only; June–Aug and Labour Day weekend daily 10am–9pm. Parking C$8 (US$5.35). Métro: Papineau and bus no. 169, or Île Ste-Hélène and bus no. 167.

Montréal's ambitious amusement park fills the northern reaches of the Île Ste-Hélène with 35 rides, an international circus, a medieval village, roller coasters, and places to eat and drink. Thrill-seekers like the rides called Le Boomerang, Le Monstre, and Le

Cobra, a stand-up roller coaster that incorporates a 360° loop and reaches speeds in excess of 60 miles per hour. A big attraction every year is the International Fireworks Competition, held on Saturdays in June and Sundays in July (postponed in bad weather). The pyromusical displays are launched at 10pm and last at least 30 minutes. (Many Montréalers choose to watch them from the Jacques Cartier Bridge, which is closed to traffic during the display. Take along a Walkman to listen to the accompanying music.)

The future of the park is uncertain. The fact that it has been losing money for several years is evident in its visible need for improved maintenance, and Montréal has been chosen as the site for a new $900 million indoor theme park to be called Technodome. That project, which has been subject to delays, is tentatively sited at the west end of the Old Port.

Planétarium de Montréal. 1000 rue St-Jacques (at Peel). ☎ **514/872-4530.** www. planetarium.montreal.qc.ca. Admission C$6 (US$4.15) adults, $4.50 (US$3.10) seniors and students, C$3 (US$2.05) children 6–17. MC, V. Schedule of shows changes frequently, call ahead. Métro: Bonaventure (Cathédrale exit).

A window on the night sky with mythical monsters and magical heroes, Montréal's planetarium is right downtown, only 2 blocks south of Windsor Station. Changing shows under the 65-foot (20m) dome dazzle and inform kids at the same time. Shows change with the seasons, exploring time and space travel and collisions of celestial bodies. The special Christmas show, "Star of the Magi," which can be seen in December and early January, is based on recent investigations of historians and astronomers into the mysterious light that guided the Magi. Shows in English alternate with those in French.

The future location of the Planetarium, if not its existence, is in doubt. It stands on desirable downtown acreage that is being eyed by developers for a new baseball stadium and, possibly, two new hotels.

4 Special-Interest Sightseeing

Centre Canadien d'Architecture (CCA). 1920 rue Baile (at rue du Fort). ☎ **514/ 939-7026.** www.cca.qc.ca. Admission C$6 (US$4.15) adults, C$4 (US$2.75) seniors and students, free for children under 12. June–Sept Tues–Sun 11am–6pm (until 9pm Thurs); rest of year Wed–Fri 11am–6pm (until 8pm Thurs), Sat–Sun 11am–5pm. Guided tours available on request. Métro: Atwater or Guy-Concordia.

The understated but handsome Canadian Center of Architecture building occupies a city block, with lawns, joining a thoughtfully contemporary structure with an older building, the 1875 Shaughnessy House. The CCA doubles as a study center and a museum, with changing exhibits devoted to the art of architecture and its history, including architects' sketchbooks, elevation drawings, and photography. The collection is international in scope and encompasses architecture, urban planning, and landscape design. Texts are in French and English. Opened in 1989, the museum has received rave notices from scholars, critics, and serious architecture buffs. That said, it is only fair to note that the average visitor is likely to find it somewhat less than enthralling. The bookstore has a special section on Canadian architecture with emphasis on Montréal and Québec City. The sculpture garden across the Ville-Marie autoroute is part of the CCA, designed by artist/architect Melvin Charney.

Centre d'Histoire de Montréal. 335 place d'Youville (at St-Pierre). ☎ **514/872-3207.** www.ville.montreal.qc.ca/jard_mus/chm. Admission C$4.50 (US$3.10) adults; C$3 (US$2.05) seniors, students, and children 6–17; free for children under 6. May–Sept daily 10am–5pm; Sept–Dec Tues–Sun 10am–5pm. Closed Jan–Apr. Métro: Square-Victoria.

Built in 1903 as Montréal's Central Fire Station, the redbrick and sandstone building is now the Montréal History Center, which traces the development of the city from its first residents, the Amerindians, to the European settlers who arrived in 1642, to the present day. Throughout its 14 rooms, carefully conceived presentations chart the contributions of the city fathers and mothers and subsequent generations. The development of the railroad, Métro, and related infrastructure are recalled, as is that of domestic and public architecture, in imaginative exhibits, videos, and slide shows. On the second floor, reached by a spiral staircase, is memorabilia from the early 20th century. Labels are in French, so ask at the front desk for a visitor's guide in English. One or two rooms are given over to temporary exhibitions.

Lieu Historique de Sir George-Étienne Cartier. 458 rue Notre-Dame Est (at Berri). ☎ **514/283-2282.** Admission C\$4.50 (US\$3.10) adults, C\$3.75 (US\$2.60) seniors, C\$1.75 (US\$1.20) children 6–16, free for children under 7. Late May to early Sept daily 10am–6pm; Sept–May Wed–Sun 10am–5pm. Closed Jan–mid-May. Métro: Champ-des-Mars.

Operated by Parks Canada, this off-the-tourist-track historic site is actually two houses. One has been reconstructed to its appearance in the 1860s as the Victorian residence of Sir George-Étienne Cartier (1814–73), one of the fathers of Canada's 1867 Confederation. The adjacent house is devoted to Cartier's career and work. During the summer, the site has costumed guides, and hosts concerts and other activities.

Hours and admission fees change with some frequency, so check ahead before you plan a visit.

Musée de la Banque de Montréal. 119 and 129 rue St-Jacques (at place d'Armes). ☎ **514/877-6810.** Free admission. Museum Mon–Fri 10am–4pm; bank Mon–Tues and Thurs–Fri 9am–5pm, Wed 10am–5pm. Métro: Place d'Armes.

Facing Place d'Armes is Montréal's oldest bank building, with a classic facade beneath a graceful dome, a carved pediment, and six Corinthian columns, the outside dimensions and appearance largely unchanged since its completion in 1847. The interior was renovated from 1901 through 1905 by the famed U.S. firm McKim, Mead, and White with Ionic and Corinthian columns of Vermont granite, walls of pink marble from Tennessee, and a counter of Levanto marble. The bank contains a small museum with a replica of its first office (and its first bank teller, Henry Stone from Boston), gold nuggets from the Yukon, a \$3 bill (one of only two known), and a collection of 100-year-old mechanical banks. A bilingual guide is available to answer questions.

Musée Marc-Aurèle Fortin. 118 rue St-Pierre (at rue d'Youville). ☎ **514/845-6108.** Admission C\$4 (US\$2.75) adults, C\$2 (US\$1.40) seniors and students, free for children under 12. Tues–Sun 11am–5pm. Métro: Square Victoria.

This is Montréal's only museum dedicated to the work of a single French-Canadian artist. Landscape watercolorist Marc-Aurèle Fortin (1888–1970) interpreted the beauty of the Québec countryside, especially the Laurentians and Charlevoix. His paintings are on the ground floor, while temporary exhibits—varied in style, but typically representative rather than nonobjective or abstract—usually feature the work of other Québec painters.

Musée Redpath. 859 rue Sherbrooke Ouest (McGill University). ☎ **514/398-4086.** Free admission. Sept–June Mon–Fri 9am–5pm, Sun 1–5pm; July–Aug Mon–Thurs 9am–5pm, Sun 1–5pm (except holiday weekends). Métro: McGill. Bus: 24.

If the unusual name seems slightly familiar, think of the wrappings on sugar cubes in many Canadian restaurants. John Redpath was a 19th-century industrialist who built Canada's first sugar refinery and later distributed much of his fortune in philanthropy.

This modest museum housed in an 1882 building is on the McGill University campus. The main draw is its collection of Egyptian antiquities, the second-largest in Canada, but also on view are fossils and geological fragments.

St-Lambert Lock. Route 132 under the east end of Victoria Bridge. ☎ **514/672-4110.** Free admission. Mid-Apr–mid-Nov daily. Drive or take a taxi across Victoria Bridge to the exit marked ÉCLUSES; park in the Observatory lot, and walk from there to the observation deck overlooking St-Lambert Lock.

The St. Lawrence Seaway was inaugurated by Queen Elizabeth II and President Eisenhower in 1959, after a century of planning and a remarkably short 5 years of actual construction. The system of canals and 15 locks meant that oceangoing vessels could sail all the way to Lake Superior in the North American heartland, 2,300 miles (3,700km) from the Atlantic. In the mammoth lock, 860 feet long by 80 feet wide, ships are raised about 15 feet, and then the upriver gates are opened for them to continue the journey to the center of the continent. The specially constructed ships, called "salters" or "lakers," are narrow, to fit the locks, but often more than 700 feet long. Obviously, the ideal time to be here is when a ship enters the lock, but there's no way to predict that circumstance. January to March, ice on the river prevents ships from using the system.

5 Organized Tours

A generalized guided tour is often the most desirable way to begin explorations of a new city. Even a mediocre tour with a guide who imagines himself a wit can provide a timesaving sense of the topography of the city, its history, and which attractions are most likely to reward an in-depth return visit.

For a complete listing of tours and tour operators, check under "Guided Tours" in the index of the annually revised *Montréal Tourist Guide,* or at **Infotouriste** (☎ **800/363-7777** or 514/873-2015). Most of the land tours leave from downtown at Square Dorchester, near the Infotouriste office. Boat tours depart from the port bordering Vieux-Montréal. Parking is free at the dock, or take the Métro to the Champ-de-Mars or Square-Victoria station and walk 6 blocks.

BOAT TOURS

Among numerous opportunities for experiencing Montréal and environs by water, a few of the more popular include the following:

Le Bateau-Mouche (☎ **800/361-9952** or 514/849-9952; **www.bateau-mouche.com**), an air-conditioned, glass-enclosed vessel reminiscent of those on the Seine in Paris. It plies the St. Lawrence River from mid-May to mid-October. Cruises depart for 90-minute excursions at 10am, noon, 2pm, and 4pm, and for a 3½-hour dinner cruise at 7pm (boarding at 6:30pm). The shallow-draft boat takes up to 158 passengers on a route inaccessible by traditional vessels. It passes under seven bridges and provides sweeping views of the city, Mont-Royal, the St. Lawrence, and its islands. Daytime snacks are available on board, and dinners are prepared by the kitchens of the Queen Elizabeth Hotel. Families get a discount on the first trip of the day, at 10am. Day tours cost C$18.75 (US$12.95) adults, C$16 (US$11.05) students and seniors, C$9 (US$6.20) children 5 to 12, children under 5 free; dinner cruises C$62.25 to C$95 (US$43 to US$66) adults, C$59 to C$92 (US$41 to US$63) students and seniors (no special rate for children under 12). *Le Bateau-Mouche* departs from the Jacques Cartier Pier, opposite Place Jacques-Cartier.

Rollin' Down the River

River cruises are a wholly different experience from that provided by the ships that sail the Caribbean and the Mediterranean. The vessels plying North America's rivers are far smaller than the monsters calling at Barcelona and San Juan, with shallower drafts to glide over closer bottoms and to negotiate channels their big brothers can't enter. Typically, riverboats have only one dining room, requiring separate sittings and kitchens and crews too small to prepare six meals from morning to midnight. Staterooms are, at best, compact, with few extras beyond hair dryers and a two-channel radios and with bathrooms of telephone booth dimensions.

In compensation, schedules are less frantic, social directors more subdued, the urge to flaunt status all but absent. Informality and casual conversation reign. Characteristic are the cruises offered by the **St. Lawrence Cruise Lines Inc.,** 253 Ontario St., Kingston, Ontario K7L 2Z4, ☎ **800/267-7868** or 613/ 549-8091, fax 613/549-8410; **www.stlawrencecruiselines.com**. The company lays out itineraries of varying lengths and port connections. A five-night version runs from Kingston through the Thousand Islands to Montréal, and then up the Ottawa River to the national capital. Stops along the way include Boldt Castle, a millionaire's unfinished monument to the love of his life; Upper Canada Village, a museum settlement of restored early 19th-century buildings; several locks in the Seaway; and a wildlife park in Québec. An especially popular 6-night cruise goes from Kingston all the way downriver to Québec City. The food served is adequate, the onboard staff friendly and eager to please, the nightly entertainment missable. (Take books.)

Best of all, compared to the big guys, are the fares, ranging from a low of $899 per person in shoulder season to a high of $1,788 in peak season in the best stateroom on the longest trip, all meals and attractions included.

Croisières du Port de Montréal (AML Cruises) (☎ 800/667-3131 or 514/ 842-3871; **www.croisieresaml.com**) also travels the harbor and the St. Lawrence. The boats depart up to five times a day from May to mid-October from the Clock Tower Pier at the foot of rue Berri in Vieux-Montréal, for tours, dinner and dancing, or extended sightseeing for 1 to 9 hours. Fares are C$14 to C$32 (US$9.65 to US$22) adults, C$12 to C$29 (US$8.30 to US$20) students and seniors, C$7 to C$25 (US$4.85 to US$17.25) children 12 and under. The higher prices above are for dinner cruises. AML also offers cruises down the St. Lawrence to Québec City, Charlevoix, and for whale-watching at and up the Saguenay River.

For an exciting—and wet—experience, consider a ride with **Saute Moutons** (☎ 514/284-9607; **www.jetboatingmontreal.com**). Their wave-jumper powerboats take on the roiling Lachine Rapids of the St. Lawrence River. The streamlined hydrojet makes the 90-minute trip May to mid-October daily, with departures every 30 minutes from 11am to 7pm. It takes half an hour to get to and from the rapids, which leaves 30 minutes for storming up the river. Arrive 45 minutes early to obtain and don rain gear and life jacket. Wearing a sweater and bringing a change of clothes are good ideas, because you almost certainly will get splashed or even soaked through. Fares are C$20 (US$13.80) adults, C$16 (US$11.05) ages 13 to 18, C$14 (US$9.65) ages 6 to 12. Cruises depart from the Clock Tower Pier.

A much milder water voyage, with great views, is the **ferry** (☎ 514/281-8000) from Jacques-Cartier Pier in Vieux-Montréal to Île Sainte-Hélène, a good way to begin and end a picnic outing or visits to the old fort or La Ronde amusement park. It operates from mid-May to mid-October.

BUS TOURS

Commercial guided tours in air-conditioned buses are offered two to eight times daily year-round by **Autocar Connaisseur/Gray Line** (☎ 514/934-1222). The basic city tour takes 3 hours; the deluxe, 5 hours, which includes an hour-long stop at the Botanical Garden. Other tours take you to the Île Ste-Hélène, the St. Lawrence Seaway, the Laurentians, and Québec City. Tours depart from Dorchester Square. Similar tours, but fewer in number, are provided by **Autocar Royal** (☎ 514/871-4733).

Montréal's romantic *calèches* (☎ 514/934-6105) are horse-drawn open carriages whose drivers serve as guides. In winter they hitch their steeds to old-fashioned sleighs for a ride around the top of Mont-Royal, the horses puffing steam, the passengers bundled in lap rugs. Prices run about C$45 (US$30) for an hour's tour in the carriage or sleigh, which can seat four comfortably, five if one sits with the driver. In addition to Mont-Royal, calèches depart from Square Dorchester and in Vieux-Montréal at Place Jacques-Cartier and rue de la Commune, and Place d'Armes opposite Notre-Dame Basilica. The carriages run year-round, but the schedules vary in the off-season, so call first.

WALKING & CYCLING TOURS

Walking tours of Vieux-Montréal, the Underground City, or any other section that piques interest are available through **Guidatour** (☎ 514/844-4021) or **Visites de Montréal** (☎ 514/933-6674). Cycling tours in French or English are available through **Vélo-Tour Montréal** (☎ 514/236-8356) at 99 rue de la Commune in Vieux-Montréal.

6 Spectator Sports

Montréalers are as devoted to ice hockey as are other Canadians, with plenty of enthusiasm left over for baseball, football, and soccer. There are several prominent annual sporting events of other kinds, such as the Grand Prix Air Canada (☎ 514/350-0000 for information) in June, The Player's Ltd. International men's tennis championship in late July, and the Montréal Marathon in September.

BASEBALL

The **Montréal Expos,** part of the National League, will continue to play at Stade Olympique (Olympic Stadium), 4549 Pierre-de-Coubertin, at least until a proposed new $200 million stadium opens downtown. Until further notice, ticket reservations can be made by telephone, with a credit card. Call ☎ 514/790-1245 for information or log on to **www.montrealexpos.com**. Subject to anticipated increases, tickets are C$7 (US$4.85) for general admission to C$23 (US$15.85) for box seats. Métro: Pie-IX.

HARNESS RACING

Popularly known as Blue Bonnets Racetrack, the **Hippodrome de Montréal** at 7440 bd. Décarie, in Jean-Talon (☎ 514/739-2741), is the host facility for

The Great American Pastime Goes North

U.S. broadcast networks and the team owners of Major League Baseball suffer night sweats over worse things than labor strife, misbehaving superstars, and laws banning the sale of beer in their stadiums. It's the terror of a World Series featuring either the Toronto Blue Jays or the Montréal Expos (or—*quelle calamité!*—both) that truly keeps them up at night. Ratings plummet whenever a playoff game takes place in either of those cities, as happened with Toronto in the early 1990s. When colorless teams from undesirably small TV markets in the Midwest match up, network executives shrug their shoulders and comfort themselves with a resigned, "Well, at least they ain't Canadians."

This is an unfortunate analysis, for Canadians are as enthusiastic about the American game as anyone—at least after their national secular religion, hockey, is taken into account. Even though there is the ever-present possibility of early and late-season games being called off on account of snow, professional baseball has been a fixture in Montréal—off and on, admittedly—since the last century. The Expos were preceded by the Royals, who played their first game in 1828 in the Eastern League. There was a gap from 1916 to 1928. The Royals were reincarnated in the International League, as a Triple-A farm club associated with the Brooklyn Dodgers. They signed Jackie Robinson in 1945, two years before Branch Rickey brought him up to The Show. Robinson paid off handsomely: In his first game for the Royals, he hit a three-run homer, scored four times, and stole two bases.

Many of the game's greats passed through Montréal—usually on their move up, although occasionally when they were headed the other way. Future Dodgers manager Walter Alston guided them in the 1950s, and his and other Royals teams of the postwar era had batting orders that included, however briefly, Don Newcombe, Bobby Morgan, Junior Gilliam, Gil Hodges, Roy Campanella, Chuck Connors (yes, the actor), and a pitcher by the name of Tommy Lasorda.

The Royals expired for good in the early 1960s but were followed by the Expos in 1969, named for the '67 World's Fair held in Montréal and later housed in a stadium built for the 1976 Olympics. Persistent success has not been their lot, but they, too, have had their favorite stars—as well as fanciful linguistic turns you won't find south of the border. When red-headed Rusty Staub was playing, Montréalers gave him the nickname "Le Grand Orange."

international harness-racing events, including the Coupe des Élevers (Breeders Cup). Restaurants, bars, a snack bar, and pari–mutuel betting can make for a satisfying evening or Sunday-afternoon outing. There are no races on Tuesday and Thursday. General admission is free, C$5 (US$3.45) for the VIP section. Races begin at 7:30pm on Monday, Wednesday, Friday, and Saturday; on Sunday at 1:30pm. Métro: Namur, and then take the shuttle bus.

HOCKEY

The NHL's **Montréal Canadiens** play at the new Centre Molson, which opened in 1996 at 1260 rue de la Gauchetière, replacing the beloved old Forum. The team has won 24 Stanley Cup championships since 1929. The season runs from October into

April, with playoffs continuing to mid-June. Tickets range from about C$16 to C$95 (US$11.05 to US$65.50). Ticket and schedule information can be obtained by phone at ☎ **514/932-2582** (CLUB). Métro: Bonaventure.

FOOTBALL

Canadian professional football returned to Montréal after a 3-year experiment with U.S. teams. The team that briefly was the Baltimore Colts is now in its second incarnation as the **Montréal Alouettes.** Lately, the CFL team plays at the McGill University stadium on a schedule that runs from June into October. Call for information at ☎ **514/254-2400.**

7 Outdoor Activities

BICYCLING

Cycling is hugely popular in Montréal, and the city enjoys a network of 174 miles of cycling paths, with another 60 miles expected to be completed soon. Heavily used routes include the nearly flat 6.8-mile (11km) *piste cyclable* (bicycle path) along the Lachine Canal that leads to Lac St-Louis, the 10-mile (16km) path west from the St-Lambert Lock (see "Special-Interest Sightseeing," above) to the city of Côte Ste-Catherine, and Angrignon Park with its 4-mile biking path and inviting picnic areas (take the Métro, which accepts bikes in the last two doors of the last car, to Angrignon station). Bikes can be rented at the Vieux-Port (at the end of boulevard St-Laurent) for C$6.50 to C$7 (US$4.35 to US$4.65) an hour or C$20 to C$22 (US$13.35 to US$14.65) a day. **Velo Aventure** on Quai King Edward is a principal source (see also "In-Line Skating" below). Bikes, along with the popular four-wheel "Q Cycles," may also be rented at the Place Jacques-Cartier entrance to the Old Port. The Q Cycles, for use in the Old Port only, cost C$4.25 (US$2.85) per half hour for adults and C$3.50 (US$2.35) per half hour for children.

A useful booklet, *Pédaler Montréal,* is available at the Infotourist office on Square Dominion. For additional information, log on to **www.velo.qc.ca**.

CROSS-COUNTRY SKIING

Parc Mont-Royal has a 1.3-mile (2.1km) cross-country course called the *parcours de la croix.* The Botanical Garden has an ecology trail used by cross-country skiers. The problem for either is that skiers have to supply their own equipment. Just an hour from the city, in the Laurentides, are almost 20 ski centers, all offering cross-country as well as downhill skiing. See chapter 10.

HIKING

The most popular—and obvious—hike is up to the top of Mont-Royal. Start downtown on rue Peel, which leads north to a stairway, which in turn leads to a half-mile (800m) path of switchbacks called Le Serpent. Or opt for the 200 steps that lead up to the Chalet Lookout, with the reward of a panoramic view of the city. Figure about 1¼ miles one way.

IN-LINE SKATING

More than 230 pairs of in-line skates and all the requisite protective gear can be rented from **Velo Adventure** (☎ **514/847-0666**) on Quai King Edward in the Vieux-Port. The cost is C$8.50 (US$5.65) weekdays or C$9 (US$6) weekends for the first hour and C$4 (US$2.65) for each additional hour, up to a maximum of C$30 (US$20) for an 8-hour day. Protective gear is included. A deposit is required. Lessons on skates are available for C$25 (US$16.65) for 2 hours.

JOGGING

There are many possibilities for running. One is to follow rue Peel north to Le Serpent switchback path on Mont-Royal, continuing uphill on it for half a mile (800m) until it peters out. Turn right and continue 1 mile (2km) to the monument of George-Étienne Cartier, one of Canada's fathers of confederation. From here, either take a bus back downtown or run back down the same route or along avenue du Parc and avenue des Pins (turn right when you get to it). It's also fun to jog along the Lachine Canal.

7

Montréal Strolls

Cities best reveal themselves to the traveler on foot, and Montréal is one of the most amenable to walkers in North America. There's much to see in the more concentrated districts—the old town, the center city, around rue Crescent, the Latin Quarter, and on "the mountain"—and the city's layout is fairly straightforward and easily navigated.

Walking Tour 1: Vieux-Montréal

Start: La Maison Pierre du Calvet, opposite Chapelle Notre-Dame-de-Bonsecours.
Finish: Vieux-Port.
Time: 2 to 3 hours.
Best Times: Almost any day the weather is decent. Vieux-Montréal is lively and safe day or night. Note, however, that most of the museums in the area close on Monday. On warmer weekends and holidays, Montréalers turn out in full force, enjoying the plazas, the 18th- and 19th-century architecture, and the ambience of the most picturesque part of their city.
Worst Times: Evenings, when attractions are closed and rue St-Paul can get a little rowdy with young barhoppers.

Take the Métro to the Champ-de-Mars station and follow the signs to Vieux-Montréal (Old Montréal), proceeding up the hill to rue Notre-Dame. Turn left, then right on rue Bonsecours, descending 1 block. Near the bottom, at no. 401 on the left, is a house that offers a look at what life was like in Montréal in the late 18th century, the:

1. **Maison Pierre du Calvet (Calvet House).** Built in 1725 (or maybe 1771) and restored between 1964 and 1966, it appears to be a modest dwelling. In the early days, though, such a house would have been inhabited by a fairly well-to-do family. Pierre du Calvet, believed to be the original owner, was a French Huguenot who supported the American Revolution. Calvet met with Benjamin Franklin here in 1775 and was imprisoned from 1780 to 1783 for supplying money to the Americans. The house, with its characteristic sloped roof meant to discourage snow buildup and the raised end walls that served as firebreaks,

Will you have enough stories to tell your grandchildren?

©2000 Yahoo! Inc.

Yahoo! Travel

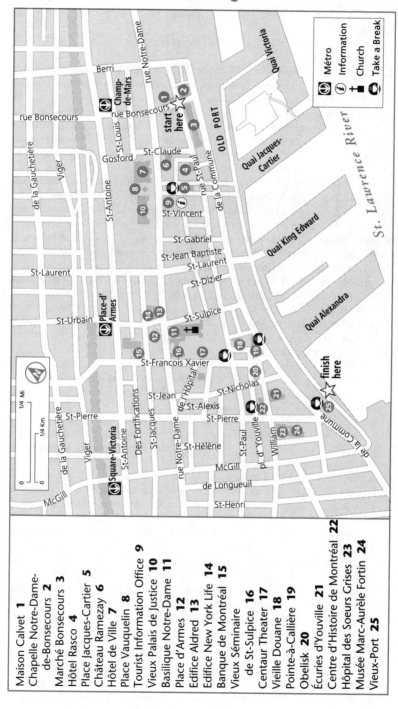

Walking Tour: Vieux-Montréal

Legend:
- Métro
- i Information
- ✛ Church
- Take a Break

St. Lawrence River

OLD PORT

start here

finish here

Streets labeled on map:
rue Notre-Dame, Berri, Champ-de-Mars, rue Bonsecours, St-Louis, Gosford, St-Claude, St-Paul, rue de la Commune, Quai Victoria, Quai Jacques-Cartier, St-Antoine, de la Gauchetière, Viger, St-Vincent, St-Gabriel, St-Jean Baptiste, St-Laurent, St-Dizier, Quai King Edward, Place-d'Armes, St-Urbain, St-Sulpice, St-Francois Xavier, Des Fortifications, St-Jacques, St-Jean, de l'Hôpital, St-Alexis, St-Nicholas, Quai Alexandra, St-Pierre, rue Notre-Dame, St-Hélène, McGill, de Longueuil, St-Henri, Square-Victoria, pl. d'Youville, William, St-Paul

1/4 Mi
1/4 Km

Maison Calvet **1**
Chapelle Notre-Dame-
  de-Bonsecours **2**
Marché Bonsecours **3**
Hôtel Rasco **4**
Place Jacques-Cartier **5**
Château Ramezay **6**
Hôtel de Ville **7**
Place Vauquelin **8**
Tourist Information Office **9**
Vieux Palais de Justice **10**
Basilique Notre-Dame **11**
Place d'Armes **12**
Edifice Aldred **13**
Edifice New York Life **14**
Banque de Montréal **15**
Vieux Séminaire
  de St-Sulpice **16**
Centaur Theater **17**
Vieille Douane **18**
Pointe-à-Callière **19**
Obelisk **20**
Écuries d'Youville **21**
Centre d'Histoire de Montréal **22**
Hôpital des Soeurs Grises **23**
Musée Marc-Aurèle Fortin **24**
Vieux-Port **25**

119

is constructed of Montréal graystone. It is now part of an inn, with an entrance at no. 405.

Continue to rue St-Paul, the oldest thoroughfare in Montréal (1672). There stands the small:

2. **Notre-Dame-de-Bonsecours Chapelle** (1673), or Sailors' Church. The church was founded by Marguerite Bourgeoys, a nun and teacher who was made a saint in 1982. Although recent excavations in the basement have unearthed foundations of her original 1675 church, the building has been altered often, and the present facade was built in the late 19th century. A museum tells the story of her life and incorporates a newly opened archaeological site. Historically, sailors saved at sea have made pilgrimages to the church to give thanks. Climb up to the tower for a view of the port and the Old Town.

Just beyond the Sailor's Church, heading west down rue St-Paul, is an imposing building with a colonnaded facade and silvery dome, the limestone:

3. **Marché Bonsecours (Bonsecours Market).** Completed in 1847, it was briefly used as the Parliament of United Canada, the City Hall, the central market, a music recital hall, and later the home of the municipality's housing and planning offices. The building was restored in 1992 to serve as a center for temporary exhibitions and musical performances during the city's 350th-birthday celebration. It continues to be used for exhibitions, celebrations, and the like. There are retail stalls inside, a new food market, and a sidewalk cafe near the entrance.

When the Bonsecours Market was first built, the dome could be seen from everywhere in the city. The Doric columns of the portico were cast of iron in England, and the prominent dome has long served as a landmark for seafarers steaming into the harbor.

Continue down rue St-Paul. At no. 281 is the former:

4. **Hôtel Rasco,** built in 1836 for Francisco Rasco, an Italian who came to Canada to manage a hotel for the Molson family and later became successful with his own hotel. The 150-room Rasco was the Ritz of its day in Montréal, hosting, among other honored guests, Charles Dickens and his wife in 1842 when the author was directing some of his plays at the theater that used to stand across the street. The hotel lives on in legend if not in fact, devoid of much of its original architectural detail. Rasco left in 1844, and the hotel slipped into decline. Between 1960 and 1981 it stood empty, but the city took it over and restored it in 1982. Now, however, its future again looks uncertain, despite the presence of a restaurant on the ground floor, for city officials can't seem to decide what to do with it.

Continue along rue St-Paul 1 more block to arrive at the focus of activity in Vieux-Montréal, a magnet for both citizens and tourists year-round, the:

5. **Place Jacques-Cartier.** Opened as a marketplace in 1804, it is easily the most appealing of the Old Town's squares. Its cobbled cross streets, gentle downhill slope, and ancient buildings set the mood, while outdoor cafes, street entertainers, itinerant artists, and flower vendors invite lingering, at least in warm weather. Calèches (horse-drawn carriages) depart from both the lower and upper ends of the square for tours of Vieux-Montréal.

🍵 **TAKE A BREAK** Some of the old buildings in and around Place Jacques-Cartier harbor restaurants and cafes. For a drink or a light meal, try to find a seat in **Le Jardin Nelson** (no. 407), on the east side of the square near the bottom of the hill. Sit in the courtyard in back when the weather is good—there often is live music—or on the terrace overlooking the activity of the square.

Walk slowly uphill, being sure to take in the old buildings that bracket the plaza. Plaques in French and English tell about some of them: the **Vandelac House** (no. 433), the **del Vecchio House** (nos. 404 to 410), and the **Cartier House** (no. 407). All these houses were well suited to the rigors of life in the raw young settlement. Their steeply pitched roofs shed the heavy winter snows rather than collapsing under the burden, and small windows with double casements let in light while keeping out wintry breezes. When shuttered, the windows were almost as effective as the heavy stone walls in deflecting hostile arrows or the antics of trappers fresh from raucous evenings in nearby taverns.

At the upper (northern) end of the plaza stands a monument to Horatio Nelson, hero of Trafalgar, erected in 1809. Originally, this monument preceded the much larger version in London by several years. However, after years of being subjected to vandalism, presumably by Québec separatists, the original statue was replaced by the one currently occupying the crown of the column.

At the top of the plaza, turn right. Past the new terraced park with its orderly ranks of trees, on the right, is:

6. Château Ramezay. Built by Claude de Ramezay between 1705 and 1706 in the French regime style of the period, this was the home of the city's French governors for 4 decades, starting with de Ramezay, before being taken over and used for the same purpose by the British.

In 1775 an army of American rebels invaded and held Montréal, using the château as their headquarters. Benjamin Franklin was sent to persuade Montréalers to join the American revolt against British rule. He stayed in the château but failed to sway Québec's leaders to join his cause.

The house has had other uses over the years. It was a courthouse, government office building, teachers' college, and headquarters for Laval University before becoming a museum in 1895. Inside are furnishings, tools, oil paintings, costumes, and other objects related to the economic and social activities of the 18th century and the first half of the 19th century.

Cross rue Notre-Dame from the Château Ramezay and walk west to the impressive:

7. Hôtel de Ville (Town Hall). Built between 1872 and 1878 in the florid French Second Empire style, the edifice houses the city's administrative offices, which moved here from Bonsecours Market, where they had been for 25 years. In 1922 the building barely survived a disastrous fire. Only the exterior walls remained, and after substantial rebuilding and the addition of another floor, it reopened in 1926.

Take a minute to look inside at the generous use of Italian marble, the art deco lamps, and the bronze-and-glass chandelier. The sculptures at the entry are *Woman with a Pail* and *The Sower,* both by Alfred Laliberté.

Continuing west, alongside City Hall is:

8. Place Vauquelin. This small public square, with a splashing fountain and a view of the Champ-de-Mars park (which lies behind and beneath the city hall), was created in 1858. The statue is of Jean Vauquelin, commander of the French fleet in New France. It stares across rue Notre-Dame at his counterpart, Nelson, two symbols of Montréal's duality. On the opposite corner is a small but helpful:

9. Tourist information office. A bilingual staff is ready to answer questions and hand out many useful brochures and maps (only from Thursday to Sunday in winter). On this site once stood the famed Silver Dollar Saloon, long since torn down. The tavern was named for 350 silver dollars embedded in its floor.

To the left of Place Vauquelin stands the imposing:

10. Vieux Palais de Justice (Old Court House). Most of the structure was built in 1856. The third floor and dome were added in 1891, as can be discerned on close examination. The Organizing Committee for the 1976 Olympic Games resided inside, and the city's civil cases continued to be tried here until a new courthouse, the Palais de Justice, was built next door in 1978. Civic departments for the city of Montréal are housed here now. The statue beside the Old Court House, called *Homage to Marguerite Bourgeoys,* is by sculptor Jules LaSalle.

Continue along rue Notre-Dame 5 more blocks, crossing rue St-Sulpice, to the magnificent Gothic Revival:

11. Basilique Notre-Dame (1829). This brilliant basilica was designed by James O'Donnell, an Irish architect living in New York. Transformed by his experience in building the church, he later converted to Roman Catholicism and is the only layman buried here. The main altar is made from a hand-carved linden tree. Behind the altar is the Chapel of the Sacred Heart (1982), a perennially popular choice for weddings. The chapel's altar, 32 bronze panels by Montréal artist Charles Daudelin, represents birth, life, and death. The church can seat 4,000 people, and its bell, one of the largest in North America, weighs 12 tons. There's a small museum beside the chapel.

The basilica faces:

12. Place d'Armes. The centerpiece of this square is a monument to city founder Paul de Chomedey, sieur de Maisonneuve (1612–76). It marks the spot where the settlers defeated Iroquois warriors in bloody hand-to-hand fighting, with de Maisonneuve himself locked in combat with the Iroquois chief. De Maisonneuve won and lived here another 23 years. The inscription on the monument reads, YOU ARE THE BUCKWHEAT SEED WHICH WILL GROW AND MULTIPLY AND SPREAD THROUGHOUT THE COUNTRY. The sculptures at the base of the monument represent three prominent citizens of early Montréal—Charles Lemoyne (1626–85), a farmer; Jeanne Mance, the founder of the first hospital in Montréal; and Raphael-Lambert Closse, a soldier and the mayor of Ville-Marie—and an Iroquois brave. Closse is depicted with his dog, Pilote, whose bark once warned the early settlers of an impending Iroquois attack.

On the opposite corner of the square from the basilica is the 23-story art deco:

13. Édifice Aldred, 507 place d'Armes. If the building looks somehow familiar, there's a reason: Built in 1931, it clearly resembles the Empire State Building in New York, also completed that year. The building's original tenant was Aldred and Co. Ltd., a New York–based multinational finance company with offices in New York, London, and Paris. Beside it stands the eight-story, red-sandstone:

14. Édifice New York Life, 511 place d'Armes, a Richardson Romanesque building with a striking wrought-iron door and clock tower. At all of eight stories, this was Montréal's first skyscraper back in 1888, and it was equipped with a technological marvel, an elevator.

Directly across the square from the statue of de Maisonneuve and the basilica is the domed, colonnaded:

15. Banque de Montréal. Montréal's oldest bank building dates from 1847. Besides being impressively proportioned and lavishly appointed inside and out, it houses a small banking museum that illustrates its early operations. Admission is free. From 1901 to 1905, American architect Stanford White was in charge of extending the original building beyond Ruelle des Fortifications to what is now rue St-Antoine. In this enlarged space he created a vast chamber with high, green-marble columns topped with golden capitals. The public is welcome to stop in for a look.

Opposite the square from the bank and adjacent to the basilica on rue Notre-Dame is the:

16. Vieux Séminaire de St-Sulpice. A seminary in the city's oldest building, which is surrounded by equally ancient stone walls, it was erected by the Sulpician priests who arrived in Ville-Marie in 1657, 15 years after the colony was founded. (The Sulpicians are part of an order founded in Paris by Jean-Jacques Olier in 1641.) The clock on the facade dates from 1701 and has a movement made almost entirely of wood. Unfortunately, the seminary is not open to the public.

Walk past the seminary, heading west on rue Notre-Dame, and turn left at rue St-François-Xavier. At rue de l'Hôpital, to the left, is the stately:

17. Centaur Theater. The home of Montréal's principal English-language theater is housed in a former stock-exchange building. The beaux arts architecture is interesting in that the two entrances are on either side rather than in the center of the facade. The building, erected in 1903, was designed by American architect George Post, who was also responsible for the New York Stock Exchange. It served in its original function until 1965, when it was redesigned as a theater with two stages.

Continue down rue St-François-Xavier. At rue St-Paul, turn left. **L'Air du Temps,** one of the city's most enduring jazz clubs, is on the corner, at no. 191.

Walk the short distance to 150 rue St-Paul and the neoclassical:

18. Vieille Douane (Old Customs House). Erected from 1836 to 1838, the building was doubled in size in 1882 to its present proportions by extending it to the south; walk around to the other side of the building for a look. That end of the building faces place Royale, the first public square in the early settlement of Ville-Marie. Europeans and Amerindians used to come here to trade.

Across the way, the modern, wedge-shaped building is the:

19. Pointe-à-Callière. Housing the Museum of Archaeology and History, with artifacts unearthed here during more than 10 years of excavation, this site was where Ville-Marie (Montréal) was founded in 1642. The museum also incorporates, via an underground connection, the Old Customs House you just passed.

A fort stood on this spot in 1645 as did, 30 years later, the château of a monsieur de Callière, from whom the building and triangular square take their names. At that time, the St. Pierre River separated this piece of land from the mainland; it was made a canal in the 19th century and later filled in.

☕ **TAKE A BREAK** One possibility for lunch or an afternoon pick-me-up is the casual, second-floor **L'Arrivage Café** at the museum. Another is the moderately priced **Stash** at 200 rue St-Paul Ouest, at rue St-François-Xavier, which specializes in Polish fare and is open from 11am until late in the evening.

Proceeding west of Pointe-à-Callière, near rue St-François-Xavier, stands an:

20. Obelisk commemorating the founding of Ville-Marie on May 18, 1642. The obelisk was erected here in 1893 by the Montréal Historical Society and bears the names of the city's early pioneers, including de Maisonneuve and Jeanne Mance.

Continuing west from the obelisk 2 blocks, look for the:

21. Écuries d'Youville (Youville Stables), on the left at 296–316 place d'Youville. Despite the name, the rooms in the iron-gated compound, built in 1825 on land owned by the Gray Nuns, were used mainly as warehouses, rather than to stable horses. Like much of the waterfront area, the "U"-shaped Youville building (the actual stables, next door, were made of wood and disappeared long ago) was run-down and forgotten until the 1960s, when a group of enterprising business people decided to buy and renovate the property. Today the compound contains offices and a popular restaurant, **Gibbys.** Go inside the courtyard and take a look if the gates are open, as they usually are.

Continue another block west to 335 rue St-Pierre and the:

22. Centre d'Histoire de Montréal (Montréal History Center). Built in 1903 as Montréal's Central Fire Station, it now houses exhibits, including many audio-visual ones, about the city's past and present. Visitors learn about the early routes of exploration, the fur trade, architecture, public squares, the railroad, and life in Montréal from 1920 to 1950.

Less than a block away, on the left at 138 rue St-Pierre, pass the former:

23. Hôpital des Soeurs Grises (Gray Nuns Hospital), which was in operation from 1693 to 1851 and now houses the administrative offices and a novitiate for future nuns. The order, founded by the widow Marguerite d'Youville in 1737, is officially known as the Sisters of Charity of Montréal. The present building incorporates several additions and was part of the city's General Hospital, run by the Charon Brothers but administered by d'Youville, who died here in 1771. The wing in which she died was restored in 1980. The wall of the original chapel remains. Visits inside must be arranged in advance. Call ☎ **514/842-9411** to arrange.

From here, look down rue St-Pierre for the brown awning at no. 118 that marks the entrance to the:

24. Musée Marc-Aurèle Fortin. This museum is devoted to a single Canadian artist. Fortin, who died in 1972, was known for his watercolors of the Québec countryside, including Charlevoix and the Laurentian Mountains. His depictions of elms recall the time when giant Dutch elms lined rues Sherbrooke and St-Joseph in Montréal, before blight decimated them.

Continue past the museum and cross rue de la Commune and the railroad tracks to enter the:

25. Vieux-Port (Old Port). Montréal's historic commercial wharves are now recycled as a waterfront park and frequented by cyclists, in-line skaters, joggers, walkers, strollers, lovers, and picnickers in good weather. This is the entry to **Parc des Écluses (Locks Park),** where the first locks on the St. Lawrence River are located.

☕ **TAKE A BREAK**   Enjoy a cafeteria-style snack at the **Maison des Écluses Café** (Locks House Café), open in summer only, in the new structure near the entry to Parc des Écluses.

From there, stroll back north along rue McGill to reach **Square Victoria** and its Métro station. Or pick up the beginning of the path along the **Lachine Canal** at Parc des Écluses and follow it for an hour or so to arrive at Montréal's colorful indoor/outdoor Atwater Market.

Walking Tour 2: Downtown Montréal

Start: Bonaventure Métro stop.
Finish: Musée McCord.
Time: 1½ hours.
Best Times: Weekdays in the morning or after 2pm, when the streets hum with big-city vibrancy but aren't too crowded.
Worst Times: Weekdays from noon to 2pm, when the streets, stores, and restaurants are crowded with businesspeople on lunch-break errands; Monday, when museums are closed; and Sunday, when most stores are closed and the area is virtually deserted (museums, however, are open).

After a tour of Vieux-Montréal, a look around the heart of the new 20th-century city provides ample contrast. To see the city at its contemporary best, take the Métro to the Bonaventure stop. Emerging from that station, the dramatic skyscraper immediately to the west is:

1. **1000 rue de la Gauchetière.** This recent contribution to the already memorable skyline is easily identified by its copper-and-blue pyramidal top, which rises to the maximum height permitted by the municipal building code. Inside, past an atrium planted with live trees, is the **Bell Amphitheatre,** a huge indoor skating rink bordered by cafes with seating for more than 1,500 spectators.

Walk west on rue de la Gauchetière. In 1 block, on the left, is:

2. **Le Marriott Château Champlain.** The hotel's distinctive facade of half-moon windows inspired its nickname, the "cheese grater."

Turn right next on rue Peel, walking north. In another block, this arrives at:

3. **Square Dorchester.** Its tall old trees and benches invite lunchtime brown-baggers. This used to be called Dominion Square, but it was renamed for Baron Dorchester, an early English governor, when the adjacent street, once named for him, was changed to boulevard René-Lévesque. Along the east side of the square is the **Sun Life Insurance building,** built in three stages between 1914 and 1931, and the tallest building in Québec until the skyscraper boom of the post–World War II era. This is also a gathering point for tour buses and calèches. In winter, the calèche drivers replace their carriages with sleighs and give rides around the top of Mont-Royal.

At the northeast corner of the square is the main office of:

4. **Infotouriste.** Many useful maps and brochures are in stock here, most of them free for the taking. Visitors can ask questions of bilingual attendants, change money, make hotel reservations, or rent a car.

From that office, go back to the other end of the square and turn left (east) on:

5. **Boulevard René-Lévesque.** Formerly Dorchester Boulevard, it was renamed in 1988 following the death of the Parti Québécois leader who led the movement in favor of Québec independence and the use of the French language. Boulevard René-Lévesque is the city's broadest downtown thoroughfare, and the one with the fastest traffic.

On the right is the:

6. **Cathédrale Marie-Reine-du-Monde (Mary Queen of the World Cathedral).** Built between 1875 and 1894 as headquarters for Montréal's Roman Catholic bishop, the cathedral is a less-than-successful copy of St. Peter's Basilica in Rome, built to roughly one-quarter scale. The statue in front of the cathedral is of Bishop Ignace Bourget (1799–1885), the force behind the construction of the basilica. It was sculpted in 1903 by Louis-Philippe Hébert, who was also responsible for the statue of de Maisonneuve in place d'Armes in Vieux-Montréal.

Walking Tour: Downtown Montréal

1 1000 rue de la Gauchetière
2 Le Marriott Château Champlain
3 Square Dorchester
4 Infotouriste
5 Boulevard René-Lévesque
6 Cathédral Marie-Reine-du-Monde
7 Le Reine Elisabeth/
     Queen Elizabeth Hotel
8 Place Ville-Marie
9 Carré Phillips
10 Christ Church Cathedral
11 Rue Ste-Catherine
12 Ogilvy
13 Rue Crescent
14 Musée des Beaux-Arts

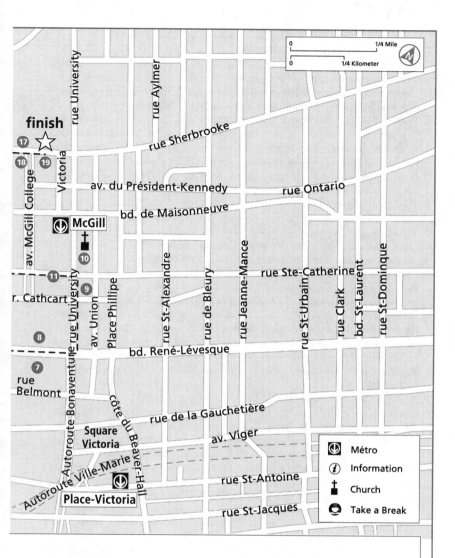

15 Maison Alcan
16 McGill University
17 Musée Redpath
18 *The Illuminated Crowd*
19 Musée McCord

Continuing past the cathedral and crossing rue Mansfield is the:

7. **La Reine Elizabeth/Queen Elizabeth Hôtel.** Opened in 1958, Montréal's largest hotel stands above **Gare Centrale,** the main railroad station, making it most convenient for people arriving by train. It also has direct access to the Underground City, and buses leave for Dorval and Mirabel airports from here.

Across boulevard René-Lévesque from the Queen Elizabeth is:

8. **Place Ville-Marie.** Known as PVM to Montréalers, this massive structure was keystone of the postwar urban redevelopment efforts in Montréal. The skyscraper, with its cross-shaped floor plan, was designed by I. M. Pei. It is meant to recall Cartier's cross, planted on Mount Royal to claim the island for France, and de Maisonneuve's first little settlement, Ville-Marie. The complex, completed in 1962, has a fountain in its plaza called *Feminine Landscape* (1972), executed by Toronto artist Gerald Gladstone.

At the end of the hotel, turn left along rue Université, crossing boulevard René-Lévesque and walking 2 blocks to rue Ste-Catherine. On the right is:

9. **Carré Phillips.** This plaza contains a statue of Edward VII and, much of the year, a farm stand. Over to the left, across rue Ste-Catherine, is:

10. **Cathedral Christ Church.** Built from 1856 to 1859, the neo-Gothic building is the seat of the Anglican bishop of Montréal. The cathedral's 127-foot aluminum-covered steel steeple replaced a heavier stone original that was threatening to collapse. Its garden is modeled on a medieval European cloister. The cathedral donated the land on which place de la Cathédrale and the shopping complex underneath it, Promenades de la Cathédrale, were built, in return for eventual ownership of the skyscraper and the underground complex. All those subterranean corridors and levels have caused some to dub it the "floating" or "flying" church.

Turn left on:

11. **Rue Ste-Catherine.** Then head west through the center of Montréal's shopping district. Most of the remaining department stores are along here, including, to the right of the church, La Baie (or "The Bay," short for Hudson's Bay Company, successor to the famous fur-trapping firm). Movie houses, cafes, and shops line rue Ste-Catherine for several blocks. At the corner of rue de la Montagne is:

12. **Ogilvy,** the most vibrant of a breed of store that appears to be fading from the scene. Founded in 1866, it strives to maintain its up-market stature by blending tradition with tasteful marketing strategies. Its Christmas windows are eagerly awaited each year, and a bagpiper announces openings, closings, and high noon. Note that Québec's language laws have rendered Ogilvy apostrophe-less.

Continue 1 more block to:

13. **Rue Crescent.** This and nearby streets are the locus of the center-city social and dining district, largely yuppie Anglo in character, if not necessarily in strict demographics. Pricey boutiques, inexpensive pizza joints, upscale restaurants, and dozens of bars and dance clubs draw enthusiastic, stylish consumers looking to spend money and find love or undemanding lust. This center of gilded youth and glamour was once a run-down slum area slated for demolition. Luckily, buyers with a good aesthetic sense saw the possibilities of these late 19th-century row houses and brought them back to life.

Turn right on rue Crescent and:

☕ **TAKE A BREAK**   For a quiet spot to munch on a croissant or sip some strong coffee, choose **Café Via Crescent,** on the left side, on the ground floor of the Château Royal Hotel. Walkers who prefer a livelier setting can opt for **Thursdays,** opposite, or walk a little farther up rue Crescent and get a sidewalk table at **Sir Winston Churchill Pub.**

Continue up rue Crescent, past boulevard de Maisonneuve, to the corner of rues Crescent and Sherbrooke. On this left corner, and on the opposite side of Sherbrooke, is the:

14. Musée des Beaux-Arts (Museum of Fine Arts). You've arrived at Canada's oldest and Montréal's most prominent museum. The modern annex on this side was added in 1991 and is connected to the stately beaux arts original building (1912) across the way by an underground tunnel that doubles as a gallery. Both buildings are made of Vermont marble.

Turn right on rue Sherbrooke, passing, at the next corner, the Holt Renfrew department store, identified on its marquee only as HOLTS. Continue on rue Sherbrooke, soon passing, on the right, the:

15. Maison Alcan. This structure has been frequently lauded for its incorporation of 19th-century houses into its late–20th-century facade. Step inside the lobby to see the results, especially over to the right.

In 4 more blocks in the same direction, on the opposite side of rue Sherbrooke, is the entrance to:

16. McGill University. The gate is usually open to this, Canada's most prestigious university. Step inside and see, just to the left, a large stone that designates the site of the native Horchelaga settlement that existed here before the arrival of the Europeans.

Also on the campus is the:

17. Musée Redpath. The building dates from 1882, and the museum's main draw is the Egyptian antiquities collection, the second largest of its kind in Canada.

Opposite the university, and just half a block south of rue Sherbrooke, on the left, is a now cream-colored resin sculpture called:

18. The Illuminated Crowd (1979). Toronto artist Raymond Mason's sculpture is frequently photographed and widely admired for its evocation of the human condition, although its detractors find it sentimental and obvious. Circle it at leisure and then return to rue Sherbrooke, turning right.

One block east is the:

19. Musée McCord, 690 rue Sherbrooke. The private museum of Canadian history first opened in 1921 and was substantially renovated and expanded in 1992. Named for its founder, David Ross McCord (1844–1930), the McCord has an eclectic and often eccentric collection of 80,000 artifacts. Furniture, clothing, china, silver, paintings, photographs, and folk art reveal elements of city and rural life from the 18th to the 20th century. Amerindians are represented in the First Nations room.

Walking Tour 3: Plateau Mont-Royal

Start: The corner of avenue du Mont-Royal and rue St-Denis.
Finish: Square St-Louis.
Time: At least 2 hours, but allow more time to explore this intriguing neighborhood at length.
Best Times: Monday through Saturday during the day, when the shops are open. Boulevard St-Laurent is at its liveliest on Saturday.
Worst Times: Sunday, when most stores are closed, if shopping is important to you. But for barhopping, evenings are fine, too.

This is essentially a browsing and grazing tour, sampling the sea of ethnicities known as Plateau Mont-Royal, north of downtown Montréal and due east of Mont-Royal Park. The neighborhood, which in recent years has seen an explosion of restaurants, cafes, clubs, and shops, is bounded on the south by rue Sherbrooke, on the north by boulevard St-Joseph, on the east by avenue Papineau, and on the west by rue St-Dominique. Monuments and obligatory sights are few along these commercial avenues and the residential side streets, whose row houses are home to students, young professionals, and immigrants old and new. This walk is, more than an architectural tour, an opportunity to get to know established and freshly minted Montréalers and the way they live and amuse themselves.

To begin, take the Métro to the Mont-Royal station. There's a fruit stand out front. Turn left, walking west on avenue du Mont-Royal to St-Denis. Turn left. In the coming blocks, there's much to discover. Some highlights follow, with the caveat that things change with considerable frequency: stores and bistros open and close, businesses change hands.

On the left side of the street is:

1. **Quai des Brumes,** 4481 rue St-Denis. This popular gathering spot for jazz, blues, and beer offers live music most evenings, and even some afternoons. Its name means "Foggy Dock." (Ignore the overhead CAFE CENTRAL sign.)

Go back to the corner and cross the street to:

2. **Requin Chagrin,** 4430 rue St-Denis. Check out this retro shop with a good selection of secondhand clothing. Farther along is:

3. **Champigny,** 4380 rue St-Denis. A large bookstore with mostly French stock, it carries travel guides and literature in English, as well as CDs, magazines, and newspapers in many languages from all over the world. It's open 7 days until midnight.

Cross rue Marie-Anne. On the left corner is:

4. **Interversion Mobilier—Creations Québécois,** 4349 rue St-Denis. Here you'll find a showroom that displays and sells contemporary Québécois furniture.

☕ **TAKE A BREAK** At 4325 rue St-Denis, ✪ **Fonduementale** specializes in what it says—fondues as appetizers, as main courses, as desserts. Excess is not without its virtues. The turn-of-the-century house has a terrace in front and a garden.

If you don't need a break just yet, continue down the right side of St-Denis to:

5. **Côte Sud,** 4338 rue St-Denis. Shelves of distinctive glassware make room for cooking and dining implements, including chef's knives, flatware, china, and related items, such as aluminum canisters and candles. They fill two floors of connecting buildings.

Not far down the street is:

6. **Départ en Mer,** 4306 rue St-Denis. A nautical theme prevails, with brass navigation instruments, bells, fisherman shirts, and a variety of ship models ranging in price from a handful of loonies to several hundred dollars. Most of the merchandise is produced in France.

A few doors further along is:

7. **Le Centre d'Artisanat,** 4274 rue St-Denis. Its wares are Afghan rugs and Pakistan jewelry, and wall hangings, small furniture pieces, and crafts from the Middle East and south Asia.

Continue down to:

8. **Zone,** 4246 rue St-Denis, where contemporary housewares are purveyed, most of them sleekly monochromatic, some brightly hued.

Walking Tour: Plateau Mont-Royal

Quai de Brumes **1**
Requin Chagrin **2**
Champigny **3**
Interversion Mobilier–
   Creations Québecois **4**
Côte Sud **5**
Départ en Mer **6**
Le Centre d'Artisanat **7**
Zone **8**
Antiques Puces-Libre **9**
Continental Bistro Américain **10**

Artefact **11**
Kaliyana **12**
Senteurs de Provence **13**
Rue Duluth **14**
Boulevard St-Laurent **15**
Schwartz's **16**
La Vieille Europe **17**
Androgyne **18**
Le Swimming **19**
Rue Prince-Arthur **20**
Square St-Louis **21**

Nearby is the wonderfully cluttered:

9. **Antiques Puces-Libre,** 4240 rue St-Denis. It offers three floors of 19th-century French-Canadian country collectibles—pine and oak furniture, lamps, clocks, vases, and much more.

From there, at rue Rachel, cross to the left side of the street and continue south to:

10. **Continental Bistro Américain,** 4169 rue St-Denis. Despite the name, this bistro is no more American than the Café Deux Magots on the Left Bank. It's populated with people who look as if they read *Le Monde* and smoke Gauloises, and men who see no point in shaving more than twice a week.

Just down the street is:

11. **Artefact,** 4117 rue St-Denis. Québécois designers and artists display (and sell) clothing and paintings at this shop.

After that, look for:

12. **Kaliyana,** 4107 rue St-Denis. Loose and comfortable clothing for women is created by a Czech-born designer who uses hand-printed fabrics.

Next, you'll come upon:

13. **Senteurs de Provence,** 4077 rue St-Denis. One of a small chain, it displays hand-painted pottery and printed linens, as well as bath soaps, shower gels, and lotions of high order, all from France.

At the corner of St-Denis and rue Duluth, cross over and walk west along:

14. **Rue Duluth.** The street is dotted with Greek, Portuguese, Italian, North African, Malaysian, and Vietnamese eateries, as well as several small antique shops.

Continue along rue Duluth until it ends at a north-south thoroughfare—one so prominent in the cultural history of the city that it's known to Anglophones, Francophones, and Allophones alike simply as "The Main."

Turn left on:

15. **Boulevard St-Laurent.** Traditionally a beachhead for immigrants to Montréal, St-Laurent has increasingly become a street of chic bistros and clubs. The late-night section runs for several miles, roughly from rue Laurier all the way down to rue Sherbrooke. This trend has been fueled by low rents and the large number of industrial lofts in this area, a legacy of St-Laurent's heyday as a garment-manufacturing center. Today these cavernous spaces have been converted into restaurants and clubs, many of which have the life spans of fireflies, but some of which pound on for years.

Soon, there is:

16. **Schwartz's,** at 3895 bd. St-Laurent. The language police insisted on the exterior sign with the French mouthful CHEZ SCHWARZ CHARCUTERIE HÉBRAÏQUE DE MONTRÉAL, but everyone just calls it Schwartz's. This narrow, no-frills deli serves the smoked meat against which all other versions must be measured. Vegetarians and those who require more (or some) distance from their neighbors' elbows will hate it.

Next, a few steps along, is:

17. **La Vieille Europe,** at 3855 bd. St-Laurent. The "Old Europe" delicatessen sells aromatic coffee beans from many nations, sausages and meats, cheeses, and cooking utensils.

Cross to the other side and continue south to:

18. **Androgyne,** at 3636 bd. St-Laurent. This gay, lesbian, and feminist bookstore is one of the best places to connect with activities in Montréal's gay community.

On the opposite side of the street is:

19. Le Swimming, 3643 bd. St-Laurent. If you stop by, you'll find a bar downstairs and an upstairs hall with a dozen pool tables.

Continue down boulevard St-Laurent and turn left (east) into:

20. Rue Prince-Arthur. Named after Queen Victoria's third son, who was governor-general of Canada from 1911 to 1916, it's a pedestrian street filled with bars and restaurants, most of which add more to the liveliness of the street than to the gastronomic reputation of the city. Establishments go by such names as La Caverne Grecque, La Gourmet Grec, Cabane Grecque, Casa Grecque—no doubt you will discern an emerging theme. Their owners vie constantly with gimmicks to haul in passersby, including two-drinks-for-the-price-of-one and dueling table d'hôte prices that plummet to C$7 (US$4.85) or lower for three courses. Beer and sangría are the popular drinks at the white resin tables and chairs set out along the sides of the street. Mimes, vendors, street performers, and caricaturists also compete for the tourist dollar.

Five blocks along, rue Prince-Arthur ends at:

21. Square St-Louis. This public garden plaza is framed by attractive row houses erected for well-to-do Francophones in the late 19th and early 20th centuries. People stretch out on the grass to take the sun or sit bundled on benches willing March away. Among them are usually a few harmless derelicts and street people. On occasional summer days, there are impromptu concerts. The square ends at rue St-Denis.

From here, bear left onto rue Cherrier to catch the Métro at the Sherbrooke station, less than half a block away.

Walking Tour 4: Mont-Royal

Start: At the corner of rue Peel and avenue des Pins.
Finish: At the cross on top of the mountain.
Time: Two hours, allowing for some dawdling. If you're pressed for time, it's possible to get to the lookout in a little more than half an hour and back down the mountain in 15 minutes.
Best Times: Spring, summer, and autumn mornings.
Worst Times: Winter, when snow and slush make a sleigh ride to the top of the mountain much more enticing than a hike.

Assuming a reasonable measure of physical fitness, a most enjoyable way to explore Parc Mont-Royal is simply to hike up from downtown. Joggers, cyclists, in-line skaters, and anyone in search of a little greenery and space head here in warm weather. In winter, cross-country skiers follow the miles of paths within the park, and snow-shoers tramp along trails laid out especially for them. The 494-acre (200-hectare) park was created in 1876 to a plan by American landscape architect Frederick Law Olmsted, who designed Central Park in New York City, as well as parks in Philadelphia, Boston, and Chicago.

Start this tour at the corner of rue Peel and avenue des Pins, at the:

1. Downtown park entrance. A handy map at the site helps to set bearings. From here, it's possible to ascend the mountain by several routes. Hearty souls can choose the quickest and most strenuous approach—scaling the steep slope directly to the lookout at the top. Those who prefer to take their time and gain altitude slowly can take one short set of stairs followed by a switchback bridle path (turn left onto it) leading to the top. The approach outlined here falls somewhere in between but points out the other alternatives as they arrive.

Take the gravel path to the right (facing the map of the park). It has intervals of four to six steps, and parallels the wall that separates the park from the outside world. When the path dead-ends, turn left (away from the steep steps seen beside a small lookout).

Those who have chosen the athletic route can take the next:

2. Stairs on the right. *Fair warning:* There are more than 250 steps in all, and the last 100 go almost straight up. For a less taxing route, stay on the wide:

3. Chemin Olmsted (Olmsted Road), named for the park's designer and actually the only part of his design that became a reality. Following this road will bypass a few of this tour's stops and get to the next stop (no. 6) in about 45 minutes.

Frederick Law Olmsted designed the road at such a gradual grade not only for pedestrians, but also for horse-drawn calèches. Horses could pull their loads up the hill at a steady pace, and on the way down would not be pushed from behind by the weight of the carriage. Chemin Olmsted is closed to automobiles. Early on, it passes some beautiful stone houses off Redpath Circle, to the left. A couple of paths lead up the mountain to the right. They get walkers to their destination more quickly but aren't as strenuous as the steps recently bypassed. So if the road begins to seem a little too slow, take the:

4. Steps that eventually appear on the right. They lead to an old pump station, to the right. From here, continue in an uphill direction until you arrive at a:

5. Covered picnic area. At this open-air stone-and-wood structure with a copper roof—take a snack break, if you wish—walk around behind the shelter and take the stairway behind it down the hill, which descends again to Chemin Olmsted, minus a couple of big loops edited out of the walk. Up ahead is the back of the:

6. Maison Smith. Built in 1858, this structure has been used as a park rangers' station and park police headquarters. From 1983 to 1992 it served as a small nature museum. Nearby is the 300-foot-high Radio Canada Tower.

From the house, walk through the field of rather undistinguished sculptures, away from the radio tower, until you reach:

7. Lac des Castors (Beaver Lake). The name refers to the once-profitable fur industry, not to the actual presence of the long-gone animals. In summer it's surrounded by sunbathers and picnickers and filled with boaters. In the cold winter months before the snow sets in, it becomes an ice-skater's paradise. Once the pond is covered with snow, the small ski tow starts operation, tugging novice skiers up the gentle slope for practice runs down and across the pond's face.

There's a small concession stand in the pavilion here, but if you're planning to have something to eat or drink on the mountain, wait for the snack bar at the chalet at the nearby lookout. Both the chalet and the pavilion have rest rooms and telephones.

Walk across the road, called Chemin de la Remembrance (Remembrance Road), behind the pavilion, to enter:

8. Notre-Dame-des-Neiges Cemetery. From this, the city's Catholic cemetery, you can visit the adjacent Protestant Mount Royal graveyard and then behind it (to the north), if you're up for a time-consuming walk, see the small adjoining Jewish and Spanish-Portuguese cemetery. Notre-Dame-des-Neiges Cemetery reveals much of the ethnic mix in Montréal. There are headstones, some with likenesses in photos or tiles, for Montréalers with surnames as diverse as Zagorska, Skwyrska, De Ciccio, Sen, Lavoie, Barrett, O'Neill, Hammerschmid, Fernandez, Müller, Giordano, Haddad, and Boudreault.

Walking Tour: Mont-Royal

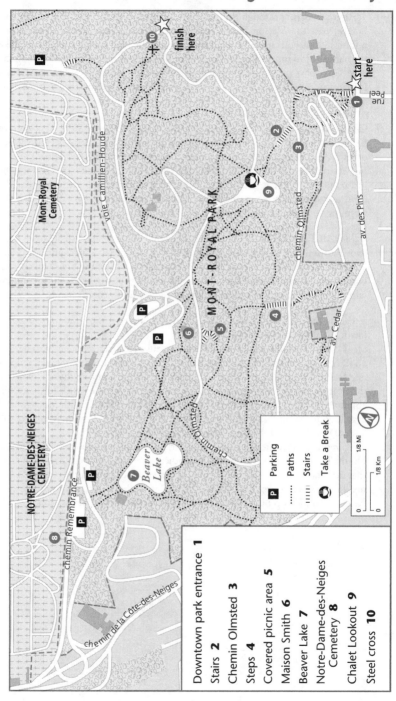

Key to map labels:

1 Downtown park entrance
2 Stairs
3 Chemin Olmsted
4 Steps
5 Covered picnic area
6 Maison Smith
7 Beaver Lake
8 Notre-Dame-des-Neiges Cemetery
9 Chalet Lookout
10 Steel cross

Map legend:
- P Parking
- ········ Paths
- |||||||| Stairs
- ⬤ Take a Break

Labels on map: start here, finish here, rue Peel, av. des Pins, chemin Olmsted, av. Cedar, voie Camillien-Houde, Mont-Royal Cemetery, NOTRE-DAME-DES-NEIGES CEMETERY, chemin Remembrance, chemin de la Côte-des-Neiges, chemin Olmsted, Beaver Lake, MONT-ROYAL PARK

Scale: 1/8 Mi, 1/8 Km

After wandering through this part of the cemetery, return to Chemin Remembrance, pass the Maison Smith again, and continue along the road for a few minutes until you arrive at a water spigot embedded in a granite slab. Take the narrow blacktop path (not the dirt one) below it through the trees. Along the way, look for a tree trunk carved by artist Jacques Morin in 1986; part of the inscription explains: an "old, sick tree, sculpted and transformed, neither male nor female . . ."

The path leads to the:

9. Chalet Lookout. The chalet was constructed in 1931 to 1932 at a cost of $230,000 and has been used over the years for receptions, concerts, and various other events. Inside the chalet, note the 17 paintings hanging just below the ceiling, starting to the right of the door that leads into the snack bar. They tell the history of the region as well as of the French explorations in North America. The front terrace offers a panoramic view of the city and the river. In winter, there's a warming room for skiers here.

☕ **TAKE A BREAK**   The concession stand in the chalet, usually open daily 9am to 5pm, sells sandwiches, muffins, apples, ice cream, milk, juice, tea, and coffee. Heed the signs that ask patrons to refrain from feeding the squirrels seen begging so adorably. These cute scavengers can find plenty to eat on the mountain, but they're not above snatching food right out of people's hands.

Facing the chalet from the terrace, locate the path running off to the right. Follow it for about 8 minutes to a giant:

10. Steel cross. Tradition has it that de Maisonneuve erected a wooden cross here in 1642. The present incarnation, erected in 1924, is lighted at night, making it visible from all over the city. Beside the cross is a plaque marking the spot where a time capsule was placed in August 1992, during Montréal's 350th-birthday celebration. Some 12,000 children ages 6 to 12 filled the capsule with messages and drawings depicting their visions for the city in the year 2142, when Montréal will be 500 years old and the capsule will be opened.

To return to downtown Montréal, return along the path to the chalet terrace. On the left, just before the terrace, is another path. It leads to the 250 or so steps that descend to where this tour began, at the entrance to the park. Or catch bus no. 11 at Beaver Lake, hop off at Chemin de la Remembrance and Côte-des-Neiges, and pick up bus no. 165, which goes to the Guy Métro station.

Montréal Shopping 8

Whether you view shopping as a focus of your travels or just a diversion, you won't be disappointed in Montréal. It ranks right up there with dining out as a prime activity among the natives. Most Montréalers are of French ancestry, after all, and seem to believe that impeccable taste bubbles through the Gallic gene pool. The city has produced a thriving fashion industry, from couture to ready-to-wear, with a history that reaches back to the earliest trade in furs and leather. In any event, it is unlikely that any reasonable consumer need—and even outlandish fantasies—cannot be met here. There are more than 1,500 shops in the Underground City alone, and many more than that at street level and above.

1 The Shopping Scene

American visitors have the advantage of a markdown on all prices encountered in Montréal shops due to the contrast in exchange rates between the Canadian and U.S. dollars. When traveling with U.S. dollars, go to a bank to exchange cash or traveler's checks for Canadian currency—or, better yet, withdraw Canadian dollars from a local ATM with either a credit card or debit card. While stores typically accept U.S. currency (in both dollars and traveler's checks), the exchange is likely to be less favorable than that obtained in a bank. There are exceptions, however, as some stores, in an attempt to attract customers carrying U.S. funds, put out signs offering better exchange rates.

Note that when you're making purchases with a credit card, the charges are automatically converted at the going bank rate before appearing on the following monthly statement. In most cases, this is the best deal of all for visitors. Visa and MasterCard are the most popular bank cards in this part of Canada, while Discover is less frequently accepted by shops, and American Express only reluctantly.

THE BEST BUYS

Most items are priced at approximately the same costs as in their countries of origin, including such big international names as Burberry and Ralph Lauren.

Exceptions are British products, including **tweeds, porcelain,** and **glassware,** which tend to cost less. While not cheap, **Inuit sculptures** and 19th- to early–20th-century **country furniture** are handsome and

---

Store Hours _____

Most stores are open Monday to Wednesday 9:30am to 6pm, Thursday and Friday 10am to 9pm, and Saturday and Sunday 10am to 5pm. Department stores downtown tend to open at 10am and are closed on Sundays.

---

authentic. Less expensive crafts than the intensely collected Inuit works are also produced, including quilts, drawings, and carvings by Amerindian and other folk artists. While demand has diminished somewhat, superbly constructed furs and leather goods are high-ticket items for which you can retrieve the high sales taxes. In addition, Québec's daring clothing designers produce some appealing fashions at often reasonable prices.

THE BEST SHOPPING AREAS

Rue Sherbrooke is a major shopping street for international and domestic designers, luxury items such as furs and jewelry, art galleries, and the Holts department store. **Rue Crescent** has a number of scattered upscale boutiques and numerous cafes for a break from shopping. **Boulevard St-Laurent** covers everything from budget practicalities to off-the-wall handmade fashions. Look along **avenue Laurier** between St-Laurent and de l'Epée for French boutiques, home accessories shops, and young Québécois designers. **Rue St-Paul** in Vieux-Montréal has a growing number of art galleries, a few jewelry shops, souvenir stands, and a shop that sells kites.

    Antiques can be found along rue Sherbrooke near the Musée des Beaux-Arts and on the little side streets near the museum. More antiques and collectibles, in more than 50 tempting shops one after another, can be found along the lengthening "Antiques Alley" of **rue Notre-Dame,** especially concentrated between Guy and Atwater. Artists display and sell their largely undistinguished but nevertheless often-competent works along compact **rue St-Amable,** just off place Jacques-Cartier. From there, meander into a walkway called **Le Jardin Amable** to find a courtyard filled with kiosks stocked with eye-catching costume jewelry and items crafted in silver and gold. **Rue St-Denis** north of Sherbrooke has strings of shops filled with fun and funky items.

    Some of the best shops in Montréal are found in city museums; tops among them are **Pointe-è-Callière,** the Montréal Museum of Archaeology and History in Vieux-Montréal, and the **Musée des Beaux-Arts** and the **Musée McCord,** both on rue Sherbrooke in the center city.

    Rue Ste-Catherine is home to the city's four top department stores and myriad satellite shops, while **rue Peel** is known for its men's fashions and some crafts. **Avenue Greene** in Anglophone Westmount has some decidedly English stores. Most of Montréal's big department stores were founded when Scottish, Irish, and English families dominated the city's mercantile class, and most of their names are identifiably English, albeit shorn of their apostrophes. The principal exception is La Baie, French for "The Bay," itself a shortened reference to an earlier name, the Hudson's Bay Company. Montréal's long history as a center for the fur trade buttresses the many wholesale and retail furriers, with outlets downtown and in Plateau Mont-Royal, but nowhere more concentrated than the "fur row" of **rue Mayor,** between rue de Bleury and rue City Councillors.

    For those who delight in the hunt for bargains and possess a willingness to plunge into barely managed chaos to find them won't want to miss **rue Chabanel.** It's a long trek north from downtown (nearest Métro station: Crémazie), a street that runs west of boulevard St-Laurent and is lined with factory buildings and warehouses. On

Saturday mornings from 8:30am to 1pm—very much more-or-less—the clothing manufacturers and importers use ground and mezzanine level showrooms and suites to put out all manner of men's, women's, and children's clothing for sale just those few hours a week (usually not in January or July). Coats, leather goods, sportswear, suits, sweaters—all are on offer at deeply discounted prices, and diligence and a willingness to bargain are rewarded. Prowl the 8 blocks numbered 99 to 555; the higher the number, the better the quality, or at least so goes the commonly held conviction.

SHOPPING COMPLEXES

A unique facet of Montréal, the **Underground City** is a warren of passageways connecting more than 1,500 shops in 10 shopping complexes that have levels both above and below street level. **Complexe Desjardins** is bounded by rues Jeanne-Mance, Ste-Catherine, St-Urbain, and boulevard René-Lévesque (☎ 514/281-1870). It has waterfalls and fountains, trees and hanging vines, music, lanes of shops going off in every direction, and elevators whisking people up to one of the four tall office towers or into the Wyndham hotel (formerly Le Meridien). **Les Cours Mont-Royal,** 1455 rue Peel at boulevard de Maisonneuve (☎ 514/842-7777), is a recycling of the old Mount Royal Hotel, lately adding a 20,000-square-foot Harry Rosen fashion emporium. **Place Bonaventure,** at rues de la Gauchetière and University (☎ 514/397-2325), has some 125 boutiques beneath the Bonaventure Hilton. **Place Montréal Trust,** at 1500 rue McGill at rue Ste-Catherine (☎ 514/843-8000), is a five-story shopping complex incorporating a Planet Hollywood. **Place Ville-Marie,** opposite La Reine Elizabeth hotel, between boulevard René-Lévesque and Cathcart (☎ 514/861-9393), was Montréal's first major postwar shopping complex, known locally simply as "PVM." **Les Promenades de la Cathédrale,** at the corner of rue University and rue Ste-Catherine (☎ 514/849-9925), has more than 100 shops on the levels below the Cathédrale Christ Church. The new **Ruelle des Fortifications,** on rue St-Pierre between St-Antoine and St-Jacques (☎ 514/982-9888), is in the Centre Mondial du Commerce (World Trade Center), at the edge of Vieux-Montréal. There are more than 80 upscale boutiques, centered on two fountains, one modern and one traditional. **Westmount Square,** at rue Wood and rue Ste-Catherine (☎ 514/932-0211), combines a shopping center, an office complex, and a condominium complex designed by the famed Mies van der Rohe.

2 Shopping from A to Z

ANTIQUES

The best place to find antiques and collectibles is in the more than 50 storefronts along Rue Notre-Dame between rues Guy and Atwater. Or visit:

Antiques Puces-Libres. 4240 rue St-Denis (near rue Rachel). ☎ **514/842-5931.**

Three fascinatingly cluttered floors are packed with pine and oak furniture, lamps, clocks, vases, and more, most of it 19th- and early–20th-century French-Canadian art nouveau.

ARTS & CRAFTS

Boutique Canadiana Worn Doorstep. 350 St-Paul Est, Vieux-Montréal. ☎ **514/397-0666.**

The ongoing development of the Bonsecours Market has altered focus from temporary exhibitions to shops and food stalls. This one concentrates on crafts, children's storybooks, maps, small furniture, and packaged foods, all with a Canadian connection.

Taxes & Refunds

Although taxes are high, visitors can obtain refunds of those incurred for lodgings or shop purchases (but not for food or drink, auto rentals, or other transportation). Save your sales receipts from any store in Montréal or the rest of Québec, and ask shopkeepers for tax-refund forms. After returning home, mail the originals (not copies) to the specified address with the completed form. Refunds usually take a few months but are in the currency of the applicant's home country. A small service fee is charged. For faster refunds, follow the same procedure, but hand in the receipts and form at a duty-free shop designated in the government pamphlet *Tax Refund for Visitors to Canada,* available at tourist offices and in many stores and hotels.

Guilde Canadienne des Métier d'Art Québec. 2025 rue Peel (at bd. de Maisonneuve). ☎ **514/849-6091.**

A small but choice collection of craft items is displayed in a meticulously arranged gallery setting. Among the objects are blown glass, paintings on silk, pewter, tapestries, and ceramics. The stock is particularly strong in avant-garde jewelry and Inuit sculpture. A small carving might be had for C$100 to C$200 (US$69 to US$138), but the larger, more important pieces go for hundreds, even thousands, more.

L'Empreinte. 272 rue St-Paul Est, Vieux-Montréal. ☎ **514/861-4427.**

This is a *coopérative artisane* (a craftspersons' collective) 1 block off place Jacques-Cartier at the corner of rue du Marché Bonsecours. The ceramics, textiles, glassware, and other items on sale often occupy that vaguely defined territory between art and craft. Quality is uneven but usually tips toward the high end.

La Guilde Graphique. 9 rue St-Paul Ouest, Vieux-Montréal. ☎ **514/844-3438.**

More than 200 contemporary artists are represented here, working in a variety of media and techniques but producing primarily works on paper, including drawings, serigraphs, etchings, lithographs, and woodcuts. Some of the artists can often be seen working in the upstairs studio.

BOOKS

Canadian Centre for Architecture Bookstore. 1920 rue Baile (rue du Fort). ☎ **514/939-7020.**

This bookstore may be the Centre's most engrossing department; it features a comprehensive selection of books on architecture, with emphasis on Montréal in particular and Canada in general. Volumes are also available on landscape and garden history, photography, preservation, conservation, design, and city planning.

Champigny. 4380 rue St-Denis (at rue Marie-Anne). ☎ **514/844-2587.**

For those who know the language or want to brush up, this two-level French bookstore is a valuable resource. It also sells tapes, CDs, and newspapers and magazines from all over the world. Authors read here on Saturday and Sunday.

Chapters. 1171 rue Ste-Catherine Ouest (at rue Stanley). ☎ **514/849-8825.**

This is the flagship store of a chain with many branches, the result of a merger between the Smithbooks and Coles booksellers. Thousands of titles are available in French and English on both general and specialized subjects.

Paragraphe. 2220 av. McGill College (south of rue Sherbrooke). ☎ **514/845-5811.**

Prowl the rows of shelves in this long storefront, then take your purchases to the adjoining Second Cup cafe, popular with students from the McGill campus, a block away. The store hosts frequent autograph parties, author readings, and occasional musical performances.

Ulysse. 4176 rue St-Denis. ☎ **514/843-9447.** Also 560 av. du Président-Kennedy (at Alymer). ☎ **514/843-7222.**

Traveler needs are served by this good stock of guidebooks, many in English, as well as accessories, including maps, day packs, money pouches, electrical adapters, sewing kits, coffeemakers, and pill cases.

CLOTHING
FOR MEN
America. 1101 Ste-Catherine Ouest (at rue Peel). ☎ **514/289-9609.**

One of the many links in a popular Canadian chain, it carries casual and dressy clothes, including suits, jackets, and slacks. There's a women's section upstairs. Among several other local outlets is the one at Place Montréal Trust.

Brisson & Brisson. 1472 rue Sherbrooke Ouest (near rue Mackay). ☎ **514/937-7456.**

Apparel of the nipped-and-trim British and European cut fills three floors, from makers as diverse as Burberry, Brioni, and Valentino.

Club Monsieur. 1407 rue Crescent (near bd. de Maisonneuve). ☎ **514/843-5476.**

Hugo and Boss styles prevail, for those with the fit frames to carry them and the required discretionary income.

L'Uomo. 1452 rue Peel (near rue Ste-Catherine). ☎ **514/844-1008.**

Largely Italian menswear by such forward-thinking designers as Cerruti, Missoni, Ungaro, Versace, Armani, and Dolce & Gabbana. A branch, Via Uomo, is down the street at 1478 rue Peel (☎ **514/284-0104**).

FOR WOMEN
Ambre. 201 rue St-Paul Ouest (at place Jacques-Cartier). ☎ **514/982-0325.**

Sonia Kozma is the star designer here, of fashionable suits, cocktail dresses, and dinner and casual wear made of linen, rayon, and cotton. And to go with the clothes, there are bold but complementary accessories.

Artefact Montréal. 4117 rue St-Denis (near rue Rachel). ☎ **514/842-2780.**

Browse here among articles of clothing and paintings by up-and-coming Québecois designers and artists.

Kyoze. Centre Mondial du Commerce, 393 rue St-Jacques Ouest, second floor. ☎ **514/847-7572.**

The eye-catching creations of Québecois and other Canadian designers are featured, including jewelry and accessories. There's a downtown outlet at 1455 rue Peel in Les Cours Mont-Royal (☎ **514/849-6552**).

UNISEX
Aritmetik. 3688 bd. St-Laurent (north of Sherbrooke).

This fun shop features sportswear by young, forward-looking Toronto and California designers of a sort you don't see everywhere. There are other branches at 2011 rue

St-Denis (☎ **514/847-8965**) and in the Cours Mont-Royal mall downtown
(☎ **514/ 286-0565**).

Club Monaco. 1455 rue Peel (north of rue Ste-Catherine). ☎ **514/499-0959.**

Awareness of this expanding Canadian-owned international chain is growing, as is
appreciation of its minimalist, monochromatic garments for men and women, along
with silver jewelry, eyewear, and cosmetics. Think Prada but affordable, with a helpful
young staff.

EnrgXchange. 1455 rue Peel (in Les Cours Mont-Royal). ☎ **514/2823-0912.**

If you're young and sleek, male or female, the stretchy garments purveyed here
shouldn't put you off, nor will the substantial discounts on items from terminated
lines by Dolce & Gabbana, Moschino, Helmut Lang, and others of their acknowledged loftiness.

Felix Brown. 1233 rue Ste-Catherine Ouest (at rue Drummond). ☎ **514/287-5523.**

A diverse selection of designers and manufacturers, mostly Italian, makes choices difficult. Among them are Bruno Magli, Moschino, Casadel, and Vicini.

Gianni Versace. 1188 rue Sherbrooke (near rue de la Montagne). ☎ **514/285-1188.**

Lifestyle designers who go well beyond clothes, in the manner of Ralph Lauren, the
inheritors of the Versace name set out exquisite porcelains and glassware, as well as
cushions and throws on classically inspired settees and chairs.

Les Cuirs Danier. 730 rue Ste-Catherine Ouest (near av. McGill College). ☎ **514/
392-0936.**

This coast-to-coast national chain got that way with quality leather garments, belts,
bags, and such—mostly for women, but men aren't ignored. There's another branch
in Place Ville Marie (☎ **514/874-0472**).

Marks & Spencer. Place Montréal Trust, 1500 av. McGill College (at rue Ste-Catherine).
☎ **514/499-8558.**

The British origins of this store grow less obvious as the mother chain continues to
spread over several continents, but the clothing still represents a favorable price-to-
value ratio. Quality foods and confections are also available. Open 7 days.

Polo Ralph Lauren. 1290 rue Sherbrooke (near rue de la Montagne). ☎ **514/288-3988.**

As he has elsewhere, the international designer has set up shop in a townhouse in the
poshest part of town, near the Ritz-Carlton. Apparel for the well-heeled family, plus
house accessories.

COFFEES & TEAS
Brulerie St-Denis. 3965 rue St-Denis (at Duluth). ☎ **514/286-9158.**

This enticingly aromatic shop has an international selection of coffees from more than
two dozen countries, whole or ground to order. There are tables at which to try a cup
of a likely selection, and some desserts to go with it. There are several other branches,
including a convenient one in the Alcan Building, at 1188 rue Sherbrooke Ouest
(☎ **514/985-9159**).

DEPARTMENT STORES
Montréal's major shopping emporia stretch along rue Ste-Catherine (except for Holt
Renfrew), from rue Guy eastward to Carré Phillips at Aylmer. An excursion along this

12-block stretch can keep a diligent shopper busy for hours, even days. Most of the stores mentioned below have branches elsewhere, including the Underground City.

Eaton. 677 rue Ste-Catherine Ouest (at rue University). ☎ **514/284-8411.**

Established in 1925, Montréal's largest store offered middle-of-the-road fashions and home furnishings. However, its future following its recent bankruptcy and sale is clouded.

Henry Birks et Fils. 1240 Carré Phillips (at av. Union). ☎ **514/397-2511.**

Across from Christ Church Cathedral stands Henry Birks et Fils, a highly regarded jeweler since 1879. This beautiful old store, with its dark-wood display cases, stone pillars, and marble floors, is a living part of Montréal's Victorian heritage. Valuable products displayed go beyond jewelry to encompass pens and desk accessories, watches, ties, leather goods, belts and other personal accessories, glassware, and china.

Holt Renfrew. 1300 rue Sherbrooke Ouest (at rue de la Montagne). ☎ **514/842-5111.**

Begun as a furrier in 1837, this showcase for International Style focuses on fashion for men and women. Such prestigious names as Giorgio Armani, Prada, Gucci, and Chanel are displayed with a tastefulness bordering on solemnity. The marquee outside reads only HOLTS. An actual human operates the elevator.

La Baie. 585 rue Ste-Catherine Ouest (near rue Aylmer). ☎ **514/281-4422.**

No retailer has an older or more celebrated name than that of the Hudson's Bay Company, a name shortened in recent years to "The Bay," then transformed into "La Baie" by the language laws. The company has done business in Canada for the better part of 300 years. Its main store emphasizes clothing, but also offers crystal, china, and Inuit carvings. Its Canadiana Boutique features historical souvenir items and wool merchandise, including their famous Hudson's Bay blankets.

La Maison Simons. 977 rue Ste-Cathrine Ouest (at rue Mansfield). ☎ **514/282-1840.**

This is the first foray out of its home area for Québec City's long-established family owned department store. Most Montréalers had never heard of it, but attention has been captured by the imaginative displays of fashions that fill the refurbished first three floors of a building that once housed the old Simpson's. One guidebook describes it as "swanky," but the actuality is closer to "softer side of Sears."

Ogilvy. 1307 rue Ste-Catherine Ouest (at rue de la Montagne). ☎ **514/842-7711.**

Established in 1866, Ogilvy has been at this location since 1912. Besides having a reputation for quality merchandise, the store is known for its eagerly awaited Christmas windows. Once thought of as hidebound with tradition—a bagpiper still announces the noon hour—it now contains a collection of high-profile international boutiques, including Guy Laroche, Escada, Anne Klein, Aquascutum, and Rodier Paris. Wide aisles and glowing chandeliers make the experience a pleasure.

GIFT ITEMS

Atelier-Boutique de Cerfs-Volants. 224 rue St-Paul Ouest (at rue St-Pierre). ☎ **514/845-7613.**

This corner shop in Vieux-Montréal is filled with sturdy, dazzling cloth kites created by the owner, who is often seen at his workbench in back. He has flown or hung kites in many of the city's public places, including Eaton Center.

Collection Méli Mélo. 205 St-Paul Ouest (at rue St-François-Xavier). ☎ **514/285-5585.**

Quality shops are increasingly challenging Vieux-Montréal's purveyors of mock moccasins, trashy T-shirts, and related claptrap. Here's one, a pleasure to poke about with its mix of exotica originating in the band of nations reaching from Morocco to Pakistan. Find here carpets, jewelry, carved chests, mirrors, and objects of polished camel bone. With essence of sandalwood and drifting incense, it even smells good.

Franc Jeu. 4152 rue St-Denis (near rue Rachel). ☎ **514/849-9253.**

Expectant parents (and new grandparents) will want to make a detour to browse through the expansive collections of Corolle dolls and the clothes, jewelry, and accessories with which to dress them.

Les Artisans du Meuble Québécois. 88 rue St-Paul Est (near Place Jacques-Cartier). ☎ **514/866-1836.**

A mix of crafts, jewelry, and other objects—some noteworthy, others mediocre—make this an intriguing stop in Vieux-Montréal. Among the possibilities are clothing and accessories for women, greeting cards, woven goods, items for the home, and handmade quilts.

Musée des Beaux-Arts Boutique. 380 rue Sherbrooke Ouest (at rue Bishop). ☎ **514/285-1600,** ext. 342.

Next to the annex of the Museum of Fine Arts, this unusually large and impressive shop sells everything from folk art to furniture. The expected art-related postcards and prints are at hand, along with ties, jewelry, watches, scarves, address books, toys, games, clocks, and even designer napkins and paper plates. The boutique is to the right of the museum entrance, a large bookstore to the left.

Musée McCord Shop. 690 rue Sherbrooke Ouest (at rue Victoria). ☎ **514/398-3142.**

Part of the newly expanded museum that tells the history of the province, this shop has a small, carefully chosen selection of cards, books with an emphasis on history, coloring books, jewelry, and handcrafts.

Pointe-è-Callière Gift Shop. 150 rue St-Paul Ouest (at place Royale). ☎ **514/872-9150.**

Located in the Old Customs House, at the end of the underground tour of the Museum of Archaeology and History, this boutique sells collectibles for the home, gift items, paper products, souvenirs, toys, and books (in French). Some are worthwhile, some not.

Senteurs de Provence. 363 rue St-Paul Est, Vieux-Montréal. ☎ **514/395-8686.**

The sunny south of France is evoked in pottery hand-painted in the creamy-bright colors of Provence, complemented by cunning collections of bath soaps and gels, printed linens, and lightly perfumed lotions and creams. Open daily. There are two other branches, at 4077 rue St-Denis (☎ **514/845-6867**) and 4859 rue Sherbrooke (☎ **514/369-7888**).

Urban Outfitters. 1246 rue Ste-Catherine Ouest (near rue de lat Montagne). ☎ **514/874-0063.**

Impossible to categorize, this outpost of the sizeable North American chain is more hoot than harbinger, with an unpredictable stock that ranges from women's tops and skirts to off-kilter lamps and glassware to such life essentials as the *Star Wars Cookbook* and a nun doll that walks and spits fire.

MUSIC

Archambault Musique. 500 rue Ste-Catherine Est. ☎ **514/849-6201.**

French-Canadian singers are gaining fans across the border—Céline Dion only the most popular among them—and their music can be found here, along with recordings by the Montréal Symphony Orchestra, Ensemble I Musici, and others, some of which may be hard to find outside of Québec. This store is across the park from the Voyageur bus terminal, but recent expansion has brought about new outlets, including the one at Place des Arts (☎ **514/281-0367**).

WINES & FOODS

Although wine and beer are sold in supermarkets and convenience stores, liquor and other spirits can be sold only in shops operated by the provincial Société des Alcools du Québec (SAQ). Though it was once as bureaucratic as most state-run agencies, successful efforts have made the stores more inviting. Some serve particular needs, others strive to be comprehensive. One of the largest is the **SAQ Selection** at 440 bd. de Maisonneuve Ouest at rue City Councillors (☎ **514/873-2274**), a virtual supermarket of wines and liquors, with more than 3,000 labels from some 55 countries. Prices run from C$10 (US$6.90) to C$1,000 (US$690) for some Bordeaux vintages. **SAQ Whiskey & Cie** at 998 bd. de Maisonneuve Ouest at rue Metcalf (☎ **514/ 282-9445**) specializes in single-malt scotches, whiskeys, brandies, and liqueurs and has a bar for tastings. Smaller and less fancy, the **SAQ Express** at 1108 Ste-Catherine Ouest is meant for quick in-and-out purchases; it's open daily and later, 11am to 10pm.

In addition, the food markets described at the end of chapter 5 in "Picnic Fare: Where to Get It, Where to Eat It" shouldn't be overlooked. They carry abundant assortments of cheeses, wines, and packaged food products that can serve as gifts or delicious reminders of your visit when you get home.

9

Montréal After Dark

Montréal's reputation for effervescent nightlife reaches back to the Roaring Twenties, specifically the 13-year experiment with Prohibition in the United States. Canadian distillers and brewers made fortunes—few of them with meticulous regard for legalistic niceties—and Americans streamed into Montréal for temporary relief from alcohol deprivation. That the city already enjoyed a both sophisticated and slightly naughty reputation as the Paris of North America added to the allure. Nightclubbing and barhopping remain popular activities, with places keeping much later hours than those of archrival Toronto, still in thrall to Calvinist notions of propriety and early bedtimes.

Montréalers' nocturnal pursuits are often as cultural as they are social. The city boasts its own outstanding symphony, French- and English-speaking theater companies, and the incomparable Cirque du Soleil (Circus of the Sun). It's also on the standard concert circuit that includes Chicago, Boston, and New York, so internationally known entertainers, rock bands, orchestra conductors and classical virtuosos, and ballet and modern-dance companies pass through frequently. A decidedly French enthusiasm for film, as well as the city's strengthening reputation as a movie-production center, ensures support for cinemas showcasing experimental, offbeat, and foreign films, as well as the usual Hollywood blockbusters.

And in summer, the city becomes even livelier than usual with several enticing events: the **Festival de Théâtre des Amériques** (late May to early June), the flashy **Benson & Hedges International Fireworks Competition** (June to July), the renowned **Festival International de Jazz** (early July), the **Juste pour Rire/Just for Laughs Festival** (late July), and, in late September to early October, the **Festival International de Nouvelle Danse** attracts modern-dance troupes and choreographers from around the world. To this bursting roster has been added the **Montréal Highlights Festival/Festival Montréal en Lumière** (mid-February to early March), dedicated to the arts, which, by this gastronomic city's measure, includes chefs the caliber of Paul Bocuse. The first opening night presented Jessye Norman and Michel Legrand, followed by 3 weeks of film, dance, special museum exhibits, performance art, and classical and modern music.

Concentrations of pubs and discos underscore the city's linguistic dichotomy, too. While there's a great deal of crossover mingling, the parallel blocks of **rue Crescent,** rue Bishop, and rue de la Montagne

Finding Out What's On

For details of current performances or special events, pick up a free copy of *Montréal Scope,* a weekly ads-and-events booklet, at any large hotel reception desk, or the free weekly newspapers *Mirror* and *Hour* (in English) or *Voir* (in French). Place des Arts puts out a monthly calendar of events *(Calendrier des Spectacles)* describing concerts and performances to be held in the various halls of the performing-arts complex. Pick one up in most large hotels, or near the box offices in Place des Arts. Montréal's newspapers, the French-language *La Presse* and the English *Gazette,* carry listings of films, clubs, and performances in their Friday and Saturday editions. The self-described "bilingual queer newspaper" *Village* provides news and views of gay and lesbian events, clubs, restaurants, and activities. For extensive listings of largely mainstream cultural and entertainment events, log on to **www.montrealonline.com**; a similar service is provided by the alternative newspaper, *Hour,* at **www. afterhour.com**. Also try the Place des Arts page, **www.infoarts.net**, and the official Web site of the Tourisme Montréal, **www.tourism-montreal.org**.

north of rue Ste-Catherine have a pronounced Anglophone character, while Francophones dominate the **Latin Quarter,** with college-age patrons most evident along the lower reaches of rue St-Denis and their yuppie elders gravitating to the nightspots of the slightly more uptown blocks of the same street. **Vieux-Montréal,** especially along rue St-Paul, has a more universal quality, where many of the bars and clubs feature live jazz, blues, and folk music. In the **Plateau Mont-Royal** area, boulevard St-Laurent, parallel to St-Denis and known locally as "The Main," has become a miles-long haven of hip restaurants and clubs, roughly from rue Laurier to rue Sherbrooke. Boulevard St-Laurent is a good place to wind up in the wee hours, as there's always some place with the welcome mat still out.

1 The Performing Arts

THEATER

The **Festival de Théâtre des Amériques** (☎ 514/842-0704), held in odd-numbered years from late May to early June, presents innovative dramatic and musical stage productions that are international in scope, not simply North American, as the name suggests. There have been works from Vietnam and China as well as from Canada, the United States, and Mexico. The plays are performed in the original languages, as a rule, with simultaneous translations in French and/or English, when appropriate. Call for information.

Centaur Theatre. 453 rue St-François-Xavier (near rue Notre-Dame). ☎ **514/288-3161.** Tickets C$20–C$36 (US$13.80–US$25). Métro: Place d'Armes.

A former stock-exchange building (1903) is home to Montréal's principal English-language theater. A mix of classics, foreign adaptations, and works by Canadian playwrights is presented, including such past productions as *Driving Miss Daisy, Oliver!, The Gin Game, Waiting for Godot, W;t, Dancing at Lughnasa,* and *Cabaret,* as well as such new works as *Venus of Dublin.* Off-season, the recently refurbished theater is rented out to other groups, both French- and English-speaking. Performances are held October to June, Tuesday through Saturday at 8pm and Sunday at 7pm, with 2pm matinees on Saturday and most Sundays. Box office hours are Sunday and Monday noon to 5pm, and Tuesday through Saturday noon to 8pm.

Saidye Bronfman Centre for the Arts. 5170 Côte-Ste-Catherine (near bd. Décarie). ☎ **514/739-2301** for information, or 514/739-4816 for tickets. Tickets C$15–C$35 (US$10.35–US$24.15). Métro: Côte-Ste-Catherine. Bus: no. 129 Ouest.

Montréal's Yiddish Theatre, founded in 1937, is housed in the Saidye Bronfman Centre for the Arts, not far from St. Joseph's Oratory. It stages plays in both Yiddish and English, usually running 3 to 4 weeks in June and October. At other times during the year, the 300-seat theater hosts dance and music recitals, a bilingual puppet festival, occasional lectures, and three English-language plays. There's also an art gallery on the premises, with exhibits that change almost monthly. Across the street, in the Edifice Cummings House, is a small Holocaust museum and the Jewish Public Library. The center takes its name from philanthropist Saidye Bronfman, widow of Samuel Bronfman, founder of the Seagram Company. She died in 1995 at the age of 98. The box office is usually open Monday through Thursday 11am to 8pm and Sunday noon to 7pm—call ahead. Performances are held Tuesday through Thursday at 8pm and Sunday at 1:30 and 7pm.

DANCE

Frequent appearances by notable dancers and troupes from other parts of Canada and the world—among them Paul Taylor, the Feld Ballet, and Le Ballet National du Canada—augment the accomplished resident company. During the summer, Les Grands Ballets Canadiens often perform at the outdoor Théâtre de Verdure in Parc Lafontaine. In winter, they're scheduled at various venues around the city, but especially in the several halls at the Place des Arts. The fall season is kicked off by the always-provocative **Festival International de Nouvelle Danse,** in late September and early October.

Les Grands Ballets Canadiens. Salle Wilfrid-Pelletier, Place des Arts, 200 bd. de Maisonneuve Ouest. ☎ **514/849-8681.** Tickets C$12–C$40 (US$8.30–US$28). Métro: Place des Arts.

This prestigious company has developed a following far beyond national borders for more than 35 years, performing a both classical and modern repertoire. In the process, it has brought prominence to many gifted Canadian choreographers and composers. It tours internationally and was the first Canadian ballet company to be invited to the People's Republic of China. The troupe's production of *The Nutcracker* the last couple of weeks in December is always a big event in Montréal. The box office is open Monday to Saturday noon to 8pm. Performances are held late October to early May at 8pm.

Tangente. Agora de la Danse, 840 rue Cherrier. ☎ **514/525-5584.** Tickets C$5–C$15 (US$3.45–US$10.35). Metro: Sherbrooke.

A September-to-June season of contemporary dance and often out-there performance art is laid out by this nonprofit organization. Housed in a new building devoted exclusively to the dance, its approximately 90 performances per year give priority to Quebéc artists, but leavened by appearances by other Canadian and international artists and troupes.

CLASSICAL MUSIC & OPERA

L'Opéra de Montréal. Salle Wilfrid-Pelletier, Place des Arts, 260 bd. de Maisonneuve Ouest. ☎ **514/985-2222** for information, or 514/985-2258 for tickets. Tickets C$32–C$99 (US$22–US$68). Métro: Place des Arts.

Founded in 1980, this outstanding opera company mounts six productions a year in Montréal, with artists from Québec and abroad participating in such shows as

A Circus Extraordinaire

Through the exposure generated by its frequent tours across North America, Europe, and Australia, the hip ✪ **Cirque du Soleil,** 8400 2e Av., St-Michel (☎ **514/722-2324;** www.cirquedusoleil.com), is enjoying an ever-multiplying following. One reason, curiously, is the absence of animals in the troupe, which means no one need be troubled by the possibility of mistreated lions and elephants. What is experienced during a Cirque du Soleil performance is nothing less than magical, a celebration of pure skill and theater, with plenty of acrobats, clowns, trapeze artists, tightrope walkers, and contortionists. Since 1984, more than 15 million people in over 120 cities have seen the Cirque du Soleil in action. The troupe is so much in demand it's difficult to track from year to year how long it will alight in its hometown, although most recently it stayed from mid-April to mid-June. Check ahead to discover its current plans. Last time out, performances were scheduled Tuesday and Wednesday at 8pm, Thursday and Friday at 5:30 and 9:30pm, Saturday at 4 and 8pm, and Sunday at 1 and 5pm. Tickets run C$49 to C$87 (US$34 to US$60) adults and C$35 to C$61 (US$24 to US$42) children.

La Traviata, Don Carlo, Carmen, Salome, La Bohème, Otello, and *Mefistofele.* Video translations are provided from the original languages into French and English. The box office is open Monday to Friday 9am to 5pm. Performances are held from September to June, usually at 8pm, in three theaters at Place des Arts and occasional other venues.

Orchestre Métropolitain de Montréal. Maisonneuve Theatre, Place des Arts, 260 bd. de Maisonneuve Ouest. ☎ **514/598-0870.** Tickets C$13–C$40 (US$8.95–US$27.60). Métro: Place des Arts.

This orchestra has a regular season at Place des Arts but also performs in the St-Jean-Baptiste Church and tours regionally. Most musicians are in their mid-30s or younger. The box office is open Monday to Saturday noon to 8pm. Performances are held mid-October to early April, usually at 8pm. Outdoor concerts are given in Parc Lafontaine in August.

L'Orchestre Symphonique de Montréal (OSM). Salle Wilfrid-Pelletier, Place des Arts, 260 bd. de Maisonneuve Ouest. ☎ **514/842-9951.** Tickets C$15–C$55 (US$10.35–US$38). Métro: Place des Arts.

This world-famous orchestra, under the baton of Swiss conductor Charles Dutoit (and Zubin Mehta before him), performs at Place des Arts and the Notre-Dame Basilica, as well as around the world, and may be heard on numerous recordings. In the well-balanced repertoire are works from Elgar to Rabaud to Saint-Saëns, in addition to Beethoven and Mozart. The box office is open Monday to Saturday noon to 8pm. Performances are usually at 8pm, during a full season that runs September to May, supplemented by Mozart concerts in Notre-Dame Basilica in June and July, interspersed with free performances at three parks in the metropolitan region.

CONCERT HALLS & AUDITORIUMS

Montréal has a score of venues, so check the papers upon arrival to see who's playing where during your stay. Big-name rock bands and pop stars that used to play at the Forum now show up at the new downtown arena, Centre Molson (below), which is also the new home of the Montréal Canadiens hockey team.

Centre Molson. 1260 rue de la Gauchetière Ouest. ☎ **514/932-2582.** www.centre-molson.com. Métro: Atwater.

The home of the Montréal Canadiens also hosts big international pop stars on the order of Ricky Martin, R.E.M., Shania Twain, and Alanis Morissette, as well as such dissimilar attractions as Disney's World On Ice. They used to be booked into the old Forum but are now diverted to this sparkling new facility, which opened in 1996. Most people agree it's vastly superior to the old Forum on all but the nostalgia scale, and the location is better. If a concert is scheduled, printed flyers, posters, and radio and TV ads make certain that everyone knows. Up to 20,000 can be seated. The box office is open Monday through Friday 10am to 6pm (or to 9pm on days of events). Performances are at 7:30pm or 8pm. Ticket prices vary greatly, depending on the attraction.

Place des Arts. 175 rue Ste-Catherine Ouest. ☎ **514/285-4200** for information, 514/ 842-2112 for tickets, or www.pdarts.com for tickets online. AE, DC, MC, V. Métro: Place des Arts.

Founded in 1963 and in its striking present home in the heart of Montréal since 1992, Place des Arts mounts performances of musical concerts, opera, dance, and theater in five halls: **Salle Wilfrid-Pelletier** (2,982 seats), where the Orchestre Symphonique de Montréal often performs; the **Maisonneuve Theatre** (1,460 seats), where the Orchestre Métropolitan de Montréal and the McGill Chamber Orchestra perform; the **Jean-Duceppe Theatre** (755 seats); the **Cinquième Salle** (350 seats); and the small **Studio-Théâtre du Maurier Ltée** (138 seats). Traveling productions of Broadway classics on the order of *Smokey Joe's Café* and *Showboat* have limited runs at the center. Noontime performances are often scheduled. The box office is open Monday through Saturday noon to 8pm, and performances are usually at 8pm. Ticket prices vary according to hall and the group performing.

Pollack Concert Hall. On the McGill University campus, 555 rue Sherbrooke Ouest. ☎ **514/398-4547.** www.music.mcgill.ca. Métro: McGill.

In a landmark building dating from 1899 that's fronted by a statue of Queen Victoria, this hall is in nearly constant use, especially during the university year. Among the attractions are concerts and recitals by professionals, students, or soloists from McGill's music faculty. Recordings of some of the more memorable concerts are available on the university's own label, McGill Records. Concerts are also given in the campus's smaller **Redpath Hall,** 3461 rue McTavish (☎ **514/398-4547**). Performances are at 8pm; they are often free, but tickets for some events can cost up to $22.

Spectrum de Montréal. 318 rue Ste-Catherine Ouest (at rue de Bleury). ☎ **800/ 361-4595** or 514/790-1245. www.admission.com (for tickets). Métro: Place des Arts; then take the Bleury exit.

A broad range of Canadian and international performers, usually of a modest celebrity unlikely to fill the larger Centre Molson, use this converted movie theater. Rock acts on the order of Musical Box and Phish are among the higher-profile acts, comedians are sometimes booked, and the space also hosts segments of the city's annual jazz festival. Seats are available on a first-come, first-served basis, and all ages are admitted. The box office is open Monday through Friday noon to 9pm and Saturday and Sunday noon to 5pm. Performances are at 8:30 or 9pm.

Théâtre de Verdure. In Lafontaine Park. ☎ **514/872-2644.** Métro: Sherbrooke.

Nestled in a popular park in Plateau Mont-Royal, this open-air theater presents free music and dance concerts and theater, often with well-known artists and performers.

Sometimes they show outdoor movies. Many in the audience pack picnics. Performances are held from June to August; call for days and times.

Théâtre St-Denis. 1594 rue St-Denis (at Emery). ☎ **514/849-4211.** Métro: Berri-UQAM.

Recently refurbished, this theater in the heart of the Latin Quarter hosts a variety of shows, including pop singers and groups and comedians, as well as segments of the Juste pour Rire (Just for Laughs) Festival in summer. It's actually two theaters, one seating more than 2,000, the other almost 1,000. The box office is open daily noon to 9pm. Performances are usually at 8pm.

2 The Club & Music Scene

COMEDY

The once enthusiastic market for comedy clubs across North America has cooled, but Montréal still has a couple of laugh spots, mostly because it's the home to the **Juste pour Rire/Just for Laughs Festival** held every summer (for information, call ☎ 514/845-2322). Those who have so far eluded the comedy-club experience should know that profanity, bathroom humor, and assorted ethnic slurs are common fodder for performers. If patrons wish to avoid becoming objects of the comedians' barbs, it's wise to sit well back from the stage. Performances are in French or English (about 50/50, it seems) or both.

Comedy Nest. 1740 bd. René-Lévesque (at rue Guy). ☎ **514/932-6378.** www. comedynest.com. Cover C$10 (US$6.90). Métro: Guy-Concordia.

Mostly local talent is showcased at this club in the Nouvel Hotel, but among the comics who stopped off here on their way up were Howie Mandel, Norm MacDonald, and superstar Jim Carrey. Shows are held Wednesday through Sunday at 8:30pm, with added shows on Friday and Saturday at 11:30pm. Drinks cost C$5 to C$8 (US$3.45 to US$5.50). The dinner-and-show package costs C$25 (US$17.25); dinner starts at 6:30pm.

Comedyworks. 1238 rue Bishop (at rue Ste-Catherine). ☎ **514/398-9661.** Cover up to C$12 (US$8.30), plus a one-drink minimum. Métro: Guy-Concordia.

There's a full card of comedy at this long-running club, up the stairs from Jimbo's Pub on a jumping block of rue Bishop south of rue Ste-Catherine. Monday is open-mike night, while on Tuesday and Wednesday, improvisation groups usually work off the audience. Headliners of greater or lesser magnitude—usually from Montréal, Toronto, New York, or Boston—take the stage Thursday through Sunday. No food is served, just drinks. Reservations are recommended, especially on Friday, when early arrival may be necessary to secure a seat. Shows are daily at 8:30pm, and also 11:15pm on Fridays and Saturdays. Most drinks cost C$5 to C$8 (US$3.45 to US$5.50).

FOLK, ROCK & POP

Scores of bars, cafes, theaters, clubs, and even churches present live music on at least an occasional basis, even if only at Sunday brunch. The performers, local or touring, traffic in every idiom, from metal to funk and reggae to grunge and unvarnished Vegas. In most cases, acts play a venue for only a night or two. Here are a few places that focus their energies on the music.

Café Campus. 57 rue Prince-Arthur Est (near bd. St-Laurent). ☎ **514/844-1010.** Cover usually C$4–C$12 (US$2.75–US$8.30). Métro: Sherbrooke.

When anyone over 25 shows up inside this bleak club on touristy Prince-Arthur, he or she is probably a parent of one of the musicians. Alternative rock prevails, but metal and retro-rock bands also make appearances. Followers of the scene may be familiar with such groups as Liquid Soul, Come, and Duke Robillard, all of whom have hit the stage here. Dance parties are often scheduled Wednesday nights.

Club Soda. 1225 bd. St-Laurent (at Ste-Catherine). ☎ **514/786-1010,** ext. 200 (box office). www.clubsoda.ca. Cover C$5 (US$3.45) and up. AE, MC, V. Métro: St-Laurent.

This long-established club changed its name and moved into these new quarters, which are even larger than the old location on avenue du Parc. It remains one of the prime destinations for attractions below the megastar level and is a principal venue for the "Just for Laughs" festival. Performers are given a stage in a hall that seats several hundred fans. Five bars pump audience enthusiasm. Musical choices hop all over the charts—folk, rock, blues, country, Afro-Cuban, heavy metal—you name it. Representative performers have included Kid Koala, Brendan Perry, and Moist Show. Acts for the annual jazz and comedy festivals are booked here, too.

Hard Rock Café. 1458 rue Crescent (near bd. de Maisonneuve). ☎ **514/987-1420.** No cover. Métro: Guy-Concordia.

No surprises here, not with clones sprouting all around the world. The hamburgers are good enough and not overly expensive, guitars and costumes and other rock memorabilia decorate the walls, and the usual Hard Rock Café souvenirs are available. The formula continues to work, and it gets crowded at lunch and on weekend evenings. Open Sunday to Thursday from 11:30am to midnight, Friday to Saturday from 11:30am to 3am; the disco starts up at 10pm. Drinks cost C$4 to C$8 (US$2.75 to US$5.50).

Hurley's Irish Pub. 1225 rue Crescent (south of rue Ste-Catherine). ☎ **514/861-4111.** No cover. Métro: Peel or Guy-Concordia.

The Irish have been one of the largest immigrant groups in Montréal since the famine of the 1840s, and their musical tradition thrives here. Celtic instrumentalists and dancers perform every night of the week, often both on the ground floor and upstairs, usually starting around 9:30pm. Guinness and other drinks go for C$3 to C$7 (US$2 to US$4.65).

✪ Le Pierrot/Les Deux Pierrots. 114 and 104 rue St-Paul Est (west of place Jacques-Cartier). ☎ **514/861-1270.** www.lespierrots.com. Cover: Le Pierrot, C$3 (US$2.05) Fri–Sat, free other nights; Aux Deux Pierrots, C$5 (US$3.45). Métro: Place d'Armes.

Perhaps the best known of Montréal's *boîtes-à-chansons*—song clubs—Le Pierrot is an intimate French-style cabaret. The singer interacts animatedly with the crowd, often bilingually, and encourages them to join in the lyrics. Le Pierrot is open year-round, daily from early June to late September, Thursday through Sunday the other months, with music into the wee hours. Its sister club next door, the larger Les Deux Pierrots, features live bands playing rock and roll Friday and Saturday nights, half in French and half in English. The terrace joining the two clubs is open on Friday and Saturday nights in summer. Le Pierrot is open only May to September, nightly. Drinks cost C$3 to C$6 (US$2.05 to US$4.15).

Le Swimming. 3643 bd. St-Laurent (north of rue Sherbrooke). ☎ **514/282-7665.** Cover C$5 (US$3.45) Thurs–Sat (when live bands are booked). AE, MC, V. Métro: Sherbrooke.

A nondescript entry and a stairway that smells of stale beer lead to a trendy pool hall that attracts as many men and women who come to drink and socialize as to play pool (*le swimming*, get it?). Many Montréal bars have a pool table, but this one has 13, along with nine TVs and a terrace. Thursday through Saturday nights they usually have bands embracing ska, funk, reggae, and jazz. Open daily noon to 3am.

O'Donnell's. 1224 rue Bishop (near rue Ste-Catherine). ☎ **514/866-0512.** www.bar-resto. com/odonnell. No cover. Métro: Guy-Concordia.

Replacing a rock/blues club called Déjà Vu, this casual family owned room feeds a current enthusiasm for Gaelic music and libations. It's a fun, friendly place, relatively inexpensive, with a couple of dance floors and live Irish music every weekend.

JAZZ & BLUES

The respected and heavily attended **Festival International de Jazz,** held every summer in the city, sustains interest in the most original American art form. During the 10 days of the event, more than 2,000 musicians perform on 16 stages for an average total audience of one million. (For information, call ☎ **800/361-4595** or 514/871-1881, or visit **www.montrealjazzfest.com.**) Scores of events are scheduled, indoors and out, many of them free. *Jazz* is broadly interpreted, including everything from Dixieland to reggae, world beat, and the unclassifiable experimental. Artists who have performed at the festival have included Thelonious Monk, Pat Metheny, John McLaughlin, Dave Brubeck, and B.B. King. Piano legend Oscar Peterson grew up here and often returns to perform in his hometown. There are many more clubs than the sampling that follows. Pick up a copy of *Mirror* or *Hour,* distributed free everywhere, or buy the Friday or Saturday editions of the *Gazette* for the entertainment section. These publications have full listings of the bands and stars appearing during the week.

Biddle's. 2060 rue Aylmer (south of rue Sherbrooke). ☎ **514/842-8656.** No cover, but a drink minimum Fri–Sat. Métro: McGill.

Right downtown, where there isn't much after-dark action, this longtime stalwart is a club-restaurant with hanging plants and faux art nouveau glass. It fills up early with lovers of barbecued ribs and jazz. The live music starts around 5:30pm (at 7pm on Sunday and Monday) and continues until closing time. Charlie Biddle plays bass Thursday through Saturday nights when he doesn't have a gig elsewhere. He and his stand-ins favor jazz of the swinging mainstream variety, with occasional digressions into more esoteric forms. It's open Sunday 4pm to 12:30am, Monday through Thursday 11:30am to 1:30am, and Friday and Saturday 11:30am to 2:30am. Drinks cost C$5 to C$7.50 (US$3.45 to US$5.15), and there's a mandatory paid coat check.

✪ **L'Air du Temps.** 191 rue St-Paul Ouest (at rue St-François-Xavier). ☎ **514/842-2003.** Cover C$5–C$25 (US$3.45–US$17.25), depending on the attraction. Métro: Place d'Armes.

A Montréal tradition since 1976, L'Air du Temps is an ardent jazz emporium of the old school—a little seedy and beat up, and no gimmicks or frippery to distract from the music. The main room and an upper floor in back can hold more than 135, and the bar stools and tables fill up quickly. Get there by 9:30pm or so to secure a seat. The bands go on at 10:30pm or thereabouts. L'Air du Temps doesn't serve food, just a wide variety of drinks, but there are several good mid-priced restaurants nearby. The club, the most likely of Montréal's jazz clubs to get seminame acts, doesn't take reservations. It's open Thursday through Monday 9pm to 3am. Drinks cost C$4 to C$8 (US$2.75 to US$5.50).

Le Quai des Brumes. 4481 and 4479 rue St-Denis (at av. du Mont-Royal). ☎ **514/499-0467.** No cover. Métro: Mont-Royal.

Loosely translated, the name means "foggy dock," a reference of elusive significance. But it's an atmospheric place in which to listen to jazz, blues, and rock. Upstairs, the Bar Central attracts its share of Plateau notables and has a small dance floor. The crowd has been described as "a fairly uniform group of post-sixties Francophone smokers." A short menu of nibbles is available in each place. Open daily 2pm to 3am. Drinks cost C$3 to C$7 (US$2.05 to US$4.85).

Maestro S.V.P. 3615 bd. St-Laurent (north of Sherbrooke). ☎ **514/842-6447.** No cover. Metro: Sherbrooke.

Good eats and live music aren't strangers in Montréal. Although this bistro is best known for seafood, especially its oyster bar (see page 88), the owner brings in a trio Sunday nights at 6:30. That justifies the name and the musical instruments that constitute most of the decor.

DANCE CLUBS

As elsewhere, Montréal's dance clubs change in tenor and popularity in mere eye blinks, and new ones sprout like toadstools after a heavy rain; they also wither as quickly. For the latest feverish spots, quiz concierges, guides, waiters—all those who look as if they might follow the scene. Here are a few that appear more likely to survive the whims of night owls and landlords. At some, you'll encounter steroid abusers with funny haircuts guarding the doors. Usually, they'll let you inside; the admittance game is not as strict nor as arbitrary as the "hipper than thou" criteria encountered at some New York and Los Angeles clubs.

Batalou. 4372 bd. St-Laurent (at rue Marie-Anne). ☎ **514/845-5447.** Cover C$7 (US$4.85). Métro: Mont-Royal.

An infectious, sensual tropical beat issues from this club-with-a-difference on The Main, a hot, happy variation from the prevailing grunge and murk of what might be described as mainstream clubs. Although most of the patrons revel in their ancestral origins in the Caribbean and Africa, the sources of the live and recorded music, everyone is welcome. Admittedly, the hip-waggling expertise of the dancers might be intimidating to the rhythmically challenged. Things get going about 10pm every night but Monday. The cover charge includes one beer or glass of wine; additional drinks are C$4 to C$7 (US$2.75 to US$4.85).

Les Foufounes Électriques. 87 Ste-Catherine Est (near St-Denis). ☎ **514/844-5539.** www.foufounes.qc.ca. Cover C$10 (US$6.90) and up. Métro: Berri-UQAM.

On the scene for more than a decade, this multilevel disco-rock club has mellowed somewhat from its outlaw days, although you can't tell from a list of the live bands— Over Kill, Last Breath, Martyr. An occasional one-hit wonder puts in a latter-day appearance—Vanilla Ice, anyone? With three dance floors and a couple of beer gardens in back, there's plenty to keep you busy, starting with the C$1.50 (US$1) beers during the 4 to 6pm happy hour, shooters for C$1.25 to C$2.50 (US85¢ to US$1.70), and pitchers for C$6 to C$9.50 (US$4.15 to US$6.55), the higher prices applied at the weekend. Look for the rocket ship over the door.

Metropolis. 59 rue Ste-Catherine Est (near bd. St-Laurent). ☎ **514/844-3500.** Cover C$10 (US$6.90) and up, depending on attraction. Métro: Berri-UQAM.

Housed in a handsome old opera house dating from the 1890s, this monster club can accommodate 2,200 gyrating bodies. The sound system and the light show are state-of-the-art, and there are six bars on three levels. Past attractions included Tito Puente, Steve Winwood, Björk, and Ben Harper. The neighborhood is scruffy but not especially worrisome, and not far from the campus of the Université du Québec. It's open Thursday through Saturday 10pm to 3am. Drinks cost C$4 to C$7 (US$2.75 to US$4.85). Box office and hours are the same as at the Spectrum (above).

Salsathèque. 1220 rue Peel (at Ste-Catherine). ☎ **514/875-0016.** Cover C$5 (US$3.45) Fri–Sat. Métro: Peel.

It's been on the scene for years, so they're obviously doing something right. The big upstairs room is all glittery, bouncing, mirrored light, the better to get the dancers moving to mambo, merengue, and other hot tropical beats. Open Wednesday through Sunday 9pm to 3am, it rarely kicks into high gear before midnight. The house band comes on at 11pm or thereabouts, and they bring in other acts. The main source of entertainment, though, is the patrons themselves, a highly proficient lot on the dance floor. Drinks run about C$4 to C$8 (US$2.75 to US$5.50).

Wax Lounge. 3481 bd. St-Laurent (north of rue Sherbrooke). ☎ **514/282-0919.** Cover C$5 (US$3.35) Mon–Thurs, C$7 (US$4.65) Fri–Sat. Metro: Sherbrooke.

A jovial, racially mixed crowd ankles over to this second-floor club after dinner at one of the half-dozen scene restaurants clustered around this busy south end of The Main. The velvet-rope policy is more in the interest of crowd control than exclusivity. When the live band (usually soul/rock with rap undertones) takes a break, the DJ pumps the house music right up through the soles of your shoes. Good brands of booze are poured, most from C$4 to C$8 (US$2.75 to US$5.50) per drink.

3 The Bar & Cafe Scene

An abundance of restaurants, bars, and cafes masses along the streets near the downtown commercial district, from rue Stanley to rue Guy between rue Ste-Catherine and boulevard de Maisonneuve. **Rue Crescent,** in particular, hums with activity from late afternoon until far into the evening, especially after 10pm on a cool summer weekend night, when the street swarms with people careening from club to bar to restaurant. **Boulevard St-Laurent,** or "The Main," as it's known, is another nightlife hub, abounding in bars and clubs, most with a distinctive European—particularly French—personality, as opposed to the Anglo flavor of the rue Crescent area. Increasingly active **rue St-Paul,** west of place Jacques-Cartier in Vieux Montréal, falls somewhere in the middle on the Anglophone-Francophone spectrum. It's also a little more likely to get rowdy on late weekend nights. In all cases, bars tend to open around 11:30am and go late. Many of them have *heures joyeuses*—happy hours—from as early as 3pm to as late as 9pm, but usually for a shorter period within those hours. At those times, two-for-one rather than discount drinks are the rule. Last call for orders is 3am, but patrons are often allowed to dawdle over those drinks until 4am.

DOWNTOWN/RUE CRESCENT

✪ **Le Tour de Ville.** In the Delta Centre-Ville Hôtel, 777 rue University. ☎ **514/879-1370.** Métro: Square Victoria.

Memorable. Breathtaking. The view, that is, from Montréal's only revolving restaurant and bar (the bar doesn't revolve, but you still get a great view). The best time to go is when the sun is setting and the city lights are beginning to blink on. In the bar, one floor down from the restaurant, the same wonderful vistas are augmented by a dance floor, with a band Thursday through Saturday 9pm to 1 or 2am. There's no cover, but drinks range from C$5.50 to C$9 (US$3.65 to US$6). The bar opens at 6pm. (Note that the name of the lounge may be changed since this just became a Delta hotel.)

Lutetia Bar. In L'Hôtel de la Montagne, 1430 rue de la Montagne (north of rue Ste-Catherine). ☎ **514/288-5656.** Métro: Guy-Concordia.

Within sight of the trademark lobby fountain with its nude bronze sprite sporting stained-glass wings, this appealing bar draws a standing-room–only crowd of youngish to middle-aged professionals after 5:30pm. Later on, there's often music by jazz duos. In summer the hotel opens the terrace bar on the roof by the pool.

Ritz Bar. In the Ritz-Carlton Hôtel, 1228 rue Sherbrooke Ouest (at rue Drummond). ☎ **514/842-4212.** Métro: Peel.

A mature, prosperous crowd seeks out the quiet Ritz Bar in the Ritz-Carlton, adjacent to its semilegendary Café de Paris restaurant. Anyone can take advantage of the tranquil room and the professionalism of its staff, but because the atmosphere is rather formal, most men will be more at ease with a jacket. Piano music dances softly around conversation during cocktail hour Monday through Friday 5 to 8pm and at dinnertime (5 to 11pm) from September to mid-May. The bar is just off the hotel lobby, to the right.

Sir Winston Churchill Pub. 1459 rue Crescent (near rue Ste-Catherine). ☎ **514/ 288-0623.** Métro: Guy-Concordia.

The three levels of bars and cafes incorporated here are rue Crescent landmarks. One reason is the sidewalk terrace, open in summer, enclosed in winter, and a vantage for checking out the pedestrian traffic all the time. Inside and down the stairs, the pub, with English ales on tap, attempts to imitate a British public house, with marginal success. Pretty waitresses in miniskirts bring food, but the burgers and such have to look up to reach mediocrity. A mixed crowd of questing young professionals mills around a total of 17 bars and two dance floors. Winnie's, on the second floor, is a restaurant with a terrace of its own and a new cigar lounge. Open daily noon to 2am. During the 5 to 8pm happy hour, drinks are two-for-one.

Thursday's. 1441–1449 rue Crescent (near rue Ste-Catherine). ☎ **514/288-5656.** Métro: Guy-Concordia.

A prime watering hole of Montréal's young professional set—those who are ever alert to the possibilities of companionship. The pubby bar spills out onto the terrace that hangs over the street, and there's a glittery disco in back, both in the Hôtel de la Montagne. Thursday's presumably takes its name from the Montréal custom of prowling nightspots on Thursday evening in search of the perfect date for Friday.

Ziggy's. 1470 rue Crescent (near rue Ste-Catherine). ☎ **514/285-8855.** Metro: Guy-Concordia.

Maybe they get away with that Francophobic apostrophe because this place looks so bloody Brit. Steps down from a shelf of outdoor tables, the long, low-ceilinged pub has two bars with hockey sticks and celeb (Alan Thicke) and sports photos on the walls. A mixed crowd partakes of the eight brews on draft. Drinks range from C$2.50 to C$7 (US$1.70 to US$4.85).

PLATEAU MONT-ROYAL

Bleu Est Noir. 812 rue Rachel Est (near St-Hubert). ☎ **514/524-4809.** Metro: Mont-Royal.

Wear anything better than a tank top and jeans or the January equivalent thereof and you'll feel conspicuously overdressed. Grungy and beery it is, with a battered sheet-metal bar, a pool table, and a beat-up fireplace—all the better to receive neighborhood regulars from 3pm to dinnertime, and clogs of students from then until the third wee hour. A DJ works the turntables most nights, with live bands appearing many Sundays. When there's a cover charge, it's usually C$5 to C$7 (US$3.45 to US$4.85).

Blizzarts. 3956a bd. St-Laurent (near rue Duluth). ☎ **514/843-4860.** Cover up to C$5 (US$3.45). Metro: Mont-Royal.

Remnants of fifties modern, much of it mismatched, fill the space around the small dance floor. Most nights, heavy-beat dance music is designed to get the 20ish crowd up and moving. Next to the DJ booth is a full bar with an espresso machine. On weekends, there's usually a band. Last we saw, the bartender on duty poured with a generous tilt of the bottle. His efforts go for about C$3 to C$7 (US$2.05 to C$4.85).

C@fé Internet. 3672 bd. Saint-Laurent (north of rue Prince Arthur). ☎ **514/842-1726.** Metro: Sherbrooke.

Keep in touch, word-process, play games, or just cruise the Net on any of 16 computers with big 21-inch monitors. Time at the keyboard costs just C$8 (US$5.50) per half hour. There's no booze, just coffee and soft drinks. It's open Monday to Friday 10am to 11pm, Saturday 11am to 11pm, Sunday 11:30am to 11pm.

Champs. 3956 bd. St-Laurent (near rue Duluth). ☎ **514/987-6444.** Metro: Mont-Royal.

Montréalers are no less enthusiastic about sports, especially hockey, than other Canadians, and fans both avid and casual drop by this three-story sports emporium to catch up with their teams and hoist a few. Games from around the world are fed to 35 TV monitors through 20 satellites, so they don't miss a goal, run, or TD. Food is what you expect—burgers, steaks, and such.

Laïka. 4040 bd. St-Laurent. (near rue Duluth). ☎ **514/842-8088.** Metro: Mont-Royal.

Newer than most of the St-Laurent watering stops, this bright little boîte has an open front in summer and fresh flowers on the bar and some of the tables. Tasty sandwiches, tapas, and meze are served, and the Sunday brunch is popular. The DJ spins house, funk, and the mirrored ball from 8pm to 3am for the mostly 18- to 35-year-old crowd. Drinks range from C$3 to C$7 (US$2.05 to US$4.85).

Le Continental Bistro Américain. 4169 rue St-Denis (at rue Rachel). ☎ **514/845-6842.** Métro: Mont-Royal.

The after-curtain crowd from the Théâtre St-Denis gathers here for drinks or late meals, which range far enough afield to be called "international." Designer Jacques Sabourin fashioned the revivalist deco decor, including the bar, which doubles as a display counter. Drinks cost C$4 to C$8 (US$2.75 to US$5.50).

Shed Café. 3515 bd. St-Laurent (north of rue Sherbrooke). ☎ **514/842-0220.** Métro: Sherbrooke.

This bar/resto, in a lively stretch of The Main near rue Sherbrooke, used to look as if the ceiling was caving in. Now it's been transformed to a Gothic dungeon look, and it's not a whit less frenetically popular. There are local beers on tap, as well as good fries and oversize portions of cake. The crowd skews young, but with enough diversity to make an hour or two interesting.

Sugar. 3616 bd. St-Laurent (north of rue Prince Arthur). ☎ **514/287-6555.** Metro: Sherbrooke.

You can't miss it, not with the 12-foot painted concrete figures of a man and woman forming the entrance. Their identity and function are unknown and soon forgotten, for the interior looks like the underpass of a construction site in a crowded European city, a heavily scarred wall on one side, and a fretwork of upright metal rods down the middle. There is a DJ station at back and an open deck upstairs. A short beer is C$3 (US$2.05), with other drinks up to C$8 (US$5.50).

Whisky Café. 5800 bd. St-Laurent (at rue Bernard). ☎ **514/278-2646.** Métro: Outremont.

Those who enjoy scotch, particularly single-malts like Laphraoig and Glenfiddich, find 30 different labels to sample here. Trouble is, the Québec government applies stiff taxes for the privilege, so most of the patrons seem to stick to beer. The decor is sophisticated, with exposed beams and vents, handmade tiled tables, and large wood-enclosed columns, but the real decorative triumph is the men's urinal, with a waterfall for a *pissoir.* Women are welcome to have a look.

QUARTIER LATIN/LATIN QUARTER

✪ **Jello Bar.** 151 rue Ontario Est (near bd. St-Laurent). ☎ **514/285-2621.** www. jello-bar.com. Metro: St-Laurent or Berri-UQAM.

Central to the burgeoning rep of this goofy fifties throwback is that it offers more than 30 kinds of martinis. Most of those, like wine coolers, are flavored excuses for people who don't really like liquor, but the classic gin and vodka versions are stalwarts to be savored. Live music helps fuel the rollicking good mood (Bruce Willis stopped by with his band). Martinis are C$5 (US$3.45).

Le Sainte-Elisabeth. 1412 rue Ste-Elizabeth (north of rue Ste-Catherine). ☎ **514/ 286-4302.** Metro: Berri-UQAM.

Aided by Guinness "on draught," this place comes closer to resembling an Irish pub than most of the many efforts in town. Past the Queen Anne Victorian facade is a copper-topped bar near the fireplace with a smattering of heavily used sofas, and beyond all that is a boxy, tree-shaded, vine-covered open courtyard, known as a *terrasse* in these parts. University and grad students predominate but don't overwhelm. Blues and jazz are on the stereo and in situ (Tuesday, usually).

Le Saint-Sulpice. 1680 rue St-Denis (near rue St-Catherine). ☎ **514/844-9458.** Metro: Berri-UQUAM.

Adjoining four-story buildings still can't absorb the youthful crowds longing to be a part of the scene here. Expect lines up to six people deep and a block long on any night of even slightly tolerable weather. Lately, the mix has included a growing number of gays and lesbians. The club has a crowded terrace, a DJ most nights and live music on some, and dance floors and bars always. Beer is the favored quaff, with drinks going for C$2.50 to C$7 (US$1.70 to US$4.85).

4 The Gay & Lesbian Scene

The city's lively **Quartier Gai/Gay Village** comprises a stretch of rue Ste-Catherine from rue St-Hubert to rue Papineau.

L'Entre-Peau. 1115 rue Ste-Catherine (near rue Amherst). ☎ **514/525-7566.** Cover C$5 (US$3.45) and up. Métro: Beaudry.

This drag-queen cabaret has prospered for more than 10 years, drawing an increasingly straight audience. As many as 20 female impersonators, done up as the usual suspects, plus some unexpected figures, take to the stage every night, year-round. The name of the club, we're told, means "between the skins," which couldn't be more apt. The owner and star boasts a personal wardrobe of more than 200 dresses, 100 wigs, and more shoes than Imelda the Shod. Drinks cost about C$3 to C$6 (US$2.05 to US$4.15).

Mozza. 1208 rue Ste-Catherine (east of rue Montcalm). ☎ **514/524-0295.** Table d'hôte C$9.50–C$13.95 (US$6.55–US$9.60). Prices include taxes. No credit cards. Metro: Beaudry.

Mozza is not a club, but rather a place to save a few loonies on dinner before setting off on a Village pub crawl. It's BYOB, so pick up a bottle first at the *depannéur* across the street. A salad starts the meal, followed by soup or, maybe, an appetizer-sized vegetable pizza. The main course is a substantial serving of pasta—you pick the type and the sauce from a dozen choices. Dessert and coffee or tea follow. Nothing about it qualifies as elegant, not with plastic tablecloths and lank service, but it's more than sustenance and the price is right.

Sisters. 1313 rue Ste-Catherine Est (near rue St-Hubert). ☎ **514/523-0292.** No cover. Métro: Berri-UQAM.

It comes and goes, so to speak, but this dance club above the Saloon restaurant is thriving once again. Lesbians and bi women constitute most of the celebrants and contribute to the high energy level. Men, straight or gay, are likely to find more congenial surroundings elsewhere.

Sky Complex. 1474 rue Ste-Catherine Est (near rue Amherst). ☎ **514/529-6969.** No cover. Métro: Beaudry.

Thought by many to be the city's best gay club, Sky continues to thrive. In the open-fronted ground-floor pub, a couple of go-go boys in Calvin briefs and waffle-stomper boots dance continuously on platforms between the two bars. Spiffy decor and thumping (usually house) music in the upstairs disco contribute to the popularity. Up to six transvestite performers constitute a cabaret show 2 or 3 nights a week. There's an outdoor terrace in summer, and frequent two-for-one beer hours. A leather bar called Sky Jack, with a separate entrance, is around the corner on rue Alexandre-de-Sève.

✪ Unity. 1400 rue Montcalm (corner rue Ste-Catherine). ☎ **514/523-4429.** Cover C$2 (US$1.40) most nights. Métro: Beaudry.

Easily the Village's biggest nightclub, with several rooms, dance floors, a top-floor terrasse (popular for viewing the fireworks from La Ronde in summer), and five bars on different levels. There's plenty of room for dancing to house and techno music and a modest light show. On the third floor are drag shows, in French, mostly. Nothing too raunchy, except for Thursdays, designated "Sex Nights." Women are welcomed Fridays. Drinks are two-for-one during happy hours Friday and Saturday from 4 to 10pm. Open Thursday to Sunday 10pm to 3am.

5 More Entertainment

CINEMA

In Montréal, English-language films are usually presented with subtitles in French. However, when the initials "VF" (for *version française*) follow a movie title, they mean that the movie has been dubbed into French. Policies vary on English subtitles on non–English-language films—the best idea is to ask at the box office. Besides the many first-run movie houses that advertise in the daily newspapers, Montréal is rich in "ciné-clubs," which tend to be slightly older and show second-run, foreign, and art films at reduced prices. Old movies are shown at no charge at the unusual eatery, **Café Ciné-Lumière,** 5163 bd. St-Laurent (☎ **514/495-1796**), where headsets are provided for individual listening while dining.

In first-run movie houses, admission is usually C$8 (US$5.50) for adults in the evening, C$5 (US$3.45) for adults in the afternoon, and C$4.50 (US$3.10) for seniors and children all the time. Some cinemas offer C$5 (US$3.45) tickets until 6pm, and at least one, the **Imperial Cinema** at 1430 rue de Bleury (☎ **514/ 848-0300**), shows first-run films all the time for only C$3 (US$2.05). The **Centre Eaton,** 705 rue Ste-Catherine Ouest, near the corner of rue McGill, has a multiplex cinema with six modern theaters.

The **National Film Board of Canada** (Cinema ONF), 1564 rue St-Denis (☎ **514/496-6895**), shows Canadian and international films, primarily in English and French, particularly classics. Shows are Tuesday through Sunday; call for times.

Imposing images surround viewers of the seven-story screen in the **IMAX theater** in the new Interactive Science Centre in the Old Port, (☎ **514/496-4629**). Available productions are limited, so efforts are made to create films suitable for the entire family. See "Especially for Kids" in chapter 6 for more details.

GAMBLING

In autumn 1993, the **Montréal Casino** (☎ **800/665-2274** or 514/392-2746; **www.casinos-quebec.com**), Québec's first, opened on Île Notre-Dame in the former French Pavilion, which was left over from the world's fair called Expo '67. The casino has 118 game tables, including roulette, craps, blackjack, and baccarat, and more than 3,000 slot machines on several floors. It can accommodate 8,000 people, most of whom come to try their luck, of course; but the four restaurants get good notices, especially **Nuances** (see chapter 5). There are four bars, live shows, and two shops selling gifts and souvenirs. No alcoholic beverages are served in the gambling areas. Patrons must be 18 or over. The casino is now open around the clock. Tickets to the show can be purchased at the casino or on the Net, at **www.admission.com**. They are priced from C$37 (US$26) for the show alone, from C$59 (US$41) for the show and dinner. The originally strict dress code has been relaxed somewhat, but the following items of clothing are still prohibited: "cut-off sweaters and shirts, tank tops, jogging outfits, cut-off shorts and bike shorts, beachwear, work or motorcycle boots, and clothing associated with violence or with an organization known to be violent." Admission and parking are free. To get to the casino, take the Métro to the Île Ste-Hélène stop, which is adjacent to Île Notre-Dame, and walk or take the shuttle bus from there.

Side Trips from Montréal 10

For respite from urban stresses and demands, Montréalers need only drive 30 minutes or so to the north or east of the city to find themselves in the hearts of the resort regions of the Laurentides or Estrie. The lakes and mountains of both areas have invited development of year-round vacation retreats and ski centers. The pearl of the Laurentides is Mont-Tremblant, the highest peak in eastern Canada, but the region has 18 other ski centers with scores of trails at every level of difficulty, many of them less than an hour from Montréal.

Bucolic Estrie, formerly known as the Eastern Townships when it was a haven for English Loyalists and their descendants, is blessed with a trio of memorable country inns on beautiful Lake Massawippi. The region promotes four seasons of outdoor diversions. It has fewer ski centers than the Laurentides, and the resort hotels that serve them are generally smaller and less extensive in their facilities, but its many lakes and gentler pastimes give it the edge for warm-weather vacations. Because the people of both regions rely heavily on tourism for their livelihoods, knowledge of at least rudimentary English is widespread, even outside such obvious places as hotels and ski resorts.

In Estrie, many of the same trails and settings developed for winter sports are used for parallel activities in summer. Bromont, for example, has 62 miles (100km) of marked trails for mountain biking, and Mont-Orford Park is the focal point for another 99 miles (160km) of hiking trails linking six regional parks. Rock climbing, white-water kayaking, sailing, and fishing are additional options. Appropriate equipment is readily available for rent on-site, wilderness shelters and trail cabins are at hand, and even meals can be catered in the woods.

1 North into the Laurentians (Laurentides)

34–80 miles (55–129km) N of Montréal

Expect no spiked peaks or high ragged ridges. The rolling hills and rounded mountains of the Laurentian Shield are among the oldest in the world, worn down by wind and water over eons. They average between 980 and 1,700 feet (300m and 520m), with the highest being Mont-Tremblant, at 3,175 feet (968m). In the lower precincts, nearer Montréal, the terrain resembles a rumpled quilt, its folds and hollows cupping a multitude of lakes large and small. Farther north the summits are higher and craggier, with patches of snow persisting well into spring, but these are still not the Alps or the Rockies. They're welcoming and embracing rather than awe inspiring.

Half a century ago the first ski schools, rope tows, and trails began to appear; today there are 19 ski centers within a 40-mile radius, and cross-country skiing has as enthusiastic a following as downhill. (The best cross-country trails are at Far Hills in Val-Morin and L'Esterel in Ville d'Esterel and on the grounds of a monastery called Domaine du St-Bernard near Villa Bellevue in Mont-Tremblant.) Sprawling resorts and modest lodges and inns are packed each winter with skiers, some of them through April. Trails for advanced skiers typically have short pitches and challenging moguls, with broad, hard-packed avenues for beginners and the less experienced.

But skiing is only half the story. As transportation improved, people took advantage of the obvious opportunities for water sports, golf (courses in the area now number 30), tennis, mountain biking, hiking, and every other kind of summer sport. Before long the region had gained an often-deserved reputation for fine dining and a convivial atmosphere that survives to this day. Bird-watchers of both intense and casual bent are fully occupied. Loon lovers, in particular, know that the lakes of Québec province's mountains are home to an estimated 16,000 of the native waterfowl that gives its name to the dollar coin. Excellent divers and swimmers, the birds are unable to walk on land, which makes nesting a trial, and they're identified by a distinctive call that might be described as an extended mournful giggle.

Winter or summer, a visit to any of the villages and resorts in the Laurentians is likely to yield pleasant memories. The busiest times are in February and March, in July and August, and during the Christmas to New Year holiday period. Other times of the year, reservations are easier to get, prices of virtually everything are lower, and crowds are less dense. May and September are often characterized by warm days, cool nights, and just enough people that the streets don't seem deserted. In May and June, it must be said, the indigenous black flies and mosquitoes can seem as big and as ill-tempered as buzzards, so prepare for them with some sort of repellent. Some of the resorts, inns, and lodges close down for a couple of weeks in the spring and the fall. A handful are open only for a few winter months.

March and April are the season when the maple trees are tapped, and *cabanes à sucre* ("sugar shacks") open up everywhere, some selling only maple candies and syrup, others serving full meals featuring the principal product and even staging entertainment.

In mid-July, the region's annual **Fête de Vins** (Wine Festival) is held for 2 days in St-Jérôme, and the emphasis is on gastronomy and wine tasting; a dozen restaurants in the area participate. In August, St-Jean-sur-le-Richelieu hosts an **International Hot Air Balloon Festival.**

July and August bring glorious summer days to the Laurentians, and during the last 2 weeks in September the leaves put on a stunning show of autumnal color. Skiers can usually expect reliable snow from early December to mid-April.

As for prices, they can be difficult to pin down: The large resorts have so many types of rooms, suites, cottages, meal plans, discounts, and packages that you may need a travel agent to pick through the thicket of options. In planning, remember that Montréalers fill the highways when they "go up north" on weekends, particularly during the top skiing months of February and March, so plan ahead when making reservations. An unfortunate note for pet owners: Few Laurentian resorts accept animals.

ESSENTIALS
GETTING THERE

BY CAR The fast and scenic Autoroute des Laurentides, also known as Autoroute 15, goes straight from Montréal to the Laurentian mountains. Just follow the signs to

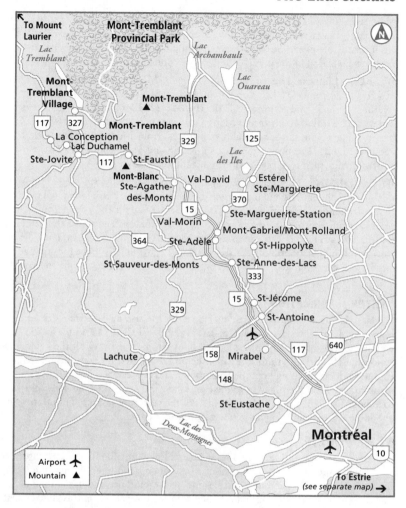

St-Jérôme. The exit numbers are actually the distance in kilometers the village is from Montréal. One likely early stop, for instance, is La Maison du Tourisme (Tourism House) at Exit 39 in St-Jérôme, and St-Jérôme is 39 kilometers (24 miles) from Montréal. This is a comely drive, once you're out of the clutches of the tangle of expressways surrounding Montréal. The Autoroute des Laurentides gives a sweeping, panoramic introduction to the area, from the rolling hills and forests of the lower Laurentians to the mountain drama of the upper Laurentians.

Those with the time to meander can exit at St-Jérôme and pick up the older, parallel Route 117, which plays tag with the autoroute all the way to Ste-Agathe-des-Monts, where the highway ends. Most of the region's more appealing towns are strung along or near Route 117. Approaching each town, signs direct drivers to the local tourism information office, where attendants provide helpful tips on lodging, restaurants, and things to do. North of Ste-Agathe, the Autoroute ends and Route 117 becomes the major artery for the region, continuing deep into Québec's north country and finally ending at the Ontario border hundreds of miles from Montréal.

Be aware that Québec's equivalent of the Highway Patrol maintains a strong presence along the stretch of Autoroute 15 between St-Faustin and Ste-Adèle. While enforcement of speed limits is flaccid, if you are pulled over, remember that radar detectors are illegal in the province and can be confiscated.

BY BUS   Limocar Laurentides buses depart Montréal's **Terminus Voyageur,** 505 bd. de Maisonneuve Est, stopping in the larger Laurentian towns, including Ste-Agathe, Ste-Adèle, and St-Jovite; call ☎ **514/842-2281** for schedules. An express bus can make the run to St-Jovite and Mont-Tremblant in less than 2 hours, while a local bus, making all the stops, takes almost 3 hours. From Montréal to Ste-Adèle takes about 1½ hours, 15 minutes more to Val-Morin and Val-David. Some of the major resorts provide their own bus service at an additional charge.

BY LIMOUSINE   Taxis and limousines await arrivals at Dorval Airport in Montréal, where all domestic and international commercial flights arrive, and will take you to any Laurentian hideaway—for a price. While the fare for the 1-hour trip by limo from Dorval is steep, four or five people can share the cost and lessen the pain. Ask for the standard fare to your inn or lodge when calling to make reservations. The inn usually will take responsibility for seeing that a taxi or limo is indeed waiting at the airport and may even help to find other guests arriving at the same time to share the cost.

VISITOR INFORMATION

For an orientation to the entire region, stop at **La Maison du Tourisme des Laurentides,** 14142 rue de la Chapelle, St-Jérôme, PQ J7J 2CB (☎ **450/436-8532**), a regional tourist information office located in St-Jérôme at Exit 39 off the Laurentian Autoroute 15. In addition to its racks of helpful brochures, the staff can make reservations for lodging throughout the Laurentides, and the service is free. The red-roofed stone cottage is off the highway to the east; follow the signs. It's open daily mid-June to Labour Day 8:30am to 8:30pm; the rest of the year, 9am to 5pm. For information about the entire region, log on to **www.laurentides.com**.

ST-HIPPOLYTE

A detour off Route 117 leads to a residential village with a body of water known as the "Millionaire's Lake"—an appellation you'll understand after viewing the stately homes facing its shores and the seaplanes and sleek motorboats moored at their docks. Lac Achigan is also known for an inn long admired for its cuisine. It is close enough for a day trip from Montréal.

To get there, take Exit 39 off Autoroute 15 and pick up Route 117 north. After about 3.7 miles (6km), branch right on Route 333 north and continue another 10 miles (16km) to the village center. Turn right on boulevard du Lac Achigan, then right again before the lake, following signs to the inn described below.

WHERE TO STAY & DINE

Auberge des Cèdres. 26 av. 305e, St-Hippolyte, PQ J8A 3P5. ☎ **877/563-2083** or 450/563-5050. Fax 450/563-1663. www.aubergedescedres.com. E-mail: info@aubergedescedres.com. 7 units. A/C TV. C$95–C$175 (US$66–US$121) double. Rates include breakfast. AE, MC, V.

Built in 1906, this shambling lakeside house operated as an inn for many years, drifting into somnolence and then closing as the owners aged. Now it has been reawakened, the new proprietors installing a bar and a computer room, redecorating the bedrooms and public areas, and converting a carriage house. Original sleeping quarters are on the second and third floors of the main building. Most of them are on the small side, and closet space is from little to none; but six rooms have lake views. The biggest room, up a very narrow staircase, has a double whirlpool, a sofa bed, and a balcony.

Emphasis is on the dining room. The diffident young chef assembles such dishes as curried salmon fillets and little sprays of seven different steamed vegetables. His seasonings could be perked up and the bread improved, but these quibbles are negligible when you get a load of the knockout view of the lake from the dining room's long windows.

ST-SAUVEUR-DES-MONTS

Only 37 miles (60km) north of Montréal, St-Sauveur-des-Monts (pop. 5,864) can easily be visited on a day trip. The village square is dominated by a handsome church, and the streets around it bustle with activity much of the year, so be prepared to have difficulty finding a parking place in season (try the large lot behind the church). Dining and snacking on everything from crepes to hot dogs are big activities here, evidenced by the many beckoning cafes. In season, there's a tourist kiosk on the square.

The area is well-known for its night skiing—23 well-lit trails, only 3 fewer than those available during the day. The mountain is wide, with a 700-foot vertical drop and a variety of well-groomed trails, making it a good choice for families. In summer, St-Sauveur-des-Monts becomes Canada's largest water park, featuring a wave pool and a mountain slide where you go up in chairlifts and come down in tubes. The first 2 weeks in August are given to the annual **Festival des Arts** (☎ 450/227-0427), with an emphasis on music and dance, including jazz and chamber concerts and ballet troupes as celebrated as the Kirov Ballet and the José Greco Flamenco Group.

The **tourist information office** serving the area is at Exit 60 of Autoroute 15, at 605 Chemin des Frênes, Piedmont, PQ J0R 1K0 (☎ 450/227-4072), is open year-round, daily from 9am to 5pm. There is also a seasonal booth (☎ 450/227-2564) in St-Sauveur in the park in front of the church.

WHERE TO STAY

Le Relais St-Denis. 61 rue St-Denis, St-Sauveur-des-Monts, PQ J0R 1R4. ☎ **888/997-4766** or 450/227-4766. Fax 450/227-8504. 41 units. A/C MINIBAR TV TEL. C$145–C$155 (US$100–US$107) double; C$175 (US$121) suite. Meal plans available. AE, DC, ER, MC, V. Pets are allowed.

Set back from the road, the cream-colored "U"-shaped building is surrounded by birch and evergreens and extensive flower gardens. The Relais resembles a country club, complete with a heated outdoor pool and nearby golf. Rooms are of good size, with fireplaces and large bathrooms. Those in the new wing are larger and more polished, with whirlpool baths. Note that the one-bedroom suites are only C$20 (US$13.80) more than the regular rooms, a deal worth considering. Ski and golf packages are available, as are therapeutic massages. Reception is in the building with the green awning. Pets are allowed, unusual in these hills.

Manoir Saint-Sauveur. 246 Chemin du Lac-Millette, St-Sauveur-des-Monts, PQ J0R 1R3. ☎ **800/361-0505** or 450/227-1811. Fax 450/227-8512. www.manoir-saint-sauveur.com. E-mail: admin@manoir-saint-sauveur.com. 216 units. A/C MINIBAR TV TEL. Mid-June to mid-Oct C$209–C$225 (US$144–US$155) double; from C$220 ($152) suite. Mid-Oct to mid-June C$99–C$138 (US$68–US$95) double; from C$180 (US$124) suite. Extra person C$10 (US$6.90). Children 17 and under stay free in parents' room. Packages available. AE, DC, ER, MC, V. Take Exit 60 off Autoroute 15.

This is one of the region's several large resort hotels, with a monster outdoor pool and a comprehensive roster of four-season activities. Its facilities include a fitness center with weight machines and a sauna, an indoor pool, racquetball, squash, tennis, in-house movies, and a shop. A warm personality isn't included. It isn't really necessary, considering that the rooms are roomy and comfortable, blandly modern with lightwood furnishings that hint vaguely of 19th-century Gallic inspirations, both provincial and royal. The main building is easily spotted from the road, with its green roof and many dormers. The front desk adjusts room prices up or down according to season, demand, and the occupancy rate on any given night, so keep asking if they have anything cheaper. Book online, and the hotel cuts 10% off the rack rates.

WHERE TO DINE

L'Armorique. 231 rue Principale. ☎ **450/227-0080.** Main courses C$3–C$14 (US$2.05–US$9.65). DC, MC, V. Summer daily 8am–2am; rest of year Tues–Sun 11am–10:30pm. CREPES/LIGHT FARE.

Using a well-preserved Victorian house in the middle of town, this creperie is only one of a number of casual eateries clustered along the streets radiating from the village square. Main-course fillings for the crepes run from conventional eggs and cheese or smoked salmon to chicken with ratatouille and shrimp, mushrooms, and mussels with béchamel. Other possibilities are several hearty salads and raclette, the fonduelike dish with all manner of things to dip. In summer, the front porch and a large side deck have vantages for watching the street activity.

MONT-GABRIEL

Mont-Gabriel is only 2½ miles (4km) from St-Sauveur-des-Monts. To get there, follow Autoroute 15 to Exit 64 and turn right at the stop sign. Although popular in summer, Mont-Gabriel comes into its own each winter when guests schuss down its 21 trails and slopes and then slide back up again on the seven T-bar lifts, the triple-chair, or the quadruple-chair lift. Eight trails are lit for night skiing. Cross-country trails girdle the mountain and range through the surrounding countryside. For lodgings, see "Mont-Gabriel Resort" under Ste-Adèle, below.

STE-ADÈLE

Route 117 swings directly into Ste-Adèle to become its main street, boulevard Ste-Adèle; or, take Exit 67 off Autoroute 15 North. The village (pop. 7,800), only 42 miles (67km) north of Montréal, is a near-metropolis compared to the other Laurentian villages that line the upper reaches of Route 117. What makes it seem big are its services: police, doctors, ambulances, a shopping center, art galleries, and a larger collection of places to stay and dine than is found elsewhere in the Laurentians. As rue Morin mounts the hill to Lac Rond, Ste-Adèle's resort lake, it's easily seen why the town is divided into a lower part (*en bas*) and an upper part (*en haut*).

The **Bureau Touristique de Ste-Adèle,** at rue St-Joseph, Ste-Adèle (☎ **450/229-9295**), is open daily: in July and August 9am to 7pm; until 5pm the rest of the year. Find it off exit 67 of Autoroute 15.

EXPLORING STE-ADÈLE

The main street of Ste-Adèle, **rue Valiquette,** is a busy one-way thoroughfare lined with cafes, galleries, and bakeries. But **Lac Rond** is the center of activities during the Ste-Adèle summer. Canoes, sailboats, and *pédalos* (pedal-powered watercraft), rented from several docks, glide over the placid surface while swimmers splash and play near shore-side beaches.

In winter the surrounding green hills are swathed in white, and the **ski trails** descend to the shores of the frozen lake. Downhill ski equipment can be rented and lessons obtained at **Le Chantecler** resort (see below), which has 22 trails served by six chairlifts and two T-bars. Some of the trails end right by the main hotel. At the town's

Centre Municipal, Côtes 40/80, 1400 rue Rolland (☎ **450/229-2921**), the trails are good for beginners: three T-bar lifts carry up the slopes for the run down 5 different trails.

Ste-Adèle has a **cinema** showing first-run English-language movies all year. For four days in late May, there has been a food festival, **Les Arts Gourmands de Sainte-Adèle,** featuring books, author lectures, cooking demonstrations, workshops, and wine tastings, utilizing the facilities of the École Hôtelière des Laurentides, which trains students for careers in the hospitality industry. Call ☎ **450/229-3729** for details.

Musée Village de Séraphin. 297 Montée à Séraphin, off Route 117 (Exit 72), Ste-Adèle. ☎ **450/229-4777.** Admission C$9 (US$6.20) adults, C$7 (US$4.80) children 12–17, C$6 (US$4.15) children 6–11, free for children under 5. Mid-May to mid-June and mid-Sept to mid-Oct Sat–Sun 10am–5pm; mid-June to Labour Day daily 10am–5pm. Closed mid-Oct to mid-May. Drive 1 mile north of Ste-Adèle on Route 117.

This re-creation of a 19th-century Laurentian village is a mild diversion from the prevailing activities, at least for a short visit. Among the 20 structures are log cabins and slightly more refined public buildings set along dirt streets that hint at what life was like 100 years ago. Children usually enjoy the park's old-time atmosphere, and they can ride a miniature train on a 20-minute run through the village and the forest. The on-site Bar Chez Ti-Père serves their parents' old-time Québec favorites like "caribou," "tiblanc" (both highly alcoholic), and cider.

WHERE TO STAY

Alpine. 1440 Chemin Pierre-Péladeau, Ste-Adèle, PQ J8B 1Z4. ☎ **877/257-4630** or 450/229-1545. Fax 450/229-1544. 17 units. A/C TV. C$70–C$95 (US$48–US$66) double. Rates include breakfast. Meal plans available. AE, MC, V. From the south, take Exit 69, then Route 370 east 2 miles (3km) to the hotel.

This collection of rustic log structures, begun in 1924, contains several types of accommodations. The four cabins have two-bedroom suites with fireplaces, and kitchenettes with microwave ovens. Sleeping up to eight people, they are meant for families. At the other end of the spectrum are *les suites romantiques,* with king-size beds, sofas in front of fireplaces, double Jacuzzis, cable TV, and VCR—meant for *making* families. On the grounds are a heated pool and a tennis court, with a mini-hole golf course adjacent. Meals of traditional Québec cooking are served at two communal tables.

Auberge Bonne Nuit, Bonjour. 1980 bd. Ste-Adèle (Route 117; C.P. 2168), Ste-Adèle, PQ J8B 2N5. ☎ **450/229-7500.** www.bonnenuitbonjour.com. E-mail: bonnenuitbonjour@qc.aibn.com. 6 units, 4 with bathroom. C$75 (US$52) double without bathroom, C$90–C$100 (US$62–US$69) with bathroom. Rates include breakfast. AE, MC, V.

Almost hidden in a stand of cedar beside Route 117 (on the left, driving north) stands this stone house—a B&B with dormers and shutters with carved squirrels. Inside is a sitting room with a rock fireplace, a small TV room, and a solarium looking out on a garden with a brook running through it. One of the new owners was a pastry chef, so the breakfasts are large and she's added an afternoon buffet of cookies, tea, and hot chocolate. Those are her quilts on the walls and on the beds in the simply but colorfully furnished rooms. Room 5 has a queen and its own balcony. There is an outdoor swimming pool, unusual for a small B&B.

L'Excelsior. 3655 bd. Ste-Adèle (Route 117), Ste-Adèle, PQ J0R 1L0. ☎ **800/363-2483** or 514/229-7676. Fax 514/229-9991. www.spaexcelsior.com. E-mail: hotel@spaexcelsior.com. 52 units. A/C TV TEL. C$80–C$110 (US$55–US$76) double; C$160–C$180 (US$110–US$124) suite. Rates include breakfast. Meal plans available. AE, MC, V. Coming from Montréal, take Exit 67 off the autoroute.

More distinctive architecturally and larger than most roadside resorts in the Laurentians, L'Excelsior benefits from management that maintains high standards of housekeeping, and all rooms have cable color TVs and share both indoor and outdoor pools and whirlpools, a tennis court, squash courts, an exercise room, a sauna, and Amadéus restaurant and bar. Many rooms have balconies and some are reserved for nonsmokers. Elaborate spa treatments are available, including hydrotherapy, massage, mineral and algae wraps, massages, and salt baths. Various packages include combinations of these with lodging and meals.

WHERE TO STAY & DINE

Hôtel L'Eau à la Bouche. 3003 bd. Ste-Adèle (Route 117), Ste-Adèle, PQ J8B 2N6. ☎ **450/ 229-2991.** Fax 514/229-7573. www.relaischateaux.fr/eaubouche. E-mail: eaubouche@ sympatico.ca. 25 units. A/C TV TEL. From C$165 (US$114) double; from C$280 (US$193) suite. Rates include breakfast. Packages available. AE, DC, ER, MC, V.

L'Eau à la Bouche started as a roadside restaurant, and the chef-owners later added this separate hotel. It's a member of the international Relais & Châteaux consortium of inns and small hotels, an organization that places its emphasis on gastronomy rather than physical exertion. That it does here, and admirably, as the recommendation of its restaurant suggests (see "Where to Dine" below). However, the hotel faces the Mont-Chantecler ski trails, is across the road from a golf course, and has a heated outdoor pool. Inside is a large living room with a brick fireplace and bar and sofas set about in conversation groups. Substantial breakfasts are served here, at tables with bentwood chairs and green-and-white checkered cloths. The bedrooms have queen- or king-size beds, ceiling fans, and reproductions of Québec country furniture. The large bathrooms have hair dryers and robes. All rooms have sitting areas, and six also have fireplaces and balconies or patios. No elevator and no porters, but help with luggage can be obtained if necessary.

Le Chantecler. 1474 Chemin Chantecler, Ste-Adèle, PQ J8B 1A2. ☎ **800/363-2420** or 450/229-3555. Fax 450/229-5593. www.lechantecler.com. E-mail: reservationchantecler@ gouverneur.com. 200 units. TV TEL. C$108–C$185 (US$74–C$128) double including breakfast, C$158–C$250 (US$109–US$172) double including breakfast and dinner. Children 17 and under stay free in parents' room. Many packages available. AE, CB, DC, DISC, ER, MC, V. Take Exit 67 off Autoroute 15, turn left at the fourth traffic light onto rue Morin, then turn right at the top of the hill onto Chemin Chantecler.

Sprawled across steep slopes cupping Lac à la Truite, this resort is composed of several stone buildings of varying heights, its roofs bristling with steeples and dormers. It has 22 slopes for all levels of skiers, including a 622-foot vertical drop, and a ski school. The rooms are decorated with pine furniture made locally; most have air-conditioning. Many of the suites have fireplaces, and most have whirlpool baths. A bountiful buffet breakfast is served in the glass-enclosed dining room, which over-looks the active slopes and the lake with its small beach. Apart from the dings and dents that typically afflict heavily used family resorts, it is maintained reasonably well.

Dining/Diversions: Dining room with terrace serving regional cuisine, piano bar, disco (winter only), movies in the projection room, and summer-stock theater.

Amenities: Ski school, 23 runs on four mountains (including 13 night-lit runs), ski chalet (with cafeteria and bar), cross-country trails, ice-skating, indoor sports complex (with a pool, sauna, Jacuzzi, squash, racquetball, badminton, and some fitness equipment), 18-hole and lit 9-hole golf courses, six lit tennis courts, windsurfing, canoeing, paddleboats, rowboats, mountain bikes. Baby-sitting, day camp, dry cleaning and laundry, self-service laundry, video rental, express checkout, and ski lockers.

Mont-Gabriel Resort. 1699 Chemin Montée Gabriel, PQ J8B 1A5. ☎ **450/229-3547,** 514/861-2852 in Montréal, or 800/668-5253 in Canada. Fax 450/229-7034. www.montgabriel. com. E-mail: info@montgabriel.com. 126 units. A/C TV TEL. C$139 (US$96) double. Rates include full breakfast. Meal plans and other packages available. AE, DC, ER, MC, V. Take Exit 64 from Autoroute 15.

Perched high above highways and the valley and looking like the rambling log "cottages" of the turn-of-the-century wealthy, this desirable hotel is only 20 miles from Montréal's Dorval Airport. Set on a 1,200-acre forest estate, the resort complex features golf and tennis programs in summer and ski packages in winter. The spacious rooms in the Tyrol section are the most desirable, many with views of the surrounding hills, while those in what they call the Old Lodge are more rustic, but a $7 million renovation in 1998 upgraded most of these. Coffeemakers and hair dryers are standard. With the Club Package come three meals and unlimited access to all sports facilities, and prices include tax and service charge. Rates drop for stays of 2 to 5 nights.

Dining/Diversions: Meals are served in the resort's dining rooms and at poolside. Evenings, there's dancing in the main lodge.

Amenities: Indoor facilities include a pool, a sauna, a whirlpool, and an exercise room. The outdoor swimming pool is heated, and there are a par-71 golf course and six tennis courts. In summer, there are activity programs for children.

WHERE TO DINE

✪ **L'Eau à la Bouche.** 3003 bd. Ste-Adèle (Route 117). ☎ **800/363-2582** or 514/ 229-2991. Reservations recommended. Main courses C$34–C$44 (US$23–US$30); fixed-price lunch from C$16 (US$11); fixed-price 5-course dinner C$55–C$75 (US$38–US$52). AE, MC, V. Daily 6–9pm. CONTEMPORARY FRENCH.

Owners Anne Desjardins and Pierre Audette leave no doubt where their priorities lie. Their nearby hotel (see above) is entirely satisfactory, but this, the restaurant, is their love child, and it has the glow-in-the-dark reviews to prove it. False modesty isn't a factor—*l'eau à la bouche* means "mouthwatering"—and the kitchen delivers. The faux Provençal interior employs heavy ceiling beams, white plaster walls, and pine paneling to set the mood. On one occasion, the preappetizer was a dollop of salmon tartare laced with flecks of ginger and sweet red pepper. It provided an interlude to appreciate the generous martinis that exceed the skimpy Québec norm and to study the carefully assembled wine list. Native ingredients and ample portions are meshed with nouvelle presentations, and the menu changes by the week, even daily. Advantage is taken of seasonal products as with the springtime starter of trout roe layered atop the lobster timbale with fiddleheads and baby asparagus heads; game dishes arrive in fall. Desserts are impressive, but the cheese plate—pungent nubbins of French and Québec varieties delivered with warm baguette slices—is special. The mostly young staff is both efficient and unobtrusive. A meal here might well be the most memorable (and pricey) dining experience of a Laurentian visit.

La Vanoise. 1261 Chemin du Chantecler, Ste-Adèle. ☎ **450/229-4396.** Main courses C$16.95–C$32.95 (US$11.70–US$22.70); table d'hôte lunch and dinner from C$13.95 (US$9.60). MC, V. May–Oct, Tues–Sun noon–10pm; Nov–Apr Tues–Sun noon–9pm. FRENCH BISTRO.

Diners view a lake from the deck or through wide windows of this frame house between courses of such bistro standards as pea soup, hot smoked salmon or slivers of duck confit on salad, veal medallions with cream and Calvados, and sole meunière. It's hardly out-of-the-ordinary, uncomplicated in both preparation and presentation, but entirely satisfactory, and at very reasonable prices. Degrees of novelty are found in such daily specials as caribou raviolis. It's more popular with locals than tourists, and families appreciate the child's menu at C$6.95 (US$4.80).

STE-MARGUERITE & ESTÉREL

To get to Ste-Marguerite (pop. 2,000) or the even less populous Estérel, only 2 miles apart, follow Autoroute 15 north to Exit 69. Or if driving from Ste-Adèle, look for a street heading northeast named Chemin Ste-Marguerite (Route 370). It becomes a narrow road that crosses the Laurentian Autoroute (at Exit 69), bridges the Rivière du Nord, and leads into an area of many lakes bordered by upscale vacation properties.

Ste-Marguerite and Estérel are 53 miles (85km) and 55 miles (88km) north of Montréal, respectively. In summer, information about the area is available from Pavillon du Parc, 74 Chemin Masson, in Ste-Marguerite-du-Lac-Masson (☎ **514/ 228-3525**); year-round, go to the nearby Bureau Touristique de Ste-Adèle (see above).

WHERE TO STAY IN ESTÉREL

L'Estérel. Bd. Fridolin-Simard (C.P. 38), Ville d'Estérel, PQ J0T 1E0. ☎ **888/378-3735** or 514/228-2571. Fax 514/228-4977. www.esterel.com. E-mail: info@esterel.com. 135 units. A/C TV TEL. C$252–C$309 (US$174–US$213) double, including full breakfast and dinner and use of most facilities. Lower rates Dec–May. Discounts for stays of 3 or more nights. Packages available. AE, CB, DC, ER, MC, V. Take the Limocar bus from Montréal into Ste-Adèle; the hotel picks up guests there.

One of the more prominent Laurentian resorts lies a few miles past Ste-Marguerite in the hamlet of Estérel. This year-round complex is capable of accommodating 300 guests on its 5,000-acre estate with three linked lakes. Occupying an expanse of otherwise vacant lakeshore, L'Estérel offers conventionally furnished rooms, many with balconies. Those with a view of the lake are more expensive.

Rates include use of all indoor facilities and the tennis courts. For a special winter experience, inquire about the dogsled trips through the woods and over the frozen lake. There are 53 miles (85km) of cross-country ski trails, nearby downhill skiing, ice-skating on a rink, and a heated indoor pool; in summer, an 18-hole golf course and school, tennis, nature trails, horseback riding, sailing, bicycle rental, parasailing, and waterskiing. Other resort amenities include a concierge, room service (7am to 10pm), dry cleaning and laundry, self-service laundry, and a kids' club.

WHERE TO DINE IN STE-MARGUERITE

✪ **Le Bistro à Champlain.** 75 Chemin Masson. ☎ **450/228-4988.** Reservations recommended. Main courses C$18–C$35 (US$12.40–US$24); table d'hôte C$34 (US$23); dégustation menu C$68 (US$47). AE, DC, ER, MC, V. Summer Tues–Sat 6–10pm, Sun noon–10pm; the rest of the year Thurs–Sat 6–10pm. FRENCH.

On the shore of Lac Masson is one of the most honored restaurants in the Laurentians. Its 1864 building used to be a general store, and it retains the original rough-hewn board walls, exposed beams, wood ceiling, and cash register. Gastronomy, not hardware, is now the motivation for customers who routinely motor up from Montréal for dinner. The 35,000-bottle cellar has been a big reason, its very reputation making it the recent target of thieves. The devastated owner, a practicing radiologist, carried on after the robbery and an unusually large number of wines can still be sampled by the glass. The food matches the wines, arriving both flavorful and attractively presented. For those caught up in the fad, there is a comfortably appointed cigar lounge with dozens of single-malt scotches available.

VAL-DAVID & VAL-MORIN

Follow Route 117 north to Exit 76 or 80, respectively, to reach Val-David or Val-Morin. To those who know it, the faintly bohemian enclave of Val-David (pop. 3,225), 50 miles (80km) north of Montréal, conjures up images of cabin hideaways set among hills rearing above ponds and lakes, and laced with creeks tumbling through fragrant forests. The village celebrated its 75th anniversary in 1996.

The **tourist office** is on the main street at 2501 rue de l'Église (☎ **888/322-7030** or 819/322-2900). It's open June 20 to Labour Day daily 9am to 7pm; September 5 to June 19 daily 10am to 4pm. Another possibility for assistance is **La Maison du Village,** a cultural center that mounts art exhibits in a two-story wooden building at 2495 rue de l'Église (☎ **819/322-2900,** ext. 237). Note that this far north into the Laurentians, the telephone area code changes to 819.

WHERE TO STAY & DINE IN VAL-MORIN

Far Hills. Val-Morin, PQ J0T 2S0. ☎ **800/567-6636** or 819/990-4409. Fax 819/322-1995. www.farhillsinn.com. E-mail: info@farhillsinn.com. 72 units. TEL. C$238 (US$164) double. Rates include breakfast and dinner. Children under 10 stay for half price in parents' room. Packages available. DC, MC, V. Leave the autoroute at Exit 76, go through Val-Morin, and follow the signs up into the hills for almost 3 miles.

Well away from main roads, this stone-and-clapboard resort is set in the midst of gardens and birch trees. The main building has a spacious public room with picture windows and two sitting areas. A large outdoor pool is cut into the hillside below the main building. More than half the rooms have air-conditioning, and a few have TVs. The most desirable are the 24 in the recently redecorated Spruce Lodge. Far Hills opened before World War II, and much of the furniture and decor date to major makeovers in the 1950s and late 1960s.

Dining/Diversions: The pine-paneled dining room with beamed ceiling and picture windows is the setting for meals that employ local produce whenever possible. Food is French, with fusion overtones, widely acknowledged to be some of the best in these mountains. The wine list features French bottlings, and several are available by the glass. When making reservations, ask for a table overlooking the grounds. Diners who aren't overnight guests can expect to pay about C$38 (US$26) for a five-course dinner. Patio brunches in summer are enjoyable, and the Panorama piano bar has live music some nights.

Amenities: The resort has a cross-country ski school and 62 miles of cross-country trails; a motor-free lake and indoor and outdoor pools; a sauna; tennis, squash, and racquetball courts; Ping-Pong; hiking and mountain climbing; and canoeing, sailing, and paddleboating. Golf courses and horse trails are nearby. Amenities include room service (9am to 9pm), dry cleaning and laundry, newspaper, in-room massage, babysitting, secretarial services, and express checkout.

EXPLORING VAL-DAVID

Val-David is small, so park anywhere and meander at leisure. Visiting the studios of local artists is a possible activity, and the village sponsors an annual **art festival,** in the first 2 weeks of August, when painters, sculptors, ceramicists, jewelers, pewter smiths, and other craftspeople display their work. There are concerts and other outdoor activities.

Val-David sits astride a 124-mile (200km) parkway called the **Parc Linéaire le P'Tit Train du Nord,** a former railroad right-of-way. It is now a trail that runs from St-Jérôme to Mont-Laurier, heavily used for cycling in summer and for cross-country skiing in winter. Have a picnic beside the North River in the **Parc des Amoureax,** which is 2½ miles (4km) from the main road through town. It has plenty of benches, and some parking spaces on the approach to the park. Watch for the sign SITE PITTORESQUE and turn at Chemin de la Rivière.

Le Village du Père Noël. 987 rue Morin (Route 117). ☎ **819/322-2146.** Admission C$8.50 (US$5.85), C$6.50 (US$4.50) seniors, free for children 2 and under. Mid-May to mid-June Sat–Sun; first 3 Sun in Sept 10am–6pm; mid-June to Aug daily 10am–6pm. Closed mid-Sept to early May.

Younger children may be diverted by a visit to this "summer home of Santa Claus," located in Val-David since 1954. Besides Kris's house, set in a mock alpine village painted in blazing colors, there are animals, games, boats, a picnic area, fast food, and a room filled with 38,000 balls meant for plunging.

WHERE TO STAY IN VAL-DAVID

Auberge du Vieux Foyer. 3167 Chemin Doncaster, Val-David, PQ J0T 2N0. ☎ **819/322-2686,** or 800/567-8327 in Canada. Fax 819/322-2687. www.aubergeduvieuxfoyer. qbc.net. E-mail: aub-duvieuxfoyer@citenet.net. 25 units, including 3 chalets. A/C TV TEL. C$166–C$186 (US$115–US$128) double; C$232 (US$160) chalet for 2. Rates include breakfast, dinner, and service. Extra person C$72 (US$50). Weekly rates, off-season rates, and packages available. MC, V. Follow the signs through the town about 1½ miles (3km) to the inn.

This Swiss-style inn stands beside its own private pond. Armchairs are drawn up to the big fireplace in the main sitting room. Behind doors painted to resemble gift packages, the guest rooms are smallish and plain vanilla, with views of the surrounding forested hills. Some have whirlpools. There are also three chalets that hold up to eight people. With the Auberge's popularity and limited number of rooms, advance reservations are a necessity most of the year. There are a heated outdoor pool and a skating rink. Bicycles and pedal boats are available, and there is cross-country skiing nearby. No elevator.

La Sapinière. 1244 Chemin de la Sapinière, Val-David, PQ J0T 2N0. ☎ **800/567-6635** or 819/322-2020. Fax 819/322-6510. www.sapiniere.com. E-mail: sapiniere@polyinter.com. 70 units. A/C TV TEL. C$270 (US$186) double; C$290–C$310 (US$200–US$214) suite. Rates include full breakfast and dinner. AE, DC, ER, MC, V. Drive through downtown and pick up the sign to the inn on the right.

This sedate lakeside inn celebrated its 60th anniversary in 1996 with a thorough renovation and paint job. It remains a tranquil lakeside retreat, upper middle class in tone, with a largely 40-plus clientele. They return faithfully year after year, in large part to escape excesses of childish shrieks and orchestrated hyperactivity. Demanding diners, they are treated to a menu of five-course meals that is changed daily and embellished with wines from a 10,000-bottle cellar. The lake is private, with motorized boats banned. Shuffleboard and croquet are expectably popular with the guests, but there are two tennis courts and a pool on-site, and golf and hiking and cross-country trails are available nearby. Saturday nights there is live music in the bar for dancing. Rooms have hair dryers and coffeemakers.

WHERE TO DINE TO IN VAL-DAVID

Le Grand Pa. 2481 rue de l'Église. ☎ **819/322-3104.** Pizzas and pastas C$6.25–C$15.50 (US$1.45–US$10.70); main courses C$16.95–C$24.95 (US$11.70–US$17.20). MC, V. Daily 11:30am–midnight. ITALIAN/CANADIAN.

In the middle of the town, near the tourist information office, an open deck reaches out to the sidewalk. It's crowded with white resin chairs and tables under big umbrellas, where locals dig into a dozen varieties of pizzas, baked in the brick oven inside. With their puffy crusts and fresh ingredients, in two sizes, they're the star attractions, often taken with pitchers of beer or sangría. Full meals are also available, and in summer they fire up a barbecue pit that sends out irresistible aromas. Friday and Saturday nights there's live music by small combos.

STE-AGATHE-DES-MONTS

With a population approaching 10,000, Ste-Agathe-des-Monts, 53 miles (85km) north of Montréal, is the largest town in the Laurentians and marks the end of Autoroute 15. Follow the Autoroute north to Exit 83 or 86.

Early settlers and vacationers flocked here in search of land fronting on Lac des Sables, and entrepreneurs followed the crowds. Ste-Agathe's main street, **rue Principale,** is the closest to citification in these mountains, but it's only a touch of urbanity. Follow rue Principale from the highway through town and end up at the town dock on the lake. Watch out for four-way stops along the way.

The dock and surrounding **waterfront park** make Ste-Agathe a good place to pause for a few hours. One possibility is renting a bicycle from **Jacques Champoux Sports,** 74 rue St-Vincent, for the 3-mile ride around the lake. Lake cruises, beaches, and watercraft rentals seduce many visitors into lingering for days. For a night or two, the motels near town on Route 117 are sufficient, but for longer stays, consider a lakeside lodge.

The **Bureau Touristique de Ste-Agathe-des-Monts,** 24 rue St-Paul (☎ **819/ 326-0457**), is open daily 9am to 8:30pm in summer, 9am to 5pm the rest of the year.

Les Bateaux Alouette (☎ **819/326-3656**) provides cruises on the lake that depart the dock at the foot of rue Principale from mid-May to late October. It's a 50-minute, 12-mile voyage on a boat equipped with a bar and running commentary of the sights that observes, among other things, that Ste-Agathe and the Lac des Sables are famous for water-ski competitions and windsurfing. The cost for the Alouette cruise is C$11.50 (US$7.95) adults, C$10.50 (US$7.25) seniors, and C$5.50 (US$3.80) for children 5 to 15. Children under 5 are free. There are regular departures from mid-May to June 24 10:30am to 3:30pm, with additional departures until 7:30pm late June to Labour Day.

WHERE TO STAY & DINE

Auberge du Lac des Sables. 230 rue St-Venant, Ste-Agathe-des-Monts, PQ J8C 2Z7. ☎ **800/ 567-8329** or 819/326-3994. Fax 819/326-9159. www.aubergedulac.com. E-mail: info@ aubergedulac.com. 23 units. A/C TV. C$92–C$124 (US$63–US$86) double; C$126–C$138 (US$87–US$95) suite. Extra person C$20 (US$13.80). Rates include breakfast (except for suites). AE, MC, V.

All the rooms in this small lakefront inn have whirlpool baths, their chief distinguishing feature. Those with double Jacuzzis and a view of the lake are slightly more expensive. There's a small terrace overlooking the lake, a good vantage for watching the sunset. Downstairs is a game room with a pool table and pinball machine. The inn is about 1½ miles from the village center and within walking distance of the beach and boating. Because of the many levels and stairs (no elevator), this isn't the best choice for the elderly or travelers with disabilities.

Auberge La Sauvagine. 1592 Route 329 Nord, Ste-Agathe, PQ J8C 2Z8. ☎ **88/787-7172** or 819/326-7673. Fax 819/326-9351. www.polyinter.com/sauvagine. E-mail: sauvagine@ polyinter.com. 9 units, 7 with bathroom. C$96–C$126 (US$66–US$87) double. Rates include breakfast. Packages available. MC, V. The inn is 1¼ miles (2km) north of Ste-Agathe, on the road to St-Donat.

For something a little different, check this out—an 1890s inn housed in a deconsecrated chapel. (An order of nuns added the chapel when they ran the property as a retirement home.) Antiques and near-antiques are scattered throughout, with an impressive armoire in the surprisingly elegant dining room. Chef-owner René Kissler gathered many culinary awards in his native Belgium and has started accumulating them here. If it is true that the best French cooking is Belgian, his *cuisine gastronomique* carries the flag proudly. His table d'hôte menu is C$36.50 (US$25); the menu dégustation for two is C$47.50 (US$33) each. Only two of the rooms upstairs share a bathroom; five have TVs. A new outdoor pool has been added. From June 15 to October 15, the restaurant is open nightly 6 to 9pm for dinner; in winter it's open nightly Wednesday to Sunday. If it's full, ask about the inn Kissler has bought on a nearby lake.

Chez Girard. 18 rue Principale Ouest, St-Agathe-des-Monts, PQ J8C 1A3. ☎ **819/ 326-0922.** www.polyinter.com/girard. E-mail: girard@polyinter.com. 8 units. TV C$100– C$105 (US$69–US$72) double. Rates include breakfast. Meal plans available. AE, MC, V. Restaurant closed Mon, inn closed Apr and Nov.

Head toward the town dock, and near the end of rue Principale, on the left, is a Québec-style house with a crimson roof. That's Chez Girard. In good weather, diners can sit on the terrace overlooking the lake. Game is a central interest of the kitchen in autumn, while the summer menu emphasizes lighter pasta and seafood dishes, such as the fusilli with snails in a pungent pesto sauce. Among dinner possibilities are tournedos of caribou with mushrooms and wild grain and tortellini with razor clams, langostinos, and scallops in a goat cheese sauce. The kitchen prides itself on using the freshest ingredients, and on the absence of a deep fryer. Dinner table d'hôtes are C$18.50 to C$26.50 (US$12.75 to US$18.30); lunch (served only in summer) is about 50% less.

The inn also has eight serviceable rooms and suites in a separate building behind the restaurant. Most units have fireplaces, whirlpool baths, and TV; suites have serving pantries stocked with breakfast fixings. Bikes are available, and guests have access to a private beach.

ST-JOVITE & MONT-TREMBLANT

Follow Route 117 about 23 miles (37km) north from Ste-Agathe to the St-Jovite exit. It's 76 miles (122km) north of Montréal. To get to Mont-Tremblant, turn right on Route 327, just before the church in St-Jovite. Most vacationers make their base at one of the resorts or lodges scattered along Route 327. Mont-Tremblant is 28 miles (45km) north of Ste-Agathe and 80 miles (130km) north of Montréal.

A few words of clarification about the use of the name Tremblant, a subject of considerable confusion to first-time visitors. First, there is Mont-Tremblant, the mountain. On its slope is Tremblant, the growing resort village described below. Its most important hotel, for the moment, is the Château Mont Tremblant, with a new Westin on the way. At the base of the mountain is Lac (Lake) Tremblant, and on the opposite shore is Club Tremblant, also described below, an independently owned resort that has no connection to Tremblant resort (although its guests ski the mountain). And, finally, there is the organic village of Mont-Tremblant, about 3 miles (5km) west, with its own market, post office, restaurants, and inns that have no specific affiliation with any of the aforementioned properties and geographical features. May that explanation be helpful.

Mont-Tremblant, at 2,135 feet (650m), is the highest peak in the Laurentians. In 1894 the provincial government set aside almost 1,000 square miles of wilderness as **Mont-Tremblant Park,** and the foresight of this early conservation effort has yielded outdoor enjoyment to skiers and four-season vacationers ever since. The mountain's name comes from a legend of the area's first inhabitants. Amerindians named the peak after the god Manitou. When humans disturbed nature in any way, Manitou became enraged and made the great mountain tremble—*montagne tremblante.*

St-Jovite (pop. 4,118), about 7½ miles (12km) south of Mont-Tremblant, is the commercial center for this most famous and popular of Laurentian districts. A pleasant community, it provides all the expected services. The main street, **rue Ouimet,** is lined with cafes and shops, including **Le Coq Rouge,** which sells folk art and country antiques.

Tourist information, including maps of local ski trails, is available at the **Bureau Touristique de Mont-Tremblant,** rue du Couvent at Mont-Tremblant (☎ **819/ 425-2434**), open daily 9am to 9pm in summer and 9am to 5pm the rest of the year; and from the **Bureau Touristique de Saint-Jovite/Mont-Tremblant,** 305 Chemin Brébeuf in St-Jovite (☎ **819/425-3300**), open daily in summer 9am to 7pm, the rest of the year daily 9am to 5pm.

SKIING, WATER SPORTS & MORE

Water sports in summer are as popular as the ski slopes and trails in winter, because the base of Mont-Tremblant is surrounded by no fewer than 10 lakes: Lac Tremblant, a gorgeous stretch of water 10 miles long, and also Lac Ouimet, Lac Mercier, Lac Gelinas, Lac Desmarais, and five smaller bodies of water, not to mention rivers and streams. From June to October, **Croisières Mont-Tremblant,** 360 Chemin Principale, in Mont-Tremblant (☎ **819/425-1045**), offers a 70-minute narrated tour of Lac Tremblant, focusing on its history, nature, and legends. Fares are C$12 (US$8.30) adults, C$10 (US$6.90) seniors, ages 6 to 15 C$5 (US$3.45), under 6 free.

Mont-Tremblant, which has a vertical drop of 2,131 feet, draws the biggest downhill ski crowds in the Laurentians. Founded in 1939 by the Philadelphia millionaire Joe Ryan, Mont-Tremblant is one of the oldest ski areas in North America, and the first to create trails on both sides of a mountain. It was the second in the world to install a chair lift. There are higher mountains with longer runs and steeper pitches, but something about Mont-Tremblant compels people to return time and again.

Today Mont-Tremblant has the snowmaking capability to cover 328 acres, making skiing possible from early November to late May, and keeping at least 30 of the trails open at Christmastime (as opposed to 9 in 1992). There are now a total of 77 downhill runs and trails, including the recently opened Dynamite and Verige trails, with 810-foot (245m) and 745-foot (225m) drops, respectively, and the Edge, a peak with two gladed trails. The nine lifts are gondolas (one of which is heated) and quad chairs, no T-bars. There is plenty of cross-country action on 56 miles (90km) of maintained trails. And in summer, choose from golf, tennis, horseback riding, boating, swimming, biking, and hiking—for starters.

WHERE TO STAY & DINE

Auberge Sauvignon. 2723 Chemin Principal, Mont-Tremblant, PQ J0T 1Z0. ☎ **818/ 425-5466.** Fax 819/425-9260. www.sauvignon@tremblant.com. 7 units. A/C. C$115–C$135 (US$79–US$93) double. Rates include breakfast. AE, DC, ER, MC, V. Closed first 2 weeks in May and last 2 weeks in Oct.

Known primarily as a dining place, this roadside inn a block from Lac Tremblant packs happy patrons into two rooms, with the spillover perching on stools at the bar in back. Even a short staff is able to handle the crowds, because service is very casual and preps and cooking are simple. Most of the main courses, which run C$15.95 to C$26.95 (US$11 to US$18.60), are grills—salmon, lamb, rib steak, entrecôte au poivre. Steaks come in four sizes, up to 16 ounces. A trip to the substantial salad bar is included, so you may want to skip an appetizer, or, if you're vegetarian, fill up with salad alone for C$10.95 (US$7.55). There are frequent off-menu specials, but you may have to ask. Reservations are suggested. Dress is casual.

Upstairs are seven cozy rooms, all with bathrooms, some with TV, a couple with coffeemakers, one with a sitting area and whirlpool. Smoking is not permitted in guest rooms.

✪ **Club Tremblant.** Av. Cuttle, Mont-Tremblant, PQ J0T 1Z0. ☎ **800/567-8341** in the U.S. and Canada, or 819/425-2731. Fax 819/425-5617. www.clubtremblant.com. 100 suites. TV TEL. C$230–C$314 (US$159–US$217) suite. Rates include full breakfast and dinner. Children 6–12 are charged C$115 (US$79). Rates are lower for stays of 2 days or more. Packages available. AE, DC, ER, MC, V. Turn left off Montée Ryan, then right on Lac Tremblant North and follow signs for less than a mile.

Terraced into a hillside sloping steeply to the shore of Lac Tremblant, this attractive property consists of several lodges in blessedly muted alpine style. Essentially a concentration of privately owned condominium apartments operated by a single management, the accommodations represent excellent value and that greatest of luxuries: space. Most of the rental units are suites of one to three bedrooms, for the price of a single room at many other resorts in the region. A typical suite has a fireplace, balcony, sitting room with cable TV and dining table, full kitchen with fridge, cookware and dishwasher, one or two bathrooms with Jacuzzi, and clothes washer and dryer. Nearly all have views of the lake and Mont-Tremblant, which rises from the opposite shore. This is a family resort, so expect childish yips and squeals in the dining rooms in peak months—July, August, February, and March. Included in the children's rate are supervised meals and day camp. A drawback on the hottest days of summer is the lack of air-conditioning in the suites, but they'll deliver a portable fan on request.

Dining/Diversions: The dining room employs a largely French menu, with a five-course table d'hôte. A bar with a stone fireplace and picture windows is an inviting spot any evening, and there's usually piano music Thursday through Saturday nights.

Amenities: Indoor and outdoor pools, Jacuzzi, workout room (with weight machine, Exercycles, and rowing machines), four tennis courts, and six nearby golf courses. There's a new spa with therapeutic baths and massages. Day-care program for children 3 to 13, and lifeguarded swimming areas. During ski season, a 22-passenger bus shuttles between the lodge and the slopes.

Gray Rocks. 525 Chemin Principal, Mont-Tremblant, PQ J0T 1Z0. ☎ **800/567-6767** or 819/425-2771. Fax 819/425-3474. www.grayrocks.com. E-mail: info@grayrocks.com. 178 units, including 56 condos. A/C TV TEL. C$260–C$310 (US$179–US$214) double; C$180 –C$310 (US$124–US$214) condo (4–8 persons). Rates include breakfast and dinner in hotel, but not in condos. Discounts for children sharing parents' room. Meals optional in condos. Ski-school packages available. AE, DISC, MC, V.

The area's dowager resort has been under new management since 1993, and its ministrations are evident, not least in the new 18-hole golf course that opened in 1998. The accommodations—rooms and condos—are in a huge rambling main building, in the cozier Le Château lodge, or in one of the resort's four-person cottages. The resort covers most of the recreational bases, including golf, tennis, a spa, horseback riding, and boating. And there is not only a private airport for guests who fly in, but also a seaplane base for joyrides over Lac Ouimet. There's a complete playground with attendants to provide child care, as well as a program of free swimming lessons.

Dining/Diversions: The dining room serves three meals daily, and there's a bar with piano and other music for dancing.

Amenities: Par-72 golf course, indoor pool and fitness center, 22 tennis courts and junior and adult tennis school, horseback riding, sailboat rentals, shuffleboard, croquet, bicycle rentals, skiing, lifts, ski school, access to 56 miles (90km) of cross-country skiing, business center, same-day dry cleaning and laundry, self-service laundry, baby-sitting, and express checkout.

Villa Bellevue. 845 Chemin Principale, Mont-Tremblant, PQ J0T 1Z0. ☎ **800/567-6763** or 819/425-2734. Fax 819/425-9360. 130 units. TV TEL. C$60–C$258 (US$41–US$178) double without meals, C$130–C$328 (US$90–US$226) double with half board (breakfast and dinner). Children 17 and under stay free in parents' room. Condos for 4–8 people available. Weekly rates and ski-weekend packages available. DC, ER, MC, V.

The two-level, shingled Villa Bellevue sits at the edge of Lac Ouimet. The rooms look somewhat worn but have large, sunny windows; some have air-conditioning. Choices are between those in the lodge and deluxe units in a newer building. A few rooms even have kitchenettes—of interest to families. There's an indoor swimming pool, augmented by sauna, steam baths, and weight room. In summer, staff members can take children off their parents' hands during the afternoon and evening at an extra charge. The Villa Bellevue has been run by the Dubois family for three generations. Cross-country skiing is nearby. A shuttle bus carries guests to and from the lifts.

○ Château Mont Tremblant. Mont-Tremblant, PQ J0T 1Z0. ☎ **800/441-1414.** Fax 819/681-7099. www.fairmont.com. 316 units. A/C TV TEL. C$149–C$399 (US$103–US$275) double. AE, DC, DISC, ER, MC, V.

This 1996 luxury entry of the Canadian Pacific/Fairmont chain commands a crest above the village, as befits its stature among the Tremblant hostelries. The enlarged lobby area has a north woods look, with monster fireplace. Down below is a health club with several fitness machines next to the indoor lap pool. Guests use the outdoor pool right through the winter, and they can ski-out and ski-in this close to the bottom of the chairlift. No-smoking rooms are available; all have hair dryers, coffeemakers, and unstocked fridges.

Marriott Residence Inn. Mont-Tremblant, PQ J0T 1Z0. ☎ **888/272-4000.** 127 units. A/C TV TEL. C$125–C$145 (US$86–US$100) double; C$145–C$299 (US$100–US$206) suite. Rates include breakfast. Packages available. AE, DC, ER, MC, V.

Near the terminus of the lower chairlift running through the central part of the village, this midlevel hotel has its own restaurant, a heated outdoor pool, and indoor parking. The higher-priced suites have two bedrooms and fireplaces.

Les Suites Tremblant. Mont-Tremblant, PQ, J0T 1Z0. ☎ **800/461-8711.** Fax 819/681-5990. www.tremblant.ca. 900 units. A/C TV TEL. C$100–C$249 (US$69–US$172) double; C$160–C$409 (US$110–US$282) 1-bedroom condo; C$240–C$609 (US$166–US$420) 2-bedroom condo. AE, DC, DISC, ER, MC, V.

A collection of several buildings scattered around the complex, each with slightly different profiles of decor and amenities, these are the choices for families, couples traveling together, or those who require economical accommodation. The least expensive two-bedroom units, at US$166, can accommodate up to six people, bringing the cost down to less than US$28 per person. The bedroom units also have kitchenettes, for greater savings, and many have fireplaces and/or washing machines. Hair dryers, coffeemakers, and fridges are standard.

Club Intrawest. Mont-Tremblant, PQ, J0T 1Z0. ☎ **800/799-3258.** www.clubintrawest. com. 42 units. A/C TV TEL. C$197 (US$136) double, C$274–C$495 (US$189–US$341) suite. AE, DC, ER, MC, V.

Not directly on the main resort property, but at the nearby intersection of Chemin Principal and Montée Ryan, this luxury facility has the look of an exclusive golf club, validated by the 18-hole course around which it is positioned. Accommodations are

---

Lodging at Tremblant Resort

Not merely a hotel with a pool, Tremblant is a complete and growing resort village stretching from the mountain's skirts to the shores of 10-mile-long Lac Tremblant. It'll be a pretty nice place if they ever finish it, but this is the kind of enterprise that always has another "phase" to go. It has the prefabricated look of a theme park, but at least they used the Québecois architectural style of pitched or mansard roofs in bright colors, not ersatz Tyrolean or Bavarian Alpine flourishes. At recent count, there were several hotels and condo complexes, an 18-hole golf course (with another on the way), and 14 shops, including a liquor store, as well as 15 eating places and bars. When the snow is deep, skiers here like to follow the sun around the mountain, making the run down slopes with an eastern exposure in the morning and down the western-facing ones in the afternoon.

To get to the village, drive three miles north of St-Jovite on Route 117; then take Montée Ryan and follow the blue signs for about 6 miles (10km). The Limocar bus from Montréal stops at the entrance, and there's door-to-door shuttle service from Dorval Airport; reservations are required (☎ **800/471-1155**).

Reservations for lodgings at the resort can be made through the central number (☎ **800/567-6760**) or by contacting the establishments directly. The general reception area is in a building labeled *Les Cèdres,* announced by a large brown sign with gold lettering reading RECEPTION—take the right turn just before the old church. The more prominent hotels, most of which incorporate privately owned condominium units, are described below. Add to them the new Westin Resort Tremblant, a 126-suite condo hotel that opened in late 2000.

Several of the less expensive lodgings have only limited facilities. Pools and health clubs are provided at centers located around the resort. Supervision is provided for children ages 1 to 12 in the Kidz Club with excursions, crafts, games, and activities. They and their older siblings can also get blissfully waterlogged at the new AquaClub, with indoor and outdoor pools and whirlpool baths. The facility also has a well-equipped fitness area.

In summer, extensive possible diversions include lake swimming, boat cruises, chairlift rides to the top of Mont-Tremblant, 11 lighted Har-Tru tennis courts, minigolf, and bike and in-line skate rentals. In winter, in addition to the chair and gondola lifts, shops rent and repair ski equipment and provide information about access to the cross-country trails.

---

generously proportioned with impressively tasteful appointments. One- to three-bedroom suites (the highest price quoted above) have full kitchens, deep two-person whirlpool baths, gas fireplaces, stereos, VCRs, and large TVs. There are also a small fitness center, a pool, eight tennis courts, and great views, but no restaurant.

AREA MOTELS

Several motels near Mont-Tremblant and St-Jovite offer the routine advantages of reasonable prices and predictable comforts. Bonuses sometimes include kitchenettes—great money savers for groups of skiers willing to do their own cooking—and private swimming pools open in the summer months. They may lack the spacious grounds and rosters of activities found at the larger resorts, but those amenities are accessible nearby.

Another possibility is the more conventional new **Comfort Inn** at 860 rue Lalonde (☎ **888/429-6006** or 819/429-6000). It stands on a rise beside Route 117 overlooking St-Jovite and has 94 rooms, an indoor pool, and the usual conveniences and moderate prices—C$64 to C$94 (US$44 to US$65)—of the international chain.

Auberge La Porte Rouge. Chemin Principale, Mont-Tremblant, PQ J0T 1Z0. ☎ **800/ 425-3505** or 819/425-3505. Fax 819/425-6700. www.aubergelaporterouge.com. E-mail: info@aubergelaporterouge.com. 14 units. A/C TV. From C$120 (US$83) double. Rates include breakfast and dinner. 5-night ski or summer packages available. Chalets, with kitchen and fireplace, available for 3–10 people. MC, V.

The closest motel to everything, this is in the village right across the road from the Hôtel de Ville (Town Hall). Wake to a view of Lake Mercier through the picture window or from the little balcony. Some rooms have both fireplaces and whirlpools. Later in the day, take lunch on the terrace facing the lake or wind down in the cocktail lounge. The dining room serves all three meals, including a four-course table d'hôte. A pool is positioned by the lake. Rowboats and paddleboats are available, and the motel is directly on the regional bike path.

Auberge Mountain View. 1177 rue Labelle (Route 327), St-Jovite, PQ J0T 2H0. ☎ **800/ 561-5122** or 819/425-3429. Fax 819/425-9109. www.aubergemountainviewinn.com. E-mail: mountain.view@sympatico.ca. 44 units. A/C TV TEL. C$68–C$94 (US$47–US$65) double. Extra person C$16 (US$11.05). Packages and off-season discounts available. AE, MC, V.

Just over a mile from the center of St-Jovite stands the Auberge Mountain View. The motel layout is perpendicular to the highway, minimizing traffic noise. Some rooms have fireplaces and refrigerators. There's a small heated pool. In the slack periods, when many other Laurentian lodgings are closed, its rates are lowered by 20% to 40%. Snowmobiles are available for rent.

WHERE TO DINE

Although most Laurentian inns and resorts have their own dining facilities and often require that guests use them, especially in winter, Mont-Tremblant and places in the vicinity have several decent independent dining options for casual lunches or the odd night out. Note that restaurants in the area open and close with irritating unpredictability, so call ahead before setting out. Those recommended below are among the more reliable. See also **Auberge Sauvignon,** listed above under "Where to Stay & Dine"; it serves reasonably priced steaks and grills.

Antipasto. 855 rue Ouimet, St-Jovite. ☎ **819/425-7580.** Main courses C$12–C$20 (US$8.30–US$13.80). MC, V. Daily 11am–11pm. ITALIAN.

Antipasto is housed in an old train station moved to this site, so there is the expected railroad memorabilia on the walls, but the owners have resisted the temptation to play up the theme aspect to excess. Captain's chairs are drawn up to big tables with green Formica tops. Almost everyone orders the César salad (their spelling), which is dense and strongly flavored—the half portion is more than enough as a first course. Individual pizzas emerge from the brick ovens in more than 50 versions, on a choice of regular or whole-wheat crust. Pastas are available in even greater variety; those with shellfish are among the winners. The sauces are savory, if a bit thin. There are outdoor tables in summer.

Brunch Café. 816 rue Ouimet, St-Jovite. ☎ **819/425-8233.** Main courses C$8–C$18 (US$5.50–US$12.40). Table d'hôte C$9–C$15 (US$6.20–US$10.35). MC, V. Apr–Oct daily 8am–10pm; Nov–Mar daily 8am–4pm. INTERNATIONAL.

While the menu lists many sandwiches, salads, pastas, and pizzas, the most satisfying choices are among the sausages picked from a roster of six designer varieties, served

---

Dining at Tremblant Resort

In addition to the bars and restaurants of the hotels of the Tremblant resort village described above, there are many freestanding places at which to get a meal or a snack in the pedestrian areas of the resort. That isn't to say they are very satisfying, for if there is a restaurant in the village that rises above flat mediocrity, it has yet to reveal itself. It wouldn't hurt the powers that be to consider luring a "fine dining" establishment to the resort in an attempt to elevate its gastronomical standards. Las Vegas did. In the meantime, my recommendation is to ski, sport about, have cocktails, and hear some music in the resort, but take serious meals off the premises.

That said, there are plenty of eating options for the exhausted or car-less. Serving a variety of kinds of food implicit in their names are Pizzateria, Coco Pazzo, Créperie Catherine, Aux Truffes, Le Savoie (fondues), Mexicali Rosa's, and Le Gascon. The Microbrasserie La Diable pours craft beers to accompany live jazz on weekends, and P'tit Caribou brings in pop performers weekly. On the summit of the mountain is Le Rendezvous Café, with a circular fireplace, and the 1,000-seat Le Grand Manitou restaurant complex, with a dining room called La Légende, plus a bistro and cafeteria.

---

with sauerkraut, mustard, and pan fries. They have complementary *bières en fût* (beer on tap), plus an interesting selection of regional microbrews and imports. The cafe is located downtown, not far from Antipasto, which is under the same management. There are umbrellas over the tables facing the main street, close tables inside. Live music is offered most summer weekends.

La Table Enchantée. 600 Route 117 Nord, Lac Duhamel. ☎ **819/425-7113.** Reservations usually required. Main courses C$15–C$25 (US$10.35–US$17.25). Table d'hôte C$15.75–C$28 (US$10.85–US$19.30). AE, MC, V. Tues–Sun 5–10pm. Closed mid-Oct to mid-Nov and 2 weeks in May. QUÉBECOIS.

The lace-covered tables in this tidy little restaurant support some of the most carefully prepared dishes in the region. The kitchen does riffs on the traditional Québec repertoire—the rare loin of caribou in rich gravy with wild rice and three vegetable garnishes, for instance. Clam chowder is a favored starter, then perhaps the pâté called *cretons,* followed by Québecois *cipaille,* a pot pie layered with pheasant, guinea hen, rabbit, veal, and pork. Dessert might be *grand-pères au sirop d'érable* (dumplings in maple syrup). Or, substitute the cheese course, which comes with a glass of port, for an extra C$10.25 (US$7.05).

Le Verre Bouteille. 888 rue Ouimet, Saint-Jovite. ☎ **819/425-8776.** Main courses C$8.95–C$18.95 (US$6.15–US$13.05); dinner table d'hôte C$12.95–C$23.95 (US$8.95–US$16.50). MC, V. Summer Mon–Tues 5:30–10pm, Wed–Sun noon–3pm and 5:30–10pm. Closed Sun–Tues in winter and 2 weeks in Nov and Apr. FRENCH BISTRO.

The married owners—he cooks, she handles the front—arrived here from France 6 years ago and made themselves a neighborhood bistro that would be at home anywhere in rural France. Inside, a dozen tables are positioned around the fully stocked service bar, supplemented by a few more out on the porch facing the street. Madame and her minions are warmly welcoming, bringing competent renditions of such standards as onion soup, game terrine, lamb ribs with rosemary, and 10-ounce pepper steaks. Lunch specials, C$6.95 (US$4.80) or less, typically include a soup or salad followed by pizza or mussels. Glasses of several different wines cost less than C$4 (US$2.75) each. No one leaves raving about the chef's creativity, but neither do they depart grumbling about portions or prices. More likely they return again and again, for this has a loyal local clientele.

2 East into Montérégie & Estrie

15–48 miles (24–77km) SE of Montréal

The tourist region designated as Montérégie occupies the south bank of the St. Lawrence opposite the island of Montréal, much of it within sight of the downtown skyline. Despite that proximity and the crossings of massive power lines, it has a largely rural, small-town aspect with miles of orchards and truck farms that have encouraged the authorities to dub it the "Garden of Québec." Given its relative tranquility and easy commuting distance, many Montréalers keep weekend houses here, especially along the region's principal topographical feature, the Richelieu Valley. The Richelieu River runs north and south, leaving the St. Lawrence near Sorel and flowing south 80 miles (130km) into Lake Champlain in New York State. It supports several provincial parks along the way and, primarily in its southern reaches, is the site of fortifications built during the French and Indian Wars.

Estrie, bordering Montérégie to the east, serves as breadbasket as well to Montréal and the province. Known also as the Eastern Townships and Les Cantons de l'Est, it is a largely pastoral region marked by billowing hills and the 2,600-foot (792m) peak of Mont-Orford, centerpiece of a provincial park and the region's premier downhill ski area. A short distance from Mont-Orford is Sherbrooke, the industrial and commercial capital of Estrie, and throughout the Mont-Orford–Sherbrooke area are serene glacial lakes that attract summer fishing enthusiasts, sailors, and swimmers from all around. In terms of tourism, Estrie is one of Québec's best-kept secrets, for it's mostly Québecois who occupy rental houses to ski, fish, cycle, or launch their boats.

Follow their lead: Once out of Montréal, drive east along arrow-straight Autoroute 10 past silos and fields, clusters of cows, and meadows strewn with wildflowers. Clumps of mountain rise with improbable suddenness from the rolling terrain that flattens as it approaches the St. Lawrence. Cresting the hill at km 100, there's an especially beguiling view of countryside stretching toward New England, not far over the horizon.

Unlike the Laurentians, which virtually close down in "mud time," when spring warmth thaws the ground, Estrie kicks into gear as crews penetrate every "sugar bush" (stand of sugar maples) to tap the sap and "sugar off." The result? Maple festivals and farms hosting "sugaring parties"—guests wolfing down prodigious country repasts capped by traditional maple-syrup desserts. For one popular example, hot maple syrup is poured on the fast-melting winter snow and cooled instantly to produce a kind of maple-sugar taffy. Montréal newspapers and local tourist offices and chambers of commerce keep current lists of what's happening where and when.

Autumn has its special attractions, too, for in addition to the glorious fall foliage (usually best in the weeks on either side of the third weekend in September), Estrie orchards sag under the weight of apples of every variety, and cider mills hum day and night to produce what has been described as Québec's "wine." Visitors are invited to help with the harvest, paying a low price for the baskets of fruit they gather themselves. Cider mills open their doors for tours and tastings.

Although town names such as Granby, Waterloo, and Sherbrooke are obviously English, vestiges of the time when Americans loyal to the Crown migrated here during and shortly after the Revolutionary War, Estrie is now about 90% French-speaking. A few words of French and a little sign language are sometimes necessary outside hotels and other tourist facilities, since the area draws fewer Anglophone visitors than do the Laurentides.

For extended stays in the region, consider making base in one of the several inns along the shores of Lac Massawippi, especially in and around **North Hatley,** and take day trips from there.

ESSENTIALS
GETTING THERE

BY CAR   For Montérégie, leave the island of Montréal on Route 20, taking the Sortie (Exit) 112 on the other side in the vicinity of Ste-Julie and heading north on Route 223 in the direction of Sorel. Several bridges across the Richelieu River connect Route 223 to Route 133, which skirts the east bank.

For Estrie, leave Montréal by the Champlain Bridge, which funnels into Autoroute 10, in the direction of Sherbrooke, the grungy metropolis of the Estrie Region. People in a hurry can remain on Autoroute 10—and plenty of express buses do this, too—but to get to know the countryside, turn off the autoroute at Exit 37 and go north the short distance to join Route 112 east.

BY BUS   Local buses leave Montréal to follow Route 112 more than a dozen times a day, arriving in Sherbrooke, 100 miles (160km) away, 3¼ hours later. Express buses use Autoroute 10, making a stop in Magog and arriving in Sherbrooke in 2 hours and 10 minutes (2½ hours from Québec City). Call ☎ **450/842-2281** at the Terminus Voyageur in Montréal for information. There is no bus service to the Montérégie region.

VISITOR INFORMATION

There are eight permanent **tourist offices in Montérégie** and 19 that operate only in summer. Two of the most conveniently situated are the seasonal offices in Chambly at 1900 av. Bourgogne, Route 112 (☎ **450/658-0321**), and in Beloeil at 35 bd. Laurier (☎ **450/536-2921**); they are open daily mid-June to Labour Day 9am to 5pm. On the opposite side of the river from Beloeil is a permanent information office in Mont-Ste-Hilaire, at 1080 Chemin des Patriotes Nord (☎ **450/536-0395**). It's open Monday to Friday 9am to 5pm.

La Maison du Tourisme (Tourism House) for the **Estrie Region,** at Exit 68 off Autoroute 10 (☎ **800/263-1068** or 450/375-8774; fax 450/375-3530), is open daily 10am to 6pm during the summer and 9am to 5pm the rest of the year. Or contact **Tourisme Cantons-de-l'Est,** 20 rue Don Bosco Sud, Sherbrooke, PQ J1L 1W4 (☎ **800/455-5527;** fax 819/566-4445; **www.tourisme-cantons.qc.ca**), for more information. The Sherbrooke tourist information bureau is at 3010 rue King Ouest (☎ **819/821-1919**), open daily late June to Labour Day 8:30am to 7:30pm, and the rest of the year 9am to 5pm.

Cheapest Eats

It's still possible, in rural areas of the province away from resort areas, to get a three-course table d'hôte meal for under C$7 (US$4.85). The only thing memorable about it will be the price, but sustenance is provided, along with the opportunity to chat with the friendly Québecois who run these little roadside canteens.

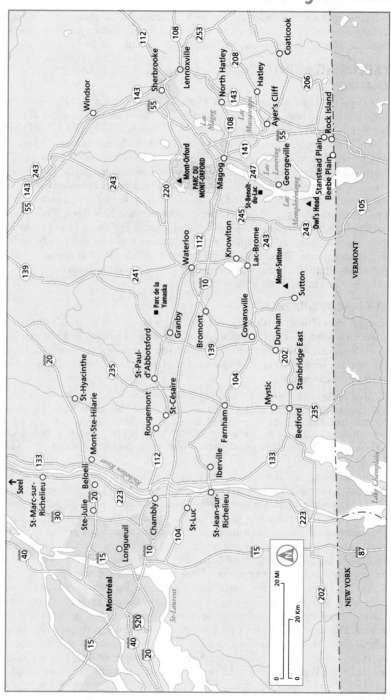

The **telephone area codes** are 450 or 819, depending on the part of the region called (towns with a 450 area code are closer to Montréal). Before June 1998, the 450 code was 514, which still appears in some tourist literature.

EXPLORING MONTÉRÉGIE
CHAMBLY

The largely residential suburb of 15,893 residents stands beside a wide basin of the Richelieu River. Today it is the site of marinas for recreational boating and windsurfing, but its history began as a frontier outpost of French Canada. In 1665, a Captain Chambly was commissioned to erect a wooden fort as defense against the Iroquois, who repeatedly attacked the colony of Ville-Marie, later to become Montréal. In 1711, the wooden fort was replaced by a stone fortress, this time for service in the several French and Indian Wars with the British. The restored **Fort Chambly Historic Site** on rue du Fort (☎ **450/658-1585**) now serves as an interpretation center, with a small museum. It's open March to May 15, October, and November, Wednesday to Sunday 10am to 5pm; May 16 to June 19, daily 9am to 5pm; June 20 to Labour Day, daily 10am to 6pm; and September 8 to 30, Monday 1 to 5pm and Tuesday to Sunday 10am to 5pm. The site is closed December to February. Admission is C$3.50 (US$2.40) adults, C$2.75 (US$1.90) seniors, C$1.50 (US$1.05) ages 6 to 16, free for children 5 and under.

ST-MARC-SUR-RICHELIEU

About 6 miles (10km) north of Autoroute 20 on Route 223, past farms, orchards, and a few small wineries, this residential and resort hamlet is strung along the west bank of the Richelieu. Among tidy houses and modest bed-and-breakfast inns stands one of the most honored hotels in all of Québec, one of only three Relais & Châteaux properties in the entire province.

Where to Stay & Dine

✪ **Hostellerie Les Trois Tilleuls.** 900 rue Richelieu, St-Marc-sur-Richelieu, PQ J0L 2E0. ☎ **800/263-2230** outside the greater Montréal area, or 450/856-7787. Fax 450/564-3146. www.relaischateaux.fr/tilleuls. 24 units. A/C TV. C$115–C$125 (US$79–US$86) double; C$390 (US$268) suite. Rates include service. Meal plans, packages available. AE, DC, ER, MC, V.

Looming directly beside the road, with the parking lot opposite, the inn doesn't look especially impressive. That perception changes once inside. The back faces the river, only a few yards away, giving water views to virtually every private and public space in the building. They look out at the inn-owned island, where guests can participate in pheasant hunts in the fall (for a price). Bedrooms all have balconies to take in the view, over room-service breakfast if you wish. While the accommodations aren't grand, except for the jaw-dropping Royal Suite, they are all comfortable enough, with hair dryers, robes, and magnifying mirrors. Some have Jacuzzis and safes.

Ah, but the food! Stop first in the atmospheric Irish Bar over a Relais & Châteaux cocktail of champagne and raspberry liqueur touched with Armagnac. Then, dinner can be by the fireplace, looking out the row of picture windows, or out on the wide terrace. The event begins with a plate of nibbles—quail pâté, perhaps, with a taste of lobster tartar or smoked ostrich and scampi. The chef emphasizes regional products, so main courses might involve sweetbreads with maple vinegar, frog leg raviolis scented with Pernod, *foie gras* harvested in nearby Granby, even caribou paired with duck—turf and wing, if you will. The headwaiter knows every bottle in the 16,000-bottle cellar.

EXPLORING ESTRIE
GRANBY
North of the Autoroute at Exit 68, this not-especially-beguiling city (pop. 45,200) does have a couple of surprises.

First is the **Granby Zoo,** 347 bd. David Bouchard (☎ **450/372-9113**). Take Exit 68 or 74 off Autoroute 10 and follow the signs. Its 70 wooded acres harbor more than 1,000 mammals, exotic birds, reptiles, and amphibians of 225 species from around the world. Founded in 1953, the zoo has an educational program for children and presents shows every day in summer, including demonstrations of raptors—birds of prey. Among the newer exhibits are a nocturnal cave, a display of robotic whales, and the "Afrika" pavilion, notable for its group of gorillas. There are restaurants, picnic areas, gift shops, and free rides. The zoo is open late May to early June Friday to Sunday; late June to Labour Day daily; and September to mid-October weekends. Open times vary but are usually 10am to 6pm in high season, until 5pm in shoulder periods. Admission is C$19.95 (US$13.75) for ages 13 and older, C$13.75 (US$9.50) for seniors and children ages 5 to 12, and C$8.95 (US$6.15) for children 2 to 4. Parking is C$4 (US$2.65). The visitor entrance is on boulevard David-Bouchard Nord.

Granby also has **Parc de la Yamaska,** with swimming from the longest beach in the area, a 2-mile (3km) hiking trail, 25 miles (40km) of cross-country ski trails, and 13½ miles (22km) of cycling trails along an old railroad track between Granby and the towns of Bromont and Waterloo.

Tourisme Granby is at 650 rue Principale, Granby, PQ J2G 8L4 (☎ **800/ 567-7273** or 450/372-7273; fax 450/372-7782). It's open in summer daily 10am to 6pm, the rest of the year Monday to Friday 9am to 5pm.

BROMONT
Take Exit 78 off Autoroute 10.

Founded in 1964 primarily to accommodate an industrial park and other commercial enterprises, this town of 5,000 is now a popular destination for day and night skiing, mountain biking (rent bikes at the entrance to the town opposite the tourist office), golf, hiking, and horseback riding. Shoppers have two of the largest **factory outlets** in Canada—Versants de Bromont and Les Manufacturiers de Bromont—and the area's largest **flea market,** with 350 stalls set up in the local drive-in from 9am to 5pm the first Sunday in May to the last Sunday in October.

Where to Stay & Dine
Château Bromont. 90 rue Stanstead, Bromont, PQ J2L 1K6. ☎ **800/304-3433** or 450/ 534-3433. Fax 450/534-0514. www.chateau-bromont.qc.ca. E-mail: chateau@chateau-bromont. qc.ca. 152 units. A/C MINIBAR TV TEL. C$170–C$200 (US$117–US$138) double; C$300 (US$207) suite. Rates include breakfast. Spa, ski, and other packages available. AE, DC, DISC, ER, MC, V.

All the rooms at the château have rocking chairs, video games, and coffeemakers; half have fireplaces. Some no-smoking rooms are available. A landscaped terrace and two hot tubs look up at the mountain. The staff is young and bilingual. Les Quatre Canards restaurant serves lunch and dinner, and there's a bistro bar, L'Equestre, and the Château Terrasse Bar-BBQ. In addition to indoor and outdoor pools and Jacuzzis, a sauna, a small gym, and squash and racquetball courts, there's a European spa featuring mud and algae baths (use of the spa facilities costs extra).

KNOWLTON
Those who shop for amusement, not mere necessity, will want to make this a destination. Knowlton is compact, but its two main shopping streets have a number of

clothing and antique stores that reveal a creeping chic influenced by refugees and day-trippers from Montréal. Ralph Lauren is here, and a shop that replaced a Liz Claiborne outlet sells outdoor gear and clothing and whimsically refers to itself as *L.L. Brome.*

The main shopping streets are **Lakeside Street** and **Knowlton Road.**

Knowlton is at the southeast corner of Brome Lake and is part of the seven-village municipality known as **Lac Brome** (pop. 5,048). It is one of the last towns in the region where a majority of the residents have English as their mother tongue. The first settler here was Paul Holland Knowlton, a Loyalist from Vermont. He arrived in 1815 and established a farm where the golf course is now. By 1834, he had added a sawmill, a blacksmith shop, a gristmill, and a store. He also founded the first high school.

Another Knowlton resident, Reginald Aubrey Fessenden, invented a wireless radio in 1906, a year ahead of Marconi, and relayed a message from Brant Rock, Massachusetts, to ships in the Caribbean. Large mansions overlook the lake on either side of town. There is a **Blue Grass Festival** in June, and the **Brome Fair** is held over Labour Day weekend.

The **tourist information office** is at 696 rue Lakeside (☎ **450/242-2870**). The major local sight is the **Musée Historique du Comté de Brome** (Brome County Historical Museum) at 130 rue Lakeside (Route 243), ☎ **450/243-6782.** It occupies five historic buildings, including the town's first school, established by Paul Holland Knowlton. Exhibits focus on the various aspects of town life, with re-creations of a schoolroom, bedroom, parlor, and kitchen. The Martin Annex (1921) is dominated by the 1917 Fokker single-seat biplane, the foremost German aircraft in World War I. Also on premises are collections of old radios and 18th- to early–20th-century weapons. The museum sells books about the area. Admission is C$3.50 (US$2.40) adults, C$2 (US$1.40) seniors, and C$1.50 (US$1.05) ages 16 and under. It's open mid-May to mid-September Monday to Saturday 10am to 4:30pm, Sunday 11am to 4:30pm, and closed the rest of the year.

Where to Stay & Dine

Auberge Lakeview. 50 rue Victoria, Knowlton (Lac Brome), PQ J0E 1V0. ☎ **800/661-6183** or 450/243-6183. Fax 450/243-0602. www.quebecweb.com/lakeview. E-mail: lakeview@telepage.com. 28 units. A/C TV TEL. C$196–C$310 (US$135–US$214) double. Rates include breakfast and dinner. Packages available. AE, MC, V. 1 block south of the town hall.

The core structure of this Victorian inn dates from 1874, and a 19th-century flavor has been sustained throughout the inevitable later extensions, the most important renovation taking place in 1986. Leather chairs are arranged around the fireplace in the lobby, stamped tin ceilings prevail, and Spencer's, the brass and mahogany pub that is a replica of the London original, is a place to settle in for an evening.

A four-course table d'hôte dinner in Sheffield's dining room is only C$38 (US$26), prepared by a chef who trained in Provence. On weekends, there's dancing to live music. The bedrooms come in four categories of relative comfort—go for the best ones and get two robes, a sitting area, access to the veranda, and a heart-shaped Jacuzzi. Much of the furniture is locally crafted in Québecois country style. Rooms in the least expensive category lack TVs, but the rest have cable. A heated pool awaits outside, banked with flowers.

SUTTON

A pleasant outing from Knowlton, or anywhere in the vicinity, Sutton (pop. 3,209) is a town with a number of promising cafes and the best bookstore in the region, **The Book Nook,** at 14 rue Principale Sud (☎ **450/538-2207**), open 7 days a week.

Estrie: Wine Country?

Canada is known more for its beers and ales than its wines, and rightly so. But that hasn't stopped a few stouthearted agriculturists from attempting to plant vines and transform the fruit into approximations of drinkable clarets, Chardonnays, and Sauternes. So far, the most successful efforts have blossomed along the Niagara Frontier in southern Ontario and in the relatively warmer precincts of British Columbia. Estrie enjoys the mildest microclimates in Québec; where apples grow, as they do in abundance in these parts, so will other fruits, including grapes. Inevitably, a few hardy entrepreneurial sorts decided to give winemaking a go.

Most of their efforts are concentrated around **Dunham,** a farming village about 18 miles (29km) west of Sutton, with several nearby vineyards along Route 202. They've been at it for only about 18 years, so their vines and the end product are still maturing. No winemaker in the valleys of Napa or the Gironde—nor, for that matter, the Hudson—is feeling the hot breath of competition from the vintages of Estrie. Still, a stop for a snack or a tour of vineyard facilities makes for an agreeable break from driving, and those demonstrating such daring deserve to be encouraged.

One possibility is the family owned and run **Les Blancs Coteaux,** at 1046 Route 202 (☎ **450/295-3503**), which opened in 1990. They serve picnic baskets and give tours in summer, but they welcome visitors all year daily 9am to 5pm. The vineyard's shop sells its Seyval Blanc and Vendange de Bacchus white wines, hard cider, apple liqueur and syrup, strawberry vinegar, relish, cider jelly, and dried wreaths and wildflower arrangements. The area's oldest vineyard, **l'Orpailleur,** 1086 Route 202 (☎ **450/295-2763**), opened in 1982. Look, too, for **Domaine des Côtes d'Ardoise,** at 879 Route 202 (☎ **450/295-2020**), and **Les Trois Clochers,** at 341 Route 202 (☎ **450/295-2034**). L'Orpailleur serves meals and all three have picnic tables, offer wine tastings, and conduct tours; but call ahead to determine schedules and hours, which vary by the season.

So far, though, the most credible bottlings in the region come out of **Le Cep d'Argent,** outside Magog, at 1257 Chemin de la Rivière (☎ **819/864-4441**). They produce eight different wines, their prizewinners being the Le Cep d'Argent dry white made from the Seyval varietal, the aperitif Mistral, and the L'Archer, a portlike fortified wine blended from red wine, brandy, and maple syrup, which sounds weird but tastes good. The cheerful owners pour samples and run a snack shop with terrace tables. They're open all year and have frequent guided tours daily May to August, weekends only the rest of the year. Tours cost C$4 (US$2.75) for visitors over age 14.

Nearby **Mont-Sutton** is known in summer for its 33 miles (54km) of hiking trails that link up with the Appalachian Trail, and for its glade skiing in winter. The surrounding country roads are popular with bikers. For more information, drop by the **Tourist Office of Sutton,** 11B rue Principale Sud (☎ **450/538-8455**), opposite the bookstore.

MONT-ORFORD

Exit 115 north off the Autoroute leads into one of Québec's most popular provincial parks. From mid-September to mid-October, **Parc du Mont-Orford** blazes with autumn color. Visitors come to try the 18-hole golf course in summer; in winter, they visit for the more than 25 miles (40km) of ski trails and slopes, with a vertical drop of more than 1,600 feet, or for the extensive network of cross-country ski and snowshoe trails.

Mont-Orford is a veteran ski area compared to Bromont (see above) and has long provided slopes of choice for the moneyed families of Estrie and Montréal. It is composed of contiguous Mont Giroux, Mont Desrochers, and Mont Orford itself, the highest peak. Children enjoy special treatment with "Kinderski," where some 100 instructors conduct a ski and snowboard school and supervise a tube slide. Aprés-ski drinks, dinner, and entertainment are provided by the Slalom Pub.

The area's other ski resorts—Bromont, Owl's Head, and Mont-Sutton—are more family oriented and less glitzy than Mont-Orford. The four have banded together to form **Ski East,** enabling skiers to purchase all-inclusive 2- to 7-day tickets good at all four areas anytime. Prices range from C$68 to C$203 (US$47 to US$140) for adults, C$56 to C$203 (US$39 to US$140) for ages 14 to 21, C$40 to C$140 (US$28 to US$97) for seniors and ages 6 to 13. Similarly economical lesson plans are available.

Orford has another claim to fame in the **Centre d'Arts Orford,** 3165 rue Parc (☎ **800/567-6155** or 819/843-3981), set on a 222-acre estate within the park and providing music classes for talented young musicians every summer. From early July to the middle of August, a series of more than 30 classical and chamber music concerts is given in connection with **Festival Orford.** Prices usually are C$12 to C$25 (US$8.30 to US$17.25) for professional organizations, free for student performances. Concerts are held Thursday to Sunday. A complete luncheon is served outside following the Saturday concert. Visual-arts exhibitions at the center are open to the public, and walking trails connect it to a nearby campground.

Where to Stay

Chéribourg. 2603 Chemin du Parc, Canton Orford, PQ J1X 3W3. ☎ **800/567-6132** or 819/843-3308. Fax 819/843-2639. www.cheribourg.com. 100 units. A/C TV TEL. C$100 (US$69). Rate includes breakfast. Meal plans, spa, ski, and other packages available. AE, DC, MC, V. Take Exit 118 from Autoroute 10 and follow Rte. 141 north.

A older property under the same ownership as the superior Manoir des Sables (see below), there has been a fair amount of needed primping and painting of late. One could wish that the fixup had gone a little further, as when confronted with a 5-foot-high showerhead. But there are compensations, including one indoor and two outdoor pools, a rejuvenated fitness room, saunas, four tennis courts, and a skating rink. The spa features massage and seaweed wraps. An Internet cafe has been added. Rooms range from the very simple in outlying cabins to duplex suites with two big beds in the main building, all with clunky pine furniture largely impervious to snowboards and ski boots. An ample breakfast buffet awaits each morning.

✪ **Manoir des Sables.** 90 av. des Jardins, Magog-Orford, PQ J1X 3W3. ☎ **800/567-3514** or 819/847-4747. Fax 819/847-3519. www.hotel.manoirdessables.com. E-mail: hotel@manoirdessables.com. 117 units. A/C TV TEL. C$135–C$235 (US$93–US$162) double. Meal plans and ski, golf, and other packages available. AE, DC, MC, V. Take Exit 118 from Autoroute 10 and follow Rte. 141 north to the hotel, on the right.

This attractive, thoroughly contemporary facility is one of the most complete resort hotels in Estrie, serving business groups, couples, families, golfers, skiers, skaters, fitness and spa enthusiasts, tennis players, and kayakers. And, as the pitchmen say, that's not all! Add indoor and outdoor pools, snowshoeing trails, snowmobiling, toboggan rides, tube slides, fishing in the hotel's lake, and Saturday-night horse-drawn sleigh rides. Bedrooms have all the big-city gadgets and niceties, which is to be expected

Fun at a Sugar Shack Near Mont-Orford

For a purely Québec experience that shouldn't be missed, take Exit 106 off Autoroute 10. Turn right, then right again. In about ⅔ mile (1km), watch for the "Camping Normand" sign. Make a left turn on rue Georges Bonnallie. In about 3 miles (5km), there is a sign for **La Sucrerie des Normand,** 426 Georges Bonnallie, Easton (☎ **450/297-2659**). Turn into the parking lot next to the long angled log-and-plank–sided building. This is a classic sugar shack, as that institution has evolved from the time when it was merely a place that processed the gathered sap from maple trees.

As you enter, the rendering room is to your right. Here the sap gathered from taps in more than 13,000 maple trees is boiled in a trough called the evaporator, then cooked further on a stove. Temperatures must be precise—216°F—for if the emerging syrup is too cold it might ferment and explode in the can; too hot, and crystals form. Lastly, the syrup is filtered and poured into cans. One popular sales device is to set up a long narrow tray of snow and pour a wriggly stream of syrup down the middle. This forms a sort of maple taffy, which is then rolled up on Popsicle sticks and eaten.

Over to your left is what happened when the producers realized that they drew audiences ripe for a wider experience. There is a full bar to one side and wooden tables next to a fireplace, the walls crowded with vintage radios, a sewing machine, apple corers, oxbows, snowshoes, and a moose head. Beyond that is a larger room with a dance floor and a stage for musicians, and finally a still-larger dining room with long plank tables.

The proprietor speaks fluent English, although that isn't really necessary. There is no menu. Sit down at a table, and she just starts bringing food: crudités with a mustard/mayo dip, a bowl of thick pea soup, a towering loaf of fragrant bread, a plate with an omelette supported by sausage and ham slices, a bowl of home fries, pork rinds, baked beans, cole slaw, and a stack of pancakes topped with samples of four maple desserts. At the ready are preserves, pickles, and all the maple syrup you can ingest. You won't be considered a bad person if you can't finish it all; few diners can. The lineup is the same for lunch or dinner. It costs all of C$17.75 (US$12.25) per person, *including* tips and taxes. If you can't move afterward, they have four basic bedrooms for rent.

Meals are served February through April, and reservations are required. Sleigh rides are arranged, they have a campground, and, when there's snow, mountain tube-sliding. The basic products are available in several sizes and forms, primarily syrup and candy. Keep in mind that the best syrup is from the first run of sap and is clear and light in color. It gets darker as the weeks of the season proceed.

Sugar shacks usually call themselves *cabane à sucre* or *érablière.* Quebéc Province has more than 400. While most restrict meal service to the sugaring off-season, some provide food through the summer for tourists. Small directional signs are often positioned at roadside. A Web site concerned with sugar shacks is **www.erabliere.com**.

since the hotel began life as a Sheraton. Coffeemakers and hair dryers are standard, and all rooms have either one queen or two double beds and sitting areas. About half have fireplaces.

MAGOG & LAC MEMPHRÉMAGOG

Orford is where people visit, but Magog (pop. 14,500) is where people live. As with countless other North American place names, Magog came by its handle through corruption of a Native Canadian word. The Abenaki name *Memrobagak* (Great Expanse of Water) somehow became Memphrémagog, which was eventually shortened to Magog (pronounced *May*-gog). The town is positioned at the northernmost end of Lac Memphrémagog (pronounced Mem-*phree*-may-gog), *not* on Lac Magog, which is about 8 miles (13km) north of Magog. The lake spills across the U.S.-Canadian border into Vermont.

The helpful **Bureau d'Information Touristique Magog-Orford,** at 55 rue Cabana (via Route 112), Magog, PQ J1X 2C4 (☎ **800/267-2744** or 819/843-2744; fax 819/847-4036), is open daily in summer 8:30am to 7:30pm, and in winter 10:30am to 6pm. Or log on to **www.mt-orford.com.**

OUTDOOR ACTIVITIES & GREGORIAN CHANTS

Magog has a fully used waterfront, and in July each year the **Lac Memphrémagog International Swimming Marathon** creates a big splash. Participants start out in Newport, Vermont, at 6am and swim 24 miles to Magog, arriving in midafternoon around 3:30 or 4pm. To experience the lake without such soggy exertion, take a 1¾-hour **lake cruise** aboard the *Aventure I* or *Aventure II* (☎ **819/843-8068**). The cost is C$12 (US$8.30) for adults, C$6 (US$4.15) for children 11 and under; a daylong cruise is C$45 (US$31). The boats leave from Point Merry Park, the focal point for many of the town's outdoor activities.

Parasailing, waterskiing, and jet-ski rentals can be arranged through **Tribord** (☎ **819/868-2222**). And while you're on or above the water, scan the ripples for Memphre, the lake's own legendary sea creature, which supposedly surfaced for the first time in 1798. It will come as no surprise that other sightings have been claimed since then.

An 11-mile (18.5km) bike path links the lake with Mont-Orford; in winter it is transformed into a **cross-country ski trail,** and a 1½-mile-long (2.5km) **skating rink** is created on the shores of the lake. Snowmobiling trails crisscross the region.

Other popular activities in the area include golf, tennis, and horseback riding. A **Vintage Festival** is held the last couple of weekends in September.

Abbaye de Saint-Benoît-du-Lac. Chemin Fisher. ☎ **819/843-4080.** Free admission; donations accepted. Daily 6am–8pm; mass with Gregorian chant at 11am, vespers with Gregorian chant at 5pm (7pm on Thurs). No vespers on Tues July–Aug. Shop, Mon–Fri 9–10:45am and 1:30–4:30pm, Sat 9–10:45am and 11:45am–4:30pm. Driving west from Magog on Rte. 112, watch for the first road on the left on the far side of the lake; take Chemin Bolton Est 12 miles (19km) south to the turnoff to the abbey.

There's no mistaking the abbey, with its granite steeple that thrusts into the sky above the lake and with Owl's Head Mountain in the background. Although Saint-Benoît-du-Lac dates only from 1912, the serenity of the site is timeless. Some 40 monks help keep the art of Gregorian chant alive in their liturgy, which can be attended by outsiders. For the 45-minute service (times above), walk to the rear of the abbey and down the stairs; follow signs for the *oratoire* and sit in back to avoid a lot of otherwise obligatory standing and sitting. The abbey receives 7,000 pilgrims a year, 60% of them between the ages of 16 and 25. It maintains separate hostels for men (☎ **819/843-4080**) and women (☎ **819/843-2340**). Make room reservations in advance, figuring about C$35 (US$24) per person. A blue cheese known as L'Ermite, among Québec's most famous, is produced at the monastery, along with a creamy version and

Swiss and cheddar types. They are on sale in the little shop, which also sells chocolate from Oka, honey, a nonalcoholic cider, and tapes of religious chants. Peek into the tiny stone chapel to the left at the entrance to the property, opposite the small cemetery. Visitors during the last 2 weeks of September or the first 2 weeks of October may want to help pick apples in the orchard.

Where to Stay

Lodging choices in Magog aren't beguiling. There are at least a number of modest B&Bs, though, three of the most convenient located along the blocks of rue Merry Nord, immediately north of its intersection with the main street, rue Principale. Otherwise, the recommendation here is to look for accommodations in one of the nearby towns described in this section.

GEORGEVILLE

Established in 1797 on the eastern shore of Lac Memphrémagog, this peaceful settlement was once a stop along the stagecoach route from Montréal to Brome, then a 5-day trip. Development has been scant. Today, the town has just enough buildings to shelter 845 residents, a general store, a little Anglican church, and a nine-hole golf course with views of the lake. It's also a summer home to actor Donald Sutherland.

The 14-mile (22km) drive along Route 247 south from Georgeville to Beebe Plain (see below) is pleasant rather than stunning. Owl's Head is the name of the prominent mountain off to the right.

Where to Stay & Dine

Auberge Georgeville 1889. 71 Chemin Channel, Georgeville, PQ J0B 1T0 (Route 247). ☎ **888/843-8686** or 819/843-8683. Fax 819/843-5045. www.fortune1000.ca/georgeville. 12 units, 8 with private bath. C$120–C$195 (US$83–US$135) double. Rates include full breakfast. Meal plans available. AE, MC, V. Take Route 247 10 miles (16km) south from Magog.

Built in 1889 to serve stagecoach traffic, new owners have reinvigorated this small inn, buffing its culinary image while perking up the dozen small upstairs bedrooms with antiques and Laura Ashley designs. The five-course table d'hôte dinner, at C$40 (US$28) per person, varies according to seasonal availability and the chef's whim, but at least 50% of his products are raised or gathered in Québec, such as the organic greens and Lac Brome duck. He comes up with such innovative fare as an *amuse-bouche* crostini of smoked Arctic char and caribou mousse, and the flavors of subsequent dishes explode like little firecrackers on a string. His head-grazing cellar is stocked primarily with top French and California labels. Reservations are essential on weekends. The fresh exterior paint job retains the house's traditional pink-and-white scheme, and there's a fancy new sign out front, so the inn is hard to miss. No smoking, and no jeans are allowed in the dining rooms. Lunch is served only to house guests, on request. They have free use of the inn's bicycles. Closed October 30 to December 16 and Sundays and Mondays off-season.

LAKE MASSAWIPPI

Southeast of Magog, reachable by Routes 141 or 108, east of Autoroute 55, is Lake Massawippi, easily the most desirable resort area in Estrie. Set among rolling hills and fertile farm country, the 12-mile-long lake with its scalloped shoreline was discovered in the early years of this century by people of wealth and power, many of whom were American Southerners trying to escape the sultry summers of Virginia and Georgia. (They came up by train and are said to have pulled down their window shades as long as they were in Yankee territory.) They built grand "cottages" on slopes in prime locations along the lakeshore, with enough bedrooms to house their extended families and friends for months at a time. Several of these have now been converted to inns. For a few days' escape from work or intensive travel, it's difficult to do better than Lake Massawippi.

In winter, the lands around the lake have 35 miles (56km) of cross-country ski trails, and a special 3- or 6-night package, called **Skiwippi,** allows any takers to spend brisk days skiing between the exemplary Auberge Ripplecove, Manoir Hovey, and Auberge Hatley (see below), reveling each night in the varied accommodations and accomplished kitchens of the three. In summer, there's a comparable golf version. For the less athletically inclined, a similar package (sans skis), called **A Moveable Feast,** is also available. Book the packages through any of the inns.

The jewel of Lake Massawippi is the town of **North Hatley** (pop. 704). Only half an hour from the United States border and 85½ miles (138km) from Montréal, the town has a river meandering through it. Old photographs show flocks of people coursing along the one main village street. Apart from impressive sunsets over the lake, it has a variety of lodgings and places to dine, shops, golf, a marina, and an unlabeled Laundromat between the general store and the post office. Horse lovers will want to know about **Équitation Jacques Robidas** at 32 Chemin McFarland, North Hatley ☎ (819/563-0166). Guides lead trail rides through forest and meadow beside the Massawippi in summer, with rates from C$20 to C$25 (US$13.80 to US$17.25) per hour. Buggy and winter sleigh rides are possibilities, and they have packages that include longer rides, meals, and vineyard visits.

An English-language theater, the **Piggery,** on a country road outside town (☎ 819/842-2431), presents plays of an often-experimental nature during the summer. For 10 Sundays from mid-April to late June, **Le Festival du Lac Massawippi** (☎ 819/823-7810) brings recitals by soloists and groups playing jazz, ethnic, and new music to North Hatley at the Ste-Élisabeth Church on Chemin Capelton.

Where to Stay

La Raveaudière. 11 Hatley Centre (P.O. Box 8), North Hatley, PQ J0B 2C0. ☎ **819/ 842-2554.** Fax 818/842-1304. www.bbcanada.com/2925.html. E-mail: aperson@accglobal. net. 7 units. C$120–C$150 (US$83–US$103) double. Rates include full breakfast. MC, V. Drive south along the lakeshore road from the center of town, bearing left up the hill. The inn is on the left. No facilities available for children under 12.

The new owners are still developing the property, most recently including the opening of an Italian restaurant. From the outside the inn looks like the ordinary 1890s farmhouse it once was. It sits next to a golf course, to which guests have access, but most visitors settle into the plush seating to read and chat with their hosts. A typical breakfast might include fruit salad with an edible flower, scones, muffins, and an egg dish. Full bar service is available to both inn and dinner guests. There are no TVs or room phones, and only four units have air-conditioning. There are three floors, no elevator.

Le Tricorne. 50 Chemin Gosselin, North Hatley, PQ J0B 2C0. ☎ **819/842-4522.** Fax 819/842-2692. www.manoirletricorne.com. E-mail: manoirletricorne@sympatico.ca. 12 units. C$125–C$275 (US$86–US$190) double. Rates include full breakfast. AE, MC, V. Take Rte. 108 west out of North Hatley and follow the signs. Children over 8 years are welcome.

While the core of this house is 125 years old, it looks as if it were erected only a few years ago. The exterior is shocking pink and white, the interior decked out in best *Good Housekeeping* manner, with lots of duck decoys, bird cages, and tartans. The decorative scheme won't be to everyone's taste, but all is immaculately kept and there is ample room to move about. Three rooms have fireplaces; five have Jacuzzis. No phones or TVs, but those are available in the common room. New guests are welcomed with glasses of port. Breakfast menus are changed regularly, with fruit omelettes one day, eggs Benedict the next. Up the hill is a pool, and one of the two ponds is stocked for fishing. There are spectacular views of Lake Massawippi from all over the hilltop property.

Where to Stay & Dine

○ **Auberge Hatley.** 325 rue Virgin (P.O. Box 330), North Hatley, PQ J0B 2C0. ☎ **819/842-2451.** Fax 819/842-2907. www.northhatley.com. E-mail: aubergehatley@northhatley.com. 24 units. A/C TV TEL. C$275–C$475 (US$190–US$328) double. Rates include breakfast, dinner, and gratuities. Ski, golf packages available. AE, MC, V. Closed Nov. 10–30. Take Exit 29 from Autoroute 55 and follow Rte. 108 east; watch for signs.

This acclaimed gastronomic resort occupies a hillside above the lake, not far from the town center. All rooms have a bathroom with tub or shower, and hair dryer, and more than half have Jacuzzis and/or fireplaces. Abundant antiques, many of them sizeable Québecois country pieces, are joined by complementary reproductions. There's a swimming pool, and the staff advises on nearby activities. But there's no uncertainty where owners Liliane and Robert Gagnon place their priorities: the pleasures of the table. The dining room has a bank of windows overlooking the lake. Tables are set with Rosenthal china, thin-stemmed glasses, fresh flowers, and candles. It's a necessarily soothing environment, since dinner can easily extend over 3 hours. Updated but essentially classical French techniques are applied to such ingredients as salmon, red deer, halibut, partridge, bison, and wild boar. Most herbs, edible flowers, and some vegetables come from the Gagnons' hydroponic farm; the ducks and pheasants, from their 100-acre game island. A particular treat is the meal-ending selection of cheeses, half French, half Québecois, served with the waiter's careful description and not a little ceremony. They've built a new wine cellar and expanded their already prodigious wine holdings to more than 10,000 bottles, still providing interesting wines by the glass and enough half bottles to satisfy lighter imbibers. Table d'hôte menus start at C$50 (US$35) and top out with the gastronomic spectacular at C$95 (US$66), and worth every last loonie.

○ **Manoir Hovey.** Chemin Hovey (P.O. Box 60), North Hatley, PQ J0B 2C0. ☎ **800/661-2421** or 819/842-2421. Fax 819/842-2248. www.manoirhovey.com. E-mail: manhovey@manoirhovey.com. 40 units. A/C TV TEL. C$195–C$470 (US$135–US$325) double. Rates include full breakfast, dinner, tax, gratuities, and use of most recreational facilities. Packages available. AE, DC, MC, V. Take Exit 29 off Autoroute 55 and follow Rte. 108 east; watch for signs.

Named for Capt. Ebenezer Hovey, a Connecticut Yankee who came upon the lake in 1793 and was the first white settler, the columned manor was built in 1899. Encompassing 20 acres and 1,600 feet of lakefront property, it's one of eastern Canada's most complete resort inns, a member of the international Romantik Hotels group. Guest rooms are ranked in five price categories, the bottom two small but adequate, with few frills; the top three desirable, even ravishingly luxurious, with fireplaces, balconies, and whirlpool baths. Several are no-smoking. Coffeemakers, hair dryers, magnifying mirrors, and radios are standard. The richly appointed library lounge has floor-to-ceiling bookshelves, deep chairs and sofas, and a stone fireplace, as beckoning a room as can be found, with chess sets and the daily newspapers laid out. A lighted tennis court, touring bikes, a heated outdoor pool, and two beaches add to the appeal. In winter, they push a heated cabin out onto the lake for ice fishing. The paneled dining room serves updated French cuisine, with a menu that changes with the seasons and features fresh herbs, vegetables, and edible flowers from the kitchen garden. All are fragrant and full-bodied, in attractive presentations. Take brandy in the atmospheric pub and work it all off the next morning in the small fitness room. Steve and Kathy Stafford are the gracious hosts.

✪ **Auberge Ripplecove.** 700 Chemin Ripplecove (P.O. Box 26), Ayer's Cliff, PQ J0B 1C0. ☎ **800/668-4296** or 819/838-4296. Fax 819/838-5541. www.ripplecove.com. E-mail: info@ripplecove.com. 25 units. A/C TV TEL. C$232–C$500 (US$160–US$345) double or cottage for 2; C$310–C$700 (US$214–US$483) suite. Rates include breakfast and dinner, gratuities, and most recreational facilities. AE, MC, V. Take Rte. 55 to Exit 21; follow Rte. 141 east and watch for signs.

A warm welcome is extended by the staff of this handsome inn, and impeccable housekeeping standards are observed throughout. The core structure dates from 1945, but subsequent expansions have added rooms, suites, and cottages. About half have gas fireplaces, balconies, whirlpool tubs, and cable TV, and the suites add kitchenettes and stocked minibars. The 12-acre property beside Lake Massawippi has a private beach, tennis courts, and a heated outdoor pool. Instruction and equipment are available for sailing, sailboarding, waterskiing, canoeing, kayaking, and cross-country skiing. Golf courses and riding stables are a short drive away. The inn's award-winning lakeside restaurant fills up most nights in season with diners drawn to the kitchen's contemporary French creations, prettily garnished and interpreted by the young chef. Wapiti and caribou appear on the card. Smoking isn't permitted. The four table d'hôte dinners range from C$42 to C$85 (US$29 to US$59). The hull of a fishing dory has been recycled as a buffet table. Check out the lobby lounge and its ornate 14-foot-high breakfront built in 1880. Innkeeper Jeffrey Stafford is the brother of the owner of Manoir Hovey in North Hatley.

Where to Dine

Le Moulin. 225 rue Mill. ☎ **819/842-2380.** Main courses C$8.50–C$18.95 (US$5.85–US$13.05); table d'hôte lunch C$13 (US$8.95), dinner C$25.95 (US$17.90). MC, V. May–Nov daily noon–2:30pm and 5:30–10pm. Closed Mon–Tues rest of year and Mar. BELGIAN.

With its big beams, wavy floors, and plywood bar, this former grist mill has an utterly casual air, the better to dig into the Belgian house specialty, *moules et frites.* That's a pot of mussels with a choice of six sauces and a plate of fries on the side. They come in large or small servings, priced accordingly, and are an agreeable variation on the burger-and-fries standard lunch. Steak is another possibility, and the table d'hôte meals are more elaborate. There's a terrace. Closings during cold months are capricious.

Pilsen. 55 rue Principale. ☎ **819/842-2971.** Reservations recommended on weekends. Main courses C$7–C$21 (US$4.65–US$14). AE, MC, V. Daily 11:30am–10:30pm (closed Mon–Tues late Oct–late Apr). The bar stays open until 3am Fri–Sat. INTERNATIONAL.

All drives through North Hatley pass the Pilsen, a pub and restaurant in the center of town. There's a terrace in front and a narrow deck overhanging the river that feeds the lake. The place fills up quickly on warm days, the better to watch boats setting out or returning. Patrons snaffle up renditions of nachos and burgers, pastas, and lobster bisque. Vegetarian plates are available. There's an extensive choice of beers, including local microbrews Massawippi Blonde and Townships Pale Ale. Park behind the restaurant.

STANSTEAD PLAIN, ROCK ISLAND & BEEBE PLAIN

For a modestly diverting half-day trip from North Hatley, follow Route 143 as far south as possible without actually crossing into the United States, and turn west to explore these three border towns. If you cross the border accidentally, which is easy to do, just report to the inspectors and come back across. There may not even be anyone on duty.

The first town is **Stanstead Plain** (pop. 1,059), some 30 miles (49km) south of North Hatley and only 9 miles (15km) north of Newport, Vermont. With a modest reputation for distinctive architecture, Stanstead Plain offers the **Centenary United Church,** with a clock face that bears the name of the person who donated the granite to build the church; the **Victorian Butler House** (1866), at 10 rue Dufferin; and the 1859 **Musée Colby Curtis,** 35 rue Dufferin (☎ **819/876-7322**), a house museum furnished accurately to the period, with two rooms for changing exhibits of such collections as antique dolls, glassware, and 19th-century tools and furnishings. Tours are given by bilingual guides. It's open mid-June to mid-September Tuesday through Sunday 10am to 5pm; the rest of the year Tuesday through Friday 10am to noon and 1 to 5pm, Saturday and Sunday 12:30 to 4:30pm. Admission is C$4 (US$2.75) for adults, C$2 (US$1.40) for seniors and students, free for kids under age six.

Stanstead East runs into the village of **Rock Island** (pop. 1,067), which is the commercial center of the area. Collectors of geographical oddities will love the **Haskell Opera House.** Dating from 1904, it's literally and logistically half Canadian and half American: the stage and performers are in Canada, and the audience is in the United States.

About 2½ miles (4km) west of Rock Island, **Beebe Plain** (pop. 975) is a center for quarrying granite, but what makes this town notable is half-mile-long **Canusa Street.** The north side is in Canada, the south side in the United States—thus its name, CAN-USA. Check the car license plates on either side. Here, it's long distance to call a neighbor across the street, and while they're free to walk across the street for a visit, they are expected, at least technically, to report to the authorities if they decide to drive.

11 Getting to Know Québec City

Québec City is the soul of New France. It was the first significant settlement in Canada, and today it is the capital of politically prickly Québec, a province larger than Alaska. The old city, a tumble of slate-roofed granite houses clustered around the dominating Château Frontenac, is a haunting evocation of a coastal town of the motherland, as romantic as any on the continent. The St. Lawrence makes a majestic sweep beneath the palisades on which the capital stands, as gray as gunmetal under dark skies, but silvered by sunlight when the clouds pass. Because of its history, beauty, and unique stature as the only walled city north of Mexico, the historic district of Québec was named a UNESCO World Heritage site in 1985—the only one so designated in North America.

Québec City is almost entirely French in feeling, in spirit, and in language; 95% of the population is Francophone. But many of its 648,000 citizens speak some English, especially those who work in hotels, restaurants, and shops where they deal with Anglophones every day. This and adjoining Sainte-Foy are also college towns, and thousands of resident young people study English as a second language. So although it is often more difficult in Québec City than in Montréal to understand and be understood, the average Québecois goes out of his or her way to communicate—in halting English, sign language, simplified French, or a combination of all three. Admitting exceptions, most of the Québecois are an uncommonly gracious lot, and it is a pleasure to spend time in their company and in their city.

In the following chapters are tips on where to stay, where to dine, and what to do in the city itself. After exploring Québec City, consider such excursions as a day trip around the Île d'Orléans, an agricultural and resort island within sight of the Château Frontenac, extended, perhaps, by a drive along the northern coast past the shrine of Ste-Anne-de-Beaupré to the provincial park and ski resort at Mont Ste-Anne and on to Charlevoix and the dramatic Saguenay River, where whales come to play.

1 Orientation

Almost all of a visit to Québec can be spent in the Old City, because many hotels and lodging places, restaurants, and tourist-oriented services are based there. The colonial city was first built right down by the St. Lawrence at the foot of rearing Cap Diamant (Cape Diamond). It was here that the earliest merchants, traders, and boatmen earned their livelihoods; but due to unfriendly fire in the 1700s, this Basse-Ville (Lower Town) became primarily a wharf and warehouse area after residents moved to safer houses atop the steep cliffs that form the rim of Cap Diamant. That trend is being reversed of late, with several new *auberges* (inns), small hotels, and many attractive bistros and shops bringing new life to the area.

Haute-Ville, or Upper Town, the Québecois later discovered, was not immune from cannon fire either, as the British General Wolfe was to prove. Nevertheless, the division into Upper and Lower Towns persisted for obvious topographical reasons. The Upper Town remains enclosed by fortification walls, and several ramplike streets and a cliff-side elevator (*funiculaire*) connect it to the Lower Town.

ARRIVING

BY PLANE   **Jean-Lesage International Airport** is small, despite the grand name. Buses into town are operated by **Autobus La Québécoise** (☎ **418/872-5525**). The 12-mile trip costs C$9 (US$6.20). Buses leave at variable times, depending on the season, but roughly every 1½ hours from 8:45am to 8:45pm Monday to Friday, every 2 hours between 9am and 8:30pm Saturday and Sunday. A taxi into town costs about C$28 (US$19.30).

BY TRAIN   The train station in Québec City, **Gare du Palais,** 450 rue de la Gare-du-Palais (☎ **418/692-3940**), was designed by Bruce Price, who was also responsible for the fabled Château Frontenac. Handsome though it is, the Lower Town location isn't central. Plan on a moderately strenuous uphill hike or a C$6 to C$8 (US$4.15 to US$5.50) cab ride to the Upper Town. That's per trip, incidentally, not per passenger, as an occasional cabbie may pretend.

BY BUS   The bus station, **Gare d'Autobus de la Vieille Capitale,** at 320 rue Abraham-Martin (☎ **418/525-3000**), is near the train station. As from the train station, it is an uphill climb or quick cab ride to Château Frontenac and the Upper Town. A taxi should cost about the same as from the train station.

BY CAR   From New York City, follow I-87 to Autoroute 15 to Montréal, picking up Autoroute 20 to Québec City. Take 73 Nord across the Pont Pierre-Laporte and exit onto boulevard Champlain immediately after crossing the bridge. This skirts the city at river level. Turn left at Parc des Champs-de-Bataille (Battlefields Park) and right onto the Grande-Allée. Alternatively, take Autoroute 40 from Montréal, which follows the north shore of the St. Lawrence. That trip takes about 2½ hours.

From Boston, take I-89 to I-93 to I-91 in Montpelier, Vermont, which connects with Autoroute 55 in Québec to link up with Autoroute 20. Or follow I-90 up the Atlantic coast, through Portland, Maine, to Route 201 west of Bangor, then Autoroute 173 to Lévis. A car-ferry there, **Traverse Québec-Lévis** (☎ **418/644-3704**), provides a 10-minute ride across the St. Lawrence River. Although the schedule varies substantially according to time of day, week, and season, the ferry leaves at least every hour (more often during rush hours) from 6am to 2am. One way, it costs C$4.50 or C$4.75 (US$3.10 or US$3.30) for the car, plus C$1.50 or $1.75 (US$1.05 or US$1.20) for each passenger age 12 to 64, C$1.10 or C$1.20 (US75¢ or US85¢) for each passenger age 5 to 11, C$1.40 or C$1.60 (US95¢ or US$1.05) for each passenger over 64.

VISITOR INFORMATION

The Greater Québec Area Tourism and Convention Bureau operates two useful provincial information centers in and near the city. One has moved from its former

Québec City Orientation

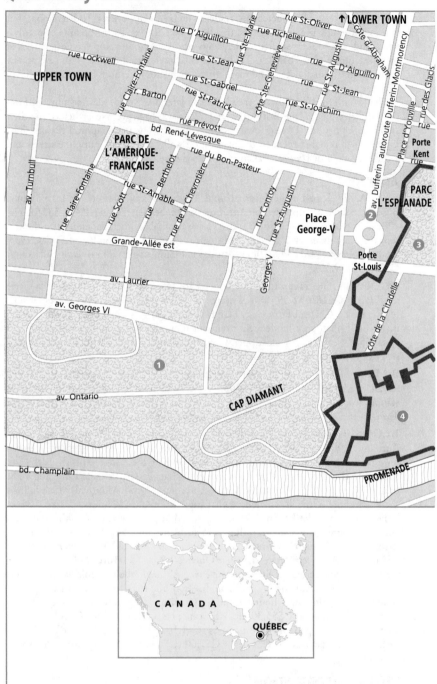

UPPER TOWN

rue Lockwell

rue D'Aiguillon

rue St-Oliver

rue Ste-Marie

rue Richelieu

↑ LOWER TOWN

côte d'Abraham

rue St-Jean

rue St-Gabriel

rue St-Patrick

rue Claire-Fontaine

r. Barton

côte Ste-Geneviève

rue St-Augustin

D'Aiguillon

rue St-Jean

rue St-Joachim

rue Prévost

bd. René-Lévesque

PARC DE
L'AMÉRIQUE-
FRANÇAISE

rue du Bon-Pasteur

Berthelot

rue St-Amable

rue Scott

rue de la Chevrotière

rue Conroy

rue St-Augustin

Place
George-V

av. Turnbull

rue Claire-Fontaine

Grande-Allée est

Georges V

av. Dufferin

autoroute Dufferin-Montmorency

Place d'Youville

rue des Glacis

rue

Porte
Kent

rue

PARC
L'ESPLANADE

②

③

Porte
St-Louis

av. Laurier

av. Georges VI

①

côte de la Citadelle

av. Ontario

CAP DIAMANT

④

bd. Champlain

PROMENADE

CANADA

QUÉBEC

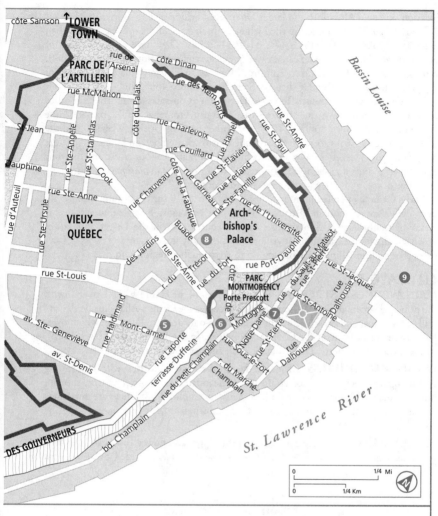

côte Samson ↑ LOWER TOWN

PARC DE L'ARTILLERIE

rue de l'Arsenal

côte Dinan

rue des Remparts

rue McMahon

côte du Palais

rue Charlevoix

rue St-André

rue St-Paul

St-Jean

rue Couillard

rue St-Hamel

rue Ste-Angèle

rue St-Stanislas

Cook

rue Chauveau

rue Garneau

rue St-Flavien

rue Ferland

Dauphine

rue d'Auteuil

rue Ste-Ursule

rue Ste-Anne

côte de la Fabrique

Buade

Ste-Famille

rue de l'Université

Archbishop's Palace

VIEUX— QUÉBEC

des Jardins

rue Ste-Anne

r. du Trésor

rue du Fort

côte de la

rue Port-Dauphin

rue du Sault-au-Matelot

rue St-Pierre

rue St-Jacques

Dalhousie

8

rue St-Louis

PARC MONTMORENCY
Porte Prescott

9

av. Ste-Geneviève

rue Haldimand

Mont-Carmel

5

rue Laporte

6

Montagne

rue Notre-Dame

7

rue St-Pierre

rue St-Antoine

av. St-Denis

terrasse Dufferin

rue du Petit-Champlain

rue Sous-le-Fort

rue Dalhousie

r. du Marché Champlain

DES GOUVERNEURS

bd. Champlain

Bassin Louise

St. Lawrence River

0   1/4 Mi
0   1/4 Km

Basilique-Cathédrale Notre-Dame **8**
Château Frontenac **5**
Fortifications of Québec **3**
Funicular **6**
Hôtel du Parlement **2**
La Citadelle **4**
Parc des Champs-de-Bataille **1**
Place Royale Information Centre **7**
Vieux-Port **9**

199

location on rue d'Auteuil to the larger Discovery Pavilion at 835 av. Wilfrid-Laurier (☎ **418/ 649-2608**), bordering the Plaines d'Abraham, and the other is in suburban Ste-Foy, at 3300 av. des Hôtels (☎ **418/651-2882**). They have rack after rack of brochures and attendants who can answer questions and make hotel reservations. Both offices are open daily 8:30am to 7pm from June 24 to Thanksgiving Day, the rest of the year 9am to 5pm Monday through Saturday, 10am to 4pm Sunday.

The **Québec Government's Tourism Department** operates an information office on Place d'Armes, down the hill from the Château Frontenac, at 12 rue Ste-Anne (☎ **514/873-2015,** or 800/363-7777 from other parts of Québec, Canada, and the U.S.). It's open 8:30am to 7:30pm late June to early September, and 9am to 5pm the rest of the year. The office has many brochures, information about cruise and bus tour operators, a souvenir shop, a 24-hour ATM (*guichet automatique*), a currency-exchange office, and a free lodging reservation service.

Parks Canada operates an information kiosk in front of the Château Frontenac; it's open daily 9am to noon and 1 to 5pm. From June to August, bilingual university students on motorbikes station themselves near tourist sites in the Upper and Lower Towns to answer the questions of visitors. Spot them by the flags on the backs of their bikes. For additional information, log on to **www.quebec-region.cuq.qc.ca.**

CITY LAYOUT

MAIN AVENUES & STREETS Within the walls of the **Haute-Ville** (Upper Town), the principal streets are rues St-Louis (which becomes the Grande-Allée outside the city walls), Ste-Anne, and St-Jean, and the pedestrians-only Terrasse Dufferin, which overlooks the river in front of the Château Frontenac. In the **Basse-Ville** (Lower Town), major streets are St-Pierre, Dalhousie, St-Paul, and, parallel to it, St-André.

FINDING AN ADDRESS If it were larger, the historic district, with its winding and plunging streets, might be confusing to negotiate. As compact as it is, though, most visitors have little difficulty finding their way around. Most streets are only a few blocks long, so when the name of the street is known, it is fairly easy to find a specific address.

STREET MAPS There are good maps of the Upper and Lower Towns and the metropolitan region in the *Greater Québec Area Tourist Guide,* provided by any tourist office.

Neighborhoods in Brief

HAUTE-VILLE The Upper Town, surrounded by thick ramparts, occupies the crest of Cap Diamant and overlooks the Fleuve Saint-Laurent (St. Lawrence River). It includes many of the sites for which the city is famous, among them the Château Frontenac, Place d'Armes, Basilica of Notre-Dame, Québec Seminary and Museum, and the Terrasse Dufferin. At a higher elevation, to the south of the Château, is the Citadel, a partially star-shaped fortress begun by the French in the 18th century and augmented often by the English well into the 19th. Since most buildings are at least 100 years old, made of granite in similar styles, the Haute-Ville is visually harmonious, with few jarring modern intrusions. The overall grayness is offset by the tin roofs and trim, coated with a silvery metallic paint, that cover the churches and many institutional buildings. When they added a new wing to the château a few years ago, they modeled it with considerable care after the original—standing policy here. The Terrasse Dufferin is a pedestrian promenade that attracts crowds in all seasons for its

For details on Web sites concerning Québec City, see "Planning Your Trip: An Online Directory" following chapter 2.

magnificent views of the river and the land to the south, ferries gliding back and forth, cruise ships, and Great Lakes freighters putting in at the harbor below.

BASSE-VILLE   The Lower Town encompasses the restored Quartier du Petit-Champlain, including pedestrian-only rue du Petit-Champlain; Place Royale and the small Notre-Dame-des-Victoires church, and, nearby, the impressive Museum of Civilization, a highlight of any visit. Basse is linked to Haute by the funicular on Terrasse Dufferin and by several streets and stairways, including one near the entrance to the funicular. Petit-Champlain is undeniably touristy, but not unpleasantly so: T-shirt vendors have been held in check, though hardly banned. It contains several agreeable cafes and shops. Restored Place Royale is perhaps the most attractive of the city's many squares, upper or lower.

GRANDE-ALLÉE   This boulevard is the western extension of rue St-Louis, from the St-Louis Gate in the fortified walls to avenue Taché. It passes the stately Parliament building, in front of which Winter Carnival takes place every year (the ice sculptures are installed across the street), as well as the numerous terraced bars and restaurants that line both sides from rue de la Chevrotière to rue de Claire-Fontaine. Later, it skirts the Musée des Beaux-Arts and the Plains of Abraham, where one of the most important battles in the history of North America took place. The city's large contemporary hotels are also on or near the Grande-Allée.

2 Getting Around

Once you're within or near the walls of the Haute Ville, virtually no place of interest nor hotel or restaurant is beyond walking distance. In bad weather, or when you're traversing between opposite ends of Lower and Upper Towns, a taxi might be necessary, but in general, walking is the best way to explore the city.

BY BUS
Local buses run quite often and charge C$2.25 (US$1.55) in exact change; tickets purchased in a *dépanneur* (convenience store) cost C$1.70 (US$1.15). A 1-day pass is C$4.60 (US$3.15). Discounts are available for seniors and students. Bus no. 7 travels up and down rue St-Jean; no. 11 shuttles along Grande-Allée/rue St-Louis and, along with nos. 7 and 8, also goes well into suburban Ste-Foy, for those who want to visit the shopping centers there.

BY FUNICULAR
Although there are streets and stairs between the Château Frontenac on the top of the cliff and Place Royale in the Lower Town, there is also a funicular, which has long operated along an inclined 210-foot track between the Terrasse Dufferin and the Quartier du Petit-Champlain. It was closed for a couple of years due to a fatal accident in 1996. Repaired now—although subject to occasional stoppages—the **upper station** is near the front of the Château Frontenac and Place d'Armes, while the **lower station** is actually inside the Maison Louis-Jolliet, on rue du Petit-Champlain. It runs all year, daily from early morning until 11:30pm. Wheelchairs are accommodated. The one-way fare is C$1.25 (US85¢).

BY TAXI

They're everywhere, cruising and parked in front of the big hotels and in some of the larger squares of the Upper Town. In theory, they can be hailed, but they are best obtained by locating one of their stands, as in the Place d'Armes or in front of the Hôtel-de-Ville (City Hall). Restaurant managers and hotel bell captains will also summon them. Fares are the same as in Montréal, meaning they're somewhat expensive here, given the short distances of most rides. The starting rate is C$2.50 (US$1.70), each kilometer costs C$1.20 (US85¢), and each minute when stopped costs another C40¢ (US30¢). A taxi from the train station to one of the big hotels is about C$6 to C$7 (US$4 to US$4.65) plus tip. To call a cab, try **Taxi Coop** (☎ **418/525-5191**) or **Taxi Québec** (☎ **418/525-8123**).

BY CAR

See "By Car" under "Getting Around" in chapter 3 for information on gasoline and driving rules in Canada.

RENTALS   Car-rental companies include **Avis,** at the airport (☎ **800/879-2847** or 418/872-2861) and in the city (☎ **418/523-1075**); **Budget,** at the airport (☎ **800/268-8900** or 418/872-9885) and in the city (☎ **418/687-4220**); **Hertz Canada,** at the airport (☎ **800/654-3131** or 418/871-1571) and in the city (☎ **418/697-4949**); **Thrifty,** at the airport (☎ **800/367-2277** or 418/877-2870) and in the city (☎ **418/648-7766**); and **National/Tilden,** at the airport (☎ **418/871-1224**) and in the city (☎ **418/692-1727**). A firm specializing in economical rates is **Discount,** in Vieux-Québec (☎ **418/692-1244**).

PARKING   On-street parking is very difficult in the cramped quarters of old Québec City. When you find a rare space on the street, be sure to check the signs for the hours when parking is permissible. When meters are in place, the charge is C25¢ (US17¢) per 15 minutes up to 120 minutes. Metered spots are free on Sundays, before 9am and after 6pm Monday through Wednesday and on Saturday, and before 9am and after 9pm Thursday and Friday.

Many of the smaller hotels have special arrangements with local garages, resulting in discounts for their guests of three or four dollars less per day than the usual C$10 (US$6.90) a day or more. Check at the hotel first before parking in a lot or garage.

If a particular hotel or auberge doesn't have access to a lot, plenty are available, clearly marked on the foldout city map available at tourist offices. Several convenient ones include the one next to the Hôtel-de-Ville (City Hall), where parking is free in the evening and on weekends; Complexe G, off the Grande-Allée on rue St-Cyrille, with twice-daily in-and-out privileges at no extra charge; and in the Lower Town across the street from the Musée de la Civilisation, on rue Dalhousie, where discounts are often offered on weekends. They are also marked on the foldout city map available at tourist offices.

BY BICYCLE

Given the hilly topography of the Upper Town, cycling isn't a particularly attractive option for most. But pedal and motorized bicycles are available at a shop in the flatter Lower Town. Bikes are about C$6 (US$4.15) an hour or C$30 to C$35 (US$20.70 to US$24) a day, mopeds about C$50 (US$35) per day. The shop, **Cyclo Services,** at C.P 1011 Québec Terminus, also rents tandems, child trailers, and in-line skates, and it's open daily throughout the year (☎ **418/692-4052**).

Fast Facts: Québec City

American Express   There is no office right in town, but for lost traveler's checks or credit cards, call ☎ **418/692-0997.** American Express keeps a customer-service desk in two shopping centers in Ste-Foy, a bus or taxi ride away: Les Galeries de la Capitale, 5401 bd. des Galeries (☎ **418/627-2580**); and Place Laurier, 2740 bd. Laurier (☎ **418/658-8820**).

Area Code   Québec City's area code is 418.

Baby-sitters   Check at the hotel concierge or front desk.

Bookstores   Most of Québec City's bookstores cater to the solidly French-speaking citizenry and the students at the university, but a few shops carry some English books and periodicals for the tourist trade. One outlet is **Maison de la Presse Internationale,** at 1050 rue St-Jean (☎ **418/694-1511**), which stocks magazines, newspapers, and paperbacks from around the world. **Librairie du Nouveau Monde,** 103 rue St-Pierre in the Lower Town (☎ **418/694-9475**), features titles dealing with Québec history and culture, including books in English. For travel books and accessories, visit **Librarie Ulysses,** 4 bd. René-Levèsque Est (☎ **418/529-5349**).

Business Hours   Banks are open from 10am to 3pm, with most also having hours on Thursday and Friday evenings. Several banks have Saturday hours, but the ones that do are mostly located outside of the Old Town.

Consulate   The U.S. Consulate is near the Château Frontenac, facing Jardin des Gouverneurs at 2 place Terrasse-Dufferin (☎ **418/692-2095**).

Currency Exchange   Conveniently located near the Château Frontenac, the Bureau de Change at 19 rue Ste-Anne and rue des Jardins is open Monday, Tuesday, and Friday from 10am to 3pm, and Wednesday and Thursday from 10am to 6pm. On weekends, it's possible to change money in hotels and shops, but you'll get an equal or better rate at an ATM, such as the one at the corner of rues Ste-Anne and des Jardins.

Dentists   Call ☎ **418/653-5412** any day or ☎ **418/524-2444** Monday through Saturday. Both numbers are hot lines that refer callers to available dentists.

Doctors   For emergency treatment, call **Info-Santé** (☎ **418/648-2626**) 24 hours a day, or the **Hôtel-Dieu de Québec** hospital emergency room (☎ **418/ 691-5042**).

Drugstores   Caron & Bernier, in the Upper Town, 38 Côte du Palais (at rue Charlevoix), is open 8:15am to 8pm Monday through Friday, and 9am to 3pm on Saturday (☎ **418/692-4252**). In an emergency, it's necessary to travel to the suburbs to Pharmacie Brunet, in Les Galeries Charlesbourg, 4250 Première Ave. (1ère or First Avenue), in Charlesbourg (☎ **418/623-1571**), open 24 hours, 7 days.

Electricity   What works in the United States works in Québec.

Emergencies   For police or ambulance, call ☎ **911.** Marine Search and Rescue (Canadian Coast Guard), 24 hours a day, ☎ **418/648-3599** (Greater Québec area) or ☎ 800/463-4393 (St. Lawrence River). Poison Control Center, ☎ **800/ 463-5060** or 418/656-8090.

Holidays   See "When to Go" in chapter 2.

Laundromat   Handy to the Château Frontenac, the new Buanderie du Vieux-Québec is open daily 7am to 10pm. It's at 41½ rue St-Louis.

Liquor & Wine   A supermarket-sized **Société des Alcools** store is located at 1059 av. Cartier. Wine and beer can be bought in grocery stores and supermarkets. The legal drinking age in the province is 18.

Luggage Storage & Lockers   Luggage storage is available in the train station, Gare du Palais, 450 rue de la Gare-du-Palais, in the Lower Town.

Mail   All mail posted in Canada must bear Canadian stamps. That might seem painfully obvious, but apparently large numbers of visitors use stamps from their home countries, especially the United States.

Newspapers & Magazines   Québec City's English-language newspaper, the *Chronicle-Telegraph,* is essentially a small-town newspaper, published weekly on Wednesday. The content is local news and advertisements, of marginal interest to visitors. Major Canadian and American English-language newspapers and magazines are available in the newsstands of the large hotels and at vending machines placed around tourist corners in the old town. The leading French-language newspapers are *Le Soleil* and *Le Journal de Québec.*

Pets   For emergency pet illnesses or injuries, call ☎ **418/872-5355** 24 hours a day. Incidentally, pet owners must by law pick up after their animals.

Police   For the Québec City police, call ☎ **911.** For the Sûreté du Québec, comparable to the state police or highway patrol, call ☎ **888/461-2131.**

Post Office   The main post office (*bureau de poste*) is in the Lower Town, at 300 rue St-Paul near rue Abraham-Martin, not far from Carré Parent (Parent Square) by the port (☎ **418/694-6175**). Hours are 8am to 5:45pm Monday through Friday. A convenient branch in the Upper Town, half a block down the hill from the Château Frontenac at 3 rue Buade (☎ **418/694-6102**), keeps the same hours.

Radio & TV   Most broadcasts on radio and TV are in French, but FM 104.7 is in English. In the large hotels, cable TV is standard, with some English-language stations, including U.S. channels.

Rest Rooms   Find them in the tourist offices and on the ground floor of the commercial complex at 41 rue Couillard, just off rue St-Jean (it's wheelchair accessible). Many cafes situate their rest rooms near the telephone.

Safety   Canadian cities are far safer than most of their U.S. counterparts. Still, tourists are particular targets of street criminals, so the usual caveats pertain. It's a good idea not to leave possessions in plain view in your car and to stay aware of the behavior of people in your vicinity.

Smoking   It is statistically true that French-speaking Québecers smoke more than other Canadians, despite heavy taxes on tobacco, and the province has not yet clamped down on smoking in public places with the determination of municipal governments in English Canada and the United States. Still, a growing number of restaurants have set aside no-smoking sections, and cigar lounges are a fading fad.

Taxes   Most goods and services in Canada are taxed 7% by the federal government. On top of that, the province of Québec has an additional 7.5% tax on goods and services, including those provided by hotels. In Québec, the federal tax appears on the bill as the TPS (elsewhere in Canada, it's called the GST), and the provincial tax is known as the TVQ. Tourists may receive a rebate on both the federal and provincial tax on items they have purchased but not used in Québec, as well as on lodging. To take advantage of this refund, request the necessary forms at duty-free shops and hotels, and submit them, with the original receipts, within a year of the purchase. Contact the Canadian consulate or Québec tourism office for up-to-the-minute information about taxes and rebates.

Telephones The telephone system, operated by Bell Canada, closely resembles the American model. All operators (dial ☎ 0—0 to get one) speak French and English, and respond in the appropriate language as soon as callers speak to them. Pay phones in Québec require C25¢ (US17¢) for a 3-minute local call. Directory information calls (dial ☎ 411) are free of charge. Both local and long-distance calls usually cost more from hotels—sometimes a lot more, so check. Directories (*annuaires des téléphones*) come in white pages (residential) and yellow pages (commercial).

Time Québec City is on the same time as New York, Boston, Montréal, and Toronto. It's an hour behind Halifax.

Tipping Waiters, waitresses, and cabbies should be given a 10% to 18% tip, depending upon the quality of the establishment and the service they provide. Bellhops usually get C$1 (US70¢) per bag, slightly more if the bags are heavy or must be carried a long distance. The doorman who hails a cab deserves some coins, up to C$1 (US70¢). Many hotel guests leave C$1 (US70¢) per night for the chambermaid.

Transit Information Call ☎ 418/627-2511 for the transit authority.

Useful Telephone Numbers For Alcoholics Anonymous, ☎ 418/529-0015, daily 8am to midnight. For Health Info, a 24-hour line answered by nurses, call ☎ 418/648-2626. For Tel-Aide, for emotional distress including anxiety and depression, call ☎ 418/686-2433. For information about tides, call ☎ 418/648-7293, 24 hours daily.

Water It's safe to drink.

Weather For the forecast, call ☎ 418/648-7766 24 hours a day.

12

Where to Stay in Québec City

Staying in one of the small hotels or inns within the walls of the Upper Town can be one of Québec City's memorable experiences. That isn't a guarantee, however, that it will be enjoyable. Standards of comfort, amenities, and prices fluctuate so wildly from one small hotel to another—even within a single establishment—that it is wise to shop around and examine any rooms offered before registering. From rooms with private bathrooms, minibars, and cable TVs to walk-up budget accommodations with linoleum floors and toilets down the hall, Québec City has a wide enough variety of lodgings to suit most tastes and wallets.

If cost is a prime consideration, note that prices drop significantly from November through April, except for such events as the Winter Festival. Or if you prefer the conveniences of large chain hotels and the Château Frontenac is fully booked, you will need to go outside the ancient walls to the newer part of town. The handful of high-rise hotels out there are within walking distance of the attractions in the Old City, or are only a quick bus or taxi ride away. Although Québec City has far fewer first-class hotels than Montréal, there are still a sufficient number to provide for the crowds of businesspeople and well-heeled tourists who flock to the city year-round. And in recent years, a clutch of new boutique hotels and small inns has greatly enhanced the lodging stock.

The prices given in the listings below are **rack rates.** That means you'll rarely, if ever, have to pay that much, unless it's the middle of Winter Carnival and everything else is booked. The higher rates given apply during the warmer months, in the Christmas season, and during the Winter Carnival in February. The cheapest rooms are usually found in smaller establishments, typically converted residences or carved out of several row houses. Often family run, they offer fewer of the usual electronic gadgets—air-conditioning and TV are far from standard at this level—and may have four or five floors, without elevators. Even with an advance reservation, always ask to see two or three rooms before making a choice in this price category. Unless otherwise noted, all rooms in the lodgings listed below have private bathrooms— *en suite,* as they say in Canada. Prices are given in both Canadian and U.S. dollars.

Similar in atmosphere and price band to these small hotels are the more than 30 bed-and-breakfasts in and around Vieux-Québec. With

Best Hotel Bets

For a roundup of my favorite Québec City hotels, see chapter 1.

---

rates in the C$75 to C$100 (US$52 to US$69) range, they don't represent substantial savings over the small hotels.

They do, however, often provide an opportunity to get to know Québecois more intimately. When calling to make arrangements, be very clear about your needs and requirements. Some hosts don't permit smoking, children, or pets. They may have only one or two bathrooms to be shared by four or five rooms, or all their rooms may be fourth-floor walk-ups, or they may be located far from the center of things. As with the other inexpensive lodging choices listed below, TVs and air-conditioning are not regular features. A deposit is typically required, and minimum stays of 2 nights are common. Credit cards may not be accepted.

A very useful *Accommodation Guide*, revised annually, is available at the tourist offices. It lists every member of the Greater Québec Area Tourism and Convention Bureau, from B&Bs to five-star hotels, providing details about number of rooms, prices, and facilities.

1 Haute-Ville (Upper Town)

VERY EXPENSIVE

✪ **Château Frontenac.** 1 rue des Carrières (at rue St-Louis), Québec City, PQ G1R 4P5. ☎ **800/828-7447** or 418/692-3861. Fax 418/692-1751. www.cphotels.ca. E-mail: agentres@ lcf.cphotels.ca. 626 units. A/C MINIBAR TV TEL. Mid-May–mid-Oct C$319–C$434 (US$220–US$299) double, C$669–C$1,250 (US$461–US$862) suite; mid-Oct–mid-May C$129–C$329 (US$89–US$227) double, C$559–C$975 (US$385–US$672) suite. AE, CB, DC, DISC, ER, MC, V. Parking C$18 (US$12.40) per day.

Québec City's magical "castle" turned 100 years old in 1993. To celebrate, the management added a new 66-room wing, and because the hotel serves as the very symbol of the city, care was taken to replicate the original architectural style throughout. In the past, the hotel hosted Queen Elizabeth and Prince Philip, and during World War II, Winston Churchill and Franklin D. Roosevelt had the entire place to themselves for a conference. The hotel was built in phases, following the landline, so the wide halls take crooked paths. The highly variable room prices depend on size, location, view or lack of one, and on how recently it was renovated. That makes the rates listed above no better than a very rough guide, for day of the week, time of year, and even the weather, if it has influenced bookings, can determine what is offered. In-room movies are available, and many rooms are no-smoking.

Dining/Diversions: The fare in Le Champlain dining room isn't yet what it might be compared to the grandeur of the physical spaces, but the kitchen is striving. It's open for dinner nightly and for Sunday brunch. The casual Café de la Terrasse offers a buffet breakfast, and dinner and dancing on Saturday nights. Two bars overlook the Terrasse Dufferin. Le Bistro is the lower-level snack bar.

Amenities: New indoor pool and kiddie pool, large gym with specialized weight machines, concierge, room service (6:30am to 11:30pm), dry-cleaning, laundry service, baby-sitting, limo service, massage, Jacuzzi, secretarial services, express check-out, valet parking, and business center.

Québec City Accommodations

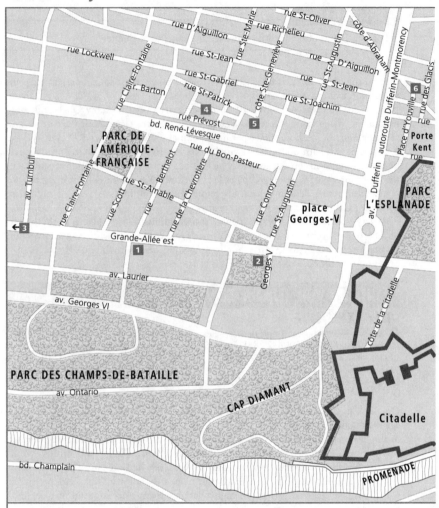

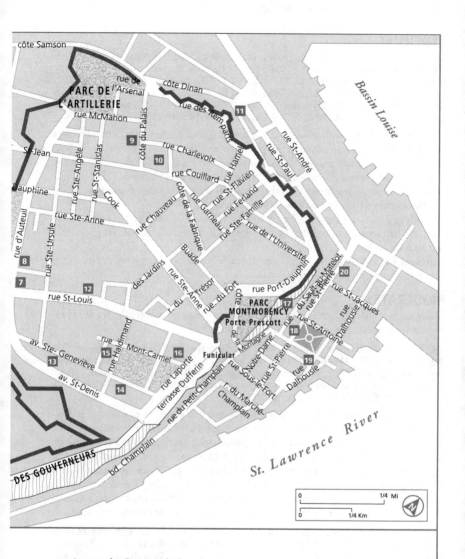

Loews le Concord **1**
Manoir de l'Esplanade **7**
Manoir Sur-le-Cap **14**
Manoir Victoria **9**
Radisson Gouverneurs **4**
Relais Charles-Alexander **3**

EXPENSIVE

Manoir Victoria. 44 Côte du Palais (rue St-Jean), Québec City, PQ G1R 4H8.
☎ **800/463-6283** or 418/692-1030. Fax 418/692-3822. www.manoir-victoria.com.
E-mail: admin@manoir-victoria.com. 145 units. A/C TV TEL. Mid-May–mid-Oct C$129–C$239
(US$89–US$165) double, C$225–C$400 (US$155–US$275) suite; late Oct–early May
C$89–C$199 (US$61–US$137) double, C$150–C$300 (US$103–US$207) suite. Extra person
C$25 (US$17). AE, CB, DC, DISC, MC, V. Children under 18 share parents' room free.

The sprawling lobby with gloomy wood paneling and chunky sofas isn't especially
beguiling; but there's a restaurant on premises, and the location beside the St-Jean
resto and bar scene is a plus for many. An added extra is the indoor pool, rare in the
city. The hotel sprawls all the way from the main entrance on Côte de Palais to adjacent St-Jean, zigzagging around a couple of stores. A long staircase reaches the lobby,
but elevators make the trip to most of the rooms.

Dining: The Resto-Bistro St-James and La Table du Manoir Victoria are serviceable, the latter serving a number of traditional Québecois dishes. Guests get a 20%
discount on meals.

Amenities: Fitness center with Nautilus machines and 10 Exercycles, dry-cleaning,
laundry, valet parking, and indoor pool.

MODERATE

Many of the hotels and inns recommended below are on or near the Jardin des Gouverneurs, immediately south of the Château Frontenac.

Cap Diamant Maison de Touristes. 39 av. Ste-Geneviève (near de Brébeuf), Québec City,
PQ G1R 4B3. ☎ **418/694-0313.** www.hcapdiamant.qc.ca. E-mail: hcapdiamant@
oricom.ca. 12 units. A/C TV. Summer C$90–C$135 (US$62–US$93) double. Winter
C$75–C$110 (US$52–US$76) double. Rates include breakfast. Extra person C$15 (US$10).
MC, V. Parking C$10 (US$6.65) in nearby lot.

Every room is different in this amiable guest house, its assortment of furniture including brass beds, Victorian memorabilia, and nonspecific retro pieces retrieved from attics.
All the rooms have small unstocked refrigerators, air-conditioning, color TV, and private
bathroom. In back of the house, which dates from 1826, there are an enclosed porch and
a garden. The Cap Diamant is only 2½ blocks from the Jardin des Gouverneurs. The
Plains of Abraham is right behind it, leading up to the Citadelle. Rooms overlook the
rooftops of the Old City. Stairs are very steep throughout, including the entrance, and
there is no elevator. When reserving, ask about the just-renovated rooms next door.

Château Bellevue. 16 rue Laporte, Québec City, PQ G1R 4M9. ☎ **800/463-2617** or
418/692-2573. Fax 418/692-4876. www.vieux-quebec.com/bellevue. E-mail: bellevue@
vieux-quebec.com. 57 units. A/C TV TEL. Late Oct–Apr 30 C$79–C$119 (US$55–US$82) double; Winter Carnival and May–late Oct C$109–C$149 (US$75–US$103). Extra person C$10
(US$6.90). Rates include breakfast (except May to mid-Oct). Packages available Oct–May.
AE, CB, DC, ER, MC, V. Free valet parking.

Money-Saving Tips

A city that combines tourism and governmental functions with a pronounced four-
season climate studded with festivals and special events inevitably produces complex
and rapidly changing rate structures for its lodgings. Simply delaying a trip or moving it up by a week or even a few days can make a significant difference in cost. To
save, skip Christmas and Winter Carnival and summer, and ask about weekend stays,
honeymoon specials, and senior-citizen or corporate discounts. Remember also that
families with children can often share a room for the cost of the parents alone.

ⓘ Family-Friendly Hotels

Château Frontenac (*see p. 207*)   Sleep in a fairy-tale castle that is the symbol of a city, with an indoor pool just for kids and street performers just outside the door.

L'Hôtel du Vieux Québec (*see p. 211*)   Popular with families and school groups, it's in a good location for exploring Upper or Lower Town.

Radisson Gouverneurs (*see p. 213*)   The rooftop swimming pool is a treat, with its indoor water route to the outside. Winter Carnival activities are a quick and easy walk away.

Occupying several row houses at the top of the Parc des Gouverneurs, this minihotel has a pleasant lobby with leather couches and chairs and a helpful staff, as well as some of the creature comforts that smaller inns in the neighborhood lack. Although the rooms are small and often suffer from unfortunate decorating choices, they are quiet for the most part and have private bathrooms. A few higher-priced units overlook the park. The hotel's private parking is directly behind the building, a notable convenience in this congested part of town, although there are only a few spaces. A first-night deposit by check or credit card is required. If you're searching for a room on the spot and this is full, there are 10 other lodgings within a block in any direction.

L'Hôtel du Vieux Québec. 1190 rue St-Jean (at rue de l'Hôtel Dieu), Québec City, PQ G1R 1S6. ☎ **800/361-7787** or 418/692-1850. Fax 418/692-5637. www.hvq.com. E-mail: reserv@hvq.com. 41 units. A/C TV TEL. May to mid-Oct, Christmas week, and Winter Carnival C$135–C$185 (US$93–US$128) double; late Oct–Apr C$89–C$109 (US$61–US$75) double. Extra person C$15 (US$10.35). DC, ER, MC, V. Parking C$9 (US$4.30).

This century-old brick hotel has been renovated with care. Guest rooms are equipped with sofas, two double beds, cable color TVs, hair dryers, unstocked fridges, and modern bathrooms. Most have kitchenettes. Ask for one of the 24 rooms recently redone with new carpeting and furniture; two of these are junior suites with Jacuzzis. With these homey layouts, it's understandably popular with families, skiers, and the groups of visiting high-school students who descend upon the city in late spring. In addition to Les Frères de la Côte on the ground floor, there are many moderately priced restaurants and night spots nearby.

Manoir de L'Esplanade. 83 rue d'Auteuil (at rue St-Louis), Québec City, PQ G1R 4C3. ☎ **418/694-0834.** Fax 418/692-0456. 36 units. A/C TV TEL. Summer C$70–C$115 (US$48–US$79) double; winter 45% less. Extra person C$10 (US$6.90). AE, MC, V. Parking C$7.25 (US$5) a day.

Though not as well appointed as similar places around the Grande-Allée, this is a clean hotel, and all rooms have private bathrooms—not something you can take for granted at this rate level. Some rooms have double beds. Students like this place, which used to be a nunnery. The Porte St-Louis is a block away.

Manoir Sur-le-Cap. 9 av. Ste-Geneviève (near rue Laporte), Québec City, PQ G1R 4A7. ☎ **418/694-1987.** Fax 418/667-4235. www.manoir-sur-le-cap.com. E-mail: manoir@mediom.qc.ca. 14 units. TV. May–Oct C$95–C$125 (US$65–US$86) double, C$225 (US$155) suite; Nov–May C$70–C$105 (US$48–US$72) double, C$150 (US$103) suite. Additional person C$15 (US$10.35) AE, MC, V.

All is fresh, painted, and shellacked at this inn on the south side of the Parc des Gouverneurs, opposite the Château Frontenac. Overhauled from top to bottom, all its bedroom floors gleam, and many have exposed stone or brick walls. Obviously the price is right, unless you require air-conditioning or a phone, and understand that these four floors have no elevator. Upgrade to what they call their "condo"—an apartment in a separate building in back—and get an apartment with a working fireplace, a phone, a VCR, and a kitchenette with microwave oven, coffeemaker, and basic crockery. When booking, request parking at one of the nearby lots. This is a nosmoking facility. English is spoken.

INEXPENSIVE

Auberge La Chouette. 71 rue d'Auteuil (near rue St-Louis), Québec City, PQ G1R 4C3. ☎ **418/694-0232.** 10 units. A/C TV TEL. May–Sept C$85–C$95 (US$59–US$66) double; Oct–Apr C$65–C$80 (US$45–US$55) double. AE, MC, V. Parking C$9 (US$6.20) a day.

Across the street from Esplanade Park and near the Porte St-Louis, this inn has a capable Asian restaurant, Apsara, on the main floor. Despite its presence, the rooms on three floors reached by the spiral stairway (no elevator) are quiet. All of them have full bathrooms but are without frills. Examine your room first. The Citadelle, and Winter Carnival and Québec Summer Festival activities, are only minutes away.

Auberge St-Louis. 48 rue St-Louis (between rues Ste-Ursule and Parloir), Québec City, PQ G1R 3Z3. ☎ **418/692-2424.** Fax 418/692-3797. www.quebecweb.com/aubergestlouis. E-mail: bonnesadresses@videotron.ca. 27 units (14 with bathroom). A/C TV. May–Oct 15 C$49 (US$34) double without bathroom, C$82 (US$57) double with bathroom; Oct 16–Apr 30 C$49 (US$34) double without bathroom, C$65 (US$45) double with bathroom. Rates include breakfast. Extra person C$10 (US$6.90). MC, V. Nearby parking C$8.35 (US$5.75) a day.

Guest rooms here come in a variety of configurations, with occasional features that add some visual interest, such as a carved fireplace mantel or a stained-glass window. But the reasons to stay here are the low prices and a good location near city hall. Some rooms have a sink and shower but no toilet, and some have a color or black-and-white TV.

2 On or Near the Grande-Allée

EXPENSIVE

✪ **Hilton Québec.** 1100 bd. Rene-Levesque Est, Québec City, G1K 7M9. ☎ **800/445-8667** or 418/647-2411. Fax 418/647-2986. www.hilton.com. 571 units. A/C MINIBAR TV TEL. C$149–C$275 (US$103–US$190) double; from C$375 (US$259) suite. Extra person C$20 (US$13.80). Children of any age stay free in parents' room. Packages available. AE, DC, DISC, ER, MC, V. Parking C$16 (US$11.05). Head east along Grande-Allée, and just before the St-Louis Gate in the city wall, turn left on rue Dufferin, then left again as you pass the Parliament building; the hotel is 1 block ahead.

Superior on virtually every count to the other mid-rise contemporary hotels outside the old town (excluding Le Capitole, above), this Hilton is entirely true to the breed, the clear choice for executives and those leisure travelers who can't bear to live without their gadgets. The location—across the street from the city walls and near the Parliament—is excellent. It is also connected to the Place Québec shopping complex, which has 75 shops, two cinemas, and the convention center.

The public rooms are big and brassy, Hilton-style, while the guest chambers are in the process of freshening. Most have one or two large beds plus in-room movies. Upper-floor views of the St. Lawrence River, old Québec, and the Laurentian Mountains are grand. The staff is generally efficient and congenial. No-smoking rooms are available.

Dining/Diversions: Le Caucus restaurant serves buffet-style as well as à la carte meals. Friday and Saturday evenings are theme nights, with live entertainment.

Amenities: Heated outdoor pool (summer only), health club with sauna and whirlpool, jogging track, airport shuttle, room service, dry-cleaning, laundry service, baby-sitting, car rental, and business center.

☼ Le Capitole. 972 rue Saint-Jean (1 block west of Porte Saint-Jean), Québec City, PQ G1R 1R5. ☎ **800/363-4040** or 418/694-4040. Fax 418/694-1916. www.lecapitole.com. E-mail: admin@lecapitole.com. 40 units. A/C MINIBAR TV TEL. Late May–Sept C$152–C$212 (US$105–US$146) double, C$260 (US$179) suite; Oct–early May C$99–C$185 (US$68–US$128) double, C$189–C$215 (US$130–US$148) suite. Packages available. AE, MC, V.

As gleefully eccentric as the three business hotels below are conventional, the entrance to this hotel is squeezed almost to anonymity between a restaurant, a theater, and a cinema on Place d'Youville. Rooms borrow from art deco and incorporate stars in the carpets and clouds on the ceiling. Most bathtubs have whirlpools, and beds have down comforters. All rooms have VCRs and CD players, with 120 videos available free of charge. Coffeemakers, hair dryers, and phones with data ports are standard.

Dining/Diversions: Ristorante Il Teatro, open daily 7am to 2am, is half continental and half show biz, with platinum records on the walls, boxed plates autographed by celebrities, and a busy sidewalk terrace. Down the central hall is the Théâtre Capitole, which presents live shows when it isn't hosting weddings and banquets.

Amenities: Concierge, room service, dry-cleaning, and laundry service.

Loews le Concorde. 1225 place Montcalm (at Grande-Allée), Québec City, PQ G1R 4W6. ☎ **800/463-5256** or 418/647-2222. Fax 418/647-4710. www.loewshotels.com. E-mail: dpare@loews.com. 404 units. A/C MINIBAR TV TEL. May–Oct C$109–C$245 (US$75–US$169), Nov–Apr C$99–C$149 (US$68–US$103) double; from C$225 (US$155) suite. Extra person over 17, C$25 (US$17.25). Children under 17 share parents' room free. Ski and weekend packages available. AE, CB, DC, ER, MC, V. Parking garage C$18 (US$12.40).

From outside, the building that houses this hotel is a visual insult to the skyline, blighting a neighborhood of late-Victorian town houses. Enter, and the affront might be forgotten, at least by those with business to do who can't be bothered with architectural aesthetics.

Standard rooms have marble bathrooms with hair dryers, prints of Québec City street scenes, in-room movies, and three telephones. They bestow spectacular views of the river and the old city, even from the lower floors. There are seven no-smoking floors and seven business-class floors, including the L'Exécutive level, reserved for the use of women only.

Of all the hotels listed here, this is the farthest from the old town, about a 10-minute walk to the walls, and then another 10 minutes to the center of the Haute-Ville.

Dining/Diversions: ☼ L'Astral is a revolving rooftop restaurant, with a bar and live piano music Tuesday to Sunday nights. Le Café Bar-Sur-le-Cap serves all three meals.

Amenities: Business center; fitness facility with sauna and some exercise equipment, and outdoor heated pool (April to November; access to pool in a private club during the other months).

☼ Radisson Gouverneurs. 690 bd. René-Lévesque Est, Québec City, PQ G1R 5A8. ☎ **888/910-1111** from eastern Canada, 800/333-3333 from elsewhere, or 418/647-1717. Fax 418/647-2146. www.radisson.com. 377 units. A/C TV TEL. C$235–C$295 (US$162–US$203) double; from C$305 (US$210) suite. Extra adult C$20 (US$13.80). Children under 16 stay free in parents' room. AE, DC, DISC, ER, MC, V. Parking C$15 (US$10.35). Turn left off Grande-Allée, and then left again onto Dufferin, just before the St-Louis Gate in the city wall. Once past the Parliament building, take the first left. The hotel is 2 blocks ahead.

Part of Place Québec, a multiuse complex, the hotel is also connected to the city's convention center. It is 1 block from the Hilton, 2 blocks from Porte (Gate) Kent in the city wall, and not far from the Québec Parliament building, a location likely to fit almost any businessperson's needs. It is, however, an uphill climb from the old city (like all the hotels and inns along or near the Grande-Allée). Some rooms have minibars; all have in-room movies. Hair dryers and coffeemakers are standard. There are three no-smoking floors and two executive floors. Every inch has been accorded the ministrations of a $5.2-million renovation completed in 2000. Reception is two levels up.

Dining: Le Café serves buffet and à la carte meals.

Amenities: Outdoor pool (open only in summer), fully equipped and staffed health club with Exercycles, sauna and whirlpool, concierge, business center, room service, dry-cleaning, laundry service, and baby-sitting.

MODERATE

Château Laurier. 1220 place Georges V Ouest (near corner of Grande-Allée), Québec City, PQ G1R 5B8. ☎ **800/463-4453** or 418/522-8108. Fax 418/524-8768. www.vieux-quebec. com/laurier. E-mail: laurier@vieux-quebec.com. 113 units. A/C TV TEL. May–mid-Oct C$109–C$179 (US$75–US$123) double; late Oct–Apr C$79–C$149 (US$55–US$103) double. AE, DC, ER, MC, V. Parking C$10 (US$6.65).

Anchoring the east end of the Grande-Allée action strip, this old-timer has lifted its formerly dowdy countenance by taking over an adjoining building and adding 65 newer, larger, jazzier units. Some of them have working fireplaces, Jacuzzis, and king beds; all enjoy the comforts and doodads of a first-class hotel, a giant step up from its previous incarnation. The new rooms are clearly more desirable than those in the plainer and more cramped original wing. A bar and bistro remain in front, down a few steps from Grande-Allée, while the expansive new lobby is located on the Georges V side. The hotel is only 2 blocks west of the St-Louis Gate and across the way from Parliament Hill.

INEXPENSIVE

☼ **Relais Charles-Alexander.** 91 Grande-Allée Est (Avenue Galipeault), Québec City, PQ G1R 2H5. ☎ **418/523-1220.** Fax 418/523-9556. www.quebecweb.com/rca. E-mail: relais@ oricom.ca. 23 units (19 with bathroom). A/C TV. C$85–C$105 (US$59–US$72) double. Rates include breakfast. MC, V. Parking nearby C$6 (US$4.15).

On the ground floor of this charming brick-faced B&B is an art gallery, which also serves as the breakfast room. This stylish use of space extends to the bedrooms as well, which are crisply maintained and decorated with eclectic antique and wicker pieces and reproductions. Rooms in front are larger, most have showers, not tubs, some have phones. They are quiet, for the most part, since the inn is just outside the orbit of the sometimes-raucous Grande-Allée terrace bars. Yet the St-Louis Gate is less than a 10-minute walk away from the hubbub.

3 Basse-Ville (Lower Town)

VERY EXPENSIVE

☼ **Auberge Saint-Antoine.** 10 rue St-Antoine (Dalhousie), Québec City, PQ G1K 4C9. ☎ **888/692-2211** or 418/692-2211. Fax 418/692-1177. www.saint-antoine.com/ info.html. E-mail: info@saint-antoine.com. 31 units. A/C TV TEL. C$219–C$299 (US$151–US$206) double; C$299–C$479 (US$206–US$330) suite. Rates include breakfast. Extra person C$20 (US$13.80). Children under 12 stay free in parents' room. AE, DC, MC, V. Parking C$5 (US$3.45). Follow rue Dalhousie around the Lower Town to rue St-Antoine. The hotel is next to the Musée de la Civilisation.

The centerpiece of this uncommonly attractive boutique hotel is the 1830 maritime warehouse that contains the lobby and meeting rooms, with the original dark beams and stone floor still intact. Buffet breakfasts and afternoon wine and cheese are set out in the lobby, where guests relax in wing chairs next to the hooded fireplace. Canny mixes of antique and reproduction furniture are found in both public and private areas. The bedrooms, in an adjoining modern wing and a separate, newly remodeled 1727 house, are spacious, in many different color schemes, with such extra decorative touches as custom-made iron bedsteads and tables. The owners' other occupation as interior designers is seen to great effect everywhere. The big bathrooms have robes and hair dryers. Several rooms have private terraces, one of which has a three-hole putting green. Prices are highest for the 13 rooms with river views, but since a large parking lot intervenes, those without the view are a better deal. The eight new suites have kitchenettes, fax machines, and computer jacks.

EXPENSIVE

Auberge Saint-Pierre. 79 Saint-Pierre (behind the Musée de la Civilisation), Québec City, PQ G1K 4A3. ☎ **888/268-1017** or 418/694-7981. Fax 418/694-0406. www.auberge.qc.ca. E-mail: st-pierre@auberge.qc.ca. 45 units. A/C TV TEL. May–Oct C$125–C$189 (US$86–US$130) double, C$179–C$189 (US$123–US$130) suite; Oct 15–May 16 C$119–C$179 (US$82–US$123) double, C$189–C$209 (US$130–US$144) suite. Rates include breakfast. AE, CB, DC, ER, MC, V. Parking nearby C$10 (US$6.90).

The doors were only opened in 1997, but the paint was barely dry before they expanded into the adjacent building to add another 13 rooms. That effort burnishes its welcome to the lengthening roster of Basse-Ville inns. Included full breakfasts are special, cooked to order by the chef in the open kitchen. Most of the rooms are uncommonly spacious, and the even more commodious suites are a possible luxury on a longer visit, especially since they have modest kitchen facilities. The made-to-order furnishings are meant to suggest rather than replicate traditional Québec styles. Bare floors with area rugs contribute to the minimalist feel. Some of the window air conditioners are underpowered, but they're being replaced. Robes and hair dryers are provided. The new wing is no-smoking.

✪ **Dominion 1912.** 126 rue Saint-Pierre (at rue Saint-Paul), Québec City, PQ G1K 4A8. ☎ **888/833-5253** or 418/692-2224. Fax 418/692-4403. www.hoteldominion.com. E-mail: reservations@hoteldominion.com. 40 units. A/C MINIBAR TV TEL. Oct 15–Apr 30 C$119–C$179 (US$82–US$123) double; May 1–Oct 14 C$139–C$239 (US$95–US$165) double. Rates include breakfast. AE, DC, ER, MC, V. Parking C$5–C$10 (US$3.45–US$6.90).

If there were space enough to recommend only one hotel in the city, this would be it. The owners stripped the inside of the 1912 Dominion Fish & Fruit building down to the studs and pipes and started over. Even the least expensive rooms are large, the queen- or king-sized beds heaped with linen-covered pillows and covered with feather duvets. Custom-made end tables swing into place or out of the way. Neutral colors extend to the spacious bathrooms and the robes hanging there. Hair dryers and coffeemakers are standard. A fruit basket awaits. Modem outlets are at desktop level. Chairs embrace sitters for work or leisure. Continental breakfast is set out in the handsome lobby along with a variety of morning newspapers. They can be taken out to the terrace in back. Connect to the Internet from the computer near the front desk. Even so, this remains one of the most desirable hotels in town. Go before the masses find it.

Le Priori. 15 rue Sault-au-Matelot (at rue St-Antoine), Québec City, PQ G1K 3Y7. ☎ **800/351-3992** or 418/692-3992. Fax 418/692-0883. www.quebecweb.com/lepriori. E-mail: priori@videotron.ca. 26 units. A/C TV TEL. May–Oct C$109–C$179 (US$75–US$123) double, C$219–C$309 (US$151–US$213) suite; Nov–Apr C$89–C$129 (C$61–C$89) double, C$179–C$239 (US$123–US$165) suite. Packages available. AE, DC, ER, MC, V. Parking C$8 (US$5.50) a day.

Locking Up

Don't assume the door to your hotel door automatically locks behind you. While modern hotels in Montréal and Québec City use card keys and deadbolts, many of the older inns and B&Bs in those cities and out in the country do not. Instead, you may have to (1) insert your room key and turn it twice to lock it upon leaving, or (2) turn the flanged button on the inside doorknob, or (3) push the inside doorknob in, then make a quarter-turn to the left (or, sometimes, the right) and then step outside to close. In any event, always test the door upon leaving.

A forerunner of the blossoming Lower Town hotel scene, located 2 blocks behind the Auberge Saint-Antoine, Le Priori provides a playful postmodern ambience behind the somber facade of a 1766 house. The French designer Phillipe Starck inspired the owners, who deployed versions of his conical stainless-steel sinks in the bedrooms and sensual multinozzle showers in the small bathrooms. In some rooms, a claw-foot tub sits beside the bed. Queen-sized beds have black tubular frames and soft duvets. The dim lighting doesn't help readers, however. Suites have sitting rooms with wood-burning fireplaces, a kitchen, and a bathroom with Jacuzzi. There's a casual restaurant off the lobby.

Le Saint-Paul. 229½ rue St-Paul (near rue Abraham-Martin), Québec City, PQ G1K 3W3. ☎ **888/794-4414** or 418/694-4414. Fax 418/694-0889. www.quebecweb.com/hotellest-paul. 26 units. A/C TV TEL. Late May–Oct C$130–C$275 (US$90–US$190) double; Nov–early May C$100–C$200 (US$69–US$138) double. AE, DC, ER, MC, V.

This 1854 mid-Victorian near the railroad station became the Basse-Ville's latest addition to the hotel scene with its 1997 renovation. While it isn't quite up to the considerable standards of most of those mentioned above, staying here represents no deprivation. Half the rooms have king-sized beds, the phones have data ports, the TVs are on cable. Some have small fridges and/or whirlpool baths. Tones and fabrics are crisp and muted. The Péché Véniel restaurant on the ground floor is under separate management. Rue St-Paul's antique row is steps away.

Where to Dine in Québec City

13

Once you are within these ancient walls, walking along streets that look to have been transplanted intact from Brittany or Provence, it is understandable if you imagine that you have in store one supernal dining experience after another in Québec City. Hype and expectations aside, the truth is that this gloriously scenic city has no *temples de cuisine* comparable to those of Paris or Manhattan. Although it is easy to eat well in the capital—even, in a few isolated cases, *quite* well—the remembered pleasures of a stay here will likely lie in other areas, absorbed by other senses.

But that's not to imply that you're in for barely edible meals served by sullen waiters. By sticking to any of the many competent bistros, the handful of Asian eateries, and one or two of the emerging *nuovo Italiano* trattorias, you will be content. Another step up, two or three ambitious enterprises tease the palate with hints of higher achievement. Even the blatantly touristic restaurants along rue St-Louis and around the Place d'Armes can produce decent meals, despite the fact that they aren't obliged to satisfy demanding regular clienteles. The less extravagant among them, in fact, are entirely satisfactory for breakfast or simple lunches, a useful fact to keep in mind if you're staying in one of the many Old Town guest houses that serve no meals.

As throughout the province, the best dining deals are the table d'hôte—fixed-price—meals. Virtually all full-service restaurants offer them, if only at lunch. They rarely require significant sacrifice, assuming you don't expect beluga, foie gras, and pricier cuts of meat. As a rule, they include at least soup or salad, a main course, and a dessert. Some places add in an extra appetizer and/or a beverage, all for the approximate à la carte price of the main course alone.

Curiously, for a city beside a great waterway and but a day's sail from some of the world's best fishing grounds, seafood is not given much attention. Mussels and salmon are on most menus, but look for those places that go beyond those staples. Game is popular, and everything from venison, rabbit, and duck to more exotic quail, goose, caribou, and wapiti is available.

At the better places, and even some of those that might seem inexplicably popular, reservations are all but essential during traditional holidays and the festivals that pepper the social calendar. Other times, it's usually necessary to book ahead only for weekend evenings. In the listings below, where no mention is made of reservations, they aren't necessary. Dress codes are rarely stipulated, but "dressy casual" works almost everywhere. Remember that for the Québecois, *dîner* (dinner) is lunch, and *souper* (supper) is dinner, though for the sake of consistency, the word *dinner* below is used in the common American sense. The evening meal tends to be served earlier in Québec City than in Montréal, at 6 or 7 rather than 8pm.

For a more extended discussion of Québec dining, see "Cuisine Haute, Cuisine Bas: Smoked Meat, Fiddleheads & Caribou" in the appendix following chapter 18.

1 Restaurants by Cuisine

BISTRO FRENCH
L'Ardoise (p. 224)
L'Échaudé (p. 224)
Le Marie-Clarisse (p. 225)

CONTEMPORARY FRENCH
Laurie Raphaël (p. 224)
Le Paris-Brest (p. 222)
Le Saint-Amour (p. 218)

CONTEMPORARY FRENCH/ITALIAN
Graffiti (p. 223)

CONTEMPORARY ITALIAN
Momento (p. 223)

ECLECTIC
Serge Bruyère (p. 219)

FRENCH/INTERNATIONAL
Le Café du Monde (p. 225)
Le Cochon Dingue (p. 225)

LIGHT FARE/CREPES
Chez Temporel (p. 222)
Le Casse-Crêpe Breton (p. 222)

MEDITERRANEAN
Les Frères de la Côte (p. 219)

QUÉBECOIS
Buffet de l'Antiquaire (p. 226)
Aux Anciens Canadiens (p. 218)

2 Haute-Ville (Upper Town)

EXPENSIVE

Aux Anciens Canadiens. 34 rue St-Louis (at rue Haldimand). ☎ **418/692-1627.** Reservations recommended. Main courses C$12.75–C$19.95 (US$8.80–US$13.75), table d'hôte lunch C$13.75 (US$9.50), dinner C$25–C$42 (US$17.25–US$28.95). AE, CB, DC, ER, MC, V. Daily noon–midnight. QUÉBECOIS.

Smack in the middle of the tourist swarms and inundated by the same during peak months, this venerable restaurant is in what is probably the oldest (1677) house in the city. Perhaps surprisingly, the food at this famous attraction is both well prepared and fairly priced. It is, in addition, one of the best places in La Belle Province to sample the cooking that has its roots in the earliest years of New France. Don't count on the ancient Québecois recipes tasting this good anywhere else. Caribou and maple syrup figure in many of the dishes, including the meat pie, Lac Brome duck, tournedos, and a definitive rendering of luscious sugar pie. Servings are large enough to ward off winter for a week. The kitchen's greatest sin is oversalting, so always taste first. Servers are in costume and there are carved wooden bas-reliefs of regional genre scenes.

✪ **Le Saint-Amour.** 48 rue Ste-Ursule (near rue St-Louis). ☎ **418/694-0667.** Reservations recommended for dinner. Main courses C$21–C$28.50 (US$14–US$19); table d'hôte lunch C$9.95–C$15.50 (US$6.65–US$10.35), dinner C$28.50–C$32.50 (US$19–US$21.65), gastronomic dinner C$54 (USD$36). AE, CB, DC, ER, MC, V. Mon–Fri 11:30am–2:30pm and 5:30–11pm, Sat–Sun 5:30–11pm. CONTEMPORARY FRENCH.

This is a restaurant for the coolly attractive and amorously inclined. Patrons pass a front room with lace curtains and potted greenery into a covered terrace, recently redecorated, lit by candles and flickering Victorian gas fixtures. Up above, the roof is retracted on warm nights, revealing a splash of stars. There is much greenery, most of it real. Easily the most romantic setting for dining in a city that knows about seductive atmosphere, it is distressing to report that there has been a perceptible slip in both food and service. The kitchen lacks the focused imagination it once had, and the wait staff is less attentive than the prices warrant. But if it has dipped from its award-winning stature of a few years ago, it remains a favorite for a hand-holding dinner *à deux* when nourishment is less than prime consideration. Herb-crusted rack of lamb or saffron-touched fillet of pike garnished with seafood niblets is good enough and not too distracting. Accompany exchanges of sweet nothings with selections from a dessert menu broken down into the categories "Chocolatey," "Fruity," "Warm," and "Cold."

Serge Bruyère. 1200 rue Saint-Jean (Côte de la Fabrique). ☎ **418/694-0618.** Reservations recommended for dinner. Table d'hôte lunch, Café Bruyère C$7.95–C$16.95 (US$5.50–US$11.70), Bistro Livernois C$9.95–C$17.95 (US$6.85–US$12.40); table d'hôte dinner, Café Bruyère C$15.95–C$24.95 (US$11–US$17.20), Bistro Livernois C$16.95–C$35.95 (US$11.70–US$24.80); main courses, La Grand Table C$31–C$36 (US$21.40–C$24.85), gastronomic dinners C$75 and C$120 (US$50 and US$80). AE, DC, MC, V. Daily 8am–10:30pm. ECLECTIC.

No moss grows on this place. The eponymous owner bought the wedge-shaped building in 1979 and set about creating a multilevel dining emporium that had something for everyone. Serge Bruyère, however, died young and tragically. His executive chef carries on, along a similar path, serving all meals from informal breakfasts to lavish late dinners. He keeps fiddling with the formula, though. The basement in back that served briefly as a German rathskeller is now an Irish pub with live music Friday and Saturday nights.

At ground level in front is the casual Café Bruyère. Up a long staircase at the back is the Bistro Livernois, with three semicircular windows looking down on the street. It is especially good for lunches, concentrating on grills and pastas that come with rounds of crusty, chewy bread. Foods are adroitly seasoned. Another flight up is the formal La Grand Table, offering a pricey menu that is both highly imaginative and immaculately presented. Gaps between the eight courses of the gastronomic extravaganza stretch on for an entire evening. Whether the unquestionably showy creations justify the raves and the sedate pace of the meal is up to you. Dress well, and arrive with a healthy credit card.

MODERATE

✪ **Les Frères de la Côte.** 1190 rue St-Jean (near Côte de la Fabrique). ☎ **418/692-5445.** Reservations recommended. Main courses C$10.95–C$15.50 (US$7.55–US$10.70); table d'hôte C$15.95–C$16.95 (US$11–US$11.70). AE, DC, ER, MC, V. Daily 11:30am–11pm. MEDITERRANEAN.

At the east end of the old town's liveliest nightlife strip, this supremely casual cafe-pizzeria is as loud as any dance club, all hard surfaces with patrons shouting over the booming stereo music. None of this discourages a single soul—even on a Monday night. Chefs in straw hats in the open kitchen in back crank out a dozen different kinds of pizza—thin-crusted, with unusual toppings that work—and about as many pasta versions, which are less interesting. Bountiful platters of fish and meats, often in the form of brochettes, make appetizers unnecessary. Keep this spot in mind when kids are in tow; there's no way they could make enough noise to bother other customers. Outside tables are available in warm weather, and breakfast is served June 24 to September 5 from 8 to 10am.

Québec City Dining

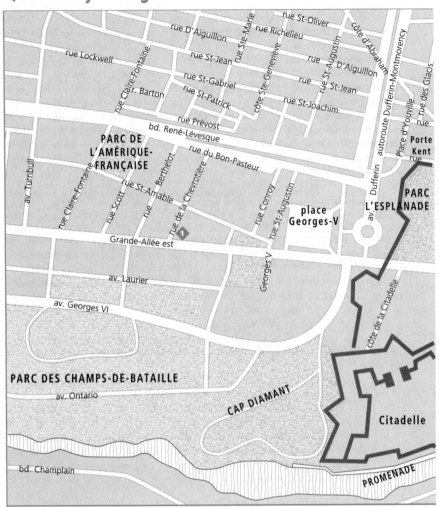

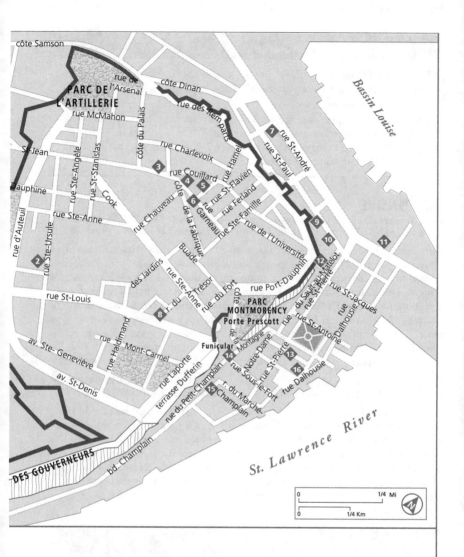

Le Saint-Amour **2**
Les Frères de la Côte **3**
Poisson d'Avril **7**
Serge Bruyère **6**

> ### ⊕ Family-Friendly Restaurants
>
> **Le Cochon Dingue** (*see p. 225*)   It's big so kids can let themselves go here (to a point). Besides, eating in a place called "The Crazy Pig" is something for show-and-tell back at school.
>
> **Les Frères de la Côte** (*see p. 219*)   This pizza place is so loud even fussy kids won't bother the other customers, the eight-year-old can have her slice with nothing on it, and the teenager can slouch over his pie with everything (except anchovies). And, it won't cost the world.

INEXPENSIVE

Chez Temporel. 25 rue Couillard (near Côte de la Fabrique). ☎ **418/694-1813.** Most items under $8 (US$5.50). MC, V. Mon–Fri 7am–1am, Sat–Sun 7am–2:30am. LIGHT FARE.

This Latin Quarter cafe with tile floors and wooden tables attracts denizens of Université Laval. They play chess, swap philosophical insights, and clack away at their laptops from breakfast until well past midnight. It could be a Left Bank hangout for Sorbonne students and their profs. Capture a table and you can hold it forever for just a cappuccino or two. Croissants, jam, butter, and a bowl of café au lait cost half as much as a hotel breakfast. Later in the day, drop by for a *croque-monsieur,* quiche, or plate of cheese with a beer or glass of wine. Just about everything is made on premises. Only 20 people can be seated downstairs, another 26 upstairs, where the light is filtered through stained-glass windows. Note that they are open up to 19 hours a day.

Le Casse-Crêpe Breton. 1136 rue St-Jean (near rue Garneau). ☎ **418/692-0438.** Most items under C$6 (US$4.15). No credit cards. Daily 7:30am–1am. LIGHT FARE/CREPES.

Eat at the bar and watch the crepes being made, or attempt to snag one of the 14 tables nearby or in the adjoining room. Often as not, you'll have to wait a while. Main-course crepes come with two to five ingredients of the customers' choice, usually a combo of ham, cheese, sweet peppers, mushrooms, eggs, or pepperoni. Dessert versions are stuffed with jams or fruit and cream. Soups, salads, and sandwiches are as inexpensive as the crepes. The name of the cafe is a play on the term *casse-croûte,* which means "break crust." It's open more than 17 hours a day, which is useful, but when it gets busy, the service is glacial. Beer is served in bottles or on tap.

3 On or Near the Grande-Allée

EXPENSIVE

✪ **Le Paris-Brest.** 590 Grande-Allée Est (at rue de la Chevrotière). ☎ **418/529-2243.** Reservations recommended. Main courses C$14–C$28 (US$9.65–US$19.30); table d'hôte lunch C$9.95–C$14.75 (US$6.85–US$10.15), dinner C$19.50–C$30 (US$13.45–US$20.70). AE, DC, ER, MC, V. Mon–Fri 11:30am–2:30pm; Mon–Sat 6–11:30pm; Sun 5:30–11:30pm. CONTEMPORARY FRENCH.

Named for a French dessert, this is easily one of the best eating places within or outside the walls, tendering a polished performance from greeting to reckoning. Within minutes after the doors are opened at lunchtime, a happy noise ensues, drowning out the cell-phone users. (Dinner is quieter.) This fashionable crowd comes in everything from bespoke suits to designer jeans—tacky T-shirts, shorts, and children are out of place. They are attended by a comely wait staff dressed in black from chin to toe who convey as much warmth as the rushed process permits. The menu shuns hyperbole—

the mere listing of component ingredients is sufficiently intriguing. One sparkling appetizer is the caramelized apple and red onion tart; another, the thinly sliced game pâté shot with pistachios and dressed with confits. Game and seafood are featured, including pheasant strudel, orange roughy, and lobster ragout. But what they do with simple pasta is impressive: The black squid-ink variety is tossed in a spicy tomato sauce with calamari and topped with leaves of crispy fried spinach, as pretty a visual and taste sensation as might be imagined. How odd that the bread is dry and woolly. Find the entrance on rue de la Chevrotière, under 200 Grande-Allée. There's a small patio for outdoor dining, and free valet parking is available after 5:30pm.

MODERATE

Graffiti. 1191 av. Cartier (near Grand-Allée). ☎ **418/529-4949.** Reservations recommended. Main courses C$18.95–C$26.75 (US$13.05–US$18.45); table d'hôte lunch C$10.25–C$14.25 (US$7.05–US$9.85), dinner C$19.95–C$28.75 (US$13.75–US$19.85). AE, CB, DC, ER, MC, V. Mon–Sat 5–11pm; Sun noon–10pm. CONTEMPORARY FRENCH/ITALIAN.

These 2 or 3 blocks of rue Cartier off Grand-Allée are just outside the perimeter of tourist Québec, far enough removed to avoid flashy banality, close enough to remain convenient. Enthusiasm for this ebullient establishment hasn't flagged a bit, stoked by an attractive male and female staff that hustles about leaving droplets of good feelings in their wake. The kitchen blends bistro with trattoria, often on the same plate. Emblematic are the pike with leeks and grilled almonds and the sautéed rabbit with pureed carrot, broccoli florets, and angel-hair pasta powerfully scented with tarragon. Choice seats are in the glassed-in terrace, the better to scope out the street scene, but there is a variety of booths and banquettes.

Momento. 1144 av. Cartier (near Grande-Allée). ☎ **418/647-1313.** Reservations recommended at dinner. Main courses C$16.75–C$21 (US$11.55–US$14.50); table d'hôte lunch C$8.75–C$15.75 (US$6.05–US$10.85), dinner C$15.95–C$24.95 (US$11–US$17.20). AE, DC, MC, V. Mon–Fri 11:30am–11pm, Sat–Sun 5–10:30pm. CONTEMPORARY ITALIAN.

Considering its manic popularity elsewhere on the continent, updated Italian cooking was late arriving in Québec. The city had the usual parlors shoveling overcooked spaghetti with thin tomato sauce, but not the kind of spiffy neotrattoria that traffics in light-but-lusty dishes meant for lives lived fast. This racy spot is helping to take up the slack, and although it lags somewhat in execution compared to its cross-street rival, Graffiti (see above), it is a welcome antidote to prevailing Franco-Italian clichés. If you don't want a full meal, the 9 pizzas and 14 pastas are uniformly satisfying and of considerable variety. Pizza crusts are almost as thin as crepes, and the "California" version, with marinated chicken, oranges, mozzarella, sun-dried tomatoes, and sesame seeds on pesto is a winner.

4 Basse-Ville (Lower Town)

EXPENSIVE

✪ **Initiale.** 54 rue St-Pierre (corner Côte de la Montagne). ☎ **418/694-1818.** Reservations recommended. Table d'hôte lunch C$12–C$19.95 (US$8.30–US$13.75), dinner C$35–C$65 (US$24–US$45). AE, DC, MC, V. Mon–Fri 11:30am–2:30pm and 6–10pm, Sat 6–10pm, Sun 10:30am–2:30pm and 6–10pm. CONTEMPORARY FRENCH.

This location hasn't been kind to restaurateurs, with two ambitious failures in the last 2 years. This latest effort, however, appears to have what it takes to chart a profitable course. Certainly the palatial setting of tall windows, columns, and deeply recessed ceiling aids in making the tone as gracious as the co-owners intend it to be. Subdued lighting and the muffled noise level help, too, but the result may be a little too sedate for diners who have little to say to their companions or prefer a little more frolicsome combustion with their food. Save on loonies at lunch, cast economy to the winds at night, when you can choose from prix-fixe menus of three to six courses. They are changed often, because the chef values freshness of ingredients over novelty, but a recent seasonal dinner started with duck slices and a grilled nubbin of foie gras with salsify. It continued with grilled smoked salmon on a patch of whipped turnip ringed with leaves of baby bok choy, herbs, and other greens. The headliner was roast guinea hen joined by the intact meat of a lobster claw and a sweet fleshy shrimp over a spoonful of spätzle. A particular treat after that was the selection of 10 impressive cheeses, all of them from Québec, followed by a tart of white wine and maple syrup. Conclusion? Laurie Raphaël (below) has competition atop that hill.

✪ **Laurie Raphaël.** 117 rue Dalhousie (at rue St-André). ☎ **418/692-4555.** Reservations recommended. Main courses C$19–C$36 (US$13.10–US$24.85); table d'hôte lunch C$10–C$17 (US$6.90–US$11.70). AE, DC, ER, MC, V. Mon–Fri noon–2pm and 6–10pm; Sat 6–10pm; Sun 6–10pm. CONTEMPORARY FRENCH.

In 1996, the owners moved from a cramped space in the Auberge Le Priori to these larger, more glamorous quarters, a suitable arena for the city's most accomplished kitchen. An *amuse-gueule* arrives with the cocktail, which might be the Kir Royale, champagne laced with crème de cassis. The waiter happily explains every dish on the menu in as much detail as his customers care to absorb. Appetizers aren't really necessary, since the main course comes with soup or salad, but they're so good that a couple might wish to share one—the little stack of lightly fried calamari rings, perhaps, with their garnish of edible nasturtium blossoms. Main courses run to caribou and salmon in unconventional guises, often with Asian touches. Coupled with an evident concern for "healthy" saucing and exotic combinations, the food closely resembles that associated with serious California restaurants. That includes something of an edifice complex in the towering presentations, held together with skewers and panache. If the service can be faulted, it is for its occasional forgetfulness. But that's quibbling, for this is a restaurant that is all but alone at the pinnacle of the local dining pantheon.

MODERATE

L'Ardoise. 71 rue St-Paul (near Navigateurs). ☎ **418/694-0213.** Reservations recommended at dinner. Main courses C$8–C$17 (US$5.50–US$11.70); table d'hôte lunch C$12.95 (US$8.95), dinner C$22.95–C$30.95 (US$15.80–US$21.35). AE, DC, MC, V. Mon–Fri 11am–10pm, Sat–Sun 9am–10pm. BISTRO FRENCH.

This is one of several bistros that wrap around the corner of rues St-Paul and Sault-au-Matelot. Most are inexpensive and cater more to locals than to tourists. Mussels are staples at Québec restaurants, prepared in the Belgian manner, with bowls of *frites* on the side. Here, they come with 14 different sauces and, with dessert and coffee, cost only C$16.95 (US$11.70). That the chef cares about what he sends out of his kitchen is evident. His food is vibrant and flavorful, served at banquettes along the walls and at tables both inside and out on the sidewalk. Piaf and Aznavour clones warble laments on the stereo. This is a place to leaf through a book, sip a double espresso, and meet neighbors.

✪ **L'Échaudé.** 73 rue Sault-au-Matelot (near rue St-Paul). ☎ **418/692-1299.** Main courses C$12–C$26.50 (US$8.30–US$18.30); table d'hôte lunch C$8.95–C$14.95 (US$6.15–US$10.30), dinner C$23–C$36 (US$15.85–US$24.85). AE, DC, ER, MC, V. Mon–Wed 11:30am–2:30pm and 5:30–10pm; Thurs–Fri 11:30am–2:30pm and 5:30–11pm; Sat 5:30–11pm; Sun 10am–2:30pm and 5:30–10pm. Closed 2 weeks in Jan. BISTRO FRENCH.

One of the necklace of restaurants rounding this Basse-Ville corner, and the most polished, it has sidewalk tables with butcher paper on top and a zinc-topped bar inside the door. The grilled meats and fishes and seafood stews blaze no new trails, but they are very satisfying and an excellent value. Good-deal lunch mains go from cheese omelette to steak tartar, wrapped around with appetizer, dessert, and coffee. Among many winners is the chilled pasta tossed in oil with a touch of lemon and a spray of dill, ringed with mussels and minced red pepper. They keep 24 brands of beer on ice and cellar 125 varieties of wine, a generous 10 of which are available by the glass. They're not so traditional that they're unaware of fads—a Cosmopolitan is C$7 (US$4.85). Aznavour on the stereo and wisps of Gitanes complete the Parisian ambience.

○ **Le Café du Monde.** 57 rue Dalhousie (at rue de la Montagne). ☎ **418/692-4455.** Reservations recommended on weekends. Main courses C$10.95–C$17.95 (US$7.55–US$12.40); table d'hôte (after 3pm) the price of your main course plus C$6.95 or C$10.95 (US$4.80 or US$7.55). AE, DC, ER, MC, V. Mon–Fri 11:30am–11pm; Sat–Sun brunch 9:30am–11pm. FRENCH/ INTERNATIONAL.

A relentlessly convivial spot near the Musée de la Civilisation, the Café du Monde enjoys a constant popularity. The international flavor to which it once aspired has been distilled down to that of a Lyonnaise brasserie. This is seen in the culinary origins of its most-ordered items—pâtés, quiches, roasted lamb knuckle, duck confit with garlic sautéed potatoes, and several versions of mussels with *frites*—classics prepared in a kitchen overseen by a chef from Brittany. Pastas and couscous are some of the less specifically French preparations. Imported beers are favored beverages, along with wines by the glass. A pot of pickles accompanies the drinks. Service is friendly, but easily distracted. Waiters and customers sit down at the upright piano for impromptu performances.

Le Cochon Dingue. 46 bd. Champlain (near rue du Marché-Champlain). ☎ **418/692-2013.** Main courses C$12.95–C$19.75 (US$8.95–US$13.60); table d'hôte C$13–C$19.95 (US$8.95–US$13.75). AE, CB, ER, MC, V. Mon–Fri 7am–11pm; Sat–Sun 8am–11pm. FRENCH/INTERNATIONAL.

This "Crazy Pig" faces the ferry dock in the Lower Town and has some sidewalk tables and several indoor dining rooms (some no-smoking) with rough fieldstone walls and black-and-white floor tiles. It is heavily used and shows it, as a result of its highly successful efforts to be a one-stop eating center with long hours to cover every possibility from breakfast to late snack. Choose from mussels, chicken liver pâté, spring rolls, smoked salmon, half a dozen salads, onion soup, pastas, quiches, sandwiches, grilled meats, and more than 20 desserts. Good shoestring *frites* accompany most dishes. Check the daily specials board for items often seen on the standard card that are discounted for the day. Wine is sold by the glass, quarter liter, half liter, or bottle, at reasonable prices. There is an offering for kids 10 and under for only C$4.95 (US$3.40). Maybe they are the target audience for the mistakenly cutesy menu urging that you eat parts of the trademark anthropomorphic pig. Service is rushed but attentive. The same people also own the nearby, smaller **Le Lapin Sauté** (☎ **418/692-5325**) at 52 rue Petit-Champlain and another **Le Cochon Dingue** (☎ **418/523-2013**) at 47 René-Lévesque, near avenue Cartier.

○ **Le Marie-Clarisse.** 12 rue du Petit-Champlain (at rue Sous-le-Fort). ☎ **418/692-0857.** Main courses C$9.75–C$27.75 (US$6.70–US$19.15); table d'hôte lunch C$9.95–C$13.75 (US$6.85–US$9.50), dinner C$16.75–C$21.75 (US$11.55–US$15). AE, DC, ER, MC, V. Mon–Sat 11:30am–2:30pm and 6–10pm; terrace open daily Apr 15–Oct 31 11:30am–10pm. BISTRO FRENCH/SEAFOOD.

Nothing much beyond sustenance is expected of restaurants stationed at the intersections of galloping tourism. That's why this ambitious cafe is such a happy surprise. There it sits, at the bottom of Breakneck Stairs, the streets awash with day-packers and shutterbugs. And yet it serves what many consider to be the best seafood in town, chosen by a finicky owner who makes his selections personally at market. A more pleasant hour cannot be passed anywhere in Québec City than here, over a platter of shrimp or pâtés, out on the terrace on an August afternoon. In January, cocoon by the stone fireplace inside, indulging in bouillabaisse—a stew of mussels, scallops, tuna, talapia, and shrimp, a plate of rice and veggies on the side with a boat of saffron mayo to slather on croutons. Try a Québec wine to wash it down, maybe the l'Orpailleur from Dunham in Estrie. The two rooms are formed of stone and brick and rafters over 200 years in place.

Poisson d'Avril. 115 quai Saint-André (in Vieux-Port, near rue St-Thomas). ☎ **418/ 692-1010.** Pastas and pizzas C$7.95–C$12.95 (US$4.80–US$8.95), table d'hôte lunch C$8.95–C$21.95 (US$6.15–US$15.15), dinner C$23.75–C$43.95 (US$16.40–US$30.30). June–Sept daily noon–3pm and 5–10pm, dinner only Oct–May. SEAFOOD.

Whoever christened this place was having a little joke: Its name means both "April Fool" and "April Fish." Nevertheless, nautical trappings that include model ships, marine prints, and mounted sailfish make the real intent clear. The dinner menu, changed daily, is replete with seafood, including some combinations of costly crustaceans responsible for the stiffer prices noted above. Two of these are the crowded bouillabaisse, which comes with half a lobster, and the "Commodore Platter," laden with snow crabs, giant shrimp, glossy sea scallops, piled mussels, and another half-lobster. A sushi bar is also operational in the evenings. Lunch is a more modest event, with more land-based dishes, pastas, and individual pizzas. In good weather, there's a covered dining terrace.

INEXPENSIVE

Buffet de l'Antiquaire. 95 rue St-Paul (near rue du Sault-au-Matelot). ☎ **418/692-2661.** Most menu items under C$10 (US$6.90); table d'hôte C$5.95–C$11.95 (US$4.10–US$8.25). AE, MC, V. Daily 7am–11pm. QUÉBECOIS.

Another inhabitant of the rue St-Paul antique row, this is the humblest eating place of the lot, with exposed brick-and-stone walls lending what there is of decor. It is the place to go when every other Lower Town cafe is closed, such as for Sunday breakfast. And, since it caters to homefolks rather than tourists, reliable versions of native Québecois cooking are always available, including, but not limited to, pea soup, *poutine,* and *fèves au lard.* Essentially a slightly upgraded luncheonette, it serves sandwiches, salads, and pastries at all hours, backed by full bar service.

Exploring Québec City   14

Wandering at random through the streets of Vieux-Québec is a singular pleasure, comparable to exploring a provincial capital in Europe. On the way, you can happen upon an ancient convent, blocks of gabled houses with steeply pitched roofs, a battery of 18th-century cannons in a leafy park, and a bistro with a blazing fireplace on a wintry day. The old city, upper and lower, is so compact that it is hardly necessary to plan precise sightseeing itineraries. Start at the Terrasse Dufferin and go off on a whim, down Breakneck Stairs to the Quartier Petit-Champlain and Place Royale, or up to the Citadel and onto the Plains of Abraham, where Wolfe and Montcalm fought to the death in a 20-minute battle that changed the destiny of the continent.

Most of what there is to see is within the city walls, or in the Lower Town. It's fairly easy walking. While the Upper Town is hilly, with sloping streets, it's nothing like San Francisco, and only people with physical limitations are likely to experience difficulty. If rain or ice discourages exploration on foot, tour buses and horse-drawn calèches are options.

Suggested Itineraries

If You Have 1 Day

Take the walking tour of the Upper Town described in chapter 15, visiting the Citadel or the Musée du Québec or both. Walk down from the Terrasse Dufferin to explore the Lower Town. Use the walking tour in chapter 15 as a guide.

If You Have 2 Days

On the second day, take the funicular or descend the Breakneck Stairs from the Terrasse Dufferin to explore the Lower Town, using the other walk described in chapter 15. Allow at least an hour or two for the Musée de la Civilisation.

If You Have 3 Days

On the third day, make a short excursion north of the city to circle bucolic Île d'Orléans, isolated from the mainland until a bridge was built in 1935. The island is home to five tranquil hamlets with several middling to good restaurants. It's preferable to drive rather than take a bus tour. Afterward, visit Montmorency Falls and the shrine of Ste-Anne-de-Beaupré, or enjoy the outdoor recreational facilities of Mont-Ste-Anne.

If You Have 4 Days or More

Spend your last day driving along the northern bank of the St. Lawrence River and exploring the small villages along the way. Take a whale-watching cruise out of La Malbaie or the ferry from Baie-Ste-Paul, returning to Québec City via the southern bank.

1 The Top Attractions

BASSE-VILLE (LOWER TOWN)

✪ **Musée de la Civilisation.** 85 rue Dalhousie (at rue St-Antoine). ☎ **418/643-2158.** Admission C$7 (US$4.85) adults, C$6 (US$4.15) seniors, C$4 (US$2.75) students over 16, C$2 (US$1.40) children 12–16, free for children under 12. Tues free to all (except in summer). June 24–Labour Day daily 10am–7pm; Sept–June 23 Tues–Sun 10am–5pm.

Try to set aside at least 2 hours for a visit to this special museum, one of the most engrossing in all Canada. Designed by Boston-based, McGill University–trained Moshe Safdie and opened in 1988, the Museum of Civilization is an innovative presence in the historic Basse-Ville, near Place Royale. A dramatic atrium-lobby sets the tone with a massive sculpture rising like jagged icebergs from the watery floor, a representation of the mighty St. Lawrence at spring breakup. Through the glass wall in back can be seen the 1752 Maison Estèbe, now restored to contain the museum shop. It stands above vaulted cellars, which can be viewed.

In the galleries upstairs are five permanent exhibitions, supplemented by up to six temporary shows on a variety of themes. The mission of the museum has never been entirely clear, leading to some opaque metaphysical meanderings in its early years. Never mind. Through highly imaginative display techniques, hands-on devices, computers, holograms, videos, and even an ant farm, the curators have ensured that visitors will be so enthralled by the experience they won't pause to question its intent. Notice, as an example of the museum's thoroughness, how a squeaky floorboard has been installed at the entrance to a dollhouse-size display of old Québec houses. If time is short, definitely use it to take in "Memoires" ("Memories"), the permanent exhibit that is a sprawling examination of Québec history, moving from the province's roots as a fur-trading colony to the present. Furnishings from frontier homes, tools of the trappers' trade, old farm implements, religious garments from the 19th century, old campaign posters, and a re-created classroom from the past envelop visitors with a rich sense of Québec's daily life from generation to generation.

A new permanent exhibition is "Encounter with the First Nations," which examines the products and metaphysical visions of the aboriginal tribes that inhabit Québec. For a year from its opening in May 2000, an important exhibition is devoted to illuminations of the civilizations that germinated and grew in what is now Syria. Exhibit texts are in French and English. There's a cafe on the ground floor.

Place Royale.

This picturesque square is the literal and spiritual heart of Basse-Ville. Royal Square is a short walk from the bottom of Breakneck Stairs, via rue Sous-le-Fort. In the 17th and 18th centuries, it was the town marketplace and the center of business and industry. The Église Notre-Dame-des-Victoires—the oldest stone church in Québec, built in 1688 and restored in 1763 and 1969—dominates the enclosed square. The paintings, altar, and large model boat suspended from the ceiling were votive offerings

Impressions

The old world rises in the midst of the new in the manner of a change of scene on the
stage . . . on its rocky promontory sits the ancient town, belted with its hoary wall and
crowned with its granite citadel . . . .
                    —Henry James, "Québec" (1871), in *Portraits of Places* (1883)

brought by early settlers to ensure safe voyages. The church usually is open to visitors during the day, unless a wedding is underway.

All the buildings on the square have been restored. For years, there was only an empty lot behind the stone facade at the northeast corner, but now it is a whole building again. On the ground floor is the new **Centre d'Interprétation de Place-Royale** (27 rue Notre-Dame, ☎ 418/646-3167). Inside, a multimedia show and other exhibitions detail the nearly 4-century history and development of the plaza. It's open daily June 24 through October 10am to 5:30pm, Tuesday to Sunday November to June 23 from 10am to 5pm. Admission is C$3 (US$2.05) adults, C$2.50 (US$1.70) seniors, C$2 (US$1.40) ages 17 and over, C$1 (US70¢) ages 12 to 16, free under age 1.

Note the ladders on some of the other roofs, a common Québec device for removing snow and fighting fires. Folk dances, impromptu concerts, and other festive gatherings are often held near the bust of Louis XIV in the center of the square. Guided tours are available from the interpretation center.

HAUTE-VILLE (UPPER TOWN)

✪ **La Citadelle.** 1 Côte de la Citadelle (enter off rue St-Louis). ☎ **418/694-2815.** Admission C$5.50 (US$3.80) adults, C$4 (US$2.75) seniors, C$2.75 (US$1.90) children 7–17, free for persons with disabilities and children under 7. Guided 55-minute tours daily, Apr to mid-May 10am–4pm; mid-May–June 9am–5pm; July–Labour Day 9am–6pm; Sept 9am–4pm; Oct 10am–3pm. Nov–Mar, group reservations only. Changing of the guard (30 mins). June 24–Labour Day daily at 10am, beating the retreat (20 mins.) July and Aug Wed–Sat at 6pm. May be cancelled in the event of rain. Walk up the Côte de la Citadelle from the St-Louis Gate.

The duke of Wellington had this partially star-shaped fortress built at the east end of the city walls in anticipation of renewed American attacks after the War of 1812. Some remnants of earlier French military structures were incorporated into the Citadel, including a 1750 magazine. Dug into the Plains of Abraham, the fort has a low profile that keeps it all but invisible until walkers are actually upon it. Never having exchanged fire with an invader, it continues its vigil from the tip of Cap Diamant. British construction of the fortress, now a national historic site, was begun in 1820 and took 30 years to complete. As events unfolded, it proved to be an exercise in obsolescence. Since 1920, it has been home to Québec's Royal 22e Régiment, the only fully Francophone unit in Canada's armed forces. That makes it the largest fortified group of buildings still occupied by troops in North America. As part of a guided tour only, the public may visit the Citadel and its 25 buildings, including the regimental museum in the former powder house and prison, and watch the changing of the guard or beating the retreat.

NEAR THE GRANDE-ALLÉE

✪ **Musée du Québec.** 1 av. Wolfe-Montcalm (near av. George VI). ☎ **418/643-2150.** Admission (excluding special exhibitions) C$7 (US$4.85) adults, C$6 (US$4.15) seniors, C$2.75 (US$1.90) students, C$2 (US$1.40) ages 12 to 16, free for children under 12; Wed free for everyone. June 1–Labour Day daily 10am–6pm (Wed until 9pm); Sept 8–May 31 Tues–Sun 11am–5pm (Wed until 9pm). Bus no. 11.

Québec City Attractions

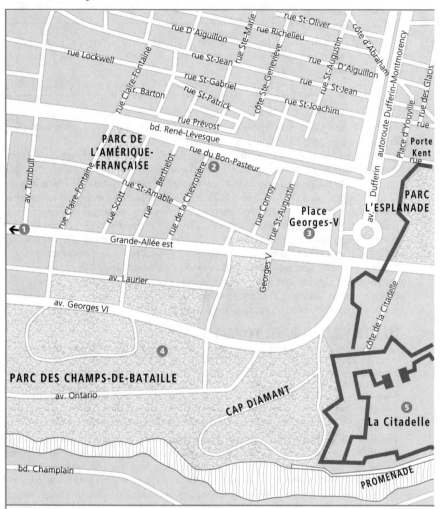

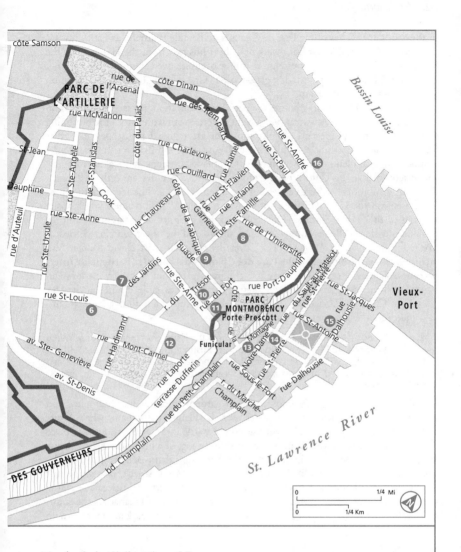

Musée de la Civilasation **15**
Musée du Fort **11**
Musée du Quebec **1**
Parc des Champs-de-Bataille **4**
Place Royal **14**

In the southern reaches of the Parc de Champs de Bataille (Battlefields Park), just off the Grande-Allée and a half-hour walk or a short bus ride from the Haute-Ville, the Museum of Québec is an art museum that now occupies two buildings, one a former prison, linked together by a soaring glass-roofed "Grand Hall" housing the reception area, a stylish cafe, and a shop.

The original 1933 building houses the permanent collection, the largest aggregation of Québec art in North America, filling eight galleries with works from the beginning of the colony to the present. On the top floor are regional landscapes and other Québec themes, with some examples of North American and British painters. On the ground floor is a splendid assortment of African masks, carvings, musical instruments, and ceremonial staffs. Unfortunately, most descriptive plaques are only in French. Traveling exhibitions and musical events are often arranged. The recent addition to the museum is the 1867 Baillairgé Prison, which in the 1970s became a youth hostel nicknamed the "Petite Bastille." One cell block has been left intact as an exhibit. In this building, four galleries house temporary shows, and the tower contains a provocative sculpture called *Le Plongeur* (The Diver) by the Irish artist David Moore. Also incorporated in the building is the **Parc des Champs-de-Bataille (Battlefields Interpretation Centre);** see below. There is a children's playroom stocked with toys and books. A surprisingly accomplished cafe-restaurant serves table d'hôte lunches for C$9.95 to C$12.95 (US$6.65 to US$8.65) Monday through Saturday, brunch Sunday, and dinner Wednesday and Saturday nights.

Parc des Champs-de-Bataille. Discovery Pavilion of the Plains of Abraham, 835 av. Wilfrid Laurier ☎ **418/648-4071.** Free admission to park. Bus tour in summer C$2 (US$1.40) for visitors ages 18–64, C$1.50 (US$1.05) ages 13–17 and 65 and over, free for ages 12 and under. Rates are expected to increase. May 18–Labour Day daily 10am–5:30pm; Sept 8–May 17 Tues–Sun 11am–5:30pm.

Covering 266 acres of grassy knolls, sunken gardens, monuments, fountains, and trees, Québec's Battlefields Park stretches over the Plains of Abraham, where Wolfe and Montcalm engaged in their swift but crucial battle in 1759. It is a favorite place for all Québecois when they want some sunshine, a jog, or a bike ride. Free concerts are given at the bandstand in the park, the Kiosque Edwin-Bélanger, during the summer. Be sure to see Jardin Jeanne d'Arc (Joan of Arc Garden), just off avenue Laurier between Loews le Concorde Hôtel and the Ministry of Justice. The statue was a gift from anonymous Americans, and it was here that "O Canada," the country's national anthem, was sung for the first time. Within the park are two martello

What a View!

For a panoramic look at the city, seek out the building that houses Québec's Education Ministry, the **Édifice Marie-Guyart** at 1037 rue de la Chevrotière (☎ **418/644-9841**). Enter the tower at the corner of de la Chevrotière and René-Lévesque, and look for signs and elevators directing to the "Observatoire de la Capitale," on the 31st floor. It's the highest overlook in the city, open June and September daily 10am to 7pm, July and August daily 10am to 10pm, October through May daily 10am to 5pm. Admission is C$4 (US$2.75) adults, C$3 (US$2.05) seniors and students, free for ages 12 and under.

Another place for an overall view is **L'Astral,** the revolving restaurant atop Loews le Concorde Hotel. It isn't necessary to plan a meal there, since the bar is as good a vantage point as any.

towers, cylindrical stone defensive structures built between 1808 and 1812, when Québec feared an invasion from the United States.

Today Battlefields Park contains almost 5,000 trees representing more than 80 species. Prominent among these are sugar maple, silver maple, Norway maple, American elm, and American ash. There are frequent special activities, including theatrical and musical events, presented in the park during the summer. Year-round, the park interpretation center provides an in-depth look at the historical significance of the Plains of Abraham to Québec over the years. The Maison de la Découverte—Discovery Pavilion—at 835 av. Wilfrid Laurier serves as a reception and information center and starting point for bus and walking tours of the park.

In summer, a shuttle bus tours the park in 45 minutes with narration in French and English.

2 More Attractions

HAUTE-VILLE (UPPER TOWN)

Basilique-Cathédrale Notre-Dame. 20 rue Buade (at Côte de la Fabrique). ☎ **418/694-0665.** Free admission to basilica and guided tours. "Act of Faith" sound-and-light show C$7.50 (US$5.15) adults, C$7 (US$4.85) seniors, C$5 (US$3.45) students 12 and over with ID, free for children 11 and under. Cathedral daily 7:30am–4:30pm. Guided tours May 1–Nov 1 Mon–Fri 9am–2:30pm, Sat 9am–4:30pm, Sun 12:30pm–4:30pm. "Act of Faith" multimedia sound-and-light show May 1–Thanksgiving (second Mon in Oct) Mon–Fri 3:30, 5, 6:30, and 8pm; Sat–Sun 6:30 and 8pm (and at 9pm July–Aug).

Notre-Dame Basilica, the oldest Christian parish north of Mexico, has weathered a tumultuous history of bombardment, reconstruction, and restoration. Parts of the existing basilica date from the original 1647 structure, including the bell tower and portions of the walls, but most of today's exterior is from the reconstruction completed in 1771. The interior, a re-creation undertaken after a fire in 1922, is flamboyantly neo-baroque, with shadows wavering by the fluttering light of votive candles. Paintings and ecclesiastical treasures still remain from the time of the French regime, including a chancel lamp given by Louis XIV. In summer, the basilica is the backdrop for a multimedia sound-and-light show called "Act of Faith," which dramatically recalls 5 centuries of Québec's history, and that of this building itself. The basilica is connected to the group of old buildings that makes up Québec Seminary. To enter that complex, go to 7 rue de l'Université (about a block away).

Chapelle/Musée des Ursulines. 12 rue Donnacona (des Jardins). ☎ **418/694-0694.** Museum C$4 (US$2.75) adults, C$3.50 (US$2.40) seniors, C$2.50 (US$1.70) students 17 and over, C$2 (US$1.40) ages 12–16, free under age 11; chapel free. Museum Oct–Apr Tues–Sun 1–4:30pm; May–Sept Tues–Sat 10am–noon and 1–5pm, Sun 1–5pm. Chapel May–Oct same days and hours as museum.

The chapel, open only from May through October, is notable for the sculptures that inform its pulpit and two retables. They were created by Pierre-Noël Levasseur between 1726 and 1736. Although the present building dates only from 1902, much of the interior decoration is nearly 2 centuries older. The tomb of the founder of this teaching order, Marie de l'Incarnation, is to the right of the entry. She arrived here in 1639 at the age of 40 and was declared blessed by Pope John Paul II in 1980. The museum displays accoutrements of the daily and spiritual life of the Ursulines. On the third floor are exhibits of vestments woven with gold thread by the Ursulines. A cape made of drapes from the bedroom of Anne of Austria and given to Marie de l'Incarnation when she left for New France in 1639 is on display. There are also musical instruments and Amerindian crafts, including the flèche, or arrow sash, still worn during Winter Carnival. Some of the docents are nuns of the still-active order. The Ursuline convent, built originally as a girls' school in 1642, is the oldest one in North America.

Le Château Frontenac. 1 rue des Carrières, Place d'Armes. ☎ **418/692-3861.**

Opened in 1893 to house railroad passengers and encourage tourism, the monster version of a Loire Valley palace is the city's emblem, its Eiffel Tower. The hotel can be seen from almost every quarter, commanding its majestic position atop Cap Diamant. Visitors curious about the interior may wish to take one of the 50-minute guided tours offered daily 10am to 6pm, May 1 to October 15; Saturday and Sunday 1 to 5pm, October 16 to April 30 (departures on the hour). They cost C$6.50 (US$4.50) for adults, C$5.50 (US$3.80) for seniors, and C$3.75 (US$2.60) for children 6 to 16. To make reservations (required) call ☎ **418/691-2166.**

Musée d'Art Inuit Brousseau. 39 rue St-Louis. ☎ **418/694-1828.** Admission C$6 (US$4.15) adults, C$4 (US$2.75) seniors and students 13 and older, free for children 12 and under with parent. Summer, daily 8:30am–10pm; winter, 9:30am–5:30pm.

A creation of the people who operate the three most reputable galleries of Inuit art in the city (see chapter 16), this private museum is an extension of the lifelong interest of collector Raymond Brousseau. The permanent collection is supplemented by occasional thematic exhibitions. In addition to carvings in stone and tusk, there are examples of fishing and hunting gear and clothing.

Musée de Cire de Québec. 22 rue Ste-Anne (near rue du Trésor). ☎ **418/692-2289.** Admission C$3 (US$2.05) adults, C$2 (US$1.40) seniors and students, children under 12 free with parent. June–Labour Day daily 9am–10pm; rest of year daily 10am–5pm.

Occupying a 17th-century house, this briefly diverting wax museum, renovated in 1994, skims across the pageant of Québec's history and heroes. Generals Wolfe and Montcalm are portrayed, of course, along with effigies of politicians, singers, Olympic gold medallists, and other newsmakers. Texts are in French and English.

Musée de l'Amérique Française. 2 Côte de la Fabrique. ☎ **418/692-2843.** Admission C$4 (US$2.75) adults, C$3 (US$2.05) seniors and students over 16, C$1 (US70¢) children 12–16, free for children under 12. June 24–Labour Day daily 10am–5:30pm; Sept 8–June 23 Tues–Sun 10am–5pm. Guided tours of exhibitions and some buildings daily in summer, Sat and Sun rest of the year. Reservations ☎ **418/692-2843.**

Housed at the site of the historic Québec Seminary, which dates from 1663, the Museum of French America focuses on the beginnings and the evolution of French

---

Checking Out the Pigeon Hotel

In Venice, they feed their pigeons in the middle of the Piazza San Marco, while New Yorkers denigrate pigeons as "rats with wings." The powers that be in Québec City chose a middle course in controlling their own feathered flocks of the family *Columbidae.* In their humane efforts to control but not exterminate the birds and their droppings, which used to despoil many a public building, authorities erected a low concrete feeding station and dwelling at the corner of the Grand-Allée and rue St-Augustin. It is supplied with fresh grain and water and is heated in winter to lure the cooing critters away from nearby windowsills and eaves. It costs the city C$28,000 a year to maintain the shelter—much less, the city says, than the expense of repeatedly scrubbing the buildings.

culture and civilization in North America. Its extensive collections include paintings by European and Canadian artists, engravings and parchments from the early French regime, old and rare books, coins, early scientific instruments, and even mounted animals and an Egyptian mummy. The mix makes for an engrossing visit.

The museum is located in three parts of the large seminary complex, the Guillaume-Couillard and Jérôme-Demers wings, and the beautiful François-Ranvoyze section, with its trompe l'oeil ornamentation, which served as a chapel for the seminary priests and students. Recent construction has added an annex to the chapel, an underground passage, and a new entrance lobby. Concerts are held in the chapel.

Musée du Fort. 10 rue Ste-Anne (near Place d'Armes). ☎ **418/692-1759.** Admission C$6.75 (US$4.65) adults, C$5.25 (US$3.60) seniors, C$4 (US$2.75) students. Apr–June and Sept 16–Oct daily 10am–5pm, July–Aug 15 daily 10am–6pm, Dec 26–Jan 4 daily noon–4pm, Feb–Mar Thurs–Sun 11am–4pm.

Bordering Place d'Armes, not far from the UNESCO World Heritage monument, this commercial enterprise presents a sound-and-light show using a 400-square-foot model of the city and surrounding region. The 30-minute production concerns itself primarily with the six sieges of Québec, including the famous battle on the Plains of Abraham. Commentary is in French or English. Military and history buffs are the ones most likely to enjoy a visit here.

BASSE-VILLE (LOWER TOWN)

The **Escalier Casse-Cou** connects the Terrasse Dufferin at the top of the cliff with rue Sous-le-Fort at the base. The name translates to "Breakneck Stairs," which is self-explanatory as soon as you see them. They lead from Haute-Ville to the Quartier Petit-Champlain in Basse-Ville. A stairway has existed here since the settlement began, but human beings weren't the only ones to ever use it. In 1698, the town council forbade citizens to take their animals up or down the stairway or face a fine.

Maison Chevalier. 60 rue du Marché-Champlain (near rue Notre-Dame). ☎ **418/643-2158.** Free admission. May–June 22 and Sept 9–Oct 31 Tues–Sun 10am–5:30pm, June 23–Sept 7 daily 10am–6pm, Nov–Apr Sat–Sun 10am–5pm.

Built in 1752 for ship owner Jean-Baptiste Chevalier, the existing structure incorporated two older buildings, dating from 1675 and 1695. It was run as an inn throughout the 19th century. The Québec government restored the house in 1960, and it became a museum 5 years later. Inside, with its exposed wood beams, wide-board floors, and stone fireplaces are changing exhibits on Québec history and civilization, especially in the 17th and 18th centuries. While exhibit texts are in French, guidebooks in English are available at the sometimes-unattended front desk. *Note:* It's also an air-conditioned refuge on hot days.

Centre d'Interprétation du Vieux-Port. 100 rue St-Andre (at rue Rioux). ☎ **418/648-3300.** Admission May–Labour Day C$3 (US$2.05) adults, C$2.25 (US$1.55) seniors and students 17 and over, C$2 (US$1.40) children ages 6–16. May–Labour Day daily 10am–5pm; schedule varies the rest of the year (call for hours).

A unit of Parks Canada, the Old Port Interpretation Center reveals the Port of Québec as it was during its maritime zenith in the 19th century. Four floors of exhibits illustrate that era. The modern port and city can be viewed from the top level, where reference maps identify landmarks. One of these is the Daishowa Pulp and Paper Mill (1927), which sells newsprint and cardboard to international markets, including *The New York Times*. Texts are in French and English, and most exhibits invite tactile interaction.

NEAR THE GRANDE-ALLÉE

Hôtel du Parlement. Grande-Allée Est (near av. Dufferin). ☎ **418/643-7239.** Free admission. Guided tours, early Sept–June Mon–Fri 9am–4:30pm; June 23–Labour Day Mon–Fri 9am–4:30pm, Sat and Sun 10am–4:30pm.

Since 1968, what the Québecois choose to call their "National Assembly" has occupied this imposing Second Empire château constructed in 1886. Twenty-two bronze statues of some of the most prominent figures in Québec's tumultuous history gaze out from the facade. The sumptuous chambers of the building may be toured with a guide for no charge, but tour times change without warning. Highlights are the Assembly Chamber, and the Room of the Old Legislative Council, where parliamentary committees meet. Throughout the building, representations of the fleur-de-lis and the initials VR (for Victoria Regina) remind visitors of Québec's dual heritage. The building can now be toured unaccompanied.

The Restaurant Le Parlementaire (☎ **418/643-6640**) is open to the public. Featuring Québec products and cuisine, it's open for breakfast and lunch Monday through Friday most of the year, and for dinner as well Tuesday through Friday in June and December.

3 Especially for Kids

Children who have responded to Arthurian tales of fortresses and castles often delight in simply walking around this storybook city. As soon as possible, head for **Terrasse Dufferin,** which has those coin-operated telescopes that kids like. In decent weather, there are always street entertainers, whether a Peruvian musical group or men who play saws or wine glasses. A few steps away at Place d'Armes are **horse-drawn carriages,** and not far in the same direction is the **Musée de Cire (Wax Museum),** on Place d'Armes at 22 rue Ste-Anne.

Also at Place d'Armes is the top of **Breakneck Stairs.** Halfway down, across the road, are giant **cannons** ranged along the battlements on rue des Ramparts. The gun carriages are impervious to the assaults of small humans, so kids can scramble over them at will. At the bottom of Breakneck, on the left, is a **glassblowing workshop,** the Verrerie la Mailloche. In the front room, craftsmen give intriguing and informative glassblowing demonstrations. The glass is melted at 2,545°F and is worked at 2,000°F. Also in the Lower Town, at 86 rue Dalhousie, the playful **Musée de la Civilisation** keeps kids occupied for hours in its exhibits, shop, and cafe. Military sites are usually a hit, at least with boys. The **Citadel** has tours of the grounds and buildings and colorful **changing of the guard** and **beating retreat** ceremonies.

The **ferry** to Lévis across the St. Lawrence is inexpensive, convenient from the Lower Town, pleasant, and exciting for kids. The crossing, over and back, takes less than an hour. To run off the kids' excess energy, head for the **Plains of Abraham,** which is also Battlefields Park. To get there, take rue St-Louis, just inside the St-Louis Gate, or, more vigorously, the walkway along Terrasse Dufferin and the Promenade des Gouverneurs, with a long set of stairs. Acres of grassy lawn give children room to roam and provide the perfect spot for a family picnic.

Even better is the **Village Vacances Valcartier** (☎ **418/844-2200**) at 1860 bd. Valcartier in St-Gabriel-de-Valcartier, about 20 minutes' drive north of downtown. In summer, it's a water park, with slides, a huge wave pool, and diving shows. In winter, those same facilities are put to use for snow rafting on inner tubes, ice slides, and skating.

4 Organized Tours

Québec City is small enough to get around quickly and easily with a good map and a guidebook, but a tour is helpful for getting background information on the history and culture of the city, grasping the lay of the land, and seeing those attractions that are a bit of a hike or require wheels to reach, such as the Musée du Québec. **Kiosque Frontenac,** facing the Château Frontenac near the upper terminal of the funicular, can make reservations for most city tours, whether by bus, boat, or foot, and is also a currency exchange. Here are some agencies and organizations that have proved reliable in the past.

BUS TOURS

Buses are obviously convenient if extensive walking is difficult for individual visitors, especially in the hilly and steeply sloping Upper Town. Among the established tour operators **Gray Line** (☎ **800/217-9722** or 418/523-9722) offers English-only tours, preferable because twice as much information is imparted in the same amount of time as on a bilingual tour. The company's city tours are in small coaches that carry 24 or fewer people, while day trips out of the city, to the casino at Charlevoix and along the south shore, for example, are in full-sized buses. Gray Line also offers a 9½-hour whale-watching excursion by bus to Tadoussac and boat into the St. Lawrence. **Maple Leaf Sightseeing Tours** (☎ **877/622-3677** or 418/622-3677) picks up passengers at their hotels in a 25-passenger "trolley bus" and embarks on a comprehensive tour of Québec, old and new, Upper and Lower Towns. They also provide walking tours. **Les Tours du Vieux-Québec** (☎ **418/664-0460**) and **Autocar Dupont** (☎ **418/649-9226**) also offer a variety of city and regional tours, with hotel pickup.

City tours tend to last 2 hours and cost about C$20 (US$13.80) for adults, half price for children ages 3 to 12. Many of the tour operators also offer half- or full-day (lunch included) tours to Ste-Anne-de-Beaupré, Montmorency Falls, and Île d'Orléans. These usually cost around C$32 (US$22) for adults.

For more information about bus tours of the city, read the "City Tours" section of the *Greater Québec Area Tourist Guide,* supplied by the tourist office.

HORSE-DRAWN CARRIAGE TOURS

A romantic but expensive way to tour the city is in a horse-drawn carriage, called a caléche. They can be hired at Place d'Armes or on rue d'Auteuil, just within the city walls near the St-Louis Gate. The 35-minute guided tour in either French or English costs C$50 (US$35) plus tax and tip. Carriages operate all summer, rain or shine. For information call ☎ **418/683-9222** or 418/624-3062.

WALKING TOURS

Points of departure for walking tours change, so to get up-to-date information on when one's leaving and from where, check at the kiosk on Terrasse Dufferin near the Château Frontenac and beside the funicular entrance. Many tours leave from there. **Visite Touristique de Québec** (☎ **418/653-9722**), which also offers bus and boat tours, has walking tours from June 15 to October 15 at a cost of C$12 (US$8) per person. The guide escorts his or her charges through the Latin Quarter down to Place Royale in the Lower Town. Tours last about 2½ hours and leave from the tourist office at 12 rue St-Anne and Place d'Armes daily at 9am and 3pm June to September, the rest of the year by appointment. As an added convenience, buses are made available to pick up guests staying in hotels outside the Old City and give them rides back at the end of the tour.

Park rangers lead free 1-hour walking tours of the Citadel most days. Walking tours of the villages of nearby Île d'Orléans (see chapter 18) are arranged by **Beau Temps, Mauvais Temps (Rain or Shine) Tours** (☎ 418/828-2275).

RIVER CRUISES

A variety of cruise possibilities are offered by **Croisières AML** (☎ 800/563-4643 or 418/692-1159). Weighing in at 900 tons, MV *Louis Jolliet* is a three-deck 1930s ferry-turned-excursion-vessel. Said to be the largest in Canada, it can carry 1,000 passengers, with bilingual guides, full dining facilities and bar. Cruises last 1½ hours in the late morning and afternoon, with three daily departures, and 2½ hours in the evening, when dancing and dining are part of the experience. Prices start at C$22 (US$15.15) for adults, C$20 (US$13.80) for seniors, C$10 (US$9.90) for children 6 to 12, but are higher for evening cruises and from late June to September.

Meals on the evening dinner and "Love-Boat" cruises are extra, from C$20 to C$29 (US$13.80 to US$20) per person over the cruise fare, tax and service not included. For more information or tickets, drop by the kiosk beside the funicular on Terrasse Dufferin. Board the boat at Quai Chouinard, 10 rue Dalhousie, near Place Royale in the Lower Town.

Croisières AML also has 3-hour **whale-watching cruises** from Baie Ste-Catherine, at the mouth of the Saguenay River. But to get to that jumping-off point from Québec City, **Croisères Dufour** (☎ 800/463-5250 or 418/692-0222) picks up passengers at Vieux-Port at 8am and sails downriver, with five intermediate ports, and spends a couple of hours in the St-Lawrence looking for whales before returning to Québec at about 6:30pm. Fares are C$129 (US$89) adults, C$119 (US$82) seniors, C$65 (US$45) children 6 to 12. Lunch is included.

5 Spectator Sports

The Nordiques, Québec's representatives in the misnamed National Hockey League, departed in 1995 for Denver, leaving the city without a team in any of the professional major leagues. For hard-core hockey fans, however, there is the new **Rafales,** the Québec team in the International Hockey League. They play at the **Colisée de Québec** (☎ 418/522-3000).

Harness races take place at the **Hippodrome de Québec,** 2205 av. du Colisée, Parc de l'Exposition (☎ 418/524-5283). General admission is only C$1 (US70¢), free with presentation of your parking ticket. Races take place year-round Thursday to Tuesday at 1:30 or 7:30pm (times vary from season to season; call ahead). Fans have been coming to the Hippodrome for afternoons or evenings of harness racing since 1916. Le Cavallo clubhouse is open year-round.

6 Outdoor Activities

The waters and hills around Québec City provide countless opportunities for outdoor recreation, from swimming, rafting, and fishing to skiing, snowmobiling, and sleigh rides. There are two centers in particular to keep in mind for most winter and summer activities, both within easy drives from the capital. Thirty minutes from Québec City, off Route 175 north, is the provincial **Parc de la Jacques-Cartier** (☎ 418/ 848-3169). Closer by 10 minutes or so is **Parc Mont-Ste-Anne** (☎ 418/ 827-1871), only 24 miles (40km) northeast of the city. Both are mentioned repeatedly in the listings below. From mid-November to late March, taxis participate in a **winter shuttle** program, picking up passengers at 16 hotels at 8:30am, taking them to Mont-Sainte-Anne and Station

Stoneham, and returning them to Québec City at about 4:30m. Round-trip fare is C$18 (US$12.40). Ask if your hotel participates when reserving a room.

BIKING

Given the hilly topography of the Upper Town, biking isn't a particularly attractive option. But rented bicycles are available at a shop on a hill that descends to the flatter Lower Town. Bikes are about C$8 (US$5.50) an hour or C$30 (US$21.40) a day. The shop, **Vélo Passe-Sport Plein Air,** at 22 Côte du Palais, also rents in-line skates; it's open daily from 9am to 11pm (☎ 418/692-3643). Bikes can also be rented at **Cyclo Services,** at 84 rue Dalhousie in the Old Port (☎ 418/692-4052). It's open all year. For more vigorous mountain biking, the **Mont-Ste-Anne recreational center** (☎ 418/827-4561) has 124 miles (200km) of trails.

CAMPING

There are almost 30 campgrounds in the greater Québec area, with as few as 20 individual campsites and as many as 368. All of them have showers and toilets available. One of the largest is in the **Parc de Mont-Ste-Anne,** and they accept credit cards. One of the smallest, but with a convenience store and snack bar, is **Camping La Loutre** (☎ 418/846-2201) on Lac Jacques-Cartier in the park of the same name. It's north of the city, off Route 175. The booklet available at the tourist offices provides details about all the sites.

CANOEING

The several lakes and rivers of **Parc de la Jacques-Cartier** are fairly easy to reach, yet in the midst of virtual wilderness. Canoes are available to rent in the park itself.

CROSS-COUNTRY SKIING

Greater Québec has 22 cross-country ski centers with 278 trails. In town, the **Parc des Champs-de-Bataille** (Battlefields Park) has 6 miles (11km) of groomed cross-country trails, a convenience for those who don't have cars or the time to get out of town. Those who do have transportation should consider **Station Mont-Ste-Anne,** which has more than 140 miles (225km) of cross-country trails at all levels of difficulty; equipment is available for rent.

DOGSLEDDING

Aventures Nord-Bec (☎ 418/889-8001) at 665 rue Ste-Aimé in Saint-Lambert-de-Lévis, about 20 minutes south of the city, offers dogsledding expeditions. While they aren't the equivalent of a 2-week mush across Alaska, there are choices of half-day to 5-day expeditions, and participants obtain a sense of what that experience is like. They get a four-dog sled meant for two and take turns standing on the runners and sitting on the sled. (Shout "Yo" to go left, "Gee" to go right.) Out on the trail it's a hushed world of snow and evergreens. With the half-day trip costing C$69 (US$48) per adult, C$59 (US$41) for students, and C$20 (US$14) for children 12 and under, it's expensive, especially for families, but the memory will stay with you. Another firm providing similar experiences is **Aventure Québec** (☎ 418/827-2227) at 3987 av. Royale in St-Ferréol-les-Neiges.

DOWNHILL SKIING

Foremost among the five area downhill centers is the one at **Parc Mont-Ste-Anne,** containing the largest total skiing surface in eastern Canada, with 51 trails (many of them lit for night skiing) and 11 lifts. From November 15 to March 30, a daily shuttle service called "HiverExpress" operates between downtown hotels and alpine and cross-country ski centers. The cars or minivans are equipped to carry ski gear and cost about C$18 (US$12.40) round-trip per person. For information call ☎ 418/525-5191.

FISHING

From May until early September, anglers can wet their lines in the river that flows through the **Parc de la Jacques-Cartier** and at the national wildlife reserve at **Cap-Tourmente** (☎ 418/827-3776), on the St. Lawrence, not far from Mont-Ste-Anne. Permits are available at many sporting-goods stores.

GOLF

Parc Mont-Ste-Anne has two 18-hole courses, plus practice ranges and putting greens. Reservations are required, and fees are C$60 to C$70 (US$41 to US$48), including golf cart. In all, there are two dozen courses in the area, most of them in the suburbs of Ste-Foy, Beauport, and Charlesbourg. All but three of the courses in the nearby suburbs are open to the public.

ICE SKATING

Outdoor rinks are located at Place d'Youville, Terrasse Dufferin, and Parc de l'Esplanade inside the walls, and at Parc de Champs-de-Bataille (Battlefields Park), where rock climbing, camping, canoeing, and mountain biking are also possible. Skates can be rented at **Vélo Passe-Sport Plein Air** (☎ 418/692-3643), at 22 Côte du Palais in the old town.

SWIMMING

Those who want to swim during their visit should plan to stay at one of the handful of hotels with pools. **Château Frontenac** has a new one, and the **Radisson Gouverneurs** has a heated outdoor pool that can be entered from inside. Other possibilities are the **Hilton** and **Loews le Concorde.**

Village Vacances Valcartier, a two-season recreational center in St-Gabriel-de-Valcartier (1860 bd. Valcartier, ☎ 418/844-2200), has an immense wave pool and water slides, as well as 38 trails for snow rafting. It's about 20 minutes west of the city.

TOBOGGANING

A toboggan run is created every winter down the stairs at the south end of the Terrasse Dufferin and all the way to the Château Frontenac. Tickets (only C$1 per person) are sold at a temporary booth near the end of the run.

Québec City Strolls

The many pleasures of walks in picturesque Québec are entirely comparable to those of similar *quartiers* in northern European cities. Stone houses huddle close together; carriage wheels creak behind muscular horses; sunlight filters through leafy canopies, falling on drinkers and diners in sidewalk cafes; and childish shrieks of laughter echo down cobblestoned streets. Not common to other cities, however, is the bewitching vista of river and mountains that the Dufferin promenade bestows. In winter, Old Québec takes on a Dickensian quality, with lamp glow flickering behind curtains of falling snow. A man who should know—Dickens himself—described the "splendid views which burst upon the eye at every turn."

Walking Tour 1: The Upper Town

Start: Terrasse Dufferin.
Finish: Hôtel du Parlement.
Time: 2 hours.
Best Times: Anytime.
Worst Times: None.

Start the walk at the:

1. **Terrasse Dufferin.** The boardwalk promenade, with its green-and-white-topped gazebos, looks much as it did 100 years ago, when ladies with parasols and gentlemen with top hats and canes strolled along it on sunny afternoons, with the Frontenac as a backdrop. The vistas of river, watercraft, and distant mountains are not soon forgotten.

   Stroll south on the terrasse, past the château. If possessed of sufficient energy and leg strength, some people may want to continue up the stairs at the end of the boardwalk to the:

2. **Promenade des Gouverneurs.** This skirts the sheer cliff wall and up past Québec's Citadel, a 20-minute uphill walk away. Return to the Terrasse Dufferin, walking as far as the battery of ancient (but not original) cannons set up as they were in the old days.

   Climb the adjacent stairs into the:

3. **Parc des Gouverneurs,** right behind—west of—the Château Frontenac. The park takes its name from the site of the mansion built to house the French governors of Québec.

Walking Tour: The Upper Town

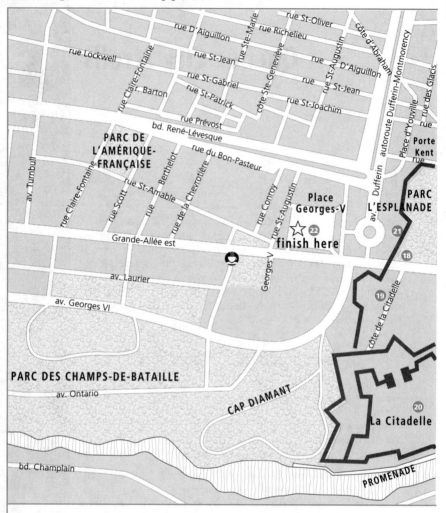

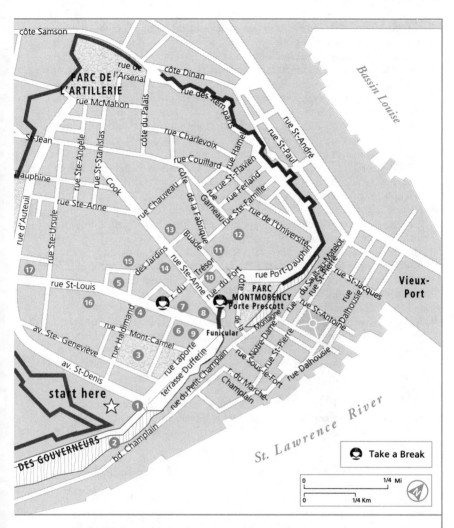

It burned in 1834, and the ruins lie buried under the great bulk of the château. The obelisk monument at the lower end of the sloping park is dedicated to both generals in the momentous battle of September 13, 1759, when Wolfe (British) and Montcalm (French) fought it out for what would be the ultimate destiny of Québec and, quite possibly, all of North America. Wolfe, wounded in the fighting, lived only long enough to hear of England's victory. In summer, the park, also known as the Jardin des Gouverneurs, is the scene of various shows and musical programs sponsored by the municipal government. Many small hotels and guest houses are gathered around or near the park. The building near the southwest corner of the park is the American consulate.

Walk up rue Mont-Carmel, which runs between the park and the Château Frontenac, and turn right onto rue Haldimand. At the next corner, with rue St-Louis, stands a white house with blue trim called:

4. **Maison Kent.** Built in 1648, it is possibly the oldest building in Québec. Although it is most famous for being the place in which France signed the capitulation to the British forces, its name comes from the duke of Kent. The duke, Queen Victoria's father, lived here for a few years at the end of the 18th century, just before he married Victoria's mother in an arranged liaison. His true love, it is said, had lived with him in Maison Kent. Today it houses the consulate general of France, as the tricolor over the door attests.

Diagonally across from Maison Kent, at rue St-Louis and rue des Jardins, is:

5. **Maison Jacquet.** This small white dwelling with crimson roof and trim dates from 1677, and now houses a popular restaurant. Among the oldest houses in the province, it has sheltered some prominent Québecois, including Philippe Aubert de Gaspé, the author of *Aux Anciens Canadiens,* who lived here from 1815 to 1824. The book recounts the history and folklore of Québec.

☕ **TAKE A BREAK**   Try Québecois home cooking right here at the restaurant named for de Gaspé's book, *Aux Anciens Canadiens,* 34 rue St-Louis. Consider caribou in blueberry wine sauce or duckling baked in maple syrup, but don't forget the sugar pie floating in cream.

Leaving the restaurant, walk downhill along attractive, if commercialized, rue St-Louis, to number 17, the:

6. **Maison Maillou.** The house's foundations date from 1736, though the house was enlarged in 1799 and restored in 1959. Note the metal shutters used to thwart weather and unfriendly fire. Now the building houses the Québec Board of Trade and Industry.

The large building across the street from Maison Maillou is the impressive:

7. **Québec Ministry of Finance.** It started out in 1799 as a courthouse, was renovated between 1927 and 1934, and was restored again from 1983 to 1987. Since then it has been Québec's Ministry of Justice, the name on the facade notwithstanding. The architect of the exterior was Eugène-Etienne Taché, Minister of Public Works at that time. The interior of the building is largely art deco. The street fronting the Ministry of Finance building is a popular parking spot for calèches, the horse-drawn carriages that tour the city.

Continue down rue St-Louis to arrive at:

8. **Place d'Armes.** This plaza was once the military parade ground outside the governors' mansion (which no longer exists). In the small park at the center of the square is the Monument to the Faith, which recalls the arrival of Recollets monks from France in 1615. The Recollets were granted a large plot of land by the king

of France in 1681 for their church and monastery. Facing the square is the monument to Samuel de Champlain, who founded Québec in 1608. Created by French artists Paul Chevre and Paul le Cardonel, the statue has stood here since 1898. The stone of the statue's pedestal is made from that used in the Arc de Triomphe and Sacré-Coeur Basilica in Paris.

Near the Champlain statue is the diamond-shaped monument designating Québec City a UNESCO World Heritage Site, the only city in North America with such a distinction. Placed here in 1985, it is made of bronze, granite, and glass. A tourist information center is also at Place d'Armes, at 12 rue Ste-Anne.

Again, up to the right, is the:

9. **Château Frontenac.** This famous edifice defines the Québec skyline. The first, lower part was built as a hotel in 1892 to 1893 by the Canadian Pacific Railway Company. The architect, Bruce Price of New York, raised his creation on the site of the governor's mansion and named it after Louis de Buade, Comte de Frontenac. Monsieur le Comte was the one who, in 1690, was faced with the threat of an English fleet under Sir William Phips during King William's War. Phips sent a messenger to demand Frontenac's surrender, but Frontenac replied, "Tell your lord that I will reply with the mouths of my cannons." Which he did. Phips sailed away.

💨 **TAKE A BREAK**   This is a great part of town to sit and watch the world go by. Grab a sidewalk table and enjoy something to drink or a bite to eat at **Au Relais de la Place d'Armes,** a red-roofed building with a mock-Tudor facade at 16 rue Ste-Anne.

Leaving there, turn right, then right again into the narrow pedestrian lane called:

10. **Rue du Trésor.** Artists hang their prints and paintings of Québec scenes on both sides of the walkway. In decent weather, it's busy with browsers and sellers. Most prices are within the means of the average visitor. Several of the artists, positioned near adjacent sidewalk cafes, draw portraits or caricatures.

Follow rue du Trésor from rue Ste-Anne down to rue Buade and turn left. On the right, at the corner of rue Ste-Famille is the:

11. **Basilique-Cathédrale Notre-Dame (1647).** The basilica has suffered a tumultuous history of bombardment and repeated reconstruction. Its interior is ornate, the air rich with the scent of burning candles. Many artworks remain from the time of the French regime. The chancel lamp was a gift from Louis XIV, and the crypt is the final resting place for most of the bishops of Québec.

Downhill from the basilica on rue Ste-Famille, just past Côte de la Fabrique, is the historic:

12. **Séminaire de Québec.** Founded in 1663 by Bishop Laval, the first bishop in North America, the seminary had grown into Laval University by 1852, and for many years it occupied the expanded seminary campus. By the middle of the 20th century, however, a new university was constructed west of the city in Sainte-Foy. The entire area is still known as the Latin Quarter—after the language that once dominated university life. An animated neighborhood at night, many visitors will want to return to rues Couillard, Garneau, and St-Jean after the sun goes down. During summer only, tours are given of the old seminary's grounds and some of its stone and wood buildings, revealing a lavish use of stone, tile, brass, and gilt-framed oil paintings. The Musée de l'Amérique Française, housed in the seminary, has an entrance at 9 rue de l'Université. It is open year-round.

From here, head back to the basilica. Take a right on rue de Buade and follow it to rue des Jardins to see the:

13. **Hôtel-de-Ville (City Hall)**, built in 1883. The building's lower level, with an entrance at 43 Côte de la Fabrique, houses the Centre d'Interpretation de la Vie Urbaine (Urban Life Interpretation Center), with a large-scale model of Québec City and its suburbs as they were in 1975. It helps strangers to get their bearings, and it might be surprising to see how spread out the city actually is. While the historic Upper and Lower Towns are compact, the city actually covers 35½ square miles (92km²).

The park next to the City Hall is often converted into an outdoor show area, and in summer, especially during the Festival d'Été (Summer Festival), concerts, dance recitals, and other programs are staged here.

Continue on rue des Jardins and cross rue Ste-Anne. On the left is the spire of the:

14. **Anglican Cathedral of the Holy Trinity.** This cathedral, said to be modeled after St-Martin-in-the-Fields in London, dates from 1804. The interior is simple but spacious, with pews of solid English oak from the Royal Windsor forest and a latticed ceiling in white with a gilded-chain motif. Visitors may happen upon an organ recital, or at least a rehearsal.

Farther along on rue des Jardins, at rue Donnacona, on the right side of the street, is the:

15. **Chapelle/Musée des Ursulines.** The museum displays the handiwork of the Ursuline nuns from the 17th, 18th, and 19th centuries. There are also Amerindian crafts and a cape made for Marie de l'Incarnation, the reverend mother and a founder of the convent, when she left for New France in 1639.

Be sure to peek into the restored chapel if it's open (May through October). It shelters the remains of General Montcalm, who was buried here after he fell in the battle that marked the end of French rule in Québec in 1759. Montcalm's tomb is actually under the chapel and not accessible to the public. His skull, on the other hand, is on display in the Ursuline Museum. The tomb of Marie de l'Incarnation, who died in 1672, is here. The altar, created by sculptor Pierre-Noël Levasseur between 1726 and 1736, is worth a look.

From the museum, turn right on rue Donnacona and walk past to the entrance of the Ursuline Convent, built originally in 1642. The present complex is actually a succession of different buildings added and repaired at various times up to 1836, for frequent fires took their toll. A statue of founder Marie de l'Incarnation is outside. The convent is a private girls' school today and is not open to the public.

Continue left up the hill along what is now rue du Parloir to rue St-Louis. Cross the street and turn right. At the next block, at rue du Corps-de-Garde, note the tree with a:

16. **Cannonball** lodged at the base of the trunk. It purportedly landed here during the War of 1759 and over the years became firmly embraced by the tree.

Continue along St-Louis another 1½ blocks to rue d'Auteuil. The house on the right corner is now the:

17. **Hôtel d'Esplanade.** Notice that many of the windows in the facade facing rue St-Louis are bricked up. This is because houses were once taxed by the number of windows they had, and the frugal homeowner found this way to get around the law, even though it cut down on his view.

Continue straight on rue St-Louis toward the Porte St-Louis, a gate in the walls. Next to it is the Esplanade powder magazine, part of the old fortifications.

Just before the gate is an:

18. Unnamed monument that commemorates the 1943 meeting in Québec of U.S. Pres. Franklin D. Roosevelt and British Prime Minister Winston Churchill, a soft-pedaled reminder to French Québecois that it was English-speaking nations that rid France of the Nazis.

Cross over St-Louis and turn along Côte de la Citadelle. On the right are headquarters and barracks of a militia district, arranged around an inner court. Near its entrance is a:

19. Stone memorial. It marks the resting place of 13 soldiers of General Montgomery's American army, felled in the unsuccessful assault on Québec in 1775. Obviously, the conflicts that swirled around Québec for centuries didn't end with the fateful 1759 battle between the British and the French.

Continue up the hill to:

20. La Citadelle. The impressive star-shaped fortress keeps watch from a commanding position on a grassy plateau 360 feet above the banks of the St. Lawrence. It took 30 years to complete, by which time it had become obsolete. Since 1920, the Citadel has been the home of the Royal 22e Régiment, which fought in both world wars and in Korea. With good timing, it is possible to both visit the regimental museum and watch the changing of the guard or the ceremony called "beating the retreat," weather permitting (see chapter 14).

Return to rue St-Louis and turn left through Porte St-Louis, which was built in 1873 on the site of a gate dating from 1692. Here the street broadens to become the Grande-Allée. To the right is a park that runs alongside the city walls. This is the:

21. Site of Winter Carnival. One of the most captivating events in the Canadian calendar, the 11-day celebration takes place every year from the first Thursday to the second Sunday of February. A palace of snow and ice, the centerpiece of the festivities, rises on this spot. Colorfully clad Québecois come to admire it, climb on it, and sample some maple-syrup candy at the nearby sugar shack set up for the occasion. On the other side of Grand-Allée, ice sculptures are created by 20 teams of artists from around the world participating in the International Snow Sculpture Competition. Each sculpture illustrates an aspect of the culture of the country it represents.

Fronting the park, on avenue Dufferin, stands Québec's stately:

22. Hôtel du Parlement. Constructed in 1884, it houses what Québecois are pleased to call their "National Assembly." Someday the label might actually be accurate. Along the facade are 22 bronze statues of prominent figures in Québec's tumultuous history. The fountain in front of the door, the work of Philippe Hébert (1890), was dedicated to Québec's original Native American, or Amerindian, inhabitants. There are tours of the sumptuous chambers inside, where symbols of the fleur-de-lis and the initials VR (for Victoria Regina) are reminders of Québec's dual heritage. If the crown on top is lit, Parliament is in session.

TAKE A BREAK   Continue along the Grande-Allée 2 more blocks to reach the strip of cafes that cause locals and visitors alike to compare it to another boulevard, the Champs-Elysées. It isn't even close, but there are plenty of places to stop for a drink or a snack, at outdoor tables in summer. One possibility is **Au Petit Coin Breton,** on the south side of the street, at 655 Grande-Allée Est.

From the Grande-Allée, walk or take the no. 11 bus back to the Old City. For a longer but scenic hike, continue along Grand-Allée to visit the Musée du Québec, on the left at 1 av. Wolfe-Montcalm; then go into Parc des Champs-de-Bataille (Battlefields Park), picking up the Promenade des Gouverneurs near La Citadelle and proceeding down onto the Terrasse Dufferin and the Château Frontenac.

Walking Tour 2: The Lower Town

Start: On the Terrasse Dufferin.
Finish: Place Royal.
Time: 1½ hours.
Best Times: Anytime.
Worst Times: None (except very late at night).

Descend to the Lower Town by the:

1a. Funicular. Its upper terminus is on Terrasse Dufferin near the Château Frontenac. As the car descends the steep slope, its glass front provides a broad view of the Basse-Ville. The mammoth grain elevators down by the harbor have a capacity of 8 million bushels. Beyond them is the river, with its constant boat traffic, and over to the left, the Laurentides Mountains rise in the distance.

Or, if you prefer a more active (and free) means of descent, use the stairs to the left of the funicular, the:

1b. Escalier Casse-Cou. "Breakneck Stairs" is the self-explanatory name given this stairway. Stairs have been in place here since the settlement began, but human beings weren't always the only ones to use them. In 1698, the town council forbade citizens from taking their animals up or down the stairway.

Both Breakneck Stairs and the funicular arrive at the intersection of rues Petit-Champlain and Sous-le-Fort. At the bottom of the stairs on the left is the:

2. Verrerie la Mailloche. In the front room, craftsmen give glass-blowing demonstrations—intriguing and informative, especially for children who haven't seen that ancient act of legerdemain. The glass is melted at 2,545°F and is worked at 2,000°F. There are displays of the results and a small shop in which to purchase them.

Exiting, walk straight ahead, passing:

3. Maison Louis Jolliet. Built in 1683, this home belonged to the Québec-born explorer who, with a priest, Jacques Marquette, was the first person of European parentage to explore the upper reaches of the Mississippi River. Jolliet died in 1700 at the age of 55. His former house is now the lower terminus for the funicular and full of tourist trinkets and gimcracks.

Then continue down:

4. Rue du Petit-Champlain. Allegedly the oldest street in North America, it is usually swarming with restaurant-goers, cafe sitters, strolling couples, and gaggles of schoolchildren ricocheting from one fetching store to another along the way. (See chapter 16 for shopping suggestions.)

At the end of the street, turn left and left again onto boulevard Champlain. A lighthouse from the Gaspé Peninsula used to stand across the street, but it has been returned to its original home, leaving the anchor and three cannons that surrounded it looking forlorn and misplaced. Following the curve of the street, pass more shops and cafes, soon arriving at the crimson-roofed:

Walking Tour: The Lower Town

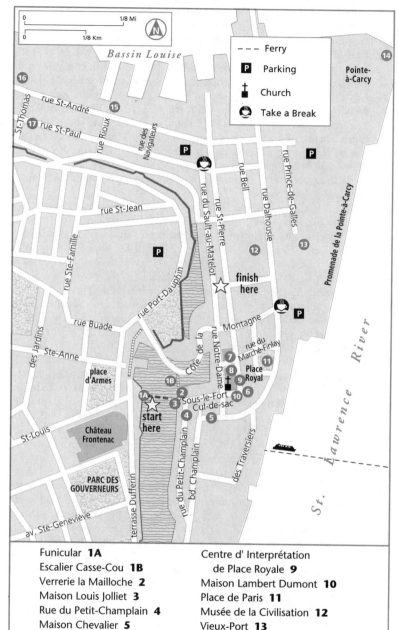

Funicular **1A**
Escalier Casse-Cou **1B**
Verrerie la Mailloche **2**
Maison Louis Jolliet **3**
Rue du Petit-Champlain **4**
Maison Chevalier **5**
Royal Battery **6**
Place Royale **7**
Église Notre-Dame-
   des-Victoires **8**
Centre d' Interprétation
   de Place Royale **9**
Maison Lambert Dumont **10**
Place de Paris **11**
Musée de la Civilisation **12**
Vieux-Port **13**
Pointe-à-Carcy **14**
Vieux-Port Interpretation Center **15**
Marché du Vieux-Port **16**
Rue St-Paul **17**

5. Maison Chevalier. Dating from 1752, this was once the home of merchant Jean-Baptiste Chevalier. Note the wealth of windows in the house, more than 30 in the facade alone. In 1763, the house was sold at auction to ship owner Jean-Louis Frémont, the grandfather of Virginia-born John Charles Frémont (1813–90). John Charles was an American explorer, soldier, and politician who mapped some 10 Western and Midwestern territories. This notable workaholic of French-Canadian heritage was also a governor of California and Arizona, a candidate for president of the United States in 1856, and a general during the Civil War.

The Chevalier House was sold in 1806 to an Englishman, who in turn rented it to a hotelier, who transformed it into an inn. From this time to the end of the century it was known, under various owners, as the London Coffee House. In 1960, the Québec government restored the house, and it became a museum about five years later, overseen by the Musée de la Civilisation, which mounts temporary exhibitions here.

Turn left after exiting the house, walking up the short block of rue Notre-Dame to rue Sous-le-Fort. Turn right, and walk 1 more block to the:

6. Royal Battery. Erected in 1691, the cannons were added in 1712 to defend the Lower Town. They got the chance in 1759, but the English victory silenced them; the exodus to the Upper Town left them to rust. Sunken foundations were all that remained of the Royal Battery by the turn of the century, and when the time came to restore this area, it had to be rebuilt from the ground up.

From the Royal Battery, return to rue Sous-le-Fort. Here you'll find a good photo opportunity: Up the street, the Château Frontenac is framed between ancient houses. Go up 1 block to rue Notre-Dame. Turn right. Half a block up the grade is the heart of Basse-Ville, the:

7. Place Royale. Occupying the center of the first permanent colony in New France, it served as the town marketplace. The square went into decline around 1860 and by 1950 had become a derelict, run-down part of town. Today it has been restored to very nearly recapture its historic appearance. The prominent bust is of Louis XIV, the Sun King, a gift from the city of Paris in 1928 that was installed here in 1931. The striking 17th- and 18th-century houses around the square once belonged to wealthy merchants. Note the ladders on some of the steep roofs, used to fight snow and fire.

Facing directly onto the square is the small:

8. Église Notre-Dame-des-Victoires. Named for French naval victories over the British in 1690 and 1711, the oldest stone church in Québec was built in 1688. It was restored in 1763 after its partial destruction by the British in the 1759 siege. The white and gold interior has a few murky paintings and a large model boat suspended from the ceiling, a votive offering brought by early settlers to ensure safe voyages. On the walls, 14 small prints depict the stages of the Passion. The church usually is open to visitors daily from 10am to 4:30pm, unless a wedding is under way.

Walk straight across the plaza, passing the new:

9. Centre d'Interprétation de Place-Royale. For decades, this was nothing but a propped-up facade with an empty lot behind it, but was now been rebuilt to serve as an interpretation center with shows and exhibitions relating the history of this historic district.

At the corner on the right is the:

10. Maison Lambert Dumont, now Geomania, a store selling rocks and crystals. Its former function as a wine store is still recalled by the large wine cask spigot jutting from the wall.

Walk past the last building on your left about 50 feet and turn around. The entire end of that building is a trompe-l'oeil mural of streets and houses and depictions of citizens from the earliest Colonial days to the present, an amusing splash of fool-the-eye trickery.

Return to Place Royale and turn left down rue du Marché-Finlay (in the far-right corner from the church), passing the:

11. **Place de Paris,** and its undistinguished white sculpture that resembles a Rubic's cube. Continue ahead to rue Dalhousie and turn left.

☕ **TAKE A BREAK** The immensely popular restaurant, **Le Café du Monde,** 57 rue Dalhousie, at rue de la Montagne, is known for its imported beers, large selection of wines by the glass, and substantial servings of mussels. It's fun, with ingratiating waiters who sometimes sit down at the upright piano to play.

Leaving the cafe, turn left on rue Dalhousie and walk to the:

12. **Musée de la Civilisation,** 85 rue Dalhousie, just past rue St-Antoine. The museum, which opened in 1988, may be situated among the cobblestoned streets in the historic Basse-Ville, but there is nothing traditional about it. Spacious and airy, with ingeniously arranged multidimensional exhibits, it is one of the most innovative museums in Canada, if not in all of North America. If there is no time now, put it at the top of the must-see list for a later visit.

Across the street from the museum is the:

13. **Vieux-Port (Old Port).** In the 17th century, this 72-acre riverfront area was the touchdown for European ships bringing supplies and settlers to the new colony. With the decline of shipping and the shifting of economic power to Montréal by the early 20th century, the port fell into precipitous decline. But since the mid-1980s, it has experienced a rebirth, becoming the summer destination for international cruise ships.

Walk across and turn left at water's edge on the port promenade, soon passing the Naturalium, a privately owned museum of natural sciences that celebrates the biodiversity of the planet, from beetles to bison. Then comes the Agora, an impressive 6,000-seat outdoor theater with a clamshell-shape stage, and behind it, the city's Customs House, built between 1830 and 1839.

Continue walking along the promenade, past the Agora, to the landscaped:

14. **Pointe-à-Carcy.** From here, look out across Louise Basin to the Bunge of Canada grain elevator, which stores the wheat, barley, corn, and soybean crop produced in western Canada before it is shipped to Europe. The bridge to rural Île d'Orléans can also be seen, the island that supplies Québec with much of its fresh fruits and vegetables.

Follow the walkway from Pointe-à-Carcy along the Louise Basin. If it is closed, as it may be because of continuing construction, follow the brick walkway toward the Customs House. On the right is the city's new Navy School.

Walk around the Customs House to rue St-André. From here, walk 4 less-than-scenic blocks to rue Rioux. On the right, at rue St-André and rue Rioux (or the left, if the pedestrian walkway along the Louise Basin was the route chosen), is a modern three-story building with blue trim, the:

15. **Vieux-Port Interpretation Center,** at 100 rue St-André. The museum illustrates what the Port of Québec was like in the 19th century, during its heyday. Be sure to see the view of the port and the city from the top level of the Interpretation

Center. Useful reference maps identify prominent landmarks. The Interpretation Center charges a small admission in summer, but at other times it's free. Texts are in English and French, and visitors are invited to touch most of the exhibits.

From the Vieux-Port Interpretation Center, go to rue St-André, turn right, and walk 1 block to the:

16. Marché du Vieux-Port, a market with jaunty green roofs and blue banners. From here look west to see the 1916 train station, designed by New York architect Bruce Price, who designed the Château Frontenac in 1893.

The colorful farmers' market has rows of booths heaped with fresh fruits and vegetables, relishes, jams, handicrafts, flowers, and honey from local hives. Above each booth hangs a sign with the name and telephone number of the seller. A lot of them bear the initials I.O., meaning they come from Île d'Orléans, 10 miles outside the city. The market is enclosed, and the central part of it, with meats and cheeses for sale, is heated. There's a little cafe inside at which to order a cup of coffee or a meal, and an ice-cream stand and a bakery.

Leaving the market, cross rue St-André at the light and walk ahead 1 short block to:

17. Rue St-Paul. Turn left onto this street, home to a burgeoning number of antique shops and cafes. Most of the shops stretch from rue Rioux, opposite the Interpretation Center, to rue du Sault-au-Matelot. There's a real sense of neighborhood here.

☕ **TAKE A BREAK** The busy **Café de Saint-Malo,** at 75 rue St-Paul and rue du Sault-au-Matelot, has low ceilings, rough stone walls, and storefront windows that draw patrons inside. Come for a full meal or, on sunny days, a drink or coffee and dessert at a sidewalk table. From here, meander back toward Place Royale and the funicular along rue du Sault-au-Matelot or rue St-Pierre.

If this walking tour has piqued your interest in Québec's history, the Librairie du Nouveau Monde (New World Bookstore), at 103 rue St-Pierre, can provide an English-language copy of the illustrated and highly readable *An Historical Guide to Québec,* by Yves Tessier.

Québec City Shopping 16

The compact size of the Old Town, with its upper and lower sections, makes it especially convenient for browsing and shopping. Though similar from one place to the next, the merchandise is generally of high quality. There are several art galleries deserving of attention, including an outdoor version in the Upper Town. Antiques shops are proliferating along rue St-Paul in the Lower Town.

1 The Shopping Scene

In the Upper Town, wander along **rue St-Jean,** both within and outside the city walls, and on **rue Garneau** and **Côte de la Fabrique,** which branch off the east end of St-Jean. There's a shopping concourse on the lower level of the Château Frontenac. For T-shirts, postcards, and other souvenirs, myriad shops line **rue St-Louis.**

Côte de la Montagne, which leads from the Upper Town to the Lower Town as an alternative to the funicular, has a gallery specializing in crafts and folk art. The Lower Town itself, particularly the **Quartier du Petit-Champlain,** just off place Royale and encompassing rue du Petit-Champlain, boulevard Champlain, and rue Sous-le-Fort (opposite the funicular entrance), offers many possibilities—clothing, souvenirs, gifts, household items, collectibles—and is avoiding (so far) the trashiness that often afflicts heavily touristed areas.

Outside the walls, just beyond the strip of cafes that line Grande-Allée, **avenue Cartier** has shops and eating places of some variety, from clothing and ceramics to housewares and gourmet foods. The 4 or 5 blocks attract crowds of generally youngish locals, and the commotion revs up on summer nights and weekends. The area remains outside the tourist orbit.

THE BEST BUYS

Indigenous crafts, handmade sweaters, and **Inuit art** are among the desirable items not seen everywhere else. An official igloo trademark identifies authentic Inuit (Eskimo) art, although the differences between the real thing and the manufactured variety become apparent with a little careful study. Inuit artwork, usually carvings in stone or bone, are "best buys" not because of low prices, but because of their high quality. Expect to pay hundreds of dollars for even a relatively small piece. Apart from a handful of boutiques, Québec City does not have the high-profile designer clothing often showcased in Montréal.

STORE HOURS

Stores tend to keep similar hours, opening and closing in tandem. With some exceptions, they are open Monday through Wednesday 9:30am to 5:30pm, Thursday and Friday 9:30am to 9pm, and Saturday 9:30am to 5pm. Many shops, including Simons department store, stay open on Sunday noon to 5pm. In the busy summer months, it's not unusual for stores to keep much longer hours—9am to 9pm daily, especially in the more obvious tourist districts and along rue St-Jean.

SHOPPING COMPLEXES

In the Upper Town, there's a small complex filled with upscale shops called **Les Promenades du Vieux Québec,** at 43 rue Buade. Here are a perfumery, a Christmas shop, Inuit carvings, cafes, a currency exchange, and clothing for men and women, including a Liz Claiborne factory outlet. Just outside the city walls at Porte Kent, **Place Québec** incorporates dozens of shops, a cinema, restaurants, a convention center, and the Hilton hotel, an easy-to-spot landmark. Place Québec is accessible from boulevard Réne-Lévesque and the Hilton. Shopping malls on a grander scale aren't found in or near the Old Town. For those, it is necessary to travel to the neighboring municipality of **Sainte-Foy.** The malls there differ little from their cousins throughout North America, in layout or available products. For sheer size, however, **Place Laurier,** at 2700 bd. Laurier, has 350 stores.

THE ANTIQUES DISTRICT

Dealers in antiques have gravitated to rue St-Paul in the Lower Town. To get there, follow rue St-Pierre from the Place Royale, and then head west on rue St-Paul. So far there are more than 20 shops, with more likely to open, filled with brass beds, knickknacks, Québec furniture, candlesticks, old clocks, Victoriana, art deco and art moderne objects, and even the increasingly sought-after kitsch and housewares of the early post–World War II period. To lend piquancy to the search for objects bearing histories, reflect that it was here that Benedict Arnold and his band of Americans were defeated in 1776 at the hands of Québec defenders (at the corner of rues St-Pierre and St-Jacques, to be exact).

2 Shopping from A to Z

ARTS & CRAFTS

Abaca. 38 rue Garneau (near rue St-Jean). ☎ **418/694-9761.**

The owners gather their own merchandise on buying trips abroad. Their inventory includes masks, jewelry, musical instruments, sculpture, and related pieces from Africa, India, Afghanistan, Japan, Korea, China, and a score of other countries. Some jewelry and handcrafts by Québec artists are also sold here. The store takes its name from a tree that grows in the Philippines. Another store around the corner also carries the owners' finds: **Origines,** at 54 Côte de la Fabrique, is filled with jewelry and sculpture.

Aux Multiples Collections. 69 rue Ste-Anne (opposite the Hôtel-de-Ville). ☎ **418/692-1230.**

Inuit, vernacular, and modern Canadian art are on offer in this gallery. The most appealing items, and those given prominence in display, are the Native Canadian carvings in stone, bone, and tusk. The shop ships purchases. Prices are high, but competitive for merchandise of similar quality. Open 7 days. Check out its siblings, the new private museum called **Galerie Brousseau et Brousseau** at 35 rue St-Louis (☎ **418/694-1828**) and the Aux Multiples branch at 43 rue de Buade (☎ **418/ 692-4298**).

Taxes & Refunds

Sales taxes on goods total 14.5%, including the 7% federal tax and 7.5% provincial tax. To get most of that tax money back, ask for and keep all receipts, and pick up a copy of the pamphlet titled *Tax Refund for Visitors to Canada,* available in many stores, in tourist offices, and at the front desks of most hotels. Inside the pamphlet is a refund application. After returning home, mail the *original* receipts (make copies for yourself) with the completed application to the address specified on the form. The refund takes a few weeks or months but eventually arrives in the currency of the applicant's home country, minus a small service charge.

Galerie d'Art du Petit-Champlain. 88 rue de Petit-Champlain (near bd. Champlain). ☎ **418/692-5647.**

This shop features the superbly detailed carvings of Roger Desjardins, who applies his skills to meticulous renderings of waterfowl. The inventory has been expanded to show lithographs, paintings, and some Inuit art. Open daily.

Galerie d'Art Trois Colombes. 46 rue St-Louis. ☎ **418/694-1114.**

Québecois and other Canadian artisans, including Inuits and Amerindians, produce the weavings, carvings, snowshoes, duck decoys, and soapstone sculptures (some by non-Inuits). Upstairs are handmade hats, coats, sweaters, high-top boots, moccasins, and rag dolls. They ship worldwide.

Outdoor Gallery. rue du Trésor (between rue Ste-Anne and rue Buade). No phone.

Sooner or later, everyone passes this alley near the Place d'Armes. Artists gather along here much of the year to exhibit and sell their work, much like the artists on St-Amable Lane in Vieux-Montréal. Although none of them are likely ever to find their etchings and serigraphs collected by major art museums, neither do they produce the equivalent of tiger and Elvis paintings on black velvet. Most of the prints on view are of Québec scenes, and one or two might make attractive souvenirs. The artists seem to enjoy chatting with interested passersby.

Version Soleil. 109 rue St-Paul (near Vieux-Port). ☎ **418/692-0032.**

In the midst of all the antique stores of rue St-Paul, this sunnily colorful shop traffics in pottery and crafts from many lands, with an evident emphasis on Latin America.

BOOKS, MAGAZINES & RECORDS

Archambault. 1095 rue St-Jean. ☎ **418/694-2088.**

The shop has two large floors of recorded music, mostly CDs with some cassettes, and the helpful staff goes to some lengths to find what you want.

Librairie du Nouveau Monde. 103 rue St-Pierre (behind the Musée de la Civilisation). ☎ **418/694-9475.**

In the Lower Town, this store has a wide variety of books, mostly in French, including the fascinating *Historical Guide to Québec,* by Yves Tessier, a good read (available in English) about the city's past, filled with illustrations, photographs, and a foldout map.

Librairie Ulysses. 4 bd. René-Lévesque Est (near av. Cartier). ☎ **418/529-5349.**

Specializing in travel, with guidebooks, travel accessories, and related items, it has smaller branches in the same building as the tourist information office at 12 rue Ste-Anne, opposite Place d'Armes, and at 2600 bd. Laurier in Ste-Foy (☎ **418/654-9779**).

Maison de la Presse Internationale. 1050 rue St-Jean (at the corner of rue Ste-Angèle). ☎ **418/694-1511.**

As the name says, this large store in the midst of the St-Jean shopping and nightlife bustle stocks magazines, newspapers, and paperbacks from around the world, in many languages. It stays open daily 7am to 11pm or midnight, and it carries *The New York Times, The Wall Street Journal,* the *International Herald Tribune,* and many U.S. periodicals. There's another branch in the Place Québec, the mall between the Hilton and Radisson hotels.

CLOTHING

America. 1147 rue St-Jean (near rue St-Stanislas). ☎ **418/692-5254.**

A link in the popular chain, it offers dependably good quality and style in casual and dress clothes for men, with intriguing half-twists away from Gap and Banana Republic norms.

Excalibor. 1055 rue St-Jean. ☎ **418/692-5959.**

If you arrive in town during Québec's August Medieval Festival, here's the place to purchase doublets and shirts with big floppy sleeves. Fabrics are muslin and velvet and mock brocade. No armor, though.

Ibiza. 57 Petit-Champlain (in midblock). ☎ **418/692-2103.**

Replacing a shop that sold toys and kids' things, this has grown up and filled its space with leather—coats, vests, and handbags. And, oddly enough, knives.

La Maison Darlington. 7 rue de Buade (near the Hôtel-de-Ville). ☎ **418/692-2268.**

The popular emporium in this ancient house comes on strong with both tony and traditional clothing for men and women produced by such makers as Burberry's, Ballantyne, and Geiger Autrician. Better still are the hand-smocked dresses produced by Québecois artisans for babies and little girls.

La Maison du Hamac. 91 rue Ste-Anne. ☎ **418/692-1109.**

Although this shop does indeed carry a wide selection of hammocks, as its name asserts, it also has clothing from Latin America—colorful hats, shirts, belts, vests, bags, and jewelry from Mexico, Nepal, Guatemala, Indonesia, and Brazil. Kites, too.

Zazou. 31 Petit Champlain (near the funicular). ☎ **418/694-9990.**

This little shop focuses primarily on the casual and dressy fashions of Québecois designers.

A DEPARTMENT STORE

La Maison Simons. 20 Côte de la Fabrique (near the Hôtel-de-Ville). ☎ **418/692-3630.**

The only department store in the Old City opened here in 1840. Small by modern standards, Simons has two floors for men's and women's clothing, emphasizing sportswear, and household linens. Most of it is pretty basic, but Tommy Hilfiger products are much in evidence. Their stores at Place Ste-Foy (2450 bd. Laurier) and Les Galeries de la Capitale (5401 bd. des Galeries) have 60,000 square feet of floor space each and carry far larger selections of fashions by such designers as Donna Karan and Hugo Boss. Another branch opened in downtown Montréal in 1999.

FOOD

La Petite Cabane à Sucre. 94 rue Petit Champlain (south end). ☎ **418/692-5875.**

Billed as a "little sugar shack," it sells ice cream, honey, maple syrup and candy, and related products, many in packaging suitable for gifts, including the tin log cabins that pour from their chimneys.

Les Halles du Petit-Cartier. 1191 av. Cartier (near rue Fraser). No phone.

This is, in effect, a mall for foodies, containing a collection of merchants in open-fronted shops purveying fresh meats and fish, cheeses, sushi, pâtés and terrines, glistening produce, deli products, pastries, confections, and fancy picnic items. There are a few fast-food counters and delis that make up sandwiches to order. Or how about a cold cooked lobster for your picnic? The mall is open 7 days a week.

GIFTS

Les Artisans Bas-Canada. 30 Côte de la Fabrique. ☎ **418/692-2109.**

Crafts and kicky hand-knits predominate, all a little on the expensive side. Duck decoys and burly sweaters for adults and kids are among the most engaging items, supplemented by lots of hats, gloves, mittens, headbands, moccasins, lumberjack coats, soapstone carvings, and Canada-themed books. The inventory has been expanded under the new third-generation owners.

Claude Berry, Inc. 6 Côte de la Fabrique. ☎ **418/692-2628.**

Find here hand-painted porcelains from Limoges, jacquard replicas of medieval tapestries, Inuit carvings, religious articles—a grab bag that might produce that elusive gift.

WINES

Société des Alcools de Québec. 1059 av. Cartier (near rue Fraser). ☎ **418/643-4334.**

A virtual supermarket of wines and spirits, with thousands of bottles in stock. They recently expanded the selling area to incorporate a section of more than 120 kinds of imported beers. There's another SAQ outlet at 888 rue St-Jean (☎ **418/643-4337**).

17

Québec City After Dark

Although Québec City can't pretend to match the volume of night-time diversions of exuberant Montréal, there is more than enough to do to occupy your evenings during an average stay. Apart from theatrical productions, almost always in French, a knowledge of the language is rarely necessary.

Drop in at the tourism information office for a list of events, such as the annual **Festival d'Été** (Summer Festival) in July, when free concerts and shows are staged all over town in the evenings and the upper portion of rue St-Jean is closed to cars to become a pedestrian promenade. The same holds true for the **Carnaval d'Hiver** (Winter Carnival) in February, when the city salutes the season with a grand ice palace, ice sculptures, and parades.

Concerts and theatrical performances usually begin at 8pm. Most bars and clubs stay open until 2 or 3am. A clear advantage of a night out in Québec is that cover charges and drink minimums are rare in the bars and clubs that provide live entertainment. Highballs aren't unusually expensive, but neither are they generously poured, which is the reason most people stick to beer, usually Canadian. Some popular brands brewed in Québec are Belle-Gueule, Saint-Ambroise, Boréale, and Maudite (with a winged Satan on the label).

1 The Performing Arts

CLASSICAL MUSIC, OPERA & DANCE

Many of the city's churches host **sacred and secular music concerts,** as well as special **Christmas festivities.** Among them are the Anglican Cathedral of the Holy Trinity, Église St-Jean-Baptiste, historic Chapelle Bon-Pasteur, and, on Île d'Orléans, the Église Ste-Pétronille. Outdoor performances in summer are staged beside City Hall in the Jardins de l'Hôtel-de-Ville, in the Pigeonnier at Parliament Hill, on the Grande-Allée, and at Place d'Youville.

L'Orchestre Symphonique de Québec, Canada's oldest, performs at the Grand Théâtre de Québec from September to May. The **Québec Opéra** mounts performances there in the spring and fall, as does, more occasionally, the **Danse-Partout** ballet company.

Check the "Night Life" section of the *Greater Québec Area Tourist Guide* for suggestions. A weekly information leaflet called *L'Info-Spectacles,* listing headline attractions and the venues in which they are appearing, is found at concierge desks and in many bars and restaurants, as is the tabloid-sized giveaway *Voir,* which provides greater detail. Both are in French, but salient points aren't difficult to decipher.

CONCERT HALLS & PERFORMANCE VENUES

Agora. 120 rue Dalhousie (Vieux-Port). ☎ **418/692-4672.**

This 5,500-seat amphitheater at the Vieux-Port is the scene of rock and occasional classical concerts and a variety of other shows in the summer. Iron Maiden, Jethro Tull, Joe Cocker, and Johnny Winter have all appeared. The city makes a dramatic backdrop. The box office, at 84 rue Dalhousie, is open daily 10am to 6pm.

Colisée Pepsi. 250 bd. Wilfrid-Hamel (Expocité). ☎ **418/691-7211.**

Rock concerts by name acts on the order of perennials Phil Collins and Led Zeppelin and new bands like New Radicals and Fun Loving Criminals are often held in this arena, located in a park on the north side of the St-Charles River. The box office is open in summer Monday through Friday 9am to 4pm, in winter 10am to 5pm.

Grand Théâtre de Québec. 269 bd. René-Lévesque Est (near av. Turnbull). ☎ **418/ 643-8131.**

Classical music concerts, opera, dance, and theatrical productions are performed in two halls, one of them containing the largest stage in Canada. Visiting conductors, orchestras, and dance companies often perform here when resident organizations are away. The Trident Theatre troupe performs in French in the Salle Octave-Crémazie. Québec's Conservatory of Music lies underneath the theater. The box office is open Monday through Friday 10am to 6pm.

Kiosque Edwin-Bélanger. 390 av. de Bernières (near the Musée de Québec). ☎ **418/ 648-4050.**

The bandstand at the edge of the Battlefields Park is the site of a 10-week summer music season, from mid-June to late August. Performances are Wednesday through Sunday and range from operas, chorales, and classical recitals to jazz, pop, and blues. All are free.

Le Capitole. 972 rue St-Jean (near Porte St-Jean). ☎ **800/261-9903** for tickets, or 418/694-9903 for information.

Mixtures of live shows and other attractions are offered on an irregular schedule in the historic 1,312-seat theater. Dramatic productions and comedic performances are in French, but they also host rock groups and occasional classical recitals.

2 The Club & Music Scene

ROCK, FOLK, BLUES & JAZZ

Most bars and clubs stay open until 2 or 3am, closing earlier if business doesn't warrant the extra hour or two. Cover charges and drink minimums are all but unknown in the bars and clubs that provide live entertainment. There are three principal streets to choose among for nightlife: the Grande-Allée, rue St-Jean, and the emerging avenue Cartier.

Only in Québec City

The **Basilique Notre-Dame** schedules son et lumière (sound-and-light) shows inside the city's loveliest church four times daily Tuesday to Friday and twice on Saturday. Tickets cost C$7.50 (US$5.15).

An after-dinner stroll and a lounge on a bench on **Terrasse Dufferin,** the boardwalk above the Lower Town, may well be the most memorable night on the town. Ferries glide across the river burnished by moonglow, and the stars haven't seemed that close since childhood.

Café des Arts. 1000 rue St-Jean (at the corner rue d'Auteuil). ☎ **418/694-1499.** Cover charge usually C$5–C$10 (US$3.45–US$6.90), depending on the attraction.

New in 1997, this unusual enterprise above the Eldorado boutique puts on theatrical pieces, mime, poetry readings, dance, *chanson,* and jazz. They serve sandwiches and cheese plates and are licensed to sell wine and beer. Open Wednesday through Saturday from 3pm.

Chez Son Père. 24 rue St-Stanislas (near rue St-Jean). ☎ **418/692-5308.** No cover.

A musical institution in Québec since 1960, this is the place where French-Canadian folksingers often get their start. The stage is on the second floor, with the usual brick walls and sparse decor. A young, friendly crowd can be found here. The club is a few steps uphill from bustling rue St-Jean.

D'Orsay. 65 rue de Buade (opposite Hôtel-de-Ville). ☎ **418/694-1582.** No cover.

Visitors whose complexions have cleared up and who are well into their mortgages will want to keep this chummy pub-bistro in mind. Most of the clientele is on the far side of 35, and they start up conversations easily—two active bars help. There's a small dance floor with a DJ, and in summer afternoons and evenings, entertainers sometime perch on a stool on the terrace out back. There is a full menu of conventional international dishes, from onion soup and fajitas to burgers and mussels.

Fourmí Atomik. 33 rue d'Auteil (south of Porte Kent). ☎ **418/694-1473.** No cover.

Up the hill from rue St-Jean is this *bar coopérative* populated exclusively by people born after 1975. The large terrace is filled every less-than-frigid afternoon and evening, most of them concerned primarily with drinking, talking, smoking, and connecting. Food, while available, is way down the list.

Kashmir. 1018 rue St-Jean (near rue St-Stanislas). ☎ **418/694-1648.** Cover depends upon performer, usually C$10 (US$6.90) or less.

Upstairs, over the Pizzeria d'Youville, the show bar that replaced Café Blues puts on an eclectic variety of musical and artistic presentations, including rock, blues, and art exhibitions, with the added attraction of dancing 3 or 4 nights a week. Scheduling is erratic. Pass the time before the evening's performances at the pool tables or poker machines.

✪ L'Emprise. 57 rue Ste-Anne (at des Jardins). ☎ **418/692-2480.** No cover.

Live jazz, usually of the mainstream or fusion variety, is a long-standing tradition in this agreeable room. The bar, off the lobby of the once-elegant Hôtel Clarendon, has large windows and art deco touches. Seating is at tables and around the bar. It has a mellow atmosphere, with serious jazz fans who come to listen. Music is nightly, from about 10pm.

Le Petit Paris. 48 Côte de la Fabrique. ☎ **418/694-0383.** Admission C$2 (US$1.40).

Singer-guitarists take the stage in this rough-hewn bar near the Hôtel de Ville, usually leaning to folk-rock, in French. There are pool tables upstairs.

Les Yeux Bleus. 1117½ rue St-Jean. ☎ **418/694-9118.** No cover.

At the end of an alleyway off rue St-Jean, it looks tumbledown from the outside but isn't intimidating inside. The music is mostly Québecois *chanson,* partly international pop.

Palais Montcalm. 995 place d'Youville (near Porte Saint-Jean). ☎ **418/670-9011** for tickets.

The main performance space is the 1,100-seat Raoul-Jobin theater, with a mix of dance programs, classical music concerts, and plays. More intimate recitals and jazz groups are found in the much smaller Café-Spectacle.

Théâtre du Petit-Champlain. 68 rue du Petit-Champlain (near the funicular). ☎ **418/692-2631.**

Québecois and French singers alternate with jazz groups in this roomy cafe-theater in the Lower Town. Have a drink on the patio before the show. The box office is open Monday through Friday 1 to 5pm, to 7pm the night of a show. Ticket prices range from C$15 to C$55 (US$10.35 to US$38) depending on the artist. Performances are usually Tuesday through Saturday.

DANCE CLUBS

Chez Dagobert. 600 Grande-Allée (near av. Turnbull). ☎ **418/522-0393.** No cover.

Long the top disco in Québec City, this three-story club has an arena arrangement on the ground floor for live bands, with raised seating around the sides. Upper floors have a large dance floor, more bars, TV screens to keep track of sports events, and video games. The sound system, whether emitting live (mostly homage or alternative bands) or recorded music, is just a decibel short of bedlam; more than a few habitués are seen donning earplugs. Things don't start jamming until well after 11pm. The crowd divides into students and their more fashionably attired older brothers and sisters. A whole lot of eyeballing and approaching goes on.

Le Bistro Plus. 1063 rue St-Jean (near rue St-Stanislas). ☎ **418/694-9252.** No cover.

At this bistro by day, things change at night on the dance floor in back, which fills with writhing young bodies—very young, in many cases. During the week, the music is recorded, with live groups on some weekends. It gets frat-house raucous and messy, especially after the 4-to-7pm happy hour, but congenial, too, with darts, a pool table, and TVs tuned to sports to keep people entertained.

Maurice. 575 Grande Allée Est. ☎ **418/640-0711.** No cover.

Bidding to challenge Chez Dagobert at the top rung of the nightlife ladder, this triple-tiered enterprise occupies a converted mansion at the thumping heart of the Grand-Allée scene. The dance room rotates live Latin and blues bands, filling the gaps with house music. Theme nights are frequent, and the balconies, cigar lounge, and Le Charlotte bar overflow with up to 1,000 postboomers. Happy hour has two-for-one drinks.

Vogue/Sherlock Holmes. 1170 d'Artgny (off Grande-Allée). ☎ **418/529-9973.** No cover.

This pair of double-decked bars is less frenetic than Dagobert, with a small disco upstairs in Vogue, and the pubby eatery Sherlock below, with a pool table and dart board. Grad students and Gen-Xers spending the disposable income of first jobs make up most of the clientele.

3 The Bar & Cafe Scene

The strip of the **Grande-Allée** between place Montcalm and place George V, near the St-Louis Gate, has been compared to the Boulevard St-Germain in Paris. That's a real stretch, but it is lined on both sides with cafes, giving it a passing resemblance. Many have terraces abutting the sidewalks, so cafe-hopping is an active pursuit. Eating is definitely not the main event. Meeting and greeting and partying are aided in some cases by glasses of beer so tall they require stands to support them. This leads, not unexpectedly, to a beery collegiate atmosphere that can get sloppy and dumb as the evening wears on. But early on, it's fun to sit and sip and watch. The following bars are removed from the Grande-Allée melée.

Aviatic Club. 450 de la Gare-du-Palais (near rue St-Paul, Lower Town). ☎ **418/522-3555.**

A favorite with the after-work crowd since 1945, it's located in the front of the city's magnificently restored train station. The theme is aviation (odd, given the venue), signaled by two miniature planes hanging from the ceiling. Food is served, ranging from Thai to Cajun to Tex-Mex in loose inspiration, along with local and imported beers.

L'Astral. 1225 place Montcalm (at the Grande-Allée). ☎ **418/647-2222.**

Spinning slowly above a city that twinkles below like tangled necklaces, this restaurant and bar in the Hôtel Loews le Concorde unveils a breathtaking 360° panorama. Many people come for dinner. Make it for drinks and the view.

Le Pape-Georges. 8 rue Cul-de-Sac (near bd. Champlain, Lower Town). ☎ **418/692-1320.**

This cozy stone-and-beamed wine bar features jazz and blues usually from Thursday through Sunday at 10pm. Light fare—cheese plates, assorted cold meats, and smoked salmon—is served during the day. Although it's in the middle of a tourist district, most of the patrons appear to be locals.

Saint Alexandre Pub. 1087 rue St-Jean (near St-Stanislas). ☎ **418/694-0015.**

Roomy and sophisticated, this is one of the best-looking bars in town. It's done in British pub mode, free of clichés, with polished mahogany, exposed brick, and a working fireplace that's a particular comfort 8 months of the year. It claims to serve 40 single-malt scotches and more than 200 beers, 24 of them on tap, along with hearty victuals that complement the brews. Sometimes it presents jazz duos and trios, usually on Monday nights from 7:30 to 11:30pm. Large front windows provide easy observation of the busy St-Jean street life; open daily 5pm to 2am.

GAY BARS

The gay scene in Québec City is a small one, centered in the Upper Town just outside the city walls, on **rue St-Jean** between **avenue Dufferin** and **rue St-Augustin,** and also along rue St-Augustin and nearby **rue d'Aiguillon,** which runs parallel to rue St-Jean. One popular bar and disco, frequented by both men and women (and by men who appear to be women), is **Le Ballon Rouge,** at 811 rue St-Jean (☎ **418/647-9227**).

Side Trips from Québec City   18

The first four excursions described below can all be combined and completed in a day. Admittedly, it will be a breakfast-to-dark undertaking, especially if much time is taken to explore each destination, but the farthest of the four destinations is only 25 miles (40km) from Québec City.

The famous shrine of Ste-Anne-de-Beaupré and the Mont Ste-Anne ski area are only about half an hour from the city by car, while bucolic Île d'Orléans, with its maple groves, orchards, farms, and 18th- and 19th-century houses, is a mere 15 minutes away. With 2 or more days available, you can continue along the northern shore to Charlevoix, where inns and a gambling casino invite an overnight, and then take the ferry across the river and drive back toward Québec City, exploring the villages along the St. Lawrence's southern bank as you make your way.

Although it is preferable to drive in this region, tour buses go to Montmorency Falls and the shrine of Ste-Anne-de-Beaupré, and circle the Île d'Orléans. Tours don't go to the southern bank at all, however, since the attractions are far more modest in scope and number.

For more information, log on to **www.quebec-region.cuq.qc.ca**.

1 Île d'Orléans

10 miles (16km) NE of Québec City

Until 1935, the only way to get to Île d'Orléans was by boat (in summer) or over the ice (in winter). The highway bridge since built has allowed the fertile fields of Île d'Orléans to become Québec City's primary market-garden. During harvest periods, fruits and vegetables are picked fresh on the farms and trucked into the city daily. In mid-July, hand-painted signs posted by the main road announce FRAISES: CUEILLIR VOUS-MÊME (Strawberries: Pick 'em yourself). The same invitation is made during apple season, September and October. Farmers hand out baskets and quote the price, paid when the basket's full. Bring along a bag or box to carry away the bounty.

ESSENTIALS
GETTING THERE

BY BUS   There are no local buses. For organized bus tours, contact **Visite Touristique de Québec** (☎ 418/563-9722), which offers

English-only tours; **Old Québec Tours** (☎ 418/624-0460); **Maple Leaf Sightseeing Tours** (☎ 418/687-9226); or **Gray Line** (☎ 418/622-7420).

BY CAR   It's a short drive from Québec City to the island. Follow avenue Dufferin (in front of the Parliament building) to connect with Autoroute 440 east, in the direction of Ste-Anne-de-Beaupré. In about 15 minutes, the Île d'Orléans bridge is seen on the right.

VISITOR INFORMATION

After arriving on the island, turn right on Route 368 East toward Ste-Pétronille. The **tourist information** office (☎ 418/828-9411) is in the house on the right, and it has a useful guidebook (C$1/US70¢) for the island. It's open daily 9am to 7pm June through August; the rest of the year, Monday through Friday only, 9am to 5pm. A good substitute for the Île d'Orléans guide is the *Greater Québec* guide, which includes a short tour of Île d'Orléans. A driving-tour cassette can be rented or purchased at the tourist office, and cycling maps are available there.

The lodgings recommended below for the Île d'Orléans are all of the *auberge* type, meaning they have five or more rooms and have full-service dining rooms open to both guests and nonguests. But there are also many bed-and-breakfast inns and *gîtes* (homes with a room or two available to travelers). Cheaper and less elaborate than auberges, many of them provide leaflets and photos to the tourist office for examination.

EXPLORING THE ISLAND

The island was long isolated from the mainland, as is evident in three **stone churches** that date from the days of the French regime. There are only seven such churches left in all of Québec, so this is a point of pride for Île d'Orléans. A firm resistance to development has kept many of its old houses intact as well. Though this could easily have become just another sprawling bedroom community, it has remained a rural farming area—and island residents work to keep it that way. They even have plans to bury their telephone lines and to put in a bicycle lane to cut down on car traffic.

A coast-hugging road circles the island, 21 miles long and 5 miles wide, and another couple of roads bisect it. Farms and picturesque houses dot the east side of the island, and abundant apple orchards enliven the west side.

There are six tiny villages on Île d'Orléans, each with a church as its focal point. It's possible to do a quick circuit of the island in half a day, but a full day may be justified if you eat in a couple of restaurants, visit a sugar shack, skip stones from the beach, and stay the night in one of the several waterside inns. If you're strapped for time, drive as far as St-Jean, then take Route du Mitan across the island, and return to the bridge, and Québec City, via Route 368 West.

STE-PÉTRONILLE

The first village reached on the recommended counterclockwise tour is Ste-Pétronille, only 2 miles (3km) from the bridge. With 1,050 inhabitants, it is best known for its Victorian inn, **La Goéliche** (see below), and also claims the northernmost stand of **red oaks** in North America, dazzling in autumn. The houses were once the summer homes of wealthy English in the 1800s; the church dates from 1871. Even if you don't stay at the inn, drive down to the water's edge, where a small public area with benches is located. Strolling down the picturesque **rue Laflamme** is another pleasant way to while away an hour or two.

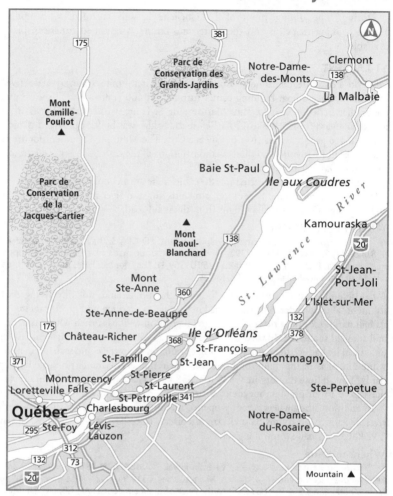

Mountain ▲

Where to Stay & Dine

La Goéliche. 22 Chemin du Quai, Ste-Pétronille, PQ G0A 4C0. ☎ **888/511-2248** or 418/828-2248. Fax 418/828-2745. www.oricom.ca/aubergelagoeliche. E-mail: aubergelagoeliche@oricom.com. 20 units. MINIBAR TEL. C$127 (US$88) double; C$147 (US$101) suite. Rates include breakfast. AE, DC, DISC, ER, MC, V. Free parking.

On a rocky point of land at the southern tip of the island stands this country house with a wraparound porch and a pool. Actually, this is a virtual replica of the 1880 Victorian that stood here until 1996. That one burned to the ground, leaving nothing but the staircase. This one was completed in record time and managed to retain the period flavor with tufted chairs, Tiffany-style lamps, and a few antiques. Only the two suites have TV. The river slaps at the foundation of the glass-enclosed terrace dining room, which is a grand observation point for watching cruise ships and Great Lakes freighters steaming past.

Dining: The dining room of La Goéliche is well regarded, with updated French cooking that's easy on the butter and cream. A modified American plan is available.

ST-LAURENT

From Ste-Pétronille, continue on Route 368 East. After 4 miles (6km), you'll arrive at St-Laurent, once a boat-building center turning out 400 crafts a year. To learn more about that heritage, visit Le Parc Maritime de St-Laurent (☎ **418/828-9672**), an active boat yard from 1908 to 1967. Before the bridge was built, it provided islanders the means to get across the river to Québec City. The Maritime Park incorporates the old Godbout Boatworks and offers demonstrations of the craft. It's open daily June 19 to Labour Day, 10am to 5pm.

The town's church was erected in 1860, and there are a couple of picturesque roadside chapels as well. Good views of farmlands and the river are available from the St-Laurent golf course—follow signs from the main road.

Where to Stay & Dine

Le Canard Huppé. 2198 Chemin Royal, St-Laurent, PQ G0A 3Z0. ☎ **800/838-2292** or 418/828-2292. Fax 418/828-2292. www.canard-huppe.qc.ca. E-mail: canard-huppe@ mediom.qc.ca. 8 units. A/C. C$100–C$125 (US$69–US$86) double. Rates include full breakfast. Meal plans available. AE, DC, ER, MC, V.

A roadside inn reminiscent of those found in the motherland, this tidy young establishment takes considerable pride in its kitchen. Local products and gentle saucings are its hallmarks. Consider this one menu item: crimson raviolis stuffed with duck confit and smoked snails and drizzled with lobster butter. All meals are served; breakfast and lunch can be had in the inviting bistro/bar or out on the terrace under the linden tree, while dinner is in the main dining room, where the service meets professional standards. Table d'hôte dinners are C$25 to C$38 (US$17.25 to US$26). Rooms upstairs don't have TV or phones, but they are attractively decorated, with firm mattresses.

In addition, the owners recently opened an annex down the road, directly on the river. Five of its six rooms have electric fireplaces, three have whirlpool tubs, all have TV. There's a small swimming pool.

Where to Dine

Le Moulin de Saint-Laurent. 754 Chemin Royal. ☎ **888/629-3888** or 418/829-3888. Reservations recommended at dinner. Main courses C$10.95–C$21 (US$7.55–US$14.50); table d'hôte, add C$11.95 (US$8.25) to the price of the main course. AE, CB, DC, ER, MC, V. Daily 10:30am–2pm and 6–9pm. Closed mid-Oct–May 1. COUNTRY FRENCH.

This former flour mill, in operation from 1720 to 1928, has been transformed into one of the island's most romantic restaurants. Rubble-stone walls and hand-wrought beams form the interior, with candlelight glinting off hanging copper and brass pots. On a warm day, sit on the terrace beside the waterfall, and be sure to wander upstairs to see the Québécois antiques. Lunch can be light—an omelette or a plate of assorted pâtés or cheeses, perhaps. There are eight main courses to choose from, only two of them fish, despite all that amply stocked water out there. On weekends, a small combo plays in the evenings.

The owners also have cottages for rent at the shore. Two-night/3-day packages are C$225 to C$249 (US$155 to US$172) per person, including breakfast, dinner, and either a 1½-hour cruise or 1-day bike rental.

ST-JEAN

St-Jean, 4 miles (6km) from St-Laurent, was home to sea captains; the homes in the village appear more prosperous than others on the island. The yellow bricks in the facades of several of the houses were ballast in boats that came over from Europe. The village church was built in 1732, and the walled cemetery is the final resting place of many fishermen and seafarers.

On the left as you enter the village is one of the largest and best-preserved houses on the island: **Manoir Mauvide-Genest,** 1451 av. Royale (☎ **418/829-2630**). Completed in 1752, it is filled with period furnishings. A "beggar's bench" on view was so named because a homeless person who appeared at the door late in the day would be offered a bed for the evening (otherwise, he might cast a spell on the house). A small chapel was added in 1930; Huron Indians made the altar. Don't make a special trip, though—it's undergoing major restoration work, so call ahead to find out if it's reopened and what the hours and prices are. The *manoir* has also served as a summertime restaurant, so you might want to check its status, too. Next door, there's an active summer theater.

If you're pressed for time, pick up **Route du Mitan,** which crosses Île d'Orléans from here to St-Famille on the west side of the island. Route du Mitan, not easy to spot, is on the left just past the church in St-Jean. A detour down that road is a diverting drive through farmland and forest. Return to St-Jean and proceed east on Route 368 to St-François.

ST-FRANÇOIS

The 5½-mile (9km) drive from St-Jean to St-François exposes vistas of the Laurentian Mountains off to the left on the western shore of the river. Just past the village center of St-Jean, **Mont Ste-Anne** can be seen, its slopes scored by ski trails. At St-François, home to about 500 people, the St. Lawrence, a constant and mighty presence, is 10 times wider than when it flows past Québec City. Regrettably, the town's original church (1734) burned in 1988. At St-François, 15 miles (24km) from the bridge, the road becomes Route 368 West.

Where to Dine

Chaumonot. 425 av. Royale, St-François. ☎ **418/829-2735.** Reservations recommended. Main courses C$18–C$27 (US$12.40–US$18.60); table d'hôte C$32 (US$22). AE, MC, V. Daily 11am–3pm and 5–9pm (until 10pm July–Aug). Closed Nov–Apr. QUÉBECOIS.

At this riverside inn, the food reflects what farmers have eaten on this island for generations—pork chops, lamb, salmon, *tourtière* (meat pie), pheasant pâté, tomato-and-onion relish, and plenty of warm bread. The kitchen mixes in a few relatively modern touches, such as quiche Lorraine and shrimp and duck pâté. Picture windows look out on the river.

The inn has eight tidy rooms available. They are quite ordinary, but if you wish to stay the night, doubles with breakfast go for C$129 to C$139 (US$89 to US$96). There's a pool. The place is named for the Jesuit priest Pierre Chaumonot, who led the Hurons to the island in 1651 to protect them from the attacking Algonquins.

STE-FAMILLE

Founded in 1661 at the northern tip of the island, Ste-Famille is the oldest parish on the island. With 1,660 inhabitants, it is 5 miles (8km) from St-François and 12 miles (19km) from the bridge. Across the road from the triple-spired church (1743) is the convent of **Notre-Dame Congregation,** founded in 1685 by Marguerite Bourgeoys, one of Montréal's prominent early citizens. This area supports dairy and cattle farms and apple orchards.

Anglers might wish to swing by **Étang Richard Boily,** 4739 Chemin Royal (☎ **418/829-2874**), where they can cast their lures for speckled or rainbow trout in a stocked pond, daily 9am to sunset. It isn't *entirely* like fishing in a rain barrel. Poles and bait are supplied—no permit is required—and customers pay only for what they catch, about C30¢ (US21¢) per inch; the fish run 9 to 12 inches. They'll clean, cut, and pack what you catch. Some island restaurants can even be persuaded to cook the fish for you. For more passive activity, buy a handful of fish pellets for C25¢ (US17¢), toss them in the water, and watch the ravenous trout jump.

On the same property is a *cabane à sucre*, the traditional "sugar shack" where maple syrup is made. See demonstrations of the equipment and get debriefed on the process that turns the sap of a tree into syrup. Free tastes are offered and several types of products are for sale in a shop on the premises.

Farther along, near the village church, you might wish to visit the **Boulangerie G.H. Blouin,** 3967 Chemin Royal (☎ **418/829-2590**), run by a family of bakers who have lived on the island for 300 years. You'll also find a little shop called **Le Mitan** (☎ **418/829-3206**) that stocks local crafts and books about the island. Unfortunately, the popular restaurant L'Arte has closed after 40 years.

ST-PIERRE

By Île d'Orléans standards, St-Pierre is a big town, with a population of about 2,000. Its central attraction is the island's oldest church (1717). Services are no longer held there; it now contains a large handicraft shop in the back, behind the altar, which is even older than the church (1695). The pottery, beeswax candles, dolls, scarves, woven rugs, and blankets aren't to every taste but are worth a look.

Thousands of migrating snow geese, ducks, and Canada geese stop by in the spring, a spectacular sight when they launch themselves into the air in flapping hordes so thick they almost blot out the sun.

Where to Stay & Dine

Le Vieux Presbytère. 1247 av. Mgr. d'Esgly, St-Pierre, PQ G0A 4E0. ☎ **888/828-9723** or 418/828-9723. Fax 418/828-2189. www.presbytere.com. 8 units (2 share a bathroom). C$65–C$90 (US$45–US$62) double. Rates include breakfast. Meal plan available. MC, V.

Down the street running past the front of the church, the former 1790 rectory has been converted to a homey inn. Filled with antiques and other old pieces, its sitting and dining rooms and glassed sun porch coax strangers into conversation. For privacy, choose one of the cottages 100 feet from the main house; for more space and enough beds for a family of five, ask for room number one.

A fireplace warms the dining room much of the year. The kitchen is fond of game, including ostrich, bison, and wapiti. Main courses run C$15.95 to C$25 (US$11 to US$17.25), with a table d'hôte of C$49 (US$33.80), which includes a bottle of wine. Bikes are rented. A neighbor raises ostriches in the adjoining lot, an unexpected sight.

Heading back across the bridge toward Québec City, there is a fine view of the next destination on a tour.

2 Montmorency Falls

7 miles (11km) NE of Québec City

At 274 feet (83m), the falls, named by Samuel de Champlain for his patron, the duke of Montmorency, are 100 feet higher than Niagara—a boast no visitor is spared. They are, however, far narrower. The waterfall is surrounded by the provincial Parc de la Chute-Montmorency, where, from early May through late October, visitors can stop to take in the view or have a picnic. In winter, the plunging waters contribute to a particularly impressive sight: The freezing spray sent up by the falls builds a mountain of white ice at the base called the "Sugarloaf," which sometimes grows as high as 100 feet. On summer nights the falls are illuminated, and toward the end of July and into

August, there is an international fireworks competition overhead. The yellow cast of the waterfall results from the high iron content of the riverbed.

ESSENTIALS
GETTING THERE
BY BUS   Programs are subject to frequent change, so check with **Visite Touristique de Québec** (☎ 418/563-9722), which offers English-only tours; **Old Québec Tours** (☎ 418/624-0460); **Maple Leaf Sightseeing Tours** (☎ 418/687-9226); or **Gray Line** (☎ 418/622-7420) to see what's currently available.

BY CAR   Take Autoroute 40, north of Québec City, going east. At the end of the autoroute, where it intersects with Route 360, the falls come into view.

VISITOR INFORMATION
A **tourist information** booth is located beside the parking area at the falls, just after the turnoff from the highway (☎ 418/663-2877). It's open early June to early September 9am to 7pm, and early September to mid-October 11am to 5pm. Admission to the falls is free.

VIEWING THE FALLS
In 1759, General Wolfe and his army of 4,000 hauled 30 heavy cannons to the heights east of the cataract, aiming them at French troops deployed on the opposite side. The British lost the ensuing firefight but 6 weeks later won the decisive battle on the Plains of Abraham. One of the earthen redoubts they constructed survives.

There are a variety of platforms from which the falls can be viewed, including a footbridge that spans the river just where it flows over the cliff, stairs that descend one side from the top to near the bottom, and a cable car (not for the vertiginous) that runs from the parking lot to a terminal near a manor house that contains an interpretation center, a cafe-bar, and restaurant. **Manoir Montmorency,** above the falls, was opened in 1994, replacing an earlier structure that burned down. Lunches and dinners of notably improved quality are served there daily, all year, except Monday and Tuesday dinners January through March. The dining room and porch have a sideways vista of the falls.

3 Ste-Anne-de-Beaupré

22 miles (35km) NE of Québec City, 15 miles (24km) NE of Montmorency Falls

Legend has it that French mariners were sailing up the St. Lawrence River in the 1650s when they ran into a terrifying storm. They prayed to their patroness, St. Anne, to save them, and when they survived they dedicated a wooden chapel to her on the north shore of the St. Lawrence, near the site of their perils. Not long afterward, a laborer on the chapel was said to have been cured of lumbago, the first of many documented miracles. Since that time, pilgrims have made their way here—over a million a year—to pay their respects to St. Anne, the mother of the Virgin Mary and grandmother of Jesus.

ESSENTIALS
GETTING THERE
BY BUS   An intercity bus to Ste-Anne-de-Beaupré leaves the Québec City bus station three times a day, at around 9:15am, 3pm, and 6:15pm. Return trips are at 2:25pm and 6pm Monday through Saturday and 8pm Sunday. Always call ahead to confirm departure times (☎ 418/525-3000). The round-trip fare is C$12

(US$8.30). Also check with **Visite Touristique de Québec** (☎ 418/563-9722), which offers English-only tours; **Old Québec Tours** (☎ 416/624-0460); **Maple Leaf Sightseeing Tours** (☎ 418/687-9226); or **Gray Line** (☎ 418/622-7420).

BY CAR   From Montmorency Falls, it's a 20-minute drive along Route 138 East to the little town of Ste-Anne-de-Beaupré. The highway goes right past the basilica, with an easy entrance into the large parking lot.

VISITOR INFORMATION

An **information booth** at the southwestern side of the basilica, 10018 av. Royale (☎ 418/827-3781), is open year-round, daily 8:30am to 4:30pm. The basilica itself is open year-round. Admission is free. Masses are held daily but hours vary.

EXPLORING THE BASILICA

Reactions to the **religious complex** that has resulted over the years at Ste-Anne-de-Beaupré inevitably vary. To the faithful, this is a place of wonder, perhaps the most important pilgrimage site in North America. To many others, it is perceived as a building that lacks the grandeur its great size is intended to impart, a raw and ponderous structure without the ennobling patina of age. The former group will want to schedule at least a couple of hours to absorb it all; the latter won't need more than 15 minutes to satisfy their curiosity.

The towering **basilica** is the most recent building raised on this spot in St. Anne's honor. After the sailors' first modest wooden chapel was swept away by a flood in the 1600s, another chapel was built on higher ground. Floods, fires, and the ravages of time dispatched later buildings, until a larger, presumably sturdier structure was erected in 1887. In 1926, it, too, lay in ruins, gutted by fire. As a result of a lesson finally learned, the present basilica is constructed in stone, following an essentially neo-Romanesque scheme. Marble, granite, mosaics, stained glass, and hand-carved wood are employed with a generous hand throughout. The pews, for instance, are of wood with hand-carved medallions at the ends, each portraying a different animal. Behind the main altar are eight side chapels and altars, each different. The hundreds of crutches, canes, braces, and artificial limbs strapped to columns and stacked on the floor of the vestibule, left behind by those who no longer needed them, attest to the conviction that miracles routinely occur here.

Note that the church and the whole town of Ste-Anne-de-Beaupré are particularly busy on days of saintly significance: the first Sunday in May, mid- through late July, the fourth Sunday in August, and early September.

Other attractions in Ste-Anne-de-Beaupré include the **Way of the Cross,** with life-size cast-iron figures, on the hillside opposite the basilica; the **Scala Santa Chapel** (1891); and the **Memorial Chapel** (1878), with a bell tower and altar from the late 17th and early 18th centuries, respectively. More commercial than devotional are the **Historial,** a **wax museum,** and the **Cyclorama,** a 360° painting of Jerusalem. Admission to the Historial is C$4 (US$2.75) adults, C$3 (US$2.05) children 6 to 13; to the Cyclorama, it's C$6 (US$3.35) adults, C$3 (US$2.05) children 6 to 15.

Driving north on Route 138 toward Mont Ste-Anne, about 1.5 miles (2km) from Ste-Anne-de-Beaupré, on the left, is a factory-outlet strip mall—about as far from the divine as you can get—called **Promenades Ste-Anne** (☎ 418/827-3555). It has shops selling discounted merchandise from Dansk, Liz Claiborne, Mondi, Marikita (crafts), and Benetton, as well as a bistro serving California-style food. The mall is open 7 days a week.

Where to Stay & Dine

✪ **Auberge La Camarine.** 10947 bd. Ste-Anne, Beaupré, PQ G0A 1E0. ☎ **800/ 567-3939** or 418/827-1958. Fax 418/827-5430. www.camarine.com. 31 units. A/C TV TEL. C$149–C$179 (US$103–US$123) double. AE, DC, MC, V. Go just past the Promenades Ste-Anne outlet center, turning left off Route 138.

Why they named it after a bitter berry is uncertain, but this inn has a kitchen that is equaled by only a bare handful of restaurants in the entire province—and that includes Montréal. (Reservations are essential for dinner.) The cuisine bears a resemblance to that variety of fusion cookery that joins French, Italian, and Asian techniques and ingredients. Salmon tartar married with leaves of smoked sturgeon and crisply sautéed lettuce is illustrative. Further specifics are fruitless, for the menu changes frequently. The owners are justly proud of their wine cellar, which includes a wide selection of half bottles. Only dinner is served (overnight guests can get breakfast and light lunch), daily from 6 to 8:30pm. A table d'hôte dinner can be had for C$48 (US$33). Reservations are required.

Guest rooms blend antique and contemporary notions, and some have fireplaces and/or Exercycles. Two have Jacuzzis. The ski slopes of Mount Ste-Anne are a short drive away by car or regular shuttle.

4 Mont Ste-Anne

25 miles (40km) NE of Québec City, about 6 miles (10km) NE of Ste-Anne-de-Beaupré

Like Montréal, Québec City has its Laurentian hideaways. But there are differences: The Laurentians sweep down quite close to the St. Lawrence at this point, so Québecois need drive only about 30 minutes to be in the woods. And since Québec City is much smaller than Montréal, the Québec resorts are more modest in size and fewer in number, but their facilities and amenities are equal to those of resorts elsewhere in the Laurentian range.

Mont Ste-Anne is a four-season getaway offering the best skiing outside Québec City as well as a plethora of outdoor activities during the summer, including golf, mountain biking, hiking, and paragliding.

ESSENTIALS
GETTING THERE
BY BUS   The **HiverExpress** (☎ **418/525-5191**) shuttle service from Québec City carries passengers to the slopes at Mont Ste-Anne, making it possible to stay in the city at night and ski the mountain by day. The round-trip fare is C$18 (US$12.40). Lodging is available (☎ **800/463-1568**).

BY CAR   Continue along Route 138 from Ste-Anne-de-Beaupré, turning onto secondary Route 360 to the recreation area.

MONT-STE-ANNE PARK
The park entrance is easy to spot from the highway. For information and rates for mountain-bike or ski rentals, call ☎ **418/827-4561** or 418/827-3121.

Mont-Ste-Anne Park, 30 square miles (49km²) surrounding a 2,625-foot-high peak, is an outdoor enthusiast's bonanza. In summer, there are camping, golfing, in-line skating, cycling, hiking, jogging, paragliding, and a 150-mile network of mountain biking trails (bikes can be rented at the park). An eight-passenger gondola to the top of the mountain operates every day for the benefit of cyclists between late June and early September, weather permitting, at ticket prices of C$10 (US$6.90) for adults, C$8 (US$5.50) for ages 14 to 20, C$6 (US$4.15) for seniors and children 7 to 13, and free for children under 7.

In winter, the park is Québec's largest and busiest ski area. Twelve lifts, including the gondola and three quad chair lifts, transport downhill skiers to the starting points of 50 trails and slopes. More than 130 miles (210km) of cross-country trails lace the park, dotted with eight heated rest huts. Cross-country skiers pay day rates of about C$16 (US$11.05) for an adult, less for students and seniors. Paragliding instruction is available in winter as well as summer.

From here it's an easy commute from the city, which is what most people do. A nearby inn is La Camarine, described above.

5 Grand Canyon & Sainte-Anne Falls

25 miles (40km) NE of Québec City, about 37 miles (6km) NE of Ste-Anne-de-Beaupré

A short drive off Route 138 is the deep gorge and powerful waterfall created by the Ste-Anne-du-Nord River. Unseen from the main road, it's worth a detour and only takes about an hour to visit.

ESSENTIALS
GETTING THERE
BY CAR   Continue along Route 138 from Ste-Anne-de-Beaupré.

CANYON STE-ANNE
Driving north, the marked entrance is on the left. A dirt road leads through the trees to a parking lot. On the far side of the adjacent picnic ground is a building containing a cafeteria and the ticket booth. Admission is C$7 (US$4.85) ages 13 and up, C$2 (US$1.40) ages 6 to 12. The site is open daily May to June 23 from 9am to 5pm, June 24 to Labour Day daily 8:30am to 5:45, and the day after Labour Day through October daily 9am to 5pm. It's closed the rest of the year. To confirm these hours, which are subject to change due to weather and season, call ☎ **418/827-4057.**

An open-sided shuttle bus takes you to the first bridge, which crosses the river just above the thundering falls, 243 feet (74 meters) high. At the turn of the last century the river was used to float logs from lumbering operations, and part of the dramatic gorge was created by dynamiting around 1917. Trails descend both sides to a second bridge, 180 feet (55 meters) above the yellowish iron-tinged water that crashes over massive rock walls. From there, a trail follows the northern rim to a third and final bridge, ending in an observation platform.

The woods that surround the gorge are privately owned, and only opened to the public in 1973. Management has wisely avoided commercial intrusions along the trails and the few descriptive signs are muted, preserving the undeniable natural beauty of the site. Visitors who have difficulty walking can get the effect of the falls without going too far from the bus, and those who suffer acrophobia can easily avoid the bridges.

6 Charlevoix

Baie-St-Paul: 61 miles (98km) NE of Québec City; La Malbaie: 92 miles (149km) NE of Québec City; St-Siméon: 113 miles (182km) NE of Québec City

The Laurentians move closer to the shore of the St. Lawrence as they approach what used to be called Murray Bay at the mouth of the Malbaie River. While it can't be pretended that the entire length of Route 138 from Beaupré is fascinating, the Route 362 detour from Baie-St-Paul is scenic, with wooded hills slashed by narrow riverbeds and billowing meadows ending in harsh cliffs plunging down to the river. The air is scented by sea salt and rent by the shrieks of gulls.

Baie-St-Paul is an artists' colony, and there are several good-to-memorable inns between there and Cap à l'Aigle, a few miles beyond La Malbaie. St-Siméon, where travelers catch the ferry to the southern shore of the St. Lawrence, affords summer visitors numerous opportunities for whale watching.

ESSENTIALS
GETTING THERE
BY CAR   Take Route 138 as far as Baie-St-Paul, then pick up Route 362 to La Malbaie, merging once again with Route 138 to reach the ferry at St-Siméon.

VISITOR INFORMATION
Baie-St-Paul has a year-round **tourist office** at 444 bd. Mgr. de Laval (☎ 418/435-4160), open mid-June through Labour Day daily 9am to 9pm, and from September to early June daily 9am to 5pm. So does La Malbaie, at 630 bd. de Comporté (☎ 418/665-4454), with the same hours. St-Siméon has seasonal tourist offices at 494 rue St-Laurent and at the ferry landing, open mid-June through Labour Day daily 9am to 7pm.

EXPLORING THE AREA
In addition to the country inns dotting the region from Baie-St-Paul to Cap à l'Aigle to La Malbaie and beyond, nearby Pointe-au-Pic has a casino, a newer, smaller off-shoot of the one in Montréal. The northern end of the region is marked by the confluence of the Saguenay River and the St. Lawrence. These waters attract six species of whales, many of which can be seen from shore from mid-June through late October, although **whale-watching cruises** are increasingly popular. In 1988, Charlevoix was named a UNESCO World Biosphere Reserve. Though only one of 325 such regions throughout the world, it was the first one to include human settlement.

BAIE-ST-PAUL
The first town of any size reached in Charlevoix via Route 138, this attractive community of 6,000 holds on to a reputation as an artist's retreat that began at the start of the 20th century. More than a dozen boutiques and galleries and a couple of small museums show the work of local painters and artisans. Given the setting, it isn't surprising that many of the artists are landscapists, but other styles and subjects are represented. Although some of their production is merely of the kitchen-hobbyist level, much is highly professional. To see selections, check the **Maison Reneé Richard,** at 58 rue St-Jean-Baptiste (☎ 418/435-5571), and **Le Centre d'Art,** 4 rue Ambroise-Fafard (☎ 418/435-3681), which specialize in landscape artists from Québec.

A Local Museum
Le Centre d'Exposition. 23 rue Ambroise-Fafard. ☎ **418/435-3681.** Admission C$3 (US$2.06) adults, C$2 (US$1.40) seniors and students, free for children under 12. Sept–May daily 9am–5pm; June–Aug daily 9am–7pm.

Opened in 1992, this brick-and-glass museum has three floors of work primarily by regional artists, both past and present. Inuit sculptures are included, and temporary one-person and group shows are mounted throughout the year.

Where to Stay & Dine

La Maison Otis. 23 rue St-Jean-Baptiste, Baie-St-Paul, PQ G0A 1B0. ☎ **800-267-2254** or 418/435-2255. Fax 418/435-2464. www.quebecweb.com/maisonotis. 30 units. A/C TV TEL. Late June–late Oct, Christmas–mid-Apr C$204–C$274 (US$141–US$189) double; late Oct–Dec 23, Apr 15–late June C$175–C$265 (US$121–US$183) double. Rates include breakfast and dinner. AE, DC, ER, MC, V.

Prices look steep at first blush, but because big breakfasts and dinners are included (and required), lunch is virtually unnecessary. A wide range of facilities and amenities allow guests who reserve far enough in advance to customize their lodgings. Combinations of fireplaces, whirlpools, stereo systems, VCRs, four-poster beds, and suites that sleep four are all available, distributed among three buildings. Housekeeping is meticulous. A long porch fronts the colorful main street, and a kidney-shaped indoor pool and sauna are on the premises, as is a jovial piano bar. The required meals are no sacrifice, served in a room with a stone fireplace and shaded candlesticks on pink tablecloths. Excellent clam chowder, salmon tartare, and pheasant have been notable in the past.

ST-IRÉNÉE

From Baie-St-Paul, take Route 362 toward La Malbaie. It roller-coasters over bluffs above the river, and in about 20 miles (32km) is this cliff-top hamlet of fewer than 800 year-round residents. Apart from the setting, the best reason for dawdling here is the lengthy music and dance festival held every summer. **Domaine Forget,** 398 Chemin les Bains (☎ **888/336-7438** or 418/452-8111 for tickets), offers concerts from mid-June through late August on Wednesday, Saturday, and some Friday evenings, and Sunday from 11am to 2pm. Ten more weekend concerts are spaced through autumn from September to late November. This performing-arts festival was initiated in 1977, with the purchase of a large hillside property overlooking the river. Stables and barns were converted to use as studios and rehearsal halls, and the surrounding lawns were used to stage the concerts and recitals. Their success prompted the construction of a new 600-seat hall, completed in time for the 1996 season. Although the program emphasizes classical music with solo instrumentalists and chamber groups, it is peppered with appearances by jazz combos. During the summer season, tickets are C$21 to C$29 (US$14.50 to US$20); children under 12 are admitted free. The fall concerts cost C$12 to C$24 (US$8.30 to US$16.55).

POINTE-AU-PIC

From St-Irénée, the road starts to bend west after 6 miles (10km), as the mouth of the Malbaie River starts to form. Pointe-au-Pic is one of the trio of villages collectively known as La Malbaie, or Murray Bay, as it was called by the wealthy Anglophones who made this their resort of choice from the Gilded Age through the 1950s. Although inhabitants of the region wax poetic about their hills and trees and wildlife "where the sea meets the sky," they have something quite different to preen about now: their new casino.

A Casino & a Museum

Casino de Charlevoix. 183 av. Richelieu (Route 362). ☎ **800/665-2274** or 418/ 665-5300. Free admission (persons 18 and over only). June–Sept daily 10am–3am; Oct–May Mon–Fri 10am–1am, Sat–Sun 11am–3am. Signs are frequent on Route 362 coming from the south, and on Route 138 from the north.

This is the second of Québec's gambling casinos (the first is in Montréal and the third opened in the Ottawa/Hull area in 1996). It is about as tasteful as such establishments get this side of Monte Carlo. Cherry-wood paneling and granite floors enclose the ranks of 800 slot machines and 21 tables, including blackjack, roulette wheels, keno, stud poker, and minibaccarat. Only soft drinks are allowed at the machines and tables, so players have to go to an adjacent bar to mourn their losses. And there is a dress code, forbidding, among other items, tank tops, bustiers, and "clothing associated with organizations known to be violent." Running shoes and "neat" blue jeans are allowed, although the management can get picky on weekends, when it gets very crowded.

Musée de Charlevoix. 1 Chemin du Havre (at the intersection of Route 362/bd. Bellevue). ☎ **418/665-4411.** Admission C$4 (US$2.75) adults, C$3 (US$2.05) seniors and students, free for children under 12. June 24–Sept 2 daily 10am–6pm; Sept 3–June 23 Tues–Fri 10am–5pm, Sat–Sun 1–5pm.

In existence since 1975, the museum moved to its present quarters in 1990. Folk art, sculptures, and paintings of variable quality by regional artists figure prominently in the permanent collection, supplemented by frequent temporary exhibitions with diverse themes.

Where to Stay & Dine

✪ **Manoir Richelieu.** 181 rue Richelieu, Pointe-au-Pic, PQ G0T 1M0. ☎ **800/441-1414** or 418/665-3703. Fax 418/665-4566. www.fairmont.com. 405 units. A/C MINIBAR TV TEL. C$199–C$299 (US$137–US$206) double, from C$459 (US$317) suite. MAP, golf, and other packages available. AE, DC, ER, MC, V.

Since 1899, there has been a resort hotel here, long the aristocratic haven of swells summering in Murray Bay. The opening of the new casino just across the drive-up circle changed the makeup of visitors. To the mix of elderly people who have been coming here since they were youngsters and families who have discovered they can be together and still have time for themselves have been added those people who will go anywhere for the fun of losing money. When it became clear that facilities had become worn and service was falling short, the hotel was closed for 9 months for a massive $140-million renovation that even involved bulldozers *inside* the building. It reopened in June 1999, bright and shiny as a new loonie, with marked improvements in every category. Rooms now brush up against deluxe standards, with all conveniences, including room safes, bathrobes, two or three phones, and easy modem connection. The Entrée Gold executive floor has 21 rooms with a lounge serving complimentary breakfasts and evening hors d'oeuvres.

Dining/Diversions: Buffet-lovers are bound to be pleased with the dozens of platters and trays of food set out for all three meals of the day in Le Saint-Laurent dining room. Le Charlevoix offers fine dining, and the informal Bistro Le Bellerive is open from 11:30am to 2am. Golf on the hillside course above the hotel provides the bonus of river views. A fitness center has weight machines and a sauna. There are indoor and outdoor pools, tennis, horseback riding, and a spa. Kids can go to day camp. The house band plays on past midnight for dancing.

CAP-À-L'AIGLE

Route 362 rejoins Route 138 in La Malbaie, the largest town in the area, with almost 4,000 inhabitants. It serves as a provisioning center, with supermarkets, hardware stores, and gas stations. There is a **tourist information office** at 630 bd. de Comporté, open mid-June through Labour Day daily 9am to 9pm, the rest of the year daily 9am to 5pm. Continue through the town center and cross the bridge on the right, making a sharp right again on the other side. This is Route 138, with signs pointing to Cap-à-l'Aigle.

William Howard Taft spent many summers in Murray Bay, starting in 1892 and extending well past his one-term presidency. For much of that time, the only way to get here was by boat; the railroad didn't arrive until 1919. Given his legendary girth, it may be assumed that Taft knew something about the good life. Some of the other folks who made this their summer home, namely the Cabots of Boston, the duke of Windsor, and Charlie Chaplin, could confirm that Taft loved the region. And if any of them could return today, they would probably choose what is arguably the premier inn in Murray Bay.

Where to Stay & Dine

☉ La Pinsonnière. 124 rue St-Raphaël, La Malbaie (secteur Cap-à-l'Aigle), PQ G5A 1X9. ☎ **800/387-4431** or 418/665-4431. Fax 418/665-7156. www.lapinsonniere.com. E-mail: pinsonniere@relaischateaux.fr. 27 units. A/C TV TEL. May–Oct 7 and Christmas–New Year C$140–C$455 (US$97–US$314) double; Nov–Apr C$125–C$455 (US$86–US$314) double. MAP available but not required. Packages available, minimum 2-night stay on weekends. AE, DISC, MC, V.

This is one of only eight member hostelries in the prestigious Relais & Châteaux organization in all of Canada. As aficionados know, properties included in this organization offer limited size, bedrooms that often border on princely luxury, and an emphasis on food and wine. Bedrooms come in five categories, the priciest of which are equipped with Jacuzzis and gas fireplaces. A substantial renovation of 10 bedrooms and the public areas has just been completed. Packages include whale-watching cruises, dogsled runs, and skiing at Mont Grand-Fonds.

Dining: You'll know where the owners focus their laserlike attention when you're seated in the serene dining room beside the picture window, anticipating a dinner that will become the evening's entertainment. With drinks and menus comes the customary *amuse-guele*—say, quail leg on a bed of slivered asparagus and fettuccine tossed with plump mussels, spiked with a spray of pungent tarragon and brightened with an edible pansy—immediately followed by soup. The main event might be a succulent veal chop with a nest of shaved carrots, fiddleheads, and purple potatoes. Wines are a particular point of pride here, and the owner needs no urging to conduct tours of his impressive cellar. Three fixed-price meals go from four to seven courses for C$50 to C$100 (US$35 to US$69).

Amenities: Indoor pool, sauna, minispa, tennis, beach (very cold water), and massages.

ST-SIMÉON

Rejoin Route 138 and continue 20 miles (32km) to St-Siméon. If you've decided to cross to Rivère-du-Loup on the other side of the St. Lawrence, returning to Québec City along the south shore, the ferry departs from here. With discretionary time left, I recommend continuing on to Baie-Ste-Catherine and Tadoussac, but if that isn't an option, it's only 93 miles (150km) back to the city the way you came on the north shore.

In St-Siméon, signs direct cars and trucks down to the ferry terminal. Boarding is on a first-come, first-served basis, and ferries leave on a carefully observed schedule, weather permitting, from April to early January. Departure times of the two to five daily sailings vary substantially from month to month, however, so get in touch with the company, **Clarke Transport Canada** (☎ **418/638-2856**), to obtain a copy of the schedule. For current fares, call ☎ **418/862-5094** or check the Web site, **www.travrdlstsim.com**. Always subject to change, fares for passengers remaining on board for the round-trip are C$10.40 (US$7.15) ages 12 to 64 years, C$9.40 (US$6.50) seniors, C$6.90 (US$4.75) children 5 to 11. For cars, the one-way fare is

C$26.40 (US$18.20). MasterCard and Visa accepted. Arrive at least 30 minutes before departure, one hour ahead in summer. Voyages take 65 to 75 minutes.

From late June through September, passengers may enjoy a bonus. Those are the months the **whales** are most active. They are estimated at more than 500 in number when pelagic (migratory) species join the resident minke and beluga whales. They prefer the northern side of the Estuary, roughly from La Malbaie to Baie-Ste-Catherine, at the mouth of the Saguenay River. Since that is the area the ferry steams through, sightings are an ever-present possibility, especially in summer.

BAIE STE-CATHERINE

To enhance your chances of seeing whales, though, continue northeast from St-Siméon on Route 138, arriving 20 miles (32km) later in Baie-Ste-Catherine, near the estuary of the Saguenay River. A half dozen companies offer cruises to see whales or the majestic Saguenay Fjord from here or from Tadoussac, on the opposite shore. The cruise companies use different sizes and types of watercraft, from powered inflatables called zodiacs that carry 10 to 25 passengers up to stately catamarans and cruisers that carry up to 500. The zodiacs don't provide food, drink, or narration, while the larger boats have snack bars and naturalists on board to describe the action. The small boats, though, are more maneuverable, darting about at each sighting to get closer to the rolling and breaching behemoths.

Zodiac passengers are issued life jackets and waterproof overalls, but expect to get wet anyway. It's cold out there, too, so layers and even gloves are a good idea. People on the large boats sit at tables inside or ride the observation bowsprit, high above the waves. Big boats are the wimp's choice for whale watching. Mine, too.

Most cruises last 2 to 3 hours. One of the most active companies offering trips is **Croisières AML,** with offices in Québec City (☎ **800/563-4643** all year, 418/692-1159 in season). From June through mid-October, they have up to four departures daily. Fares on the larger boats are C$35 (US$24) for adults, C$15 (US$10.35) for children 6 to 12, while zodiac fares are an extra C$10 each (US$6.90). Excursions of comparable duration and with similar fares are provided on the catamaran maintained by **Famille Dufour Croisières** (☎ **800/463-5250** or 418/827-8836).

From Baie Ste-Catherine, it's less than a half-hour drive back to St-Siméon and the ferry across to the opposite shore. Alternatively, continue north to the ferry, **Traverse Tadoussac** (☎ **418/235-4395**), at the mouth of the dramatic Saguenay River. Palisades rise sharply from both shores, the reason it is often referred to as a fjord. The ferry can board up to 400 passengers and 75 vehicles for the trip across to Tadoussac, which takes only 10 minutes. Departure times vary according to season and demand, of course, but in summer figure every hour from midnight to 6am, every 40 minutes from 6:20 to 8am, every 20 minutes from 8am to 8pm, and every 40 minutes from 8:20pm to midnight.

TADOUSSAC

Known as "The Cradle of New France," the oldest permanent European settlement north of Florida was established in 1600 at the point where the Saguenay and St. Lawrence Rivers meet. Missionaries followed and stayed until the middle of the 19th century. The hamlet might have vanished soon after, had a resort hotel not been built there in 1864. A steamship line brought vacationers downriver from Montréal and points farther west and deposited them here for stays that often lasted all summer. Apart from the hotel—the current building was erected in 1942—a few small support businesses, a post office, a marina, and more than a dozen small motels and B&Bs

constitute the town. Its port is an important starting point for whale watching and Saguenay cruises. Tadoussac is the southernmost point of the tourist region designated as Manicouagan.

Where to Stay & Dine

Hôtel Tadoussac. 165 rue Bord de l'Eau, Tadoussac, PQ G0T 2A0. ☎ **800/561-0718** or 418/235-4421. Fax 418/235-4607. www.familledufour.com. 149 units. TV TEL. C$120–C$246 (US$83–US$170) double. Rates include breakfast. MAP, golf, and whale-watching cruise packages available. AE, DC, DISC, ER, MC, V. Closed Nov–early May.

From the opposite shore, the bright-red mansard roof of the sprawling hotel dominates the point of land that slopes down to the river. (You might recognize it as the centerpiece in the film *Hotel New Hampshire*.) The lawns have a pétanque (lawn bowling) court and an outdoor pool, as well as groupings of chairs from which to watch the comings and goings of boats and zodiacs. Inside, the public spaces and bedrooms have a shambling, country-cottage appearance—no pretense of luxe here. Maple furnishings and hand-woven rugs and bedspreads are all made in Québec. Tennis and golf are available.

Meals in the large dining room are better than might be expected, while falling well short of impressive. The fixed-price meals have a substantial number of choices in each course, from appetizer to dessert. Advance reservations must be made for dinner, with the earlier seating drawing older guests and most of the families with children.

7 The Southern Bank

Montmagny: 31 miles (50km) E of Québec City; St-Jean-Port-Joli: 91 miles (146km) E of Québec City; Kamouraska: 130 miles (210km) E of Québec City

Here we are at truth-in-guidebook time. The south bank of the St. Lawrence River between Québec City and Kamouraska holds touristic interest only in relation to transit on the way to somewhere else—with the Gaspé Peninsula farther east as a destination, or as an alternative route back to Québec City after a drive along the north shore to Baie-Ste-Catherine and a ferry ride from St-Siméon to Rivère-du-Loup. Further, the fact that the tourist office in St-Jean-Port-Joli is closed from October through April says much about the relative desirability of a trip through here in those months.

That said, towns on the southern bank are within easy range of a day's excursion from Québec City, and in good weather the views of the river and its islands themselves are almost worth the drive. Motels and guest houses are in sufficient abundance to ensure lodging on short notice, although few of them can be described as memorable. On a day trip, St-Jean-Port-Joli makes a logical turnaround point. But if you're planning to take the ferry across the river and return by the north shore to Québec City, continue to Rivère-du-Loup.

For the first 20 miles (32km) of the drive, Île d'Orléans (see section 1 at the beginning of this chapter) will be off to the left in midstream, with the Laurentian Mountains on the north bank as a backdrop.

ESSENTIALS

GETTING THERE

BY CAR   From Québec City, take Autoroute 20 along the southern shore as far as St-Michel, and then pick up Route 132 east for the only slightly slower scenic road that keeps the river in sight. If you arrive by ferry from St-Siméon and plan to work your way back to the city, go to the end of this section and follow the itinerary backward from Kamouraska, which is 130 miles (210km) east of Québec City.

VISITOR INFORMATION

The **Montmagny Tourist Office,** 45 av. du Quai (☎ **800/463-5643** or 418/ 248-9196), is open Monday through Friday 8:30am to 4:30pm. It's in a little park with a walkway beside the river. The **St-Jean-Port-Joli Tourist Office,** at 7 place de l'Église (☎ **418/ 598-3747**), is open in summer daily 9am to 8pm, in May and early September daily 9am to 5pm, and closed the rest of the year.

MONTMAGNY

As you're driving from Québec City along the southern shore of the St. Lawrence, the first big town is Montmagny, with a population of 12,000. From here in summer, you can take a boat out to **Grosse Île,** the Ellis Island of Canada. Parks Canada is transforming it into a reminder of that period in the country's history when 4.5 million people immigrated to Canada via Québec. Thousands with cholera or typhoid fever were quarantined on the island from 1832 to 1937; almost 7,000 died there and most were buried there. Some 300,000 Irish refugees from the potato famines came through here in 1847 and 1848. A small train with a guide carries visitors around part of the island and makes stops along the way.

Off Montmagny lies the **Archipel de l'Île aux Grues,** islands known for the wild fowl that make it a hunter's destination. There are six islands in all, the largest being Île aux Grues (Cranes' Island) and Île aux Oies (Geese Island). A ferry goes to the Île aux Grues from Montmagny.

Background information on both immigrants and birds is provided by the interpretation center at 53 rue du Bassin Nord in Montmagny. Called **Théâtre Educatif des Migrations** (☎ **418/248-4565**), it is open 1 to 5pm late April through mid-June, 10am to 10pm late June through mid-August, and 9am to 6pm from late August to mid-November.

WHERE TO STAY & DINE

Manoir des Erables. 220 bd. Taché Est (Route 132), Montmagny, PQ G5V 1G5. ☎ **800/ 563-0200** or 418/ 248-0100. Fax 418/248-9507. www.manoirdeserables.com. E-mail: erable@ globetrotter.qc.ca. 23 units. TV TEL. C$80–C$160 (US$55–US$110) double, C$95–C$195 (US$66–US$135) suite. Meal plan and other packages available. AE, DC, MC, V.

Since 1975, this stately 1814 inn has enjoyed a glossy reputation for both food and lodging. Unfortunately, only a few of the large Victorian bedrooms remain due to a fire in 1982. The rest are new. All have hair dryers, and suites have fireplaces and/or whirlpool baths. Seven rooms in a stone house on the property, the Pavillon Collin (1867), are air-conditioned. There are bicycles for rent and a pool.

In the dining room, sterling glints by the light of sparkling chandeliers. The French menu changes daily. The dining room is open daily for both lunch and dinner. Reservations required for dinner.

L'ISLET-SUR-MER

Along Route 132 on the approach to L'Islet-sur-Mer are many roadside farm stands selling honey, fruits, and vegetables. About 10 miles (16km) east of Montmagny, this fishing village produced sailors who roamed the world, among them an Arctic explorer named Joseph-Elzéar Bernier, who claimed the Arctic islands for Canada. Bernier, who became a captain at the age of 17, made 269 voyages and crossed the Atlantic 45 times. In 1874, he did it in 15 days and 16 hours, quite a feat in those days.

A MARITIME MUSEUM

Musée Maritime du Québec. 55 rue des Pionniers Est. ☎ **418/247-5001.** Admission C$5 (US$3.35) adults, C$2.50 (US$1.65) children. Mid-May–mid-Oct daily 9am–6pm; rest of year Tues–Fri 9am–noon and 1:30–5pm.

Dedicated to the town's favorite son (see Joseph-Elzéar Bernier above), the museum relives the area's nautical history from the 17th century forward. The monument in front of the museum illustrates his explorations on a globe, crowned with the aurora borealis. Housed in a former 19th-century convent, the museum has three floors of exhibits. Particularly captivating are the many large ship models, ranging from fully rigged galleons to brigantines to Seaway freighters. Sound, videos, and computers are employed with a degree of sophistication. Out back are the hydrofoil Bras d'Or 400 and the icebreaker *Ernest Lapointe,* which was built in Canada before World War II and used until 1978.

ST-JEAN-PORT-JOLI

This town of 3,400 gained an early measure of fame for the traditional wood carving practiced here for generations, but in the 1930s, three brothers—Médard, André, and Jean-Julien Bourgault—gained far wider celebrity as master sculptors in wood. Dozens of students were attracted to the town and a wood-carving school was established. Today scores of active craftspeople live and work here, and the town is filled with their shops and galleries, showing textiles, pottery, and carvings in stone and wood.

Guidance is offered by the tourist information center at 7 place de l'Église (☎ **418/598-3747**), open from May through October.

EXPLORING THE TOWN

Although proclamations such as "masterful" and "exquisite" are tossed around with abandon in reference to the wood carvings of these artisans, individual responses vary widely. Stop by first at the **Musée des Anciens Canadiens** (below) to see if you have enough interest to explore further.

If you like the work, there are ample opportunities to seek out carvings for sale and to meet the people who produce them. Wander into some of the wood-carving shops strung along Route 132 for a look at what's being done today. The artists are usually happy to chat and show their studios.

Musée des Anciens Canadiens. 332 av. de Gaspé Ouest. ☎ **418/598-3392.** Admission C$4.50 (US$3.10) adults, C$2.50 (US$1.70) children 7–12, free for children under 12. May–June daily 9am–6pm; July–Aug daily 8:30am–9pm; Sept–Oct daily 8:30am–5pm; Nov–Apr by reservation only.

Museum is too grand a label for this gallery attached to a boutique, but it's a good place to start to learn about the works of the Bourgault brothers—Médard's religious sculptures and nudes, André's country folk, and Jean-Julien's religious sculptures and furniture. The work of other village artisans is also on display, including the model boats carved by members of the Leclerc family, which are also on display in the Musée Maritime Bernier in L'Islet-sur-Mer.

Église Saint-Jean Baptiste. 2 av. de Gaspé Ouest. ☎ **418/598-3023.** Free admission. June 27–Labour Day daily 9am–5pm; Labour Day–June 26 Mon–Fri 9am–5pm (or by reservation).

The church was built from 1779 to 1781 and later decorated by the early wood carvers, including the Bourgaults, who created the pulpit in 1937. A more recent addition is the 17-piece crèche, each piece carved by a different local artist and presented to the church in 1987. Buried in the church under the seigneurial pew is the author of *Anciens Canadiens,* Philippe-Aubert de Gaspé, who was the last in a line of lords of the manor (seigneurs) who owned and governed St-Jean since 1633. Look for the nearby plaque that lists all of the town's seigneurs, back to the time when the original land grant was made by the king of France.

Seigneurie des Aulnaies. 525 de la Seigneurie, St-Roch-des-Aulnaies. ☎ **418/354-2800.** Admission (including tours) C$5 (US$3.45) adults, C$2.50 (US$1.70) children 6–15. Late June–early Sept daily 9am–6pm, mid-Sept–mid-Oct daily 10am–4pm.

About 9 miles (14km) east of St-Jean-Port-Joli is this historic farm beside the Ferrée River, with a working flour mill from 1842 and a manor house from 1850. The grounds are filled with chestnuts, black locusts, and redwoods—trees not ordinarily found in this area. Six tours of the mill and manor house are given daily by costumed docents starting at 9:30am.

WHERE TO STAY & DINE

Auberge des Glacis. 46 Route Tortue, St-Eugène, PQ G0R 1X0. ☎ **877/245-2247** or 418/247-7486. Fax 418/247-7182. E-mail: aubergedesglacis@hotmail.com. 10 units. C$164–C$179 (US$113–US$123) double, C$189–C$209 (US$130–US$144) suite. Additional person C$60 (US$41) extra. Rates include breakfast and dinner. AE, DC, MC, V.

About 7½ miles (12km) west of St-Jean-Port-Joli, this 1840 stone mill–turned-inn sits beside a stream in the woods. The only steady sounds are of crickets and gurgling water. Each room has special touches—a spinning wheel, a brass bed, an antique armoire. All the bathrooms, most of which have showers only, were redone last year. Three rooms have TVs and two have VCRs; another is perfect for families, with a bedroom, separate sitting area, and loft with two single beds reached by a ladder. The innkeepers rent cross-country skis and snowshoes in winter, and horseback riding is available nearby. Bikes are free, and there's a pond for swimming. In the dining room, the French menu is changed daily.

Appendix: Montréal & Québec City in Depth

As important to your enjoyment of a new destination as deciding where you'll stay or eat is learning something about its history and culture before you arrive in order to appreciate what you'll see and experience.

1 A Look at French Canada: Now & Then

Québec province is immense, the largest province in the second-largest country in the world (after Russia) and more than three times as large as France. It encompasses almost 600,000 square miles—two times the size of Texas—stretching from the northern borders of New York, Vermont, and New Hampshire to almost the Arctic Circle. To the east of it lie Maine and the province of New Brunswick; to the west, the province of Ontario and James and Hudson Bays. (In fact, Québec would be even larger had Labrador not been awarded to Newfoundland in 1927.) Its substantial fund of natural resources include 16% of the world's supply of fresh water. Most of the province's population lives in its lower regions—the St. Lawrence lowlands and parts of the Appalachians and the Laurentians. More than 80% of its almost seven million residents lives within an area 200 miles long and 60 miles wide, one of the highest concentrations of people in sparsely populated Canada.

Montréal, home to a third of the province's population, occupies about one-third (60 square miles) of the island of Montréal, which is part of the Hochelaga Archipelago. The island is situated in the St. Lawrence River near where it joins the Ottawa River. At the city's center is a 764-foot hill (which natives like to think of as a mountain) called *Mont-Royal,* and from which the city takes its name. Nearby rise more mountains: the Laurentides (the Laurentians), the oldest mountain range in the world and the playground of the Québecois. The foothills of the Appalachian mountains separate Québec from the United States and add to the beauty of Estrie, the bucolic country on the opposite side of the St. Lawrence once known as the Eastern Townships, where many Montréalers have country homes. The capital city of Québec, 166 miles northeast of Montréal, commands a stunning location on the rim of a promontory overlooking the St. Lawrence River, which is at its narrowest point here, 1,969 feet across.

THE EUROPEANS ARRIVE The Vikings landed in Canada more than 1,000 years ago, probably followed by Irish and Basque fishermen. English explorer John Cabot stepped ashore briefly on the east coast in 1497, but it was the French who managed the first meaningful European toehold in the wilderness. When **Jacques Cartier** sailed up the **St. Lawrence** in 1535, he recognized at once the tremendous strategic potential of **Cape Diamond,** "the Gibraltar of the North." But he was exploring, not empire building, and after stepping ashore he continued on his trip upriver.

Samuel de Champlain arrived 73 years later, in 1608, determined to settle at Québec, a year after the Virginia Company founded its fledgling colony of Jamestown, hundreds of miles to the south. The British and French struggle for dominance in the new continent focused on their explorations, and there the French outdid the English. Their far-ranging fur trappers, navigators, soldiers, and missionaries opened up not only Canada but also most of what eventually became the United States, moving all the way south to the future New Orleans and claiming most of the territory to the west. This vast region later comprised the **Louisiana Purchase.** At least 35 of the subsequent 50 states were discovered, mapped, or settled by Frenchmen, who left behind some 4,000 place names to prove it, among them Detroit, St. Louis, New Orleans, Duluth, and Des Moines.

Champlain's first settlement, or "habitation," grew to become Québec City's **Basse-Ville,** or Lower Town, down on the flat riverbank beneath the cliffs of Cap Diamant—Cape Diamond. But almost from the beginning there were attacks, first by the Iroquois, then by the English, and later by the Americans. To better defend themselves, the Québecois constructed a fortress atop the cape, and gradually the center of urban life moved to the top of the cliffs.

Jacques Cartier sailed up the broad St. Lawrence River, past the spot that would become Québec City under Champlain, to what was then a large island with a fortified **Iroquois village** composed of 50 longhouses, called **Hochelaga.** Cartier, as usual, did not linger but pushed onward in his search for the sea route to China. His progress was halted by the fierce rapids just west of the island. In a demonstration of mingled optimism and frustration, he dubbed the rapids **La Chine** on the assumption that China was just beyond them. He then decided to check out the Indian settlement after all, landing at a spot in what is now

Dateline

- **1534** Jacques Cartier sails up the St. Lawrence, claiming the territory for France and marking the first European discovery of Canada.

- **1608** Samuel de Champlain founds a settlement at Kebec, at the foot of Cape Diamond. It will become the city of Québec.

- **1642** Paul de Chomedey, sieur de Maisonneuve, establishes a colony called Ville-Marie that will become Montréal.

- **1668** Québec Seminary is founded in Québec City, later to become Laval University in 1852.

- **1759** British General Wolfe defeats French General Montcalm on the Plains of Abraham in Québec City.

- **1760** Montréal falls to the British.

- **1763** The king of France cedes all of Canada to the king of England in the Treaty of Paris.

- **1775** Montréal is occupied by American Revolutionary forces, who withdraw after a few months, when an attempted siege of Québec City by Benedict Arnold fails.

- **1821** English-speaking McGill University is founded in Montréal.

- **1867** The British North America Act creates the federation of the provinces of Québec, Ontario, Nova Scotia, and New Brunswick.

- **1883** "Je me souviens" becomes the motto of Québec—an ominous "I remember."

- **1900–10** 325,000 French Canadians emigrate to the United States.

- **1922** Armand Bombardier invents the prototype for the Ski-Doo, the first

continues

snowmobile, which will make him famous and wealthy in the late 1950s.

- **1925** The Seagram Company is founded in Montréal.
- **1940** Women obtain the right to vote in provincial elections in Québec, having obtained that right in federal elections in 1917.
- **1948** The Québec flag, bearing four fleurs-de-lis, is adopted.
- **1962** Montréal's underground city is born, with the construction of Place Ville-Marie.
- **1967** Montréal hosts the successful Expo '67.
- **1968** The Parti Québecois is founded by René Lévesque, and the separatist movement begins in earnest. Québecois Pierre Elliott Trudeau is elected prime minister of Canada, and he holds that office for most of the following 18 years.
- **1976** The Parti Québecois comes to power in Québec and remains in office until 1985, when the Liberal Party succeeds it. Montréal hosts the Olympics.
- **1984** Québecois Brian Mulroney becomes prime minister of Canada.
- **1989** The North American Free-Trade Agreement goes into effect, gradually removing all tariffs on goods of national origin moving between the United States and Canada.
- **1990** The Meech Lake Accord, recognizing Québec as a "distinct society" within Canada, is voted down, and separatist agitation increases.
- **1992** Montréal celebrates its 350th birthday. The Charlottetown Accord, a reworking of Meech Lake, is defeated at the polls.
- **1993** Mulroney resigns with public approval ratings in the single digits. He is

continues

Old Montréal, and paid his respects to the native people before moving on. That was the extent of Cartier's contribution to the future city.

THE FOUNDING OF MONTRÉAL More than 100 years later, **Paul de Chomedey, sieur de Maisonneuve,** arrived in 1642 to establish a colony and to plant a crucifix atop the hill he called Mont-Royal. He and his band of settlers came ashore and founded **Ville-Marie,** dedicated to the Virgin Mary, at the spot now marked by Place Royale. They built a fort, a chapel, stores, and houses, and the energetic **Jeanne Mance** made her indelible mark by founding the hospital named Hôtel-Dieu-de-Montréal, which still exists today.

Life was not easy. Unlike the friendly Algonquins who lived in nearby regions, the Iroquois in Montréal had no intention of living in peace with the new settlers. De Maisonneuve had said he would settle at Montréal "even if the very trees of the island turn to Iroquois," and it must have seemed to the handful of inhabitants of Ville-Marie that the trees had done just that. Fierce battles raged for years, and the settlers were lucky that their numbers included such undauntable souls as la Salle, du Luth, de la Mothe Cadillac, and the brothers Lemoyne, all of whom later left their names on territories in the Great Lakes and Mississippi.

At **Place d'Armes** stands a statue of de Maisonneuve, marking the spot where the settlers defeated the Iroquois in bloody hand-to-hand fighting, with de Maisonneuve himself locked in mortal combat with the Iroquois chief. De Maisonneuve won.

From that time the settlement prospered, though in 1760 it fell to the British, the year after Wolfe defeated Montcalm on the Plains of Abraham in Québec. Until the 1800s the city was contained in the area known today as **Vieux-Montréal.** Its ancient walls no longer stand, but half of its long and colorful past is preserved in the streets, houses, and churches of the Old City.

ENGLAND CONQUERS NEW FRANCE In the 1750s the struggle between Britain and France had escalated, after a series of conflicts beginning in 1689 that had embroiled both Europe and the New World. The latest episode was known as the **French and Indian War** in North America, an extension of Europe's Seven Years' War. Strategic Québec became a valued prize. The French sent **Louis Joseph, marquis de Montcalm,** to command their forces in the town. The British sent an expedition of 4,500 men in a fleet under the command of a 32-year-old general named **James Wolfe.** The ensuing battle for Québec, fought on the **Plains of Abraham** southwest of the city on September 13, 1759, is one of the most famous in North American history, since it also resulted in a continent that was thus transferred to British culture and influence for centuries to come.

Wolfe and his forces rowed upriver to a cove west of the city and silently climbed the towering cliff face in darkness through a narrow but undefended ravine. At the top, the opposing forces met and engaged on the broad meadow. Both generals perished as a result of the 20-minute battle. Wolfe lived just long enough to hear that he had won. Montcalm died a few hours later. Told that he was mortally wounded, he replied, "All the better. I will not see the English in Québec." Today a memorial to both men overlooks Terrasse Dufferin in Québec City, the only statue in the world commemorating both victor and vanquished of the same battle. The inscription, in neither French nor English but Latin, says simply, COURAGE WAS FATAL TO THEM.

THE UNITED STATES INVADES The capture of Québec determined the course of the war, and the **Treaty of Paris** in 1763 ceded all of French Canada to England. In a sense, this victory led to Britain's worst defeat. If the French had held Canada, the British government might have been more judicious in its treatment of the American colonists. As it was, the British decided to make the colonists pay the costs of the French and Indian War, on the principle that it was their homes being defended. They slapped so many taxes on all imports that the infuriated colonists openly rebelled against the Crown.

But if the British misjudged the temper of the colonists, the Americans were equally wrong about the mood of the Canadians. **George Washington** felt sure that French Canadians would want to join the revolution, or at least be supportive. He was mistaken on both counts. Even the arguments of **Benjamin Franklin,** who was sent to Montréal to plead the case, could not convince them. The Québecois were at best ambivalent about the American cause, in part because of the virulent

succeeded by Kim Campbell, the first woman to head the Progressive Conservative Party and the first female prime minister. She and the Tories are soundly defeated by Jean Chrétien and the Liberals in October.

- **1994** Québec's separatist Parti Québecois wins provincial elections, ending 9 years of Liberal rule.

- **1995** Despite a seemingly unstoppable momentum toward independence, federalist politicians defeat separatists in important by-elections in Québec. A referendum on separation from the rest of Canada is narrowly defeated.

- **1996** Sharp cuts in federal contributions to Canada's cherished universal health-care system provoke job actions by doctors. Accounts of unsanitary hospitals, outdated equipment, and ever-lengthening delays for treatment cause mounting unease in the face of governmental demands for even greater efficiencies and cost-cutting procedures.

- **1997** Prime Minister Jean Chrétien calls early elections in hopes of strengthening his party's hold on Parliament. Results are mixed. The separatist Bloc Québecois loses its standing as the largest opposition party to the emerging western Reform Party, but Chrétien's Liberals shrink from 174 seats to 155.

- **1998** The governing provincial Parti Québecois wins reelection in November, beating off the resurgent Liberals, headed by Jean Charest. Still, the margin of victory is narrower than expected, and Premier Bouchard shelves plans for an early referendum on independence.

continues

■ **2000** Despite signs of Québec's emergence from a decade-long recession, by some measures surpassing the rest of Canada, support for Bouchard and separation falls below 40% of the electorate. He declares that it's more important to win re-election in 2003.

anti-monarchist tenor of the rebels. They detested their British conquerors, but they were also staunch Royalists and devout Catholics, and saw their contentious neighbors as godless Republicans. Only a handful supported the Americans, as often as not to sell them supplies, and three of Washington's most competent commanders came to grief in attacks against Québec. Vermonter **Ethan Allen** and his Green Mountain Boys were taken prisoner at Montréal, and Montgomery fell before Québec, where the ambitious **Benedict Arnold** was also driven back in defeat, possibly fueling his eventual perfidy.

Thirty-eight years later, in the **War of 1812,** another U.S. army marched up the banks of the Richelieu River where it flows from Lake Champlain to the St. Lawrence. And once again the French Canadians stuck by the British and drove back the invaders. The war ended essentially in a draw, but it had at least one encouraging result: Britain and the young United States agreed to demilitarize the Great Lakes and to extend their mutual border along the 49th parallel to the Rockies.

MONTRÉAL AND QUÉBEC CITY TODAY　The ancient walls that protected Québec City over the centuries are still in place today, the town within their embrace little changed, preserving for posterity the heart of New France. Montréal, though, has gone through a metamorphosis. The city's recent history is almost as intriguing as its early days, for it was "wet" when the United States was "dry" due to Prohibition. Bootleggers, hard drinkers, and prostitutes flocked to this large city situated so conveniently close to the American border and mixed with rowdy elements from the port, much to the distress of Montréal's mainly upstanding citizenry. For half a century the city's image was decidedly racy, but in the 1950s a cleanup began, with a boom in high-rise construction and eventual restoration of much of the derelict Old Town. In **1967** Montréal welcomed the world to Expo. The great gleaming skyscrapers and towering hotels, the superb Métro system, and the highly practical underground city, so much a part of this modern city, date mostly from the past 40 years.

All this activity helped to fuel a phenomenon later labeled the **"Quiet Revolution."** It was to transform the largely rural, agricultural province into an urbanized, industrial entity with a pronounced secular outlook. French Canadians, long denied access to the upper echelons of desirable corporate careers, started to insist upon equal opportunity with the powerful Anglophone minority. Inevitably, a radical fringe movement of separatists emerged, signaling its intentions by bombing Anglophone businesses. The **FLQ,** as it was known, was behind most of the terrorist attacks, reaching its nadir with the kidnapping and murder of a cabinet minister, **Pierre Laporte.**

Most Québecois separatists were not violent, and most Québecois were not even separatists. **Pierre Trudeau,** a bilingual Québecois, became prime minister in 1968. As flamboyant, eccentric, and brilliant as any Canadian who ever held the post, he necessarily devoted much of his time trying to placate voters on both sides of the issue. In 1969, the **Official Languages Act** mandated that all federal agencies provide services in both French and English. Yet by 1980, a provincial referendum on separation from the confederation was defeated by only 60% of the vote. Subsequent attempts to assuage the chafed sensibilities of French Québecois failed again and again, as often at the hands of other

> *Being ourselves is essentially a matter of keeping and developing a personality that has survived for three and a half centuries.*
> —René Lévesque, founder of the Parti Québecois (1968)

provincial premiers as by the Québecois, hounding at least three prime ministers from office.

In 1993, the governing Tories were defeated by the opposition Liberals. The new prime minister, **Jean Chrétien,** a federalist, was not aided in his task of national reconciliation by representation in the House of Commons of the militantly separatist **Bloc Québécois,** which became the largest opposition party in the same election. And in Québec the following year, the **Parti Québécois** won provincial elections to end nine years of Liberal control. The new premier, **Jacques Parizeau,** vowed to hold an early referendum on sovereignty, which was held in late October 1995 and was narrowly defeated by a bare 1% of the total vote. Parizeau resigned the day after, after making intemperate remarks about the negative role of ethnic voters in the results. Recent polls suggest that pro-confederation sentiments are gaining ground over separatism, but fluctuations have been the rule. Federalists have even floated the notion that if Québec has the right to secede from Canada, then smaller regions and municipalities have an equal right to secede from Québec. The **Crees** of northern Québec stirred the pot further, asking that the federal government affirm their right to stay in Canada. Contention over the intractable issue isn't going to end anytime soon, but conversations with ordinary Québecois suggest they are so weary of the seemingly endless sovereignty argument they no longer care what happens as long as it is decided one way or the other.

2 The Politics of Language

The defining dialectic of Canadian life is language, the thorny issue that might yet tear the country apart. Many Québecois believe that a separate independent state is the only way to maintain their culture in the face of the Anglophone ocean that envelops them. The role of Québec within the Canadian federation is the most debated and volatile issue in Canadian politics.

One attempt to smooth ruffled Francophone fur was made in 1969, when federal legislation stipulated that all services were henceforth to be offered in both English and French, in effect declaring the nation bilingual. That didn't long assuage militant Québecois. Having made the two languages equal in the rest of the country, they undertook to guarantee the primacy of French in their own province. To prevent dilution by newcomers, the children of immigrants are required to enroll in French-language schools, even if English or a third language is spoken in the home. Bill 101 was passed in 1977, which all but banned the use of English on public signage. Ogilvy's and Eaton's department stores were made to drop their offensive Anglo apostrophes, and GOING OUT OF BUSINESS posters were taken down. Stop signs now read ARRÊT, a word that actually refers to a stop on a bus or train route. (Even in France, the red signs read STOP, but then, Québecois like to believe they speak a purer—by which they mean older—form of the language than is spoken in the mother country today.) The bill funded the establishment of enforcement units, virtual language police who let no nit go unpicked.

And that was not enough. In a 1980 referendum, Québec's citizens voted on whether they favored maintaining the political status quo or wished to seek a "sovereignty-association" with the Canadian government. In sovereignty-association, they would have had political autonomy while retaining economic links with Canada. Though the latter proposition was narrowly defeated, the separatist issue was hardly put to rest. Two years later a new national constitution was adopted, though never endorsed by Québec, whose constituency felt it did not adequately protect the province's distinct linguistic and cultural heritage.

As a result of this backlash, which has resulted in the flight of an estimated 400,000 Anglophones to other parts of Canada, Canadian Prime Minister Brian Mulroney met with the 10 provincial premiers in April 1987 at a retreat at Québec's Meech Lake to cobble together a collection of constitutional reforms. The Meech Lake Accord, as it came to be known, addressed a variety of issues, but most important to the Québecois it recognized Québec as a "distinct society" within the federation. In the end, however, Manitoba and Newfoundland failed to ratify the accord by the June 23, 1990, deadline. As a result, support for the secessionist cause burgeoned in Québec, and the separatist Parti Québecois now controls the provincial government. A referendum held in 1995 was narrowly won by those Québec residents who favored staying within the union, but the vote settled nothing. The issue continues to divide families and dominate all political discourse.

People talk about separation in Québec as often as those elsewhere chat about the weather, though there are times, due to sheer exhaustion with the subject, that it seems to be the last thing anyone wants to discuss. In bars, restaurants, and hair salons, and around kitchen tables, the same questions and opinions continue to be uttered, over and over. Would a politically independent Québec continue to share a common currency, a common central bank, and a tariff-free relationship with the rest of Canada? Would the Canadian-U.S. Free-Trade Agreement be extended to an independent Québec? Would the Atlantic provinces, cut off from the rest of Canada, apply to the United States for statehood? Would the Crees of northern Québec or Anglophone parts of Montréal be allowed to remain in Canada?

In the midst of the unshakable fray, Québec remains committed to ensuring, one way or another, the survival of the province's culture and language, its bedrock loyalty to its Gallic roots. France may have relinquished control of Québec in 1763, but its influence, after its century and a half of rule, remains powerful to this day. The Québecois continue to look across the Atlantic for inspiration in fashion, food, and the arts. Culturally and linguistically, it is that tenacious French connection that gives the province its special character, which is a source of great regional pride, if considerable national controversy.

There are reasons for the festering intransigence of the Québecois, about 240 years' worth. After what they unfailingly call "The Conquest," their English rulers made a few concessions to French-Canadian pride, including allowing them a Gallic version of jurisprudence. But a kind of linguistic exclusionism prevailed, with wealthy Scottish and English bankers and merchants denying French-Canadians access to upper levels of business and government. Intentionally or thoughtlessly, Anglophones lowered an opaque

Impressions

Je me souviens. (I remember.)
　　　　　—Motto for Québec province, seen on automobile license plates

ceiling on Francophone advancement. The present strife, and the frequent foolishness and small-mindedness that attends it on both sides, is as much payback as it is pride in the French heritage.

None of this should deter potential visitors. The Québecois are exceedingly gracious hosts. While Montréal may be the largest French-speaking city outside Paris, most Montréalers grow up speaking both French and English, switching effortlessly from one language to the other as the situation dictates. Telephone operators go from French to English the instant they hear an English word out of the other party, as do most store clerks, waiters, and hotel staff. This is less the case in country villages and in Québec City, but there is virtually no problem that can't be solved with a few French words, some expressive gestures, and a little goodwill.

3 Cuisine Haute, Cuisine Bas: Smoked Meat, Fiddleheads & Caribou

French cuisine has prevailed since the arrival of Québec's earliest white settlers. At first, the food of the colony was the country cooking of the motherland adapted to the ingredients found in New France: **root vegetables, dried legumes, apples, maple sugar and syrup,** and whatever catchable **fish and game** were available. Dishes native to the region evolved, many of which are still savored by the Québecois today. Among these are *cretons,* a pâté of minced pork, allspice, and parsley; a meat pie called *tourtière,* beans and pork baked in maple syrup; and *tarte au sucre,* maple sugar pie. As time passed and food became more than sustenance, the gastronomic fervor of the old country was imported to Québec, and replications of Parisian bistros and manifestations of the Epicurean teachings of Brillat-Savarin arrived and multiplied. The entire range of Gallic cuisine was then available, from lowbrow to upper-crust. They persist in the cities and in many excellent restaurants out in the countryside. Game is still highly popular, with wild boar, venison, pheasant, quail, hare, and even caribou and wapiti appearing frequently on menus. Oddly, for a region whose identity is shaped in large part by the great river that runs through it, fish is seen less often. When it is, it is almost invariably salmon. Extremely popular shellfish are **scallops** (*pétoncles,* pronounced "pay-*tonk*"); **mussels** *(moules),* served in the Belgian manner with thin French fries *(frites),* and **lobster** *(homard),* which comes at remarkable bargain prices during the summer festival celebrating its availability.

Vegetables are largely those familiar to Americans, increasingly provided by organic or hydroponic farms, especially in winter. An exception is **fiddleheads**—*têtes des violon*—the tightly curled tips of wild ferns picked in spring just before they unfold into fronds. Their season is short, usually the last half of May and early June, and they appear on plates all over the province, usually sautéed and tossed in butter or oil with garlic. Cheese-lovers can rejoice in the delicious reality that more than 75 distinct *fromages* are produced in Québec. Many of them equal some of the best French varieties, in part because the Québecois versions are also unpasteurized. For that reason, they cannot be imported into the United States, so this is the place to sample them.

There things stood, until recently. There was French food and there was everything else, which was foreign. Ethnic eateries existed, mostly serving the immigrant groups who established them. The biggest, priciest, and longest-lived restaurants remained the French ones. The culinary revolution that rolled across the continent from California in the 1980s swallowed up Vancouver, Toronto, Chicago, and New York; but it barely touched Montréal, and it

Le Dining Terms

A little knowledge of local restaurant terminology will help you avoid confusion when dining in Québec. An *entrée* is an appetizer, not the main course, which is *le plat principal*. In fancier places, where a pre-appetizer nibble is proffered, it is an *amuse-gueule* or *amuse-bouche*, and the little plate of cookies and sweets that comes with coffee contains *les mignardises*. A tip left at the end of a meal is a *pourboire*.

bypassed Québec City entirely. That is now changing, quite dramatically. **Cal-Ital, new Canadian,** and **fusion** have arrived and are taking their place at the head of the table. Of the 10 or 12 top restaurants in the province, nine are making their own rules, improvising, inventing new combinations of textures, tastes, and ingredients. The traditional kitchens remain, but they are lightening their sauces, rethinking their assumptions, and even tossing out old recipes. More Italian, Mediterranean, and Asian restaurants are opening every year. Cosmopolitan Québec has become even more sophisticated, with remarkable restaurants found even in relatively remote rural areas.

The Québecois enjoy their comfort foods as much as anyone. In Montréal, these include **smoked meat,** a maddeningly tasty sandwich component that hovers somewhere in the neighborhood of pastrami and corned beef but is somehow different. And the Montréal rendition of the **bagel** is thinner, chewier, and better than the more famous New York prototype. Take it from someone born in *Le Bronx.*

Many lower-priced restaurants in Montréal allow patrons to bring their own wine, indicated by signs in the window that show a red hand holding a bottle or carry the words APPORTEZ VOTRE VIN. To buy wine or spirits outside a bar or restaurant, go to an outlet of the Québec Société des Alcools (SAQ), the governmental monopoly that holds the exclusive right to sell all strong liquor in the province. Licensed grocery stores may sell wine, beer, and alcoholic cider, but the Société des Alcools stores also have the largest selections of wines. A subcategory of stores, maisons des vins, also carry old, rare, and special wines.

In restaurants, wine is often offered by the liter, half-liter, quarter-liter, and glass (*verre*). The quarter-liter contains two glasses, usually a small saving over glasses ordered separately. Imported wines and spirits are very expensive, encouraging experimentation with Canadian efforts with the grape. Some are appalling, a few are...not bad. Excellent Québec beers include **Belle Gueule, Boréal,** and the darker **St-Amboise.**

4 Recommended Reading

Writing from the perspective of a minority within a minority, the Jewish Anglophone Mordecai Richler has inveighed against the excesses of Québec's separatists and language zealots in a barrage of books and critical essays in newspapers and magazines. His outrage and mordant wit can be sampled in his *Oh Canada! Oh Québec!* (Knopf, 1992) and *Home Sweet Home: My Canadian Album* (Knopf, 1984; paperback, Penguin, 1985). An amusing, less caustic look at the Anglophone-Francophone conflict is provided by *The Anglo Guide to Survival in Québec* (Eden Press, 1983). A serious, relatively balanced view—with a slight lean to the French-Canadian side of the issue—is given by Brian Young and John A. Dickinson in *A Short History of Québec: A Socio-Economic Perspective* (Copp Clark Pitman Ltd., 1988). One of the authors taught at McGill University, the other at the Université de Montréal.

Index

See also Accommodations and Restaurant indexes below.

FROMMER'S® COMPLETE TRAVEL GUIDES

FROMMER'S® DOLLAR-A-DAY GUIDES

FROMMER'S® PORTABLE GUIDES

FROMMER'S® NATIONAL PARK GUIDES

Family Vacations in the National Parks
Grand Canyon

National Parks of the American West
Rocky Mountain

Yellowstone & Grand Teton
Yosemite & Sequoia/ Kings Canyon
Zion & Bryce Canyon

FROMMER'S® MEMORABLE WALKS

Chicago
London

New York
Paris

San Francisco
Washington, D.C.

FROMMER'S® GREAT OUTDOOR GUIDES

New England
Northern California

Southern California & Baja
Southern New England

Washington & Oregon

FROMMER'S® BORN TO SHOP GUIDES

Born to Shop: France
Born to Shop: Italy

Born to Shop: London
Born to Shop: New York

Born to Shop: Paris

FROMMER'S® IRREVERENT GUIDES

Amsterdam
Boston
Chicago
Las Vegas

London
Los Angeles
Manhattan
New Orleans

Paris
San Francisco
Seattle & Portland
Vancouver

Walt Disney World
Washington, D.C.

FROMMER'S® BEST-LOVED DRIVING TOURS

America
Britain
California

Florida
France
Germany

Ireland
Italy
New England

Scotland
Spain
Western Europe

THE UNOFFICIAL GUIDES®

Bed & Breakfasts in California
Bed & Breakfasts in New England
Bed & Breakfasts in the Northwest
Bed & Breakfasts in Southeast
Beyond Disney
Branson, Missouri

California with Kids
Chicago
Cruises
Disneyland
Florida with Kids
Golf Vacations in the Eastern U.S.
The Great Smoky & Blue Ridge Mountains

Inside Disney
Hawaii
Las Vegas
London
Miami & the Keys
Mini Las Vegas
Mini-Mickey
New Orleans
New York City
Paris

San Francisco
Skiing in the West
Southeast with Kids
Walt Disney World
Walt Disney World for Grown-ups
Walt Disney World for Kids
Washington, D.C.

SPECIAL-INTEREST TITLES

Frommer's Britain's Best Bed & Breakfasts and Country Inns
Frommer's Britain's Best Bike Rides
The Civil War Trust's Official Guide to the Civil War Discovery Trail
Frommer's Caribbean Hideaways
Frommer's Adventure Guide to Central America
Frommer's Adventure Guide to South America
Frommer's Adventure Guide to Southeast Asia
Frommer's Food Lover's Companion to France
Frommer's Gay & Lesbian Europe
Frommer's Exploring America by RV
Hanging Out in Europe

Israel Past & Present
Mad Monks' Guide to California
Mad Monks' Guide to New York City
Frommer's The Moon
Frommer's New York City with Kids
The New York Times' Unforgettable Weekends
Places Rated Almanac
Retirement Places Rated
Frommer's Road Atlas Britain
Frommer's Road Atlas Europe
Frommer's Washington, D.C., with Kids
Frommer's What the Airlines Never Tell You